Praise for
A Handful of Sand

SHORTLISTED
for the Territory Read 2018 Book of the Year Award

SHORTLISTED
for the Prime Minister's Literary Awards 2017
(Australian History)

SHORTLISTED
for the Northern Territory Chief Minister's History Book Award 2017

'An epic historical work, meticulously researched and beautifully written.'
Dr Mickey Dewar

'…the narrative restores one's faith, if any were needed, in the power of well-informed, committed, passionate, even-handed historical story-telling … [a] milestone in the historiography of the decade.'
Professor Peter Read

'The definitive work on the Walk-off and the Gurindji struggle.'
The Honourable Ted Egan AO

'A narrative rich in ironies, well structured, much like a campfire tale … unfurling, exploring side channels, circling round.'
Nicolas Rothwell, *The Australian*

A HANDFUL OF SAND

THE GURINDJI STRUGGLE, AFTER THE WALK-OFF

CHARLIE WARD

© Copyright 2016 Charlie Ward
All rights reserved. Apart from any uses permitted by Australia's Copyright Act 1968, no part of this book may be reproduced by any process without prior written permission from the copyright owners. Inquiries should be directed to the publisher.

Monash University Publishing
Matheson Library and Information Services Building
40 Exhibition Walk
Monash University
Clayton, Victoria 3800, Australia
www.publishing.monash.edu

Monash University Publishing brings to the world publications which advance the best traditions of humane and enlightened thought. Monash University Publishing titles pass through a rigorous process of independent peer review.

Second printing.

www.publishing.monash.edu/books/hs-9781925377163.html

Series: Australian History

Series Editor: Sean Scalmer

Design: Les Thomas

Front cover image: Mervyn Bishop (Australia, b.1945), *Prime Minister Gough Whitlam pours soil into the hands of traditional land owner Vincent Lingiari, Northern Territory* 1975, printed 1999.
Type R3 photograph, 30.5 x 30.5 cm.
Art Gallery of New South Wales
Hallmark Cards Australian Photography Collection Fund 1991
Photo: AGNSW
© Mervyn Bishop / The Commonwealth of Australia (through the Department of the Prime Minister and Cabinet)

Back cover image: Wattie Creek, with Alan Thorpe's hut circled. Courtesy of ASIO.

National Library of Australia Cataloguing-in-Publication entry:

Creator:	Ward, Charlie, 1972- author.
Title:	A handful of sand : the Gurindji struggle, after the walk-off/ Charlie Ward.
ISBN:	9781925377163 (paperback)
Subjects:	Gurindji (Australian people), Treatment of--Northern Territory--Wave Hill Station.
	Aboriginal Australians, Treatment of--Northern Territory--Wave Hill Station.
	Aboriginal Australians--Land tenure--Northern Territory.
	Aboriginal Australians--Social conditions--Northern Territory.
	Self-determination, National--Northern Territory.
	Livestock workers, Treatment of--Northern Territory--Wave Hill Station.
	Strikes and lockouts--Cattle trade--Northern Territory--Wave Hill Station.
Dewey Number:	994.290049915

Printed in Australia by Griffin Press an Accredited ISO AS/NZS 14001:2004 Environmental Management System printer.

The paper this book is printed on is certified against the Forest Stewardship Council® Standards. Griffin Press, a member of the Opus Group, holds chain of custody certification SCS-COC-001185. FSC® promotes environmentally responsible, socially beneficial and economically viable management of the world's forests.

DEDICATION

*To Gurindji leaders of the past, present and future,
that their hopes and dreams are realised.*

CONTENTS

Dedication..v
Abbreviations viii
Glossary..xiv
Maps xviii
Acknowledgments..xxii
Preface...xxvi

Introduction: Put in Their Place, 1879–1930..................1

PART ONE: THE QUEST FOR JUSTICE 1930–72 9
Chapter 1: Finding Their Feet, 1930–1966 11
Chapter 2: Taking a Stand, 1966–1968..................... 30
Chapter 3: Friends from Afar, 1969–1970.................. 54
Chapter 4: Progress and Strain, 1971 79
Chapter 5: Vindication, 1972............................. 98

PART TWO: MAKING A FIST OF IT 1973–78 119
Chapter 6: A New Beginning, 1973 121
Chapter 7: Into the Fray, 1974.......................... 148
Chapter 8: A Handful of Sand, 1975 173
Chapter 9: A Fighting Chance, 1976 195
Chapter 10: Mixed Blessings, 1977–78 218

PART THREE: THE HARDER ROAD 1979–86................. 241
Chapter 11: 'A Fragmentation of Support', 1979–80.......... 243
Chapter 12: Testing Times, 1981–82 264
Chapter 13: Resignation, 1983–86 285

Afterword 310
Select Bibliography 321
Index... 345

ABBREVIATIONS

AACM: the Australian Agricultural Consultancy Management Company. An advisory group formed in Adelaide in 1965 by Philip Young and Newton Tiver. The company quickly grew, aided in part by contracts with government agencies such as the Department of Aboriginal Affairs. By the mid-1980s, AACM employed up to sixty consultants on projects in developing countries.

ABSCHOL: from 'Aboriginal Scholarships'. Abschol was a student body established under the auspices of the National Union of Students in 1951 to boost Indigenous enrolments in tertiary education. Abschol's mandate expanded to encompass broader pro-Aboriginal causes throughout the 1960s and early 70s, when 'branches' operated on many university campuses. In 1969 the Gorton Government began its own Indigenous scholarship program, rendering Abschol's scholarship program redundant.

ACTU: the Australian Council of Trade Unions. The ACTU was formed in 1927 to advance the cause of unionism on a sector-wide, national basis.

ADC: the Aboriginal Development Commission. The ADC was established in 1980 by the Fraser Government. It absorbed some 'development' functions from the DAA, including pastoral operations. The Commission assisted Aboriginal people to acquire land, to engage in business enterprises, and to obtain finance for housing and other needs.

AIATSIS: the Australian Institute of Aboriginal and Torres Strait Islander Studies (originally known as the Australian Institute of Aboriginal Studies, or AIAS) was established in Canberra in 1964. The Institute is Australia's foremost resource for information about the cultures and societies of Aboriginal and Torres Strait Islander peoples.

ALP: the Australian Labor Party is a major political party founded in the 1890s by striking pastoral workers. Historically, the party's

ABBREVIATIONS

principal focus was upon the rights of workers and it remains closely aligned with various labour unions.

ALRA: the *Aboriginal Land Rights (Northern Territory) Act. ALRA* provides the basis upon which Aboriginal people in the Northern Territory can claim rights to land based on traditional occupation. Although the Whitlam Government appointed Justice Woodward to chair the Aboriginal Land Rights Commission and develop the Act, *ALRA* was passed eventually by the Fraser Government on 16 December 1976.

ANZ: the Australia and New Zealand Banking Group. Proprietary owners of the ANZ Bank.

ANZAC: the Australian and New Zealand Army Corps was a First World War army corps that also fought during the Second World War and the Vietnam War.

ASIO: the Australian Security and Intelligence Organisation. ASIO was formed in 1949 to co-ordinate Australian intelligence, particularly regarding the threat of Soviet activity. Modelled along the lines of Britain's M15, ASIO played a significant role collecting data on the members and affiliates of the Communist Party of Australia throughout the 1950s and 60s. ASIO has been criticised for directing its attention towards the members of progressive social movements during the 1960s–70s, such as peace, feminist and civil rights activists, rather than those providing a threat to national security.

BTEC: the Brucellosis and Tuberculosis Eradication Campaign. A national initiative that successfully eradicated tuberculosis and brucellosis from Australian cattle between 1970 and 1997.

CAA: the Council for Aboriginal Affairs (1967–76) was established by the Government of Harold Holt in response to the 'Aboriginal' referendum of 1967. The Council was comprised of three members— H.C. 'Nugget' Coombs, Barrie Dexter and W.E.H. Stanner. The Council's purpose was to provide policy advice on Aboriginal issues directly to the office of the Prime Minister. Its recommendations were broadly resisted by successive Coalition Governments until the election of the Whitlam ALP Government in December 1972.

CCL: the NT Council for Civil Liberties. This group was active in the late 1970s and early 80s.

CLC: the Central Land Council. Established as a statutory body in 1976 under the *Aboriginal Land Rights (Northern Territory) Act (ALRA)* to represent the land-related interests of traditional owners of the southern part of the Northern Territory.

CLP: the Northern Territory Country Liberal Party is a political party affiliated with both the National (formerly 'Country') and Liberal Parties of Australia. The CLP was the dominant force in NT politics from its inception in 1974 until the turn of the century.

CPA: the Communist Party of Australia. Founded in 1920 by socialists inspired by the Russian Revolution, the CPA grew in size and influence for two decades, attracting members keen to promote alternatives to the fascist politics gaining popularity in Europe and (it was argued) the economic exploitation by capitalists responsible for the Great Depression of the 1930s. After the human rights abuses of Joseph Stalin's Soviet regime became apparent in 1956 and the Menzies Government attempted to ban it, CPA membership declined steadily. The party split into competing variants in the 1990s. One of these was the Socialist Party of Australia, which adopted the Communist Party of Australia name in 1996.

CPC: the Northern Territory Cattle Producers' Council. A peak advocacy body that represented the interests of NT pastoralists from 1963 to 1984. The CPC succeeded the NTPLA (Northern Territory Pastoral Lessees' Association) and was a forerunner to the current NTCA (Northern Territory Cattlemen's Association).

DAA: the Department of Aboriginal Affairs was a Commonwealth agency formed in 1972. Notwithstanding the creation of the Aboriginal Development Commission in 1980 (which assumed land and development functions from it), the Department was responsible

ABBREVIATIONS

for administering the nation's Aboriginal affairs until 1990.

DCGC: the Daguragu Community Government Council. From 1982 until its abolition in 2008, DCGC was the Gurindji local government body administering services to—and via an elected council board, guided by—the people of Kalkaringi and Daguragu. The Council was formed after various, less successful, 'Aboriginal-controlled' council structures were trialed by the DAA at Libanungu/Kalkaringi in the 1973–81 period.

DPP: the Northern Territory Department of Primary Production was established in 1979 and took responsibility for managing and supporting the NT's rural industries.

FCAA/FCAATSI: the Federal Council for the Advancement of Aborigines. The FCAA was established in 1958 in Adelaide, merging from a number of organisations lobbying for Aboriginal rights. In 1964 it changed its name to the 'Federal Council for the Advancement of Aborigines and Torres Strait Islanders'. From its inception until its demise in 1978, FCAA/FCAATSI was comprised of Aboriginal and non-Aboriginal activists working together for the improvement of conditions for Aboriginal people.

GBM: Government Business Manager. These public service positions were created in 2007 by the then federal department of Families, Housing, Community Services and Indigenous Affairs. As part of the NT Emergency Response (also known as 'the Intervention'), GBMs were stationed in remote Aboriginal communities and allocated the task of co-ordinating government business on behalf of the Commonwealth and states.

GDT: 'GDT' was the registered cattle brand used by the Muramulla company to identify their cattle. GDT stands for 'Gurindji Daguragu Territory'.

MLA: a Member of the (NT) Legislative Assembly (See NTLA).

NACC: the National Aboriginal Advisory Consultative Council. The first government-created body comprised of elected Aboriginal representatives to provide advice to the Commonwealth. Established by the Whitlam Government in 1973.

NAWU: the North Australian Workers' Union. NAWU was formed in 1927 as a subsidiary of the Australian Workers' Union. NAWU represented Indigenous workers in the 'equal wages' hearings in the 1960s, although the union itself had few Indigenous members.

NLC: the Northern Land Council. Established as a statutory body in 1976 under the *Aboriginal Land Rights (Northern Territory) Act (ALRA)* to represent the land-related interests of traditional owners of the 'Top End' of the Northern Territory.

NT: the Northern Territory of Australia.

NTA: the Northern Territory Administration sat within the Department of Territories (1932–1951), and then the Department of the Interior (1951–1968). The NTA contained the Welfare Branch, Education Branch and others active in Aboriginal settlements

NTCAR: the Northern Territory Council for Aboriginal Rights. A primarily Indigenous organisation formed in 1961 to fight against injustice to Aborigines, NTCAR worked in tandem with the Councils for Aboriginal Rights existing in other states.

NTCRATSI: the NT Council of Rights for Aborigines and Torres Strait Islanders. After NTCAR folded in the early 1970s, NTCRATSI was briefly active doing similar work in Darwin.

NTDCD: the Northern Territory Department of Community Development. The NTDCD was formed after NT self-government in 1978. Its responsibilities included social welfare and local government.

NTED: the Northern Territory Education Department took responsibility for providing school education in the NT from the Commonwealth Department of Education in 1979.

NTG: the Northern Territory Government was formed after the Fraser Government's *NT Self-government Act* was passed in 1978. The NTG replaced the NTLA and assumed many functions of a state government, directly funded by the Commonwealth.

ABBREVIATIONS

NTLA: the Northern Territory Legislative Assembly is a unicameral ('one-house') legislature formed after the 1974 federal election. Members with full voting rights at a federal level oversaw the transition of the Northern Territory to self-government in 1978.

NTLC: the Northern Territory Legislative Council. The NTLC was a partly-elected governing body of the Northern Territory from 1947 until its replacement by the fully elected Northern Territory Legislative Assembly (NTLA) in 1974.

NUAUS: the National Union of Australian University Students. Established in 1937 at Adelaide University to represent the interests of tertiary students, the NUAUS campaigned for a variety of causes, particularly in the 1960s. The NUAUS established Abschol (see above).

QC: Queen's Counsel. Senior lawyers appointed by the legal profession in various Commonwealth countries, including Australia.

TB: a colloquialism for tuberculosis.

VAAL: the Victorian Aborigines' Advancement League. The AAL was Australia's longest-running Aboriginal rights group, formed in Melbourne in the 1930s. An early issue it fought for was Aboriginal representation in parliament. The AAL had numerous branches and was especially active in Victoria and Tasmania. It disbanded only recently.

VRD: the Victoria River Downs station adjoins the Daguragu Land Trust. VRD is owned by the Hooker Pastoral Co. and was originally more than 20,000 square kilometres in area. VRD and surrounds, including Wave Hill station and the Gurindji's land, is often referred to as 'the VRD area'.

WWF: the Waterside Workers' Federation. Established in 1902 and registered federally in 1907, the WWF was a labour union known for its militancy and solidarity. Under the leadership of Charlie Fitzgibbon, the WWF and affiliated unions gave strong support to the Gurindji in the 1966–1974 period. In 1993 the WWF amalgamated with the Maritime Union of Australia (MUA).

GLOSSARY

Arbitration Commission: the central institution of Australian labour law, the Commonwealth Conciliation and Arbitration Commission is a tribunal with powers under the Workplace Relations Act.

Build-up: Northern Australia's pre-monsoonal season, usually extending from October to December. A hot period with high humidity, 'building up' to the wet season.

Countrymen: Aboriginal English for members of one's own language group, or Australian Indigenous people in general.

Daguragu: the Gurindji name for the place by Wattie Creek where they chose to build the Daguragu community.

Droughtmaster: a tropical breed of beef cattle developed in North Queensland by crossing Brahman and British breed cattle such as Beef Shorthorns during the early 1900s.

Dry Season: Northern Australia's cooler season (typically 18–32 degrees celsius); usually from March to September.

Ganger: the foreman or leading hand of a gang of labourers.

Gurindji: an Indigenous language group whose country centres around the upper Victoria River in the Northern Territory of Australia. The Gurindji and neighbouring groups such as Bilinarra, Nyininy, Mudburra, Malngin, and Ngarinyman groups are part of the Ngumpin-Yapa language family. Intermarriage and close relations between Ngumpin people have increased since European settlement and have been facilitated by the development of a regional Kriol. In the text, the term 'Gurindji' is used to refer to the Indigenous people who lived on Wave Hill station and who subsequently re-located to Wattie Creek. This group includes members of all of the above.

Humbug (*Aboriginal English*): to cause a nuisance, usually through begging or making repetitive requests.

Janama skin: a male *ngumpit* 'skin' name. See Skin Name/Group.

GLOSSARY

Jungurra skin: a male *ngumpit* 'skin' name. See Skin Name/Group.

Kajirri (*Gurindji*):   old woman, a term of respect.

Kalkaringi/ Kalkarindji: name(s) given to the former Wave Hill Welfare Settlement, which is still often referred to as 'Settlement' by the Gurindji. As befitting the 'Settlement's' contested history, according to linguist Patrick McConvell:

> For a few years the 'township' was known as Libanangu which was as close as people who wrote the name could get to the traditional name of the Wave Hill area—Lipananyku. However, following the upgrading of the airstrip, which was between Libanangu and Daguragu, it was decided (by whom is not clear) that the airstrip should have a new name; and soon after the township itself was assigned that name (without consultation with Aboriginal people as far as I know). The airstrip was named Kalkurung but variations, with a -ji ending unknown among the Gurindji, also circulated at the time. The town is now known as either Kalkaringi or (since 1986, officially) Kalkarindji. This was named after the waterhole on Wattie Creek downstream from Daguragu which was closest to the airstrip Kalkarriny.[1]

Karnatiti (*Gurindji*):   carrying two buckets or other goods on a shoulder-yoke, a practice perhaps adapted from Wave Hill station's Chinese gardeners.

Kartiya: white person, white people.

Karu Walija (*Gurindji*):   children.

Koori; Kooris: a general name for Indigenous people from south-east Australia, usually those in New South Wales and Victoria.

Marluka (*Gurindji*):   old man, a term of respect.

---

1   'Changing Places: European and Aboriginal Styles', in *The Land Is a Map: Placenames of Indigenous Origin in Australia*, ed. by F. Hodges, J. Simpson and L. Hercus (Canberra, Pacific Linguistics and Pandanus Press, 2002), pp. 50–61 (p. 52).

Murnnungku (*Gurindji*): a word used for 'policeman' in the Victoria River region; reportedly its original meaning was 'man with chains'.

Myall: a term formerly used by both Indigenous and non-Indigenous people to refer to Aborigines living a traditional lifestyle away from European activity.

New Generation: the people of Kalkaringi and Daguragu refer to people born during or after the 1960s as 'new generation'. The 'new generation' stands in contrast to the old people of the station era, now mostly deceased. It is commonly understood that 'new generation' have different values and interests than previous generations, the most obvious being a much greater appreciation and knowledge of mainstream cultures and technologies.

Ngumpit (*Gurindji*): Gurindji word meaning 'Aboriginal person; people'; the Gurindji's name for themselves and neighbouring Indigenous groups (See 'Gurindji').

Numamudidi: a clan group from southeast Arnhemland whose country extends along the coast north of the Roper River mouth. Members of this clan include the Daniels and Rogers families, both of whom extended strong support to the Gurindji land rights struggle.

Skin Name/Group: eg. '*Jungurra* skin': 'Skin' names refer to a classificatory system in which all *ngumpit* are members of one of sixteen 'skin groups' at birth. One's 'skin' is determined by maternity and dictates the roles and relationships a person is able or obligated to form with others.

Track mob: the Gurindji's English name for those who took part in the Wave Hill Walk-off and 'tracked' to Wattie Creek.

Warlpiri: a large Aboriginal language and cultural group whose traditional land includes the Tanami Desert, to the south of Gurindji land.

Welfare Branch: the Welfare Branch was a branch of the the Northern Territory Administration, which sat within the Commonwealth Department of the Interior. The Branch was established in 1953 with the passage of the *Welfare Ordinance*, which designated Aboriginal people deemed to require 'special care' as government 'wards' and

GLOSSARY

gave significant powers over them to a 'Director of Welfare'. This arrangement continued until 1963, when the *Social Welfare Ordinance* was passed. The Welfare Branch (or later, the Welfare Division) was disbanded in 1972 by the Whitlam Government. The Branch/Division was replaced by the DAA.

Wet Season: usually from January to February, much monsoonal rain can fall in this time in the north Australia, causing significant floods and isolation of remote areas.

Woodward Commission: the Whitlam Government's 1973–74 Royal Commission into Aboriginal Land Rights, led by Justice Edward Woodward. The Commission's findings were used to draft the *Aboriginal Land Rights (Northern Territory) Act* 1976.

Yapa: a Warlpiri word meaning 'Aboriginal'; the Warlpiri's name for themselves and neighbouring Aboriginal groups (See 'Warlpiri').

Yolngu: the collective name for the Indigenous people of north-east Arnhemland.

MAPS

The Wave Hill Area, Northern Territory

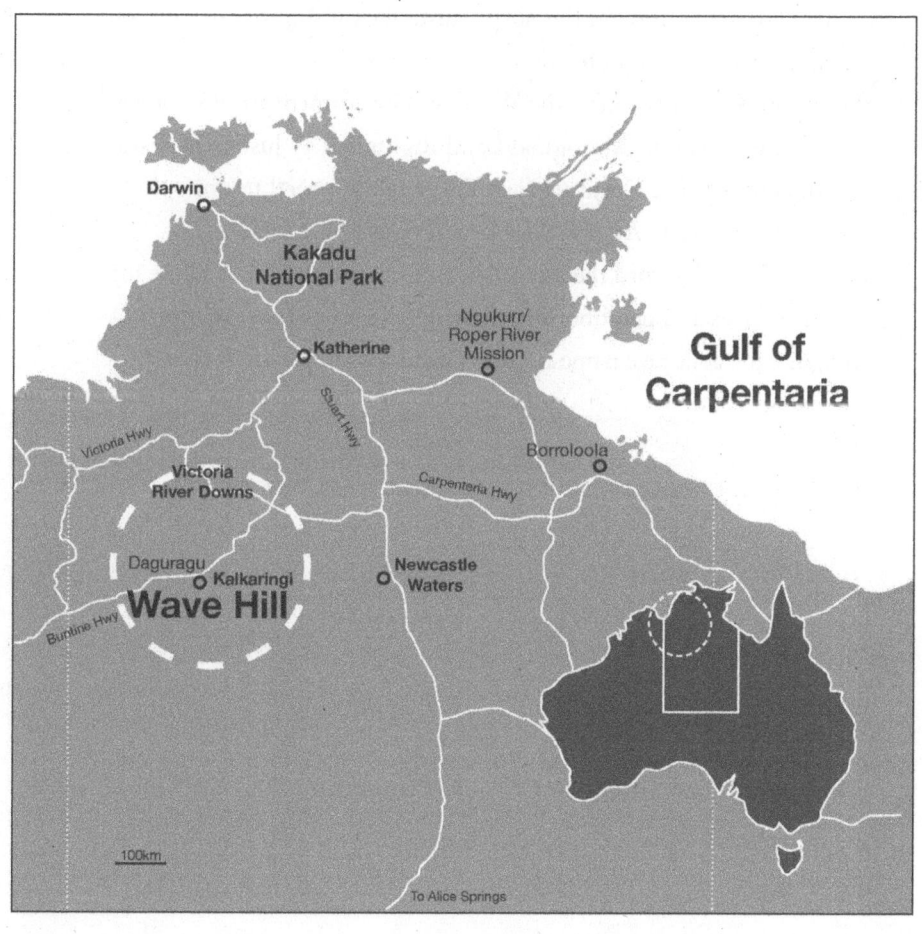

MAPS

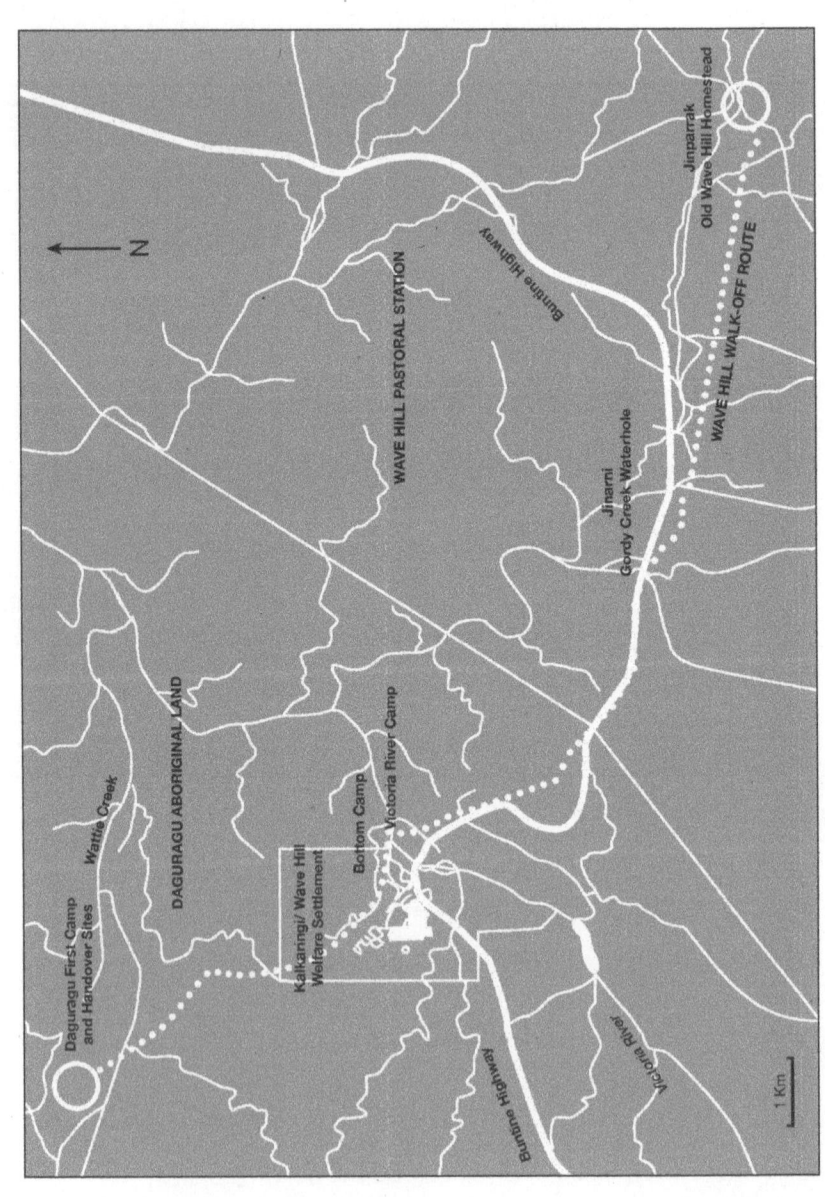

A HANDFUL OF SAND

Wattie Creek Village, October 1970
With thanks to Hannah Middleton.

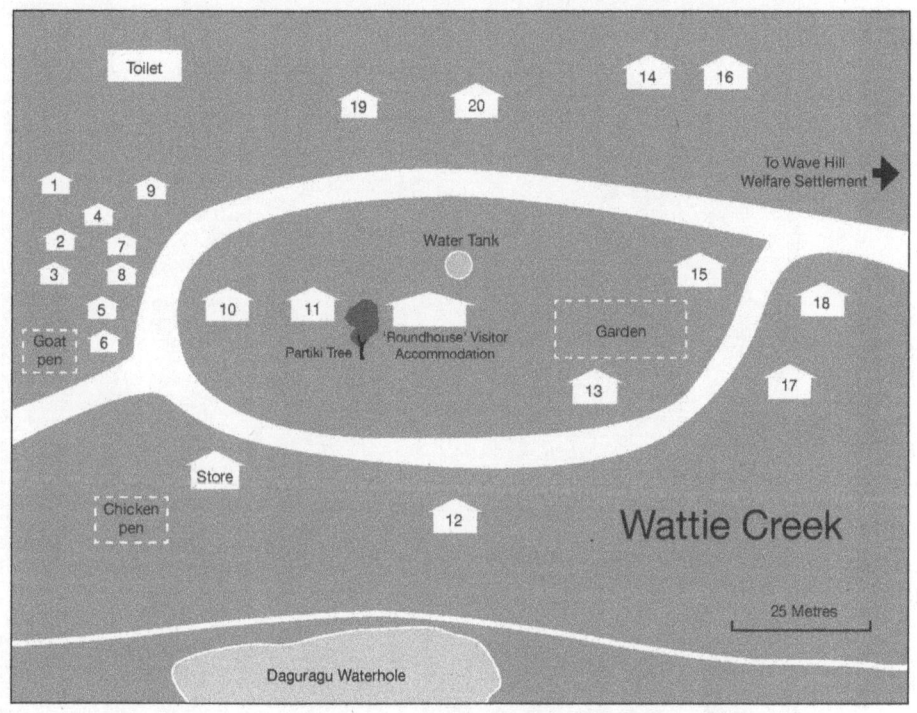

MAPS

KEY: Gurindji Camps (2–18 people)

1. Horace Wulmun
2. Barry Kadija (ex-Victoria River Downs)
3. Lupngiari (Captain Major), Amy Wurrumak
4. Freddy Algy
5. Pincher Nyurrmiarri, 'Big' Blanchie Bulngari
6. Vincent Lingiari, 'Little' Blanchie Jingaya
7. George Nidgi, Marie Djaban
8. Steven Ngalngayarri, Vera Dulngarri
9. Nugget Jinypal, Alice (_____)
10. Jerry Rinyngayarri, Melva Nanaku
11. Tommy Wodjabunga
12. Long Jack Jurumbak, Elsie Likapal
13. Donald Nangiari, Kitty Nanaku
14. Snowy Yalugura, Theresa Yupuny
15. Mick Rangiari, Lizzie Wapngarri or Ngilyawarru
16. Hobbles Danayarri, Lizzie Wartalilla
17. Long Johnny Kijngayari, Polly Lajayi
18. (Wanga) Bill Nurnngayarri, Mildred Jiwij
19. Abschol House 1.
20. Abschol House 2.

NB: In some cases the names of individuals may be misspelt, missing or wrongly included. In these instances, I apologise to the families of those concerned.

ACKNOWLEDGMENTS

During the twelve years since I first travelled to Kalkaringi and Daguragu, many people have assisted my creation of this work. I owe special thanks to the people of those communities for sharing their history with me. Notably the late Billy Bunter, Susan Cebu, Brenda Croft, Judith Donald, Paddy Doolak, Rosaleen Farquharson, Roslyn Frith, Gus George, the late Harry George, Michael George, Oscar George, the late Helen Morris, Michael Paddy, Maurie Japarta Ryan, George Sambo, William Smiler and family, Jimmy and Biddy Wavehill and Violet Wadrill.

I am permanently indebted to scores of others for their willingness to be interviewed as well. Firstly, the Gurindji's surviving Numadidi and Nunggubuyu supporters from Ngukurr: Brian Daniels, David Daniels, Kevin Rogers and Walter Rogers; and secondly their Mudburra supporters from Elliott: Claudette Albert, Johnny Devlin, Dick Kingston and Pompey Raymond.

Thanks are also due to these *kartiya* supporters of the Gurindji (or children thereof) for their interviews: Brian Aarons, Geoff Eames, Paul Fox, Kerry Gibbs, Christine Jennett, Tony Lawson, Andre Leu, Michael Leu, the late Brian Manning, Patrick McConvell, Tania McConvell, Warwick Neilley, Philip Nitschke, Barbara Pelczynska, Jack Phillips, David Quin, Jan Ridgway and Alex Romanoff.

Former Vestey's employees also answered my questions: the late Len Brodie, Neil Dudgeon, Graeme Fagan, Lauris Farrow, Jenny Lowe, Mark 'Fox' Lumsden, the late Peter Morris, Jack Noble, Dorothy Sing, Barbara Walters and the late Cec (and Dawn) Watts.

ACKNOWLEDGMENTS

Thanks also to these former public servants, mostly of the Welfare Branch and/or Department of Aboriginal Affairs: Gordon Bauman, Graham Castine, Harry Con Foo, Barrie Dexter, Ted Egan, Norm Faint, Barry Hansen, Bill Gray, Ray Hempel, Trevor LaBrooy, Barry Lamshed, John Millhouse, Ted Milliken, Gavin Perry, Ian Pitman, Colin Plowman, Brian Radunz, Len Richardson, John and Ann Rutter, Tony Scott, Essie Warmuth and Kirk Whelan.

Other former residents of Wave Hill consented to be interviewed: Bev Andrews, John and Elaine Bullock, Peter Collins, Frank Dalton, Bryce Fardell, Patricia Fardell, Marg Fenbury, Fred Friis, Keith Lansdowne, Norm and Helen McNair, Colin and Maggie Muir, Julia Pannell, Holt and Charl Thomson, and Allan Thorpe. Missionaries Rev Bernie Clarke, Gwen Dickman (née Moore), Rev Jim and Marilyn Kime, Rev Percy Leske and Lance Tremlett also kindly spoke to me.

Some interviewees also showed special generosity with records: Daphne Atkinson and family, Meredith Burgmann, John 'Jack' Cooke, Bryan Havenhand, Thea Hayes, brothers Fred and Bob Jeffrey, Hannah Middleton, Charlie Mines, Stan Pelczynski, Richard Preece, Rod Williams and Paddy Zakaria.

Lastly, among my interviewees, Jan Richardson, Lyn Riddett, Rob and Kay Oke and Rob Wesley-Smith deserve more than special mention for fielding my endless questions, providing records, feedback on the drafts and more. They were essential to this book, as was the support of the Northern Territory Government through the Northern Territory History Grants Program of the Department of Natural Resources, Environment, the Arts and Sport.

Academic staff have also assisted me. Firstly, my supervisory teams: Assistant Professor Rick Hosking, Dr Christine Nicholls and

A HANDFUL OF SAND

Dr Nathan Hollier oriented me in the jungle of academia; and thanks to Professor Tim Rowse, Dr Sarah Irving, and Professor Gillian Cowlishaw for supporting and challenging me further. Dr Rani Kerin and Professor Ann McGrath at the Australian National University, Assistant Professor Michael Christie at Charles Darwin University, Professor Mark McKenna and Professor Ann Curthoys at University of Sydney and Dr Sue Anderson at the University of South Australia are also deserving of special thanks.

Archival staff have been of great assistance, in particular Francoise Barr, Carolyn Newman, Matthew Stephen and Maureen Wilkins at the Northern Territory Archives Service; and Eve Chaloupka, Ben Heaslip and Joanne Wood at the National Archives of Australia, Darwin. Thanks is also due to Vern O'Brien, who has made as well as preserved NT history.

My appreciation to the following for providing discussion, advice, encouragement or access to records: Dr Malcolm Allbrook, Vic Barnett, Dr Anne Bartlett, Dr Debbie Bird Rose, Rob Chapman, Erika Charola, Chris Duke, Steph Forman of Global Interaction, Jason Gibson, David Hanlon, Henry Harper (H2), Dr Mary Anne Jebb, Luke Kelly, Dr Darrell Lewis, Kim Mahood, Dr Colin Salter, Dr Felicity Meakins, Hetti Perkins, Professor Nicolas Peterson, Stewart Philpott, Steve Roeger, Nicholas Rothwell, Dr Will Sanders, Murray Seiffert, Penny Smith of Karungkarni Art, Liz Sommerlad, Dr Sue Taffe, John Trezona, Professor Colin Tatz, and Dr Ailsa 'Tommy' Zainu'ddin.

Working to a very tight schedule, the team at Monash University Publishing have shown great professionalism: Dr Nathan Hollier, Joanne Mullins, Les Thomas, Sarah Cannon and Laura McNicol Smith.

ACKNOWLEDGMENTS

My longer literary slog has also been supported by many. Thanks to Susan Hampton, Charlotte Clutterbuck and the Grammar Gang, Peter Bishop and the Varuna Writers' Centre, and former staff of the Northern Territory Writers' Centre—especially Maryanne Butler, Kaye Hall, Sandra Thibodeaux, and Michael Giacometti.

Lastly, knowing I've forgotten others, heartfelt thanks to my family for their constant encouragement and assistance—especially my mother, Barbara Holloway (reader and editor extraordinaire); my very late father, Russel Ward; my partner Trang Dang; my author sister Biff; multilingual Brother Be; in-law librarian Pat Tandy; and the rest of the mob.

PREFACE

Of the extraordinary Wave Hill Walk-off, this much I knew. On the morning of 23 August 1966, in the remote Northern Territory, Aboriginal leader Vincent Lingiari led 200 Gurindji, Mudburra and Warlpiri workers and their families—90 percent of the staff of Wave Hill cattle station—from a century of servitude. They rejected the pleas of their British multinational employer 'Vestey's' to return, re-occupied an area of their own land at Wattie Creek, and fought until the nation's leaders—and its legislature—came to their cause. Chastened by the Gurindji's situation, Prime Minister Gough Whitlam and his supporters embraced Aboriginal land rights and returned their country with a symbolic handful of dirt in 1975. It seemed that after decades of denial, white Australia had extended 'a fair go' to the country's first people. Lingiari, long a thorn in the establishment's side, replied 'We're all mates now', and was awarded an Order of Australia.

When my Gurindji friends wanted to celebrate the 40th anniversary of their elders' Walk-off, in July 2006, I put my hand up to help. I was searching for Lingiari's vision of cross-cultural mateship and believed the Walk-off was a triumph. In my imagination, the tale loomed large. I'd inherited a romantic vision of the bush, from the old folk songs my father sang. They were peopled by bushrangers, shearers, drovers, alcoholics and stockmen—friends one and all—but Aboriginal people were absent. How did they fit into the Australian picture? I'd been trying to resolve that question, living and working with the Gurindji at Wave Hill.

PREFACE

I knew the 'beef road' to their country well. Cars laden with black fellas vied with serpentine road trains and government Toyotas. Flash troop carriers were so common that even when I saw one newly upended in the scrub, I wasn't shocked, just concerned it might contain my two colleagues. They'd been employed by the Gurindji to organise their 40th 'Freedom Day' too.

Termite mounds came into focus as I pulled up. A big cattleman walked towards me and held out his hand: 'I'm John Underwood. It's your fellas. They're alright'.

I doubted that. Ash, charcoal and dust were everywhere, an explosion from each of the half-dozen landings their vehicle had made. People loitered about a tarp strung off the far side of the wreck, but there was no sign of my mates. On the far side of the Toyota one of my friends leaned, the dust on his white skin streaked with blood. His pale eyes took me in. 'Charlie', he said levelly. Our colleague's neck was bulbously swollen. He was lying on the ground, and looked much worse.

With mortality on the breeze, our naive optimism dissipated with the fumes of a ruined engine. Posters depicting the iconic 'handback' of land to Lingiari by 'Saint Gough' Whitlam blew lazily about.

Whitlam had towered over me as a child and shook my hand before launching a book of my father's. Staring dumbly at these images of the great man, it felt like his famous handful of sand had blown to the world's four corners.

Enthralling as I found the Walk-off tale, the planets orbiting the saga were failing to align. How much credit, I wondered, was Whitlam due? Everyone I knew thought his self-determination policy had been the 'fair go' Aboriginal Australia desperately deserved, but three decades on, self-determination—or some bloody thing—had left

my Gurindji friends facing some serious problems. My now injured colleagues and I were possibly making the situation worse. Some blackfellas said the do-gooders of my type—indeed all the whites in their communities—were like cars: to be used until broken and replaced with a newer model.

Kneeling beside a totalled Toyota waiting for an ambulance, I had time to reflect:

Was Daguragu the 'better place' Lingiari had wanted? What was the Gurindji's freedom as they saw it? Aside from the iconic Walk-off and handback, what was their history? How much more blood—Gurindji and white—had been shed for the elders' vision?

Answering these questions would require me to explore the Walk-off's earliest roots, uncover the elders' dreams, and go beyond Whitlam's triumphal 'handful of sand'. The popular Walk-off song I knew focused on land rights alone, but Lingiari's group had also wanted to run a cattle operation and create an independent community managed by their children. To find out what happened to *those* dreams, I would need to track the restless dance of Aboriginal, government and cattle industry power playing over Wave Hill.

I would also need to talk with the old people who dreamed and strategised at Wave Hill station and Wattie Creek—but that was impossible. Who among Lingiari's generation was left? I sat with their radical spokesman Mick Rangiari while he sucked on secreted smokes, hawking into a tin, but the old fighter died months later. Luckily, I had more time with Billy Jampijinpa Bunter. From the windy morning we met on the northern edge of the Tanami desert, Mr Bunter proved himself a wise, gracious public servant and lawman, sharing his memories of the strike and the founding of Wattie Creek with me. Sadly, our last conversations occurred during his treatment

PREFACE

for lung cancer, and in September 2012 the last member of the Walk-off's inner sanctum passed away.

The leaders and spokesmen of that time were gone, and the old women of their generation were largely off-limits. Not only had the *kajirri* been less involved in political decision-making than their men, but my gender was an obstacle. Reading the archives, it emerged that scores of white men (and not a few white women) had encountered and perpetuated the same problem. The records I found were written by male *kartiya* journalists and public servants—recording and interrogating Gurindji men. Notwithstanding the attention of female activists in the early 1970s, the words and perspectives of old Gurindji women were almost entirely out of reach. With 'new generation' Gurindji women—some in their fifties now—the situation for me was different. The form of this book became clear. To understand the fate of the Walk-off leaders' vision, I knew that the stories of the European-Australians who inspired, supported, disappointed and deceived the elders must be told as well.

What follows then is a tale in which the Gurindji star; but it is not theirs alone. Scores of baby boomers with memories of Lingiari and Wattie Creek have also spoken with me, scattered from the rainforests of North Queensland to Western Australia's vineyards. I was occasionally thwarted by fires, floods, deaths and mechanical misadventures, but with few exceptions, aging activists, cattlemen, wharfies, patrol officers, nurses and missionaries gave me their time. Usually they told me that being among the Gurindji, on their country, was the most memorable period of their lives.

My decision to explore beyond the Gurindji's reputation as celebrated land rights pioneers is not one I have made lightly. Regardless of their visionary leadership in the 1960s and 70s, the residents of

Kalkaringi and Daguragu that emerge in these pages struggle like the rest of us. The problems that have assailed the Gurindji's countrymen have affected the 'Birthplace of Land Rights' as well. How could it be otherwise? No society has proved itself immune to the economic, political and cultural impact of the 'West', and the generation of Gurindji that came of age after the Walk-off—the first to exercise much individual choice about their social responsibilities—proved no different. This is the cost of the freedom their elders sought. In the Gurindji's foibles, we see our own. What sets them apart is the enormity of the challenges they faced—often presented under the guise of Aboriginal 'self-determination'.

Frank Hardy called his book about the Gurindji and their departure from Wave Hill station *The Unlucky Australians*. After Whitlam's handover of land in 1975, the currency of the old men was still adversity. While half a dozen elders fought tooth and nail for the continuation of their society and the survival of their culture, the forces arrayed against them included inexhaustible reserves of *kartiya* managing the business of the state, or merely their own interests. At most, the whitefellas involved had a two- or three-year contract riding on their engagement. When they were gone, others appeared, until their agendas or those of government were either achieved or abandoned. Though they preached consultation, none of the hundreds of officials the Gurindji dealt with learned the language of the local people.

* * *

In Part One of this book (The Quest for Land: 1930–72), Lingiari and his group struggle against the pastoral industry for equality.

PREFACE

Their plan for a future free of Vestey control is stalled until outside help arrives. Following the 'track mob's' famous 1966 Walk-off, conservative politicians—not 'British Lord Vestey'—emerge as the Gurindji's real foes regarding land rights. Country Party Ministers authorise spying on the group, and ignore Vestey's offer to give the Aborigines land. While the governments of John Gorton and William McMahon attempt to undermine the Gurindji's camp at Wattie Creek, the elders call for skilled support. Concerned students and others come to their aid. With a shifting network of supporters, the elders lobby politicians, build houses and create the foundations for their cattle operation—a far cry from 'eight long years of waiting', as this period has often been described. The Whitlam Government breaks the group's impasse when it comes to power in 1972, and makes an unprecedented offer to support the Gurindji's dream.

Part Two (Making a Fist of It: 1973–78) tells how conflict and chaos mired Whitlam's radical new Aboriginal self-determination policy at Wattie Creek and in Canberra alike. Pressured by the high expectations it has created, the government works on two fronts to obtain land for the Gurindji. Unable to postpone its delivery, during a ceremony at Daguragu Whitlam returns the Gurindji's land to them in the form of a pastoral lease. Receiving their land rights would take another ten years, but with Whitlam's handover, Lingiari's group gain tenure for their community, and funding and access to land for their cattle operation.

A surge of optimism follows, and an inflated, government-endorsed version of the elders' cattle operation gets underway. Cracks emerge quickly, though. White advisers are foisted on the elders against their will. Many younger Gurindji are unwilling—or unable—to take over the new local council created by the Department of Aboriginal

Affairs. Teenagers rebel while the conservative Fraser Government develops the 'track mob's' village. Hordes of whites arrive, to help whom—the Gurindji or themselves—is not often clear. By the late 70s, the elders' control is dissolving, a process hastened by the formation of the new Northern Territory Government.

In Part Three (The Harder Road: 1979–86), the new government in Darwin threatens the Gurindji, and the elders bar its representatives from their country in response. In radical reforms the NTG refashions the Gurindji's community council and overwhelms their cattle project. White businesses flourish, at the Gurindji's expense, it could be argued, while the young women of Daguragu mount a rebellion against the power of the old men. The police protect young Gurindji from traditional punishment and as the elders' authority declines, they worry for the future of their law and their vision.

To protest against European domination of their affairs, the families of Lingiari and other elders lead a second, little-known Gurindji walk-off in 1982. It falters, and a decade after 'self-determination', the track mob's leaders and their young trainees launch their final quest for control.

Introduction

PUT IN THEIR PLACE, 1879–1930

Ochre-drawn serpents, bats and emus watched the first white man traverse Gurindji land in 1879. Nat Buchanan, or 'Paraway,' the overlander, guided his horse across black soil plains between craggy red hills and spring-fed creeks. To the keen eyes of this country's residents, the four-legged apparition appeared as a devil-spirit. The Gurindji granted Buchanan passage, but the overlander envisioned a pastoral cornucopia and returned in 1884, droving thousands of cattle from 'par away' Queensland. The descriptions of the Gurindji's country that followed were tinged with joy and greed:

> As pretty Mitchell grass country as ever the eyes of man looked on—you have nothing like it about Adelaide![1]

The authorities of that city, two thousand miles distant, issued Buchanan with a lease over country they had never seen. With the dedication of his wife's brothers and his son Gordie, Buchanan unleashed Europe's pastoral juggernaut on the Aboriginal clans of the upper Victoria River. Their lives were changed irrevocably.

Choosing a location near a *ngumpit* river crossing that was fast becoming a drovers' route, a small stone homestead was built. The

---

1   C. Hemphill, Letter to the Editor, 'Central Australian Exploration', *The Adelaide Observer*, April 2 1891, p. 27.

'notoriously callous' 'Greenhide Sam' Croker, fancying the play of light on a layered range, named Buchanan's primitive, enormous run 'Wave Hill'. Co-existence with the Gurindji tribe was negotiated. Protecting cattle from *ngumpit* spears was a full-time occupation for half a dozen men led by Gordie Buchanan. After their first encounter with the Gurindji at the new site—in which a man was shot for attempting to steal a billy—the cattlemen chained people by the neck to build huge cattle yards near the homestead.[2] Sam Croker offered them a 'treaty': he would see the Gurindji were unharmed within a certain area if his cattle were left alone. Beyond this, Croker's 'myall' bush neighbours continued hunting his unfenced herds. In that wild country, beatings and murders continued in *ngumpit* camps, as punishment for cattle killing, or the theft of food.

In 1913 a police hut—for station is too grand a word—was built at nearby Bow Hill. The pastoralists' activities were then protected by the crude tools of European law: chaining and imprisonment. The Bow Hill police spent weeks on patrol with Aboriginal trackers, chasing cattle-killers over hundreds of miles. If caught alive, the alleged offenders were brought back and imprisoned next to their sick (and free) female relatives, who the police treated for the venereal diseases wracking the population. The authorities' impulses of control and care were paradoxically entwined from the outset.

The Gurindji's place in cattle station life became entrenched at the homestead, overlaying their extensive managerial and ceremonial responsibilities to their traditional country. Under the resulting regime—a type of rawhide feudalism repeated all over Australia's north—the Aborigines lived as second-class citizens during the dry

---

2   Oscar George, Personal Communication, 2004; Pearl Ogden, *From Humpy to Homestead: The Biography of Sabu Sing* (Winellie, Northern Territory, 1992), p. 78.

INTRODUCTION

season, and enjoyed a semblance of traditional life each monsoonal summer.

The stature of the senior Gurindji men—who were still family leaders and keepers of ceremony in the rare moments when traditional culture held sway—would diminish as they assumed their roles as head 'boys' of the stock camps among the whites. Compounding their emasculation, the months they spent in the stock camps (or droving) allowed unscrupulous whites to form sexual liaisons—by force or bartering—with Gurindji women. In country virtually devoid of their European counterparts, Gurindji women were preyed upon by frustrated white travellers as well as station staff:

> A lot of bagmen, drovers going through [...], they'd camp down on the river and have a swag full of dresses and goodies [...]. That's how they'd lure women down to those places.[3]

If an aggrieved husband retaliated against his wife's *kartiya* predator, the consequences were dire.

Despite disease and sexual predation, aspects of this situation were to the local peoples' advantage. The saving grace for many of the men was spending weeks or months at a time on country, or droving Vestey's cattle for thousands of miles. The fragile peace around Wave Hill was also life-saving. Some of the Gurindji's Warlpiri neighbours walked hundreds of miles to the station, fleeing violence and drawn by stories of sweet, easy foods and the treasured tobacco of the Europeans. Insufficient stale flour, sugar and tea were obtained on the station too, in exchange for work.

In 'the wet,' expectations were relaxed. The Gurindji stockmen and house staff would hand in the clothing offered to them as payment

---

3   Sing, quoted in Ogden, p. 63.

and return to neglected country on foot, camping for weeks on end. Catching *jungkuwurru* (echidna), *kirrawa* (goanna), and *yawu* (fish), medicine from the new season's red-rooted grass was also made. The Gurindji converged with their Warlpiri neighbours (once traditional enemies) and camped with Warlmanpa people at Catfish waterhole on the headwaters of the Victoria River. They met their Nyininy countrymen around Billiluna or Mistake Creek in the west. Dancing, ceremony and renewal ensued.

* * *

Buchanan's snuffle-nosed shorthorns trampling Gurindji land heralded the Aborigines' entwinement in a globalising industry. At the other end of the supply chain, demand for fatted beef in England was growing. Samuel Vestey, an ambitious grocer in the seaport of Liverpool, realised separate markets could be united by developments in shipping and refrigeration. Demand was so great for American corned beef that Vestey and his son William bought a section of the Liverpool docks and converted it to cold storage. Capitalising on England's new middle class, the Vesteys found themselves at the helm of a global operation. Following their expansion into China and Russia (where they bought vast quantities of frozen eggs), Australian and Latin American rangelands entered their sights. As a former colony, Australia was compliant with British power and offered plentiful land and labour at little cost.

'Vestey's', as the family's myriad companies were commonly known, bought the lease on Wave Hill station from the Buchanan clan at the start of World War One. Still largely an unfenced wilderness, Wave Hill was a minor tile in the family's global operations, though

INTRODUCTION

one they quickly worked into a huge chain of properties across northern Australia. The Australian government hoped to outsource development to wealthy pastoral lessees, and Vestey's took up the gauntlet. They rented almost 90,000 square kilometres of land in the Northern Territory and the East Kimberley for a trifle. Under the trading name of the Australian Investment Agency (AIA), the Liverpudlian merchants entered a partnership with the government, undertaking to develop ports and railways to hasten the North's economic growth.

While the Territory's Administrator curried favour with William and Samuel Vestey in 'Big England', the pair began to display the disarming candour and eccentricity which became their hallmarks. To reward themselves for their contribution to the British war effort, they brazenly requested their massive income should be exempt from taxation. Despite the objections of King George V, the Vesteys bought peerages from the British Prime Minister, and became Lords in the process. To celebrate they designed a family crest featuring chicken eggs and an iceberg, representing the keys to their success.

Meanwhile, the last massacre in Gurindji country occurred in about 1924 on a small knoll, midway between Vestey's cattle station and the police outpost at Bow Hill. Decades later, an old man remembered:

> They been coming with the horses and found this mob [at] Blackfellow's Knob. They trying to race away from them but they shot them like a dog [...]. One or two can get away. They shoot that bloke climb up the tree [...]; he fell over. Warlatarrka was his name. He was Jungurra [skin].[4]

---

4   See Pincher Nyurrmiarri, cited in *Daguragu Land Claim: Aboriginal Land Rights (Northern Territory) Act 1976* (Canberra, Australian Government, 1981).

Coinciding with this violence, the station homestead that had been rashly built on the flat by the Victoria River was destroyed by flooding. A story among the Gurindji has it that the flood was caused by 'Tinker', a rain-maker acting on a bet that he couldn't make rain. After the flood washed away the homestead and a good number of cattle, Tinker, according to a grandson, was so fearful of retribution he took off into the Tanami desert, never to return.[5] Following this disaster for the Europeans, a new station was built fifteen miles to the east. The Gurindji, bemused the whites would apply the name 'Wave Hill' at another location, followed them to the place they knew as Jinparrak. The most excessive punitive violence and gross misunderstandings ceased.

The Gurindji's residence at the 'new' Wave Hill station was another uneven patch of ground where they constructed their own 'wurlies', or 'dog houses'. A windmill-fed cattle trough lay in the next paddock. There the Gurindji washed and the women filled buckets to carry *karnatiti*-style—with a yoke over their shoulders. To the north sat neat wood-posted yards. By these were sheds housing the whites' animals, tools and equipment: the domain of a blacksmith, a saddler, and other *kartiya*. The earth was worn free of cover by donkey hooves, camel pads, hobnail boots, chicken claws and newly-introduced car tyres. The apex of European power was at the centre of all this: two veranda-ed houses for the manager and book-keeper, hemmed by a lawn and flowers.

Together, a dozen whites oversaw the management of 200 Aboriginal people and 20,000 cattle scattered over 6,000 square miles. The station's semi-indentured pool of 'natives' made it possible

---

5 Michael George, Personal Communication, Kalkaringi, Northern Territory, 27 October, 2010.

INTRODUCTION

for the Europeans to run the station. Working as 'domestics' at the homestead, the women made themselves dresses from chaff bags sewn with twine. Dubbed 'gins', 'lubras', 'bucks' and 'boys', the Gurindji became 'gate boys,' 'kitchen girls,' 'wood boys,' and 'house-gins'. Old women had the awful job of carting the homestead's sewerage. They'd 'clean it out six days a week. Those old girls used to have to carry it in four gallon tins on a yoke, poor old buggers'.[6] On summer nights small children worked the 'punkah' fan in exchange for leftovers, cooling the manager and his guests as they dined. Such was Jinparrak, the 'new' Wave Hill station in which the Gurindji's leaders came of age. It would be their lot for forty years.

---

6   Sing cited in Ogden, p. 62.

Part One

The Quest for Justice 1930–72

Chapter 1

FINDING THEIR FEET, 1930–1966

Without Vincent Lingiari, work on Vestey's Wave Hill station would have ceased. Whatever their attitudes to 'blacks', the whites depended on him to organise their workers. Aboriginal people looked up to him, regardless of their tribe. Lingiari was a Nyininy lawman and a powerful leader from country west of Wave Hill, married to a 'full' Gurindji woman.[1] A Juelama skin, he inherited the mantle of leadership from his father and emerged in middle age as the main advocate for all the Aborigines on the station. One of his protégés, the late Billy Bunter, put it this way:

> Vincent Lingiari was a really important person in the Vestey's. He was the only person to be in charge for all the tribes [...]— Gurindji, Warlpiri, Ngarinyman, Mudburra, Nyininy people— but he was also the Vestey headboy. He was a really important bloke, a Christian bloke, and a lot of people looked up to him, you know? A person on the whiteman way and the Aboriginal way, a nice old fella.[2]

Thoughtful and reflective, Lingiari usually spoke only after consideration. Even Europeans who opposed his politics were struck by

---

1   Lyn Riddett [former resident at Wattie Creek, 1971–73], Personal Communication, 12 January 2012.
2   Darwin, NTAS, Billy Bunter, Interview Recorded by Charlie Ward, October 2010, NTRS 3609, BWF 21.

his innate dignity. A woman who spent time with Lingiari when she was a teenager recalled 'He was a beautiful man. He required respect because he was so respectful'.[3]

Lingiari dwelt upon his people's circumstances from a young age. In the 1930s, a boss from Wave Hill took him for company on an eye-opening trip to Adelaide. During his time in the south, a group of young locals befriended him and invited him fishing. An old man also asked about his work conditions on Wave Hill. On hearing the young stockman's response—no wages, but food, though 'no butter, no jam', the white man said:

> 'Oh well, you want to finish up, tell them to stick their jobs up their fuckin' arses'.
>
> 'Alright', Lingiari replied, 'I will. I got enough guts to do it'.[4]

Lingiari's first visit to a crowded city kindled his later association between 'help', 'friends', and the big cities of the south.

Lingiari's main counsel—for he made no decisions alone—came from the sons of two families: brothers Mick Rangiari, Pincher Nyurrmiarri and 'Long Johnny' Kijngayari from one; and Jerry Rinyngayarri and Donald Nangiari from another. Rangiari was an extrovert, a negotiator and something of a lair. He carried the scars of the Gurindji's conditions deeper than many, having broken his pelvis in a horse fall and waited days for help. His brother Pincher was a brilliant social observer who shared Rangiari's outspokenness. These men formed a radical flank, their opinions tempered in Lingiari's judgment by Nangiari and Rinyngayarri, two of his more cautious

---

3   NTAS, Interview with Essie Warmuth [resident of Wave Hill Welfare settlement, 1965–66]. Recorded by Charlie Ward, December 2010, NTRS 3609, BWF 11.

4   Darwin, NTAS, Vincent Lingiari Interviewed by Ted Egan and Tim Bowden, 1979, NTRS 1942, TS 1237.

countrymen. Living in an open-air labour market, these men's leadership was political as well as ceremonial.

Through their work, many Gurindji men travelled to Vestey's properties in Western Australia and Queensland, droving the company's cattle for thousands of miles. They saw that the conditions of black stock workers in Queensland were better than their own, and visited the unionised mining town of Mount Isa. During the 'Japanese War', Vestey's won a contract to supply the Australian forces with meat. Hundreds of Aboriginal people—including Lupngiari ('Captain Major'), another Gurindji leader—worked with the army, interacted with more open-minded whites, and experienced 'equal pay' for the first time.

Lupngiari took 'horses from Darwin to that New Guinea place, over there', to furnish the Australian troops.[5] He was an experienced and respected stockman, buffalo shooter and drover, and later ran a stock camp on Gallipoli station for thirteen years. With a larrikin, good-natured air and an endearing shrill voice, Captain Major, as he was known to whites, had been blinded in one eye by a tree-branch. In 1935 he had stood up to Wave Hill station's manager Tiger Goddard. Terrified, Goddard had threatened him with a whip and held a gun to his head.[6] Like Vincent Lingiari, Lupngiari had serious politics, passable English, and a willingness to fight.

Lupngiari and Lingiari's generation of Gurindji matured when their people's conditions were at their worst. At Wave Hill station, spoils from Vestey's war business were nowhere to be seen, and the health of the station's Aboriginal workers was so poor that their

---

5   Frank Hardy, *The Unlucky Australians*, Sydney, Nelson, 1968 (2006 edn, Melbourne, One Day Hill), p. 30; Pearl Ogden, *From Humpy to Homestead: The Biography of Sabu Sing* (Winellie, Northern Territory, 1992), p. 95.

6   Ann McGrath, *Born In the Cattle* (North Sydney, Allen & Unwin, 1987), p. 114.

numbers were falling. Fearful of losing their labour supply, Vestey's recruited two anthropologists to advise how their workers' fertility could be improved. Newly married graduates Ronald and Catherine Berndt were dispatched by Professor AP Elkin from Sydney University. They found the living conditions and diet of the Aboriginal staff on Vestey properties (like most others) 'atrocious'.[7] During their fieldwork, they recorded four Aboriginal births on Wave Hill. Two of the mothers and three of the babies died. Dreadful events like the arrival at Wyndham hospital of a Gurindji woman with a long-dead foetus in her womb occurred, and *ngumpit* spoke of choosing not to procreate while their situation prevailed.

The health of Gurindji country was also plummeting. With still incomplete internal fencing, rampaging mobs of feral donkeys and no upper limits on stock numbers, damage to the station's waterways went unchecked. The damage was recognised as early as the 1940s, though it was twenty years before Vestey's culled ninety thousand donkeys, by then known to the Gurindji as 'Jesus horse'. The erosion that occurred through these decades can be measured by a public servant's observation in 1967: 'what was known as a spring [at the junction of Gill and Wattie Creeks] in the boyhood days of [Lingiari] is now quite a gorge'.[8]

Vestey's inflexibility was such that occasionally the stockmen—who like their white colleagues, worked sixteen hour days—were not given time to bury their dead. Although the company usually lent them a truck, sometimes families carried the bodies of their kin to a range a mile or so distant, in darkness:

---

7   Berndt and Berndt, cited in Glen McLaren and William Cooper, *Distance, Drought and Dispossession* (Darwin, Northern Territory University Press, 2001), p. 164.
8   Darwin, NAA, Report from M. Ivory to H.C. Giese in 'Sacred Sites: Wave Hill Area', 29 May 1967, *District Welfare Officer Reports, Wave Hill Area*, E242, K66/1/1.

> When people passed away [there], at that camp [...] we had to carry them [...] to the other side of that creek there [...] that far. Carry up that body—long stick on the side. [The manager said] 'You got to carry 'em up yourself'.⁹

They would leave the bodies to decay in trees so they could return for work by the dawn. Like much else, Vestey's miserliness pushed Gurindji funerals and internment ceremonies into the wet season. At the same time, thanks to a loophole identified by Vestey's lawyers, its income—and that of other foreign landlords during the 1940s—was entirely tax-free.

After the War, noises—if not actions—about improving the situation of the Territory's Aboriginal cattle workers, were emanating from Canberra. Inspired by the contribution made by Aboriginal people during the War, the Chifley Labor Government pressed for the wages of Aboriginal station workers to be set at *half* that paid to whites. The pastoralists forced a retreat, and an Aboriginal wage was set at 25 percent of the Award. As a compensatory gesture, the pastoralists undertook to build rudimentary housing for their Aboriginal workers: a huge advance—if it was delivered upon. In another humanitarian act, the government sent Doctor WA 'Spike' Langsford and his later-famous assistant, Phillip *'I, The Aboriginal'* Roberts, to survey the Gurindji's health.

In the 1950s, a newly-created 'Welfare Branch' began paying pensions for unemployable Aborigines, via the manager of Wave Hill. Welfare patrol officers also began visiting, consulting with Lingiari, and pressuring the manager to improve amenities for

---

9   Victor Vincent, on 'Conditions: Housing and General—Track Two', *Walk-off Stories, From the Darkness into the Light: Gurindji Freedom Banners Project*, Audio CD (Kalkaringi, NT, Daguragu Community Government Council, 2000).

Aboriginal workers. Along with a raft of new entitlements such as long service and sick leave, Vestey's was required to provide lamps, accommodation, and 'stretchers and mattresses [stuffed] with sufficient dry hay, straw kapok or fibre' to their staff.[10] In response to the Welfare Branch's requests for Aboriginal huts at Wave Hill, though, 'Alison' Bingle, Vestey's general Australian manager, stonewalled:

> [...] You will acknowledge that Rome was not built in a day and you do know that labour for building purposes and materials are not readily available in the Territory.[11]

In 1952, Bingle employed a rotund, balding ex-butcher named Tom Fisher as Wave Hill's manager. Mindful that his white staff were entitled to only one holiday every three years and were massively isolated, Fisher built a 'rec room' containing billiard and ping pong tables and a darts board. As a result of such gestures, white stockmen regarded Vestey's as among the Territory's better employers. The company's consistency and one-eyed fairness engendered loyalty in many whites that lasted for decades. Spontaneous gestures to make the Gurindji's lives more bearable also occurred. The wife of Fisher's predecessor dispensed second hand clothes to the Gurindji each year, while Lady Vestey herself gave a sketchbook to Dandy Jumiari, a talented Gurindji artist. These were token gestures, but the new 'Welfare' patrols and the arrival of Tom Fisher heralded a slight improvement for the Gurindji.

---

10 Darwin, NTAS, 'The Northern Territory Cattle Station Industry Award 1951', *Northern Territory Pastoral Lessees' Association, Administration and Correspondence Files, 1910–1994*, NTRS 3548, B1/2B.

11 Darwin, NAA, 'Letter to Acting Director of Native Affairs from AS Bingle, 29 January, 1954, Administrator, Northern Territory [II]—Central Registry, *Wave Hill Station*, F1, 1952/736. Another ostensible reason for Vestey's reluctance to build was the perceived difficulties that would ensue if limited staff accommodation was provided while other families missed out. See Ogden, pp. 64–65.

FINDING THEIR FEET, 1930-1966

Vestey's began an annual picnic race for staff 'jollification' at the Linnaker River near the Western Australian border. The gathering soon shifted to the Negri River on Ord River station, and after considerable lobbying from Native Affairs, was opened to Aboriginal employees. Vestey's transported Gurindji families by truck for hundreds of miles to attend, and the races were filled with revelry, storytelling and sporting misadventures.

After patrol officer Ted Evans' lobbying in 1953, the Gurindji were paid cash wages before their Negri trip, and hence handled money for the first time. A witness recorded:

> Everywhere bough sheds housed laughing groups of people. [...] Black boys [sic] built fires and brewed billies of black tea; ringers and jackeroos supervised the horses some had brought over hundreds of miles to race [...], bottles were opened hastily to greet old friends. [Later] I could hear the blacks, corroboreeing to the didgereedoo [sic] down by the creek in the age-old fashion of their people. Gorgeous in paint and feathers, they were concluding their celebrations with a dance.[12]

Although expectations differed regarding alcohol, 'the Negri' was a great opportunity to mix with others from across the northwest. While these events nurtured pride among male staff as 'Vestey men', they did little to bridge the gap between the races on Wave Hill.

* * *

While Lingiari and 'Captain Major' dreamed of better lives for their people, their vision was being honed by an older man: Tipujurn, or 'Sandy Moray'. Moray had travelled widely between Vestey's stations

---

12   Wanda Stirling [aka Marie Mahood], 'The Negri Bush Races', *Western Mail*, 9 November 1950.

in the 1920s–40s, becoming familiar with *kartiya* ways and learning English. Born around 1905, Tipujurn's father had been murdered by white men, and he harboured strong resentment. Like Lupngiari, he showed little fear dealing with unreasonable Europeans. When a fight broke out in the stock camps, Moray often cried 'You're the bloke that finished my father!'[13]

In about 1950, Tipujurn convened a meeting on his traditional country, under a Nutwood *Partiki* tree on the fertile plain by Wattie Creek. To this gathering of Gurindji men, he put forward a radical vision of living independently of Vestey's on their own land, running Gurindji-owned cattle. According to Lingiari, he told them: 'I think we got to stick-up somehow now, get own land, [find] *kartiya* people [to] work with us. [...] We go to headquarters, find people in the big city somewhere, find a mate'.[14] Many of those present, including Lingiari, thought the idea a fantasy, but each night Moray reinforced his concept, encouraging them: 'just do what we can, keep going now'.[15] He lobbied *ngumpit* on surrounding stations in the same way. Eventually Moray's plan gained acceptance among the Gurindji—a dream they would cling to, until the time was right.

Between working as the 'headboy' of Wave Hill's Number Two stock camp, providing workers to Tom Fisher, 'growing up' his nephews and children, ironing out tribal disputes and his ceremonial duties, Lingiari lobbied Wave Hill's managers to improve the lot of his people. Using his significant authority, tact and political nous,

---

13 NTAS, Lingiari, NTRS 1942, TS 1237.
14 NTAS, Lingiari, NTRS 1942, TS 1237.
15 Minoru Hokari, 'From Wattie Creek to Wattie Creek: An Oral Historical Approach to the Gurindji Walk-Off' (*Aboriginal History*, 24, 2000), p. 103.

Lingiari confronted Tom Fisher about clothing, which his people received in lieu of money:

> Next time I got wild I went to gate, waiting for Tom Fisher. He come along, said:
>
> 'You can start branding and drafting in the morning', said all this.
>
> 'Righto Tom, what about we fuckin' clothes?' I said.
>
> 'Oh no, it's not time' [he replied].
>
> [I told him] 'If [you] don't give we clothes tomorrow, we move off'.
>
> 'Oh, no, I'll bring it out tomorrow morning'.
>
> Just before sun-up [the clothes] come.
>
> 'That's more like it' [I said], 'Good one'.[16]

The consistent needling of Vestey's by both Welfare officers and the Gurindji bore results in 1959. In the lee of a small hill next to the Aborigines' wurly camp, a number of shadeless iron huts and barracks were built for the Gurindji 'headboys' and their families.[17] The huts were tiny, industry standard. They measured twelve feet along each wall and were made of tin with a rock and ant-bed floor. Although

---

16   See NTAS, Lingiari, NTRS 1942, TS 1237.
17   These huts and a primitive shower block formed the nucleus of a 'new camp', the existence of which was consistently ignored by journalists and unionists keen to convey Vestey's negligence in post Walk-off reports. Mention of the 'new camp' has even dropped out of most Gurindji narratives about Jinparrak, due in part to the fact that most Gurindji remained in the 'old camp' rather than relocating. The flooring of several cottages is still visible at the site. See Darwin, NAA, 'Wave Hill Report, 6 October 1966', and 'Wave Hill Station: Inspection and Census, 29 September 1965', *Employment and General Welfare of Aboriginals—Wave Hill Station*, F1, 1967/1113; Ralph Hayes, cited in Ogden, p. 64; Residents of Daguragu and Kalkaringi, *From the Darkness into the Light: Gurindji Freedom Banners* (Daguragu Community Government Council, Kalkaringi, NT, 2000).

they were too small to do anything except sleep in, piled together on the floor, they had been hard-won. After Vestey's exploitation of the Gurindji for fifty years, these tin boxes were an acknowledgement of their occupants' humanity and growing international recognition of 'human rights'. With the huts, four pit toilets were also built nearby.

As well as patrol officers, Christian missionaries came by. Lingiari took to the teachings of United Aborigines Missionaries at the Negri races, and declared himself a believer. When newly-ordained Baptist Minister Jim Kime visited from the nearby Hooker Creek Welfare settlement in 1964, Tom Fisher introduced him to the senior Gurindji. After Fisher left, Lingiari took the missionary into one of the new 'Welfare' huts and pointed to a poster on the wall. According to Kime:

> It was a graphic poster that featured 'two ways': an upward way and a downward way. The upward way pointed to a narrow road leading upwards with an Aboriginal person [...] looking very clean and pristine with his hair cut, walking up to what looked like heaven. The other [route] showed a very miserable group on a wide road with people [drinking], beating their wives—leading down to what appeared to be hell. Pointing to the upward road, Vincent said 'We want to go this way'.[18]

The Gurindji's plan to 'track' to a better life was already in place. Kime visited the Gurindji camp every fortnight, and was gobsmacked by the Gurindji elders' receptivity to his Bible stories—a stark contrast to the older Warlpiri at Hooker Creek.

*** * * ***

---

18   Rev Jim Kime, Interview Recorded by Charlie Ward, 3 June 2014.

Once buoyed by the promises of patrol officers, the Gurindji's belief in 'Welfare' was leeching away. Ceremonial leader Long Johnny Kijngayari described the pattern:

> 'Next year we'll improve your conditions and help you' [the patrol officers said].
>
> Then we looking out, but nothing.
>
> [We said] 'We're making big money for the whites, but we get nothing, we must go away'.
>
> Then we stayed at work and said, 'We'll watch out next year'. Then we watched out, but no, still the same way.
>
> We said, 'I don't think we'll get anything [...]. No, we must leave them'.
>
> Then 'We'll go west to the races and see if they give us big money when we get back'.
>
> [Afterwards, we asked] 'Where is it, where is it, where is it?', but there was nothing.
>
> Next year we started camp [work] again.[19]

In the early 60s, the situation was approaching breaking point, though the whites were oblivious. According to Billy Bunter, a Warlpiri teenager who was privy to the older men's strategising, Lingiari's frustration peaked in 1964, and the elders agreed to enact Moray's plan to 'track' as soon as support was available.[20]

In Darwin, Brian Manning and George and Moira Gibbs, the Gurindji's future allies, were building connections with confident,

---

19 Johnny Kijngayari, 'The Wave Hill Strike' in *This is What Happened: Historical Narratives by Aborigines*, ed. by Luise Hercus and Peter Sutton (Canberra, Australian Institute of Aboriginal Studies, 1986), pp. 305–311.
20 NTAS, Bunter, NTRS 3609, BWF 21.

politicised Aboriginal men such as Davis Daniels and Jacob Roberts from Roper River. Gibbs had been active in Darwin's Aboriginal labour struggles of the 1940s and 50s, while Manning had fallen in heavily with the local Communist Party (CPA) after his recent arrival. The home he shared with other 'reds' was known about town as 'The Kremlin'. Roberts, Daniels, Manning and Terry Robinson, another white 'red', created Darwin's Council for Aboriginal Rights (NTCAR) along the same 'mixed' lines as its powerful southern-based supporter, FCAATSI. Formed in 1961, NTCAR ensured that some years the majority of Darwin's May Day marchers were Aboriginal.

Thanks to their purchase of a wireless from a travelling hawker, the Gurindji's exposure to current affairs and social issues was growing. In between the men's time on the stock camps, Lingiari and others would lie around it in the evenings, listening to news from afar. Aboriginal issues were gaining airtime. NTCAR began to pressure the North Australian Workers' Union (NAWU) to support Aboriginal station workers, and in 1964 the union initiated the 'Aboriginal equal wages case'. Despite the national Arbitration Commission only visiting six stations, and not speaking to Aboriginal people, the men on Wave Hill knew the case related to them. According to Captain Major:

> I bin thinkin' longa time about my people not having proper wages, proper conditions. I bin thinkin' we got no one to help us, no one behind us. Then I bin hearing about them whitefellas talkin' in that court somewhere about equal wages.[21]

---

21   Cited in Hardy, 1968 (2006), p. 31; NTAS, Cooke, NTRS 3609, BWF 28; Bill Bunbury, *It's Not the Money, It's the Land: Aboriginal Stockmen and the Equal Wages Case* (North Fremantle, Western Australia, Fremantle Arts Centre Press, 2002), pp. 88–89.

FINDING THEIR FEET, 1930–1966

By March 1966, there were roughly forty huts and barracks in the barren 'new camp' built by Vestey's at Wave Hill, though, as the company had long predicted, few of them were occupied. The Gurindji's bottom line remained: *kartiya* stockmen were paid the equivalent of $33 a week, compared to the Aboriginal wage of $6.34. The Commission found that all workers in the NT pastoral industry should be paid the same rate. Only 'slow workers' would be exempt. To minimise the pain of adjustment for the cattlemen, the Commission decided the transition to full award wages should be made over three years, by December 1968. Observers were shocked. The big pastoralists, it was said, would have no hope of returning profits if they began paying their Aboriginal workers the same as whites. Thousands of Aboriginal people would lose their jobs.

At the time of the equal wages case, Dexter Daniels, the younger brother of NTCAR activist Davis, was working in a new position as NAWU's Aboriginal organiser. Dexter was outraged by the three year delay, and pushed for a general strike in protest. The union's pragmatic Irish secretary Paddy Carroll restrained him. Although Carroll knew the union couldn't sustain a large strike in the bush, he struck a deal with Daniels in April 1966 and sent him and another organiser, Curly Nixon, to assess the potential of a symbolic strike near the Territory's main road at Newcastle Waters station. As it happened, Daniels' nephews—also Nunggubuyu men from the Roper River mission—were working there, and he was related to many of the area's Mudburra people through his mother.

The response to Dexter's union mob on Newcastle Waters and surrounding stations was electric, creating a turning point in Territory history. A former ringer described the group's arrival on Vestey's Helen Springs:

It was in the evening, just on twilight. We'd just knocked off mustering and a couple of the horses were still tied to the tying rail. We were having our evening meal when a three-ton Bedford truck turned up in the blacks' camp.

'I wonder what the hell is happening over there' [I said].

No-one knew who it was. Anyway, twenty minutes later, you could see from the light of their campfire the Aboriginal boys rolling their swags and throwing them on the back of the truck. Still no-one came to tell us what was happening, and away they went. Wally Atkinson, the manager, came out in the morning and told us it was strikes, with whatever language he used.[22]

When Daniels—who probably understood some of the local language—arrived at Newcastle Waters, there was an audience keen to hear his message and relieve their pent-up grievances. The young radical passed on a message to an old pensioner named 'Prentice', who could read:

Mr Prentis,

Please tell the boys to stop work soon as they come home from mustering camp. My address is Box 132, c- NAWU, Darwin.

Dexter Daniels.[23]

Following Daniels' visit, on 21 April 1966, a couple who worked at the Newcastle Waters school, Duncan Jabada and Elsie Malyeri, went on strike. After sending Daniels and NAWU another pre-written telegram, eighty Mudburra, Gurindji and Wambaya staff

---

22   NTAS, Jack Noble, Interview Recorded by Charlie Ward, October 2011, NTRS 3609, BWF 29.
23   NAA, Telegram from Dept. of Northern Territory Administration, Darwin, to Dept. of Territories, Canberra, 28 April 1966, F1, 1966/2182.

from the station followed suit, striking for higher pay. The group 'sat down' on an old ceremony ground which quickly became known as 'Union Camp'. Situated behind the Newcastle Waters pub, the authorities urged them to leave:

> When we bin strike, policeman used to humbug there, and Welfare, longa that place where we bin live, Union Camp. Policeman and Welfare always go there, trying to put we back to work.[24]

Ironically, the conditions provided by Newcastle Waters' manager Roy Edwards were among the best of any Aboriginal station workers in the Territory. Some of the strikers had huts with electricity, and running water had been supplied to their camp. Edwards' relationship with Aboriginal people was reputedly good and when some of his most reliable staff confronted him over pay, he was dismayed.

The local Welfare officer, JA 'Jack' Cooke, aware of Aboriginal anger about the delayed introduction of the Award, observed a fact pastoralists and other public servants were about to learn:

> The atmosphere is such on most large properties that the Aboriginal workforce would go on strike at the instruction of a union organiser, particularly Dexter Daniels. Having seen the results of his agitation at Newcastle Waters I believe this man could develop into a powerful force and if he so desired he could seriously embarrass the government and temporarily cripple the Northern Territory pastoral industry […].
>
> It appears to me that Dexter Daniels has cast a messianic spell over these people and having followed his instructions they now expect great support from [him]. Their first disillusionment will

---

24 Darwin, NTAS, Interview with [Newcastle Waters strikers] Pompey Raymond, William Kingston, Claudette Albert, Alan Albert and Johnny Devlin, Recorded by Charlie Ward, October 2010, NTRS 3609, BWF 22.

probably be the non-appearance of [his promised] truck full of food.[25]

Despite the cynicism of Cooke and many pastoralists, support for Daniels and the strikers was immediate. The crews of three ships berthed in Darwin Harbour 'passed the hat', and after a large shopping trip, attempted to deliver their supplies to the 'Union Camp' personally. Unfortunately their vehicle broke down on the 500 mile drive and contrary to Cooke's expectations, Dexter Daniels completed the delivery.

One of the most receptive to Daniels' agitation was the disgruntled Gurindji stockman, Lupngiari. At the time of Daniels' visit, Lupngiari was a head 'boy' working for Roy Edwards, paid $10 ($125 in today's terms) per week.[26] Like Moray and Lingiari, he knew the taste of indignity firsthand: 'I remember once when I was a young lad I returned from a long trip with a mob of cattle and asked for my wages. They gave me a bag of lollies'.[27] When Daniels arrived, the old stockman was smarting from a potentially fatal neck injury. Edwards had refused him time off, and the manager's wife had 'treated' Lupngiari with some ointment. While suffering acute pain, the stockman had:

> [...] kept riding on it just the same. [...] I went down to the [...] yard and was thinkin' to meself, [...] 'I only get $10, and these

---

25 Darwin, NAA, Cooke to Giese, 28 April 1966, *Industrial Unrest on Pastoral Properties 1966–1969*, F1, 1966/2182.

26 Financial values in this book have been cited in the following form: £AUS/$AUD original amount ($AUD 2015 value). Current values have been calculated and rounded off using the Australian Bureau of Statistics' Australian Consumer Price Index Calculator <http://www.abs.gov.au/websitedbs/d3310114.nsf/home/Consumer+Price+Index+Inflation+Calculator> [accessed 8 November 2015].

27 Henry McCarthy, 'Two Quiet Men who ask for Dignity and Support', *Tribune*, 19 October 1966.

other men only get $6. That not right!' And I bin thinkin' again, 'Wish we had someone behind us somewhere'.²⁸

Lupngiari quickly found allegiance and friendship with the young Dexter Daniels, and assumed the role of spokesman for the mob at Newcastle Waters. When news of the strike broke, however, it was tinged by a fact which was quickly exploited by critics. Although the workers were apparently striking over pay, few could identify how much they were paid, nor what rate they were striking for.²⁹

* * *

Two hundred miles away, along the feared Murranji drovers' track, Vincent Lingiari was at *Kawarlakujarra*, or the 'Number 22' bore on Wave Hill station. While fixing a mule to a buggy, he was kicked and his leg badly broken. The camp's head stockman rode for help. Unlike many of his countrymen who had been seriously injured in the past, Lingiari was flown by Connellan Air to the Katherine hospital, and then transferred to Darwin.³⁰ Introduced by his brother Davis (then NTCAR secretary, working as a hospital orderly), Dexter

---

28   Cited in Hardy, 1968 (2006), p. 31.
29   To some, this defied the legitimacy of industrial action and it was alleged the strikers were merely the puppets of their union advocates. To others, it underscored the need for radical industrial reform. Those making such allegations against the strikers would have known, however, that only a few Aboriginal staff (like Lupgngiari) could count; none had ever been schooled in finance. Also, the pay rate for pastoral workers had varied significantly over time, and wage payments—when they had been made at all—were usually withheld in trust accounts, paid in arrears, or transferred as credit to a company store (with its own pricing system), in which case the staff never saw their money at all. In addition, pay slips were rarely given and decimal currency had been introduced only two months earlier, making any knowledge the strikers may have accrued of the value of cash to that time redundant.
30   Writers such as Minoru Hokari (2000, 2011) and Colin Salter (2009) have conjectured Lingiari feigned his broken leg to travel to Darwin to meet with unionists. Eye witness accounts contradict this. See Darwin, NTAS, Interview with Neil Dudgeon

Daniels met the respected *marluka* Lingiari during his convalescence. They discussed the Gurindji's position, and the working conditions at Wave Hill. Daniels advised the Gurindji leader 'right way is to finish up with Vestey mob'.

While Lingiari's bones mended and he considered his people's predicament, a group of men from his Number Two stock camp confronted Tom Fisher, requesting more pay. Angered by Fisher's outright refusal, the group walked from the station to the Wave Hill Welfare settlement, where Bill Jeffrey, a new manager, gave them food and sympathy. When Vestey's pastoral manager Peter Morris heard of Jeffrey's generosity, he sought the official co-operation usually given to 'big' cattlemen. Morris asked Welfare Branch director Harry Giese for an assurance that any incentive for Aboriginal workers to leave Wave Hill station would be removed:

> I understand from Mr Fisher that these natives walked down to the school at the Wave Hill police station and [...] were fed at the school. [...] I know you yourself don't agree with the principle of natives being able to walk-off employment on a station and [...] obtain rations without having to work.[31]

Sensing Dexter Daniels' 'reconnaissance' trips were having a wider impact than he wished, NAWU's Paddy Carroll attempted to 'clip his wings', giving him strict instructions only to visit Newcastle Waters. Ignoring this advice, Daniels took leave from NAWU and sought support from the more radical NTCAR. Soon afterwards—with NTCAR backing—Dexter, a young Numamudidi man named

---

recorded by Charlie Ward, November 2012, NTRS 3609, BWF 48; NTAS, Bunter, NTRS 3609, BWF 21; Manning, 2002, p. 2; Hardy, 1968 (2006), p. 72; Darwin, NTAS, *Flight Manifests and Trip Records 1941–1976, Connellan Airways*, NTRS 622.

31   Darwin, NAA, P Morris to HC Giese, 27 June 1966, *Employment and General Welfare of Aboriginals: Wave Hill Station*, F1, 1967/1113.

Walter Rogers and a nuggetty Greek wharfie, Nick Bagonis, went to visit workers on a range of stations, assessing their willingness to strike. The reception they received from management was often less than friendly, and in one instance they were 'welcomed' with a rifle.

When the NTCAR-backed firebrands eventually arrived at Wave Hill, the Gurindji were away at the Negri races. Only the female skeleton staff and Mick Rangiari were present. When Lingiari returned from hospital on 20 August 1966, he had the demeanour of a 'changed man'.[32] The activists were waiting for him. Before leaving for the next station, Daniels got straight to the point: 'What about it now?' Lingiari was ready, but wanted his people behind him. 'What about when they come back?' Daniels asked.[33]

After a lifetime of simmering, enervating conflict with his pastoral masters, it was this show of support on his own country that tipped Lingiari into action. When he had wrung promises from Vestey's or visiting public servants in the past, the *kartiya* usually reneged on them. Now, it seemed to Lingiari that by announcing outright it would do nothing about pay for three years, the commission in the south had done away with all pretences of equality. The punishments available to Europeans (and the repercussions from their use) had also changed. Tom Fisher and the new Welfare officer Bill Jeffrey were fond of the Gurindji people, and unlike in the past, a show of force by the single local policeman was unlikely. It was time. When his people returned from the Negri, Lingiari would lead them—come what may—into a future of their making.

---

32 Sing, cited in Ogden, p. 95.
33 Hardy, 1968 (2006), p. 72.

Chapter 2

TAKING A STAND, 1966–1968

> I chose this place (Wattie Creek) just for Aborigines because we on top of the bone, on top of the blood. Old people get shot all over, that's why.[1]
>
> Pincher Nyurrmiarri, 1981.

Carrying blankets, billycans and babies, with dogs ranging alongside, the Gurindji walked west in the early morning of 23 August 1966, following a fence-line to Gordy Creek. All but the most elderly and 'pumpers'—men minding bores on remote parts of the station—were part of the exodus. Their leaders, the head Aboriginal stockmen of Wave Hill, had been to the office at the homestead and told manager Tom Fisher their decision. They ignored his pleas, collected their few belongings, and set out.

The destination Lingiari had chosen was the Victoria River bed by the drovers' common, fifteen miles distant. From the middle of Wave Hill's sprawl, it was the only non-Vestey-held territory they could easily reach. The common was the site of the region's Welfare

---

1   Pincher Nyurrmiarri, cited in *Daguragu Land Claim 1981*, p. 203.

Branch ration depot, police station, and a small school, all known as the 'settlement'. The common had been used for decades by drovers, hawkers and Afghan cameleers travelling between Queensland and the Kimberley. It was the only human habitation in eighty miles.

To avoid confrontation, or worse, the group stayed off the road, following the fence. Walking in the sun for hours, the *karu* (children) became thirsty, and in the gulch of Gordy Creek, the women stopped and dug for water. Finding nothing, the people continued, joining the road their parents and grandparents had largely built by hand. As feared, the local *murnnungku* (policeman), Constable 'Bluey' Harvey, had been sent to intercept them. Harvey was tough and of the old school. In a forthright exchange, Harvey asked Lingiari:

> What are you doing?
>
> You know what I'm doing. I'm going. Lot of trouble. No food, not much tucker, just bread and beef and no money.[2]

In the face of the Gurindji's (and Warlpiri's) determination, there was little the policeman could do. In the afternoon, a friendly hawker known as 'Buckinbuckin' for his colourful language came by. Seeing children flagging, he gave many a ride on the back of his green Bedford truck.

Late that day, people at the settlement saw an extraordinary sight. Blanche Bulngari, wife of Pincher Nyurrmiarri, the new depot yardman, later told of:

> [...] something glinting and flashing in the distance [...]. She realised they [the lights] were slowly coming closer. Figures began to emerge: men, women and children walking slowly

---

2   Darwin, NTAS, Vincent Lingiari Interviewed by Ted Egan and Tim Bowden, 1979, NTRS 1942, TS 1237.

with swags and new billy cans. The sun had been catching the […] billycans and the light went on ahead and gave the word to the people sitting at the settlement.[3]

For eighty years, the Gurindji had been confined; dependent on the rations and pensions paid (or not) at Wave Hill station. Even a teenager at the settlement sensed the enormity of the occasion:

> I was in our house […] and I just saw them […], this magical group of people, coming up over the river bed, over the hill and walking towards us. I remember the feeling was of excitement […]. There was an awareness in me of how monumental it was—'This is a really big thing!'[4]

The people, numbering about 200, reunited with Bulngari, Nyurrmiarri and a dozen or so others living at the settlement. They settled on the river's low western flank, a few hundred metres from Harvey's police station and the home of Bill Jeffrey.

That night George Kalapiti, the respected 'headboy' of Wave Hill's 'Number One' stock camp, was transporting horses back to the station from the Negri races. Almost home, he slowed the truck to enter the Victoria River crossing. Glancing out of his cab in the darkness, Kalapiti was staggered to see dozens of lights flickering from the track mob's fires, scattered like stars in the river bed. His countrymen had turned the world upside down.

* * *

---

3   Lyn Riddett, *Kine, Kin and Country: The Victoria River District of the Northern Territory, 1911–1966* (Darwin, Northern Territory, Australian National University, 1990), p. 128.

4   NTAS, Darwin, Essie Warmuth [step-daughter of Bill Jeffrey], Interview Recorded by Charlie Ward January 2010, NTRS 3609, BWF 11.

TAKING A STAND, 1966–1968

Two days after the walk-off, the pastoral manager of Vestey's' enormous northern holdings, Peter Morris, flew to Wave Hill to meet Lingiari with Tom Fisher. He arrived in the river bed to ascertain what the Gurindji would require to return. This sudden willingness of Lord Vestey's foot soldiers to bargain was too little and too late for Lingiari: his people were not returning. Then, in a radical departure from the Gurindji's previous skirmishes, more outside support arrived. A Bedford truck driven by Darwin unionist Brian Manning arrived with food for the disgruntled workers. With him were Dexter Daniels, the screen star Robert Tudawali (who had risen to fame in the 1955 film *Jedda*), and Kerry Gibbs, the teenage son of activist friends George and Moira.

Since the last massacres in the 1920s, local pastoralists had kept a lid on discontent. Now, with the Gurindji's departure from Wave Hill station—in combination with smaller strikes catalysed by Daniels—the industry was cast into agitation. Pastoralists—not to mention public servants, radicals and journalists—all guessed at the outcomes. The manager of a station neighbouring Wave Hill, Rosewood, wrote to his superiors:

> Seems there is a carload of black agitators moving around this area, they visited Newry [station] and next day all Bill's blacks walked out, Spring Creek have lost a heap now. [...] The grapevine has it that the great Dexter Daniels is in the area where Mount Isa [Mining company] are planning operations in and around the Macarthur River. He will have all the coons demanding higher wages before they get work.[5]

---

5   Darwin, NTAS, D Bostock to P Shaw, 3 June 1966, *Rosewood Station Pastoral Records: Hooker Pastoral Co, Correspondence Jan 1964–Dec 1972*, NTRS 9, Box 15.

While Manning took up Bill Jeffrey's invitation to stay at the settlement and Tudawali, Daniels and young Kerry Gibbs camped with the Gurindji, others were keen to talk to the strikers. Within a fortnight, senior Welfare officer Ted Evans, radical journalist Frank Hardy and long-term activist Stan Davey arrived.

Consultations fuelled by billy tea between these whites and the Gurindji leaders ensued. Whether they were sceptical, curious, or supportive, it became apparent to them that the Gurindji were not merely protesting about wages. Lack of pay was one issue. It also emerged that the Gurindji believed they possessed the right to choose the conditions in which they lived and worked, on land they saw as their own. If taken seriously, the issues this raised for the cattle industry and the government were huge. On 8 September 1966, pastoralists, NAWU and Welfare Branch officials met in far-away Sydney to discuss the growing problems typified by the Gurindji's standoff with Vestey's.[6]

Although the Gurindji were roughing it outdoors still, their situation had changed radically. No longer relegated to their isolated humpies or 'dog-houses' until required to work by whites, Bill Jeffrey, Hardy and Manning accepted them socially at the Welfare settlement. Some of the Gurindji would take their battered Slim Dusty records—purchased from hawkers such as 'Buckinbuckin'—to Jeffrey's house in the evenings, and listen to music in the cool air

---

[6] At the time of the Walk-off, the Liberal and rural-based conservative Country Party Coalition had ruled for sixteen years. The then Prime Minister Harold Holt was a progressive liberal on social issues, though was corralled by his more conservative Country Party colleagues such as Charles 'Ceb' Barnes (Minister for Territories) and John McEwen (Minister for Trade and Industry). See Darwin, NAA, Letter from Assistant Administrator AV Atkins to Administrator RL Dean, 7 September 1966, 'Wages and Conditions of Aboriginal Pastoral Workers', *Industrial Unrest on Pastoral Properties 1966–1969*, F1, 1966/2182.

underneath. After putting in long hours every day though, exhaustion would get the better of Bill. Classical music would find its way onto the turntable—a genre unappreciated by Lingiari's countrymen. After a respectful interlude in which the strains of Mahler or Shostakovich wafted on the night air, they would take their leave. Lingiari would climb the stairs and knock respectfully: 'Thank you, *marluka* (old man). We really like that music but we're very tired now and we want to go home'.[7]

While Vestey's privately bulldozed the Gurindji's old camp at the station, the journalist and author Frank Hardy sidelined his misgivings and became primary adviser, publicist, and confidante to the elders. They could hardly have hoped for a better advocate. The battle-worn communist had stronger media and political connections in the south than Daniels, Manning, Gibbs or Carroll. He had also fallen out with the Communist Party leadership and was less politically constrained. Above all, Hardy could use his skills as a writer to shape the Gurindji's situation into something mainstream audiences could comprehend.

With articles about the Gurindji's stand proliferating, the telegraph lines were running hot in the Welfare Branch's Darwin office. Since the earlier strikes at Newcastle Waters and Helen Springs, officials had established that although they would discourage Aboriginal people from striking, the Branch still needed to ensure those who did so weren't suffering from hunger or illness, and they received government benefits.

At the settlement, this was something of a headache. There were now about 150 people in the river bed, the annual rains were

---

7   NTAS, Warmuth, NTRS 3609, BWF 11.

approaching, spare accommodation was non-existent, and even before the Gurindji's arrival there had been insufficient food.[8] Payment of Aboriginal pensions to Tom Fisher was halted and their money transferred directly to the settlement. Aside from goats' milk ice cream made by Bluey Harvey's wife, though, there was little for the Gurindji to spend it on.

To complicate matters further, the Branch's man-on-the-ground, Jeffrey, was something of a loose cannon. A jack-of-all-trades who had landed a job as a public servant, Jeffrey had been in the Territory for eighteen months and had strong political beliefs; a fact he withheld from his superiors. A volatile but 'gentle giant' with both Communist and pro-Aboriginal sympathies, Jeffrey found himself 'fighting on two fronts'—to fully support the Gurindji, against the wishes of his own department. As Vestey's Peter Morris said to me, the Gurindji had found in Bill Jeffrey someone 'thinking their way' about equal rights.[9] With the Branch's approval, the errant official oversaw a Gurindji cook called Panto ferrying pots of stew down to the river in a wheelbarrow—for children and expectant mothers. When the number of Panto's deliveries continued rising, Jeffrey quipped there were 'a lot of lactating women'.[10] When accused by his superiors of consorting with Hardy, Jeffrey protested that he knew nothing of the journalist's political activities. It was a fine line to walk, which took a toll on him personally.

---

8   About twenty Aborigines had remained on or returned to Wave Hill station. Darwin, NAA, Report from Visit to Wave Hill Station, 6 October, 1966, *Employment and General Welfare of Aboriginals - Wave Hill Station*, F1, 1967/1113.
9   Darwin, NTAS, Interview with Peter Morris Recorded by Charlie Ward, November 2009, NTRS 3609, BWF 32; Hardy, 1968 (2006), p. 167.
10 Cited in Frank Hardy, *The Unlucky Australians*, Sydney, Nelson, 1968 (2006 edn, Melbourne, One Day Hill), p. 78.

TAKING A STAND, 1966–1968

As the heat and humidity increased towards the end of 1966, Hardy, Lupngiari and Daniels went on a tour organised by Hardy's union friends. In the south, they spoke about the Gurindji's plight to hundreds of sympathetic workers, as well as to 'Ceb' Barnes, the Minister for Territories in Canberra.

With tactical dialogue now quietening at Wave Hill, the Gurindji and the Jeffreys began to feel the heaviness of political isolation. Anne became morose and her husband fell into a sour, paranoiac fog that coalesced around the other white men present—Bluey Harvey and teacher Adrian Luck. Tensions brewed until Jeffrey took a group of Gurindji to Luck's residence for a showdown over the teacher's supposed mismanagement of the *ngumpit* people's new bank accounts. The two whites abused each other, with Jeffrey calling the teacher 'Mr Vestey' and threatening to have him 'run off the place'.[11] To the Gurindji, being involved in a *kartiya* conflict was completely distasteful, and they soon excluded Bill Jeffrey and other Welfare men from their confidence. This was perhaps not an easy choice: in their new circumstances, supportive whites provided insurance against harassment by rogue jackaroos. As little as forty years earlier, some people's parents had been killed by pastoralists or their hired hands. Fears of an attack kept them awake at night and some began to doubt their choice.

* * *

The Gurindji had reason to hesitate: a series of slow, seismic changes were in motion, triggered by their Walk-off, their activism in

---

11 SA Luck to Welfare Branch Assistant Director (Northern), 5 December 1966. In possession of the author.

the south, and the equal wages decision. Fuelling talk of Aboriginal work and land issues, the public could see that the Gurindji's homeless status on their own country meant the whole status quo of race relations in the north was no longer tenable. The fate of all Aborigines on pastoral land, the direction of the nation's Aboriginal policy and the northern cattle industry would all turn on this axis.

When Hardy returned in March 1967 from a southern summer spent teaching at the University of New England, he was met by faces worn and glum. The radical journalist and raconteur was given a rusty chair among the leaders as he tried to decipher the machinations of *kartiya* politics in Canberra for them. The Gurindji were hoping for advice; Hardy was reluctant to pre-empt them. Once he told them that Lupngiari was in Darwin still, touting their idea of reclaiming land from Vestey's, their enthusiasm erupted. That night, Sandy Moray's 'right word' about starting their own community at Wattie Creek was reiterated by the leaders to everyone in the camp. Plans were made to move immediately. Bill Jeffrey returned to form, and—surely with a look over his shoulder—gave the men some government tools and fencing wire to help them establish a new, illegal camp. As Hardy recorded:

> The bearded devil [Jeffrey] said gleefully, 'I know where there is some wire lying outside the fence'. [They] followed him through the balmy moonlight across the settlement. He passed a pair of wire cutters to Pincher without a word.[12]

The next morning, six months after their Walk-off, the strikers set out to Wattie Creek. The area chosen by Moray adjoined the

---

12   Soon afterwards Anne Jeffrey was admitted to the Katherine hospital suffering nervous exhaustion. Her respite did nothing to improve the Jeffreys' situation and in June they left Wave Hill. Hardy, 1968 (2006), pp. 173, 178; Valerie Bishaw, Personal Communication, 14 December, 2010.

TAKING A STAND, 1966–1968

Daguragu waterhole, close to Mimangu, the Gurindji's most significant Dreaming and burial site at Seale Gorge. The spot had permanent water, rich soil for growing food, and was free from European activity. Returning to the nutwood tree under which their plan had been born, the Gurindji began to make their new home. Within weeks they were revitalised, erecting shelters and a fence to mark the land they had reclaimed. To proclaim their new status, Lingiari and Pincher Nyurrmiarri thought the camp needed a sign: 'We want a sign, Vestey's got a sign, Welfare got a sign, the policeman's got a sign, everybody's got a signboard. Gurindji got to have a signboard'.[13] When Hardy made one for them, it read 'Gurindji Mining Lease and Cattle Station'.

This was a rare moment on the frontier. The Gurindji had co-opted and reversed their initial dispossession. Like early European settlers, they busied themselves cutting trees and building huts in the bush. Theirs was not a project to tame nature's wildness, but one that sought to shift completely their engagement with the industry which had taken over their country. In the eyes of the public, the 'strike' at the settlement became an 'occupation' at Wattie Creek. What was becoming obvious to all though, was that more than equal pay, the Gurindji wanted their land.

Hardy had given the matter 'a bit of thought' during his southern sojourn, and sought legal advice from an eminent ALP barrister, Lionel Murphy. At Murphy's suggestion, the old activist began drafting a petition calling on the Governor-General Lord Casey to release 'about 500 square miles' of Vestey's pastoral lease. In April

---

13   Darwin, NTAS, 'Newsbeat TV Program transcript, 8 August 1968', *Northern Territory Pastoral Lessees Association, Administration and Correspondence Files*, NTRS 3548, C1–5J.

1967, he sent the petition—marked with an 'X' by Lingiari, Pincher Nyurrmiarri, Long Johnny Kijngayari and Gerry Ngalgardji, and undersigned by Hardy and Jeffrey—to Canberra.

Although the Liberal-Country Party government of Harold Holt was in power, a few politicians on both sides of parliament were sympathetic to the Gurindji. One of these, shadow Minister Gordon Bryant, read the old men's petition to the house. The language was hardly of the stock camps, but it made the Gurindji's point well:

> We, the leaders of the Gurindji people write to you requesting that you bring before the Parliament of Australia the present position of our people, and our earnest desire to regain tenure of our tribal lands [...] of which we were forcibly dispossessed in time past. [...] Morally, if not legally, the land is ours and should be returned to us. If given our rightful heritage, we would show the rest of Australia and the world that we are capable of working and planning our destiny as free citizens [...].[14]

Federal political forces began aligning themselves against land-hungry Aborigines. Minister for the Interior Doug Anthony—a dairy farmer from Bundjalung country in New South Wales—made the NT pastoralists' case against excising land for Aborigines. The cattlemen feared that conceding land to the Gurindji would lead to a mountain of similar claims.

In his tardy response to their petition, the Governor-General advised the Gurindji to apply for a lease on vacant Crown Land (around the Welfare settlement, presumably) and warned them for good measure: 'You should be careful that you do not do anything to break the law in any way, or to interfere with the rights of the pastoral

---

14 'Gurindji Claim to Wave Hill', *Smoke Signals*, 1, 6, Feb–March 1967 (Melbourne, Aborigines' Advancement League), p. 11; Hardy, 1968 (2006), p. 115.

lessee'.¹⁵ At Wattie Creek, the elders stuffed Lord Casey's letter into a powdered-milk tin and ignored it. The letter was so protective of Vestey's it could have been written by the company itself, and illustrated the power pastoral lobbyists enjoyed within the Liberal-Country Party government. Although it was the first significant blow the squatters had received since their departure from Vestey's station, the affair helped them identify their adversaries.

When news of the Governor-General's stance emerged, it backfired against Canberra and played into Gurindji hands. Sympathy in the south lay with the Aborigines and the official rejection of their demands highlighted the issues they raised further. Sensing the popular mood, Harold Holt's government planned a referendum for 27 May 1967. Commonly thought of as the Aboriginal rights, or citizenship, referendum, it was in fact primarily a vote on whether the federal government should be able to legislate on Aboriginal issues—how, was little-discussed.¹⁶ Activists and supportive celebrities nonetheless successfully framed a 'Yes' vote as a 'pro-Aboriginal', 'Australian' act. Gary Shearston, a popular folk singer, turned some of Murri activist Oodgeroo Noonuccal's poetry into a 'Yes' campaign ditty. Reporting about Wave Hill and a court case initiated by Yolngu activists at Yirrkala also formed an overture to the campaign leading up to the day, and the prominent lobby group FCAATSI prioritised

---

15   Edward G Whitlam, *Abiding Interests* (St. Lucia, University of Queensland Press, 1997), p. 298.

16   The Commonwealth already administered the affairs of NT Aboriginal people, as the Territory lacked an independent government of its own. Elsewhere, responsibility had fallen to each state. The Referendum also asked whether Aborigines should be counted in Commonwealth censuses. Contrary to popular belief, Aboriginal people were not given 'rights' or 'citizenship' as a result of the 1967 Referendum. See Bain Attwood and Andrew Markus, 'Representation Matters: The 1967 Referendum and Citizenship', in *Citizenship and Aboriginal Australians: Changing Conceptions and Possibilities*, ed. by Nicholas Peterson and Will Sanders (Cambridge University Press, 2000), pp. 118–140.

the recognition of 'traditional occupation land rights' for the first time.

Although the referendum was a landslide, delivering Canberra a huge mandate to act on behalf of Aboriginal Australians, authorities were silent about Gurindji activity at Wattie Creek. Not so Vestey's, who refused to accept damage to their leasehold lying down. After the Gurindji cut a fence-line to allow them vehicle access to their camp, Peter Morris sought legal action. The NT Police Commissioner was drawn into the dispute. Caring little about political neutrality, he advised against arresting any Aboriginal people, as this would give Frank Hardy another 'complaint to keep the issue in the limelight'.[17] Vestey's capitulated, and the offender, Long Jack Jurumbak, was let off with a warning. *Kartiya* supporters George Gibbs and Stan Smith of NTCAR were not so lucky. While assisting the squatters to measure their proposed 'excision' from Wave Hill, they were arrested for trespass. Presumably Constable Bluey Harvey relished charging those he saw as Hardy's 'trouble-making [...], scaly mates'.[18]

By 1967 the Walk-off had 'knocked the gas' out of station manager Tom Fisher, and he resigned. The strain on Bill Jeffrey and his family also overwhelmed them. After Jeffrey's wife Anne was hospitalised for stress, Jeffrey himself was transferred, then sacked, soon afterwards. Turning himself into a rogue whistle-blower and something of a *cause célèbre*, Jeffrey, dressed in cowboy boots and smoking Cuban cigars, dished dirt on the Welfare Branch to credulous reporters

---

17   Darwin, NAA, 'Report to Officer-in-Charge by Roy Harvey, 24 April 1967', *Industrial Unrest*, F1, 1966/2182.
18   Darwin, NTAS, Interview with Roy Harvey Recorded by Daniel Bacon, 1979, NTRS 1942/417.

in the south. He expanded upon the lies he'd told about himself to Frank Hardy, at length.[19]

Jeffrey's replacement, Ian Rodger, was left to repair the damaged relationship between the settlement and Wave Hill station. Despite a frosty initial response from Vestey's, he found the new station manager Frank Wilmington receptive to talks facilitated by a bottle of 'Black Label' Johnny Walker. When the pair were the last men standing, Rodger and Wilmington's friendship was sealed. Wilmington—like many pastoralists in the region—also began giving better pay and conditions to Aboriginal workers. Welfare officials saw any Gurindji leaving Wattie Creek as a sign of 'disunity', though many young men went to work on surrounding stations largely to earn money for the camp.

Despite pooling their resources, the Gurindji were in no bush idyll. The 'track mob', as they later called themselves, were surviving on basic food bought from the Welfare settlement, supplemented by bush tucker and occasional donations from the unions. Like on Wave Hill station, the women were collecting all the camp's water *karnatiti* style, by shoulder-yoke in heavy buckets. Meat was obtained every fortnight or so, by donation or time-honoured means from their cattle-rich landlord, Vestey's.

As the Gurindji's first pre-monsoon 'build-up' at Wattie Creek began, Lingiari sent Mick Rangiari and Pincher Nyurrmiarri to Darwin in a clapped-out old truck bought for a song from Bill Jeffrey. With eight others, many of whom had never seen the sea or a big town, the group were to buy supplies that would last them through

---

19   Charlie Ward, 'Red Truths and White Lies: Frank Hardy and Bill Jeffrey at Wave Hill', *Griffith Review Edition 36: What is Australia For?*, 2012. <https://griffithreview.com/articles/red-truths-and-white-lies/>. Accessed 1 December 2014.

the coming rains. After limping up the highway from Katherine, the group coaxed their vehicle to George Gibbs' house. Gibbs was an able mechanic and although he wanted to help, he told them NTCAR would be unable to pay for repairs. To raise funds, the group registered for work with the Commonwealth Employment Service while they stayed and ate at Bagot Welfare settlement. Back at Wave Hill, aside from medical assistance and schooling, a cache of food from Hooker Creek comprised the squatters' only official support.

* * *

The Holt Government considered its sweeping new referendum-delivered powers for six months before it appointed a tiny panel called the Council for Aboriginal Affairs (CAA) for advice. In the words of one of its members, 'the mountain [of the referendum] gave birth to a mouse'.[20] With a touch of biblical flair, Holt decided the Council would consist of three wise men—H.C. 'Nugget' Coombs, Barrie Dexter and W.E.H. Stanner. Each was a luminary in his field: economics; public administration; and anthropology. After giving them the brief of providing policy advice on Aboriginal issues directly to the Prime Minister, Holt drowned a week after their first meeting. Limited by its size, lack of statutory power and European heritage, the CAA nonetheless began to play a key role in the Gurindji's struggle, providing a conduit between the Aborigines' supporters and the cabinet. With Holt gone though, the learned trio were resented and stonewalled by his more conservative Coalition successors.

In a sign the Gurindji were at last attracting official attention, they hosted their first VIP at Wattie Creek in April 1968. WC 'Billy'

---

20 Darwin, NTAS, Interview with Barrie Dexter Recorded by Charlie Ward, February 2010, NTRS 3609, BWF 25.

Wentworth, the first ever federal Minister for Aboriginal Affairs, had been sent by Holt's successor, Prime Minister Gorton, to assess the Gurindji's situation firsthand. Wentworth's Country Party colleagues resisted the idea: they hoped not to bestow the squatters' camp with credibility. To his adversaries' annoyance though, Wentworth was dogged in pursuing 'the Aboriginal issue', and wanted to cement his reputation as 'first friend of the Aborigines'.[21] Although he was a vehement anti-'red' and knew of Hardy and Manning's communist connections, Wentworth didn't dismiss the Gurindji out of hand, as the Minister for Territories, Ceb Barnes, had done. The federal minister came away from Wattie Creek broadcasting that the Gurindji were only seeking eight square miles of land; enough, it was argued, on which to build a small village and run a horse plant. Even this proposal drew the ire of pastoralists. The Australian Woolgrowers' and Graziers' Council thundered:

> Once this experiment is begun there is no end to it [...]. The Territory's welfare, police, health and administrative resources will be stretched beyond capacity.[22]

In a wishful misreading of the situation, the Country Party Minister for the Interior, Peter Nixon, privately opined that:

> So long as the Gurindji people [are] allowed to stay at Wattie Creek without interference it might be possible to avoid facing

---

21 In 1966, Wentworth had proposed changes that went further than those approved in the referendum of 1967. He had suggested that power should be bestowed to the Commonwealth to prevent racial discrimination, and that the Commonwealth should be beholden to legislate positively—rather than merely legislate—for Aboriginal people. See: Tim Rowse, *Obliged to Be Difficult: Nugget Coombs' Legacy in Aboriginal Affairs* (Cambridge University Press, 2000), p. 42.

22 'Press Release: The Australian Woolgrowers' and Graziers' Council, April 1968'. Cited in *Prime Ministers at the ANU*, ed. by Michael Piggott and Maggie Shapley (Canberra, Australian National University), <http://eview.anu.edu.au/ministers_anu/pdf_instructions.php> [accessed 18 May 2012] p. 66.

up to the question of title, especially if the heat has gone out of the [...] issue.²³

Wentworth's proposal was put to Cabinet a month later, but the sway of senior conservatives held. There stalled the hopes of any idealists that the government of the day might cater to the Gurindji's wishes.

In July 1968, long after Casey's dismissive letter, Ministers Nixon and Wentworth announced the Gorton Government's official response to the squatters' petition. Instead of exploring dialogue with Vestey's about surrendering an area at Wattie Creek—as had been canvassed by the Department of Interior and recommended by the NT's own Legislative Council—the government announced it would pour its resources into a tiny location not of the Gurindji's, but the authorities' choosing: the desolate, infertile, flood-prone Wave Hill Welfare settlement. The Gurindji—and any other Aboriginal people in the area—would be housed in twenty high quality houses at the government's expense.

Irrespective of its control by 'Welfare', the settlement was an atrocious choice for the Gurindji—if it was meant to support their independence. Coaxing anything from the ground there had flummoxed successive *kartiya*, and the resident police officer was then carting soil from several miles away on which to grow a lawn. Heralded by the attention-grabbing offer of houses, the government's 'solution' to the Gurindji's land request merely amounted to expanding its local outpost at Wave Hill. This had been the Welfare Branch's plan for

---

23   Darwin, NAA, 'Telegram from Department of Interior Canberra to Northern Territory Administration Darwin, 25 March 1968', *Industrial Unrest on Pastoral Properties 1966–1969*, F1, 1966/2182.

ten years—a fact unreported at the time.²⁴ For the government, it was imperative that its 'solution' kept a lid on the Pandora's Box of Aboriginal 'land rights' on pastoral leases.

When George Gibbs arrived at Wattie Creek in August 1968 to help repair the Gurindji's truck, the elders had no idea about Minister Nixon's announcement. The government had simply not bothered to inform them. The old men were stunned, as Wentworth's enthusiasm during his visit had convinced them they would receive a ten square mile excision. According to Gibbs:

> They never knew a thing—they were absolutely bamboozled. As a matter of fact Tom Vincent [Lingiari] said, 'Oh George, that's not true, that's not true, Mr. Wentworth he been say we going to get that land'. I was absolutely dumbfounded myself [...]. It was seventeen days since the decision was made up in Darwin.²⁵

When a camera crew arrived a month later with Frank Hardy, Lingiari recounted Wentworth's visit for the reporter:

> Mr. Wentworth came along here one day and he reckoned that everything good. [He said] 'Well I give you ten square miles round that black hill over there'. I said, 'Alright'. I'll stay here till he come back. He promised. I want[ed] to see his buildings put up for me.²⁶

---

24   Authorities wished to loosen the control of pastoralists over the region's Aboriginal people. See Darwin, NAA, Report from Assistant District Welfare Officer M. Ivory to Director H.C. Giese, 'Wave Hill Camp', 23 May 1967', *District Welfare Officer Reports: Wave Hill Area*, NAA, E242, K66/1/1; Cecil Holmes, 'Their Meeting Was Vital But Doctor Coombs Missed It', *NTN*, 18 October 1969.
25   Canberra, NAA, Memo: Deputy Secretary to the Minister of the Interior, 'Wattie Creek, Channel Nine (Adelaide) Programme', September 1968, *Petition by Gurindji People to Governor-General re Wave Hill Pastoral Land, Northern Territory*, A1734, NT1968/2509, p. 97.
26   Canberra, NAA, A1734, NT1968/2509, p. 96.

The Gorton Government's decision and its miscommunication was another slap to the Gurindji. The contrast between the tiny proposed Aboriginal allotment at the settlement and Vestey's 6,158 square mile Wave Hill lease was stark. Had they known it, the Gurindji's only comfort lay in the fact the government's efforts to avoid the political morass of land rights had led it into an embarrassing corner. Due to the rough-and-ready administration of land in the north, it was discovered the area of the common the government was offering the Gurindji had accidentally been leased to Vestey's fifteen years earlier. Two weeks after announcing its refusal to seek a small excision from Vestey's, the government was forced to privately pursue the path it had publicly rejected. To its relief, this was achieved.

Also unknown to the public was the plan of senior Welfare Branch mandarins to break the Gurindji's resolve, either by cutting off the Aborigines' unemployment benefits and forcing them back to work, or exploiting the gap they perceived between old and young Gurindji. In May 1968, Welfare officer Mick Ivory was sent to spend several weeks with the squatters. Officially, he had been instructed to monitor their plans and cohesion, and assess the sacred sites mentioned in their petition. Ivory told Vestey's Cec Watts though that his brief was to 'parley with the Wattie Creek leaders and convince them to accept the government's decision to form a township on the common'.[27] Documents also show Ivory's superiors wished to establish:

> [...] how far the patrol officers may involve themselves in steps to continue the division presently existing in the Wattie Creek group, with a view to its eventual disintegration.[28]

---

27 Darwin, NTAS, 'Limbunya Natives', Australian Investment Agency, 20 August 1968, *Administration and Correspondence Files*, NTRS 3548, C1/5J.
28 Canberra, NAA, Telex from Northern Territory Administration to Department of the Interior, 25 September 1968, *Petition by Gurindji People to Governor-General re*

TAKING A STAND, 1966–1968

Ivory genuinely liked and respected the Gurindji, who showed him their usual good grace and hospitality. Senior men took him to dozens of sites, most of which he deemed not sacred, but 'only Dreaming places'.[29] Any efforts Ivory made to 'divide' the Gurindji achieved nothing.

* * *

Including such tawdry, secretive dealings, the fifteen months since the referendum had hardly been a glorious start to the Commonwealth's new 'hands-on' relationship with Aboriginal Australians. On the night of 13 August 1968, the first debate on Aboriginal issues in federal parliament was held. Here was a chance, finally, for the country's politicians to explain themselves. The potential was huge. Would the Commonwealth's unused powers herald an era of political goodwill?

The scene that evening in parliament house was inauspicious. It was a bitterly cold winter's night. Only fifteen tired MPs were in attendance—most were absent, preparing for the budget speech the next day. The only distinguishing feature was the quizzical, demanding face of 'Hoppy Mick' Rangiari looking down from the visitors' gallery. Rangiari was on a speaking tour and had arrived in Canberra from Melbourne. After the affable Lupngiari had blazed this track with Dexter Daniels, Rangiari had learned from Lupngiari how to tell the Gurindji's tale in the south. The former stockman was accompanied by FCAATSI activists Burnum Burnum (Harry

---

Wave Hill Pastoral Land, Northern Territory, (A1734) NT 1968/2509.
29   Darwin, NAA, 'Sacred Sites: Wave Hill Area', *District Welfare Officer Reports, Wave Hill Area* (E242) K66/1/1.

Penrith) and Faith Bandler, and a few supporters from Abschol, a student lobby group active at the university across the lake outside.

Gough Whitlam, the vigorous leader of the Labor Party, was preparing his notes. Dozens of issues could have been raised, but due to Frank Hardy's pestering a month earlier, it was the plight of Mick Rangiari's countrymen sleeping illegally under tin and spinifex that he brought to the government's attention. Here was a chance to drag the conservatives' paralysis right to their door. Taking the floor, Whitlam began by noting that after a leisurely interval of fifteen months, the Prime Minister had recently announced his government's response would be to do *nothing* with its powers to legislate for the country's Aboriginal people. The former lawyer made a jibe about Billy Wentworth's capitulation to his conservative colleagues:

> The Minister was to lead the Gurindji into the Promised Land. He came in out of the wilderness and found the Country Party worshipping the golden calf.[30]

Wentworth's riposte was well-worn, accusing Whitlam of duplicitous self-interest: '[...] the Leader of the Opposition is trying to use the Aboriginals for a political purpose'.

Both sides then got down to discussing the Gurindji. Their efforts to discredit each other were wildly successful, but did little to advance their Aboriginal constituents. Whitlam's foot-soldiers Gordon Bryant and Jim Cairns argued the Gorton Government had failed the Gurindji through its offer to house them at the Welfare settlement, which it was morally and legally obligated to do in any case. The government cynically replied it had in fact taken the hard

---

30   Australia, House of Representatives, *Parliamentary Debates (Hansard) Session 1968—Second Session of the 26th Parliament (Second Period)* (Canberra, Commonwealth Government Printer, 1968), pp. 16–23.

road: it would have been far easier and cheaper to give the Gurindji the land they wanted, rather than providing them with services at the common.

It would be another four years before Whitlam, Cairns and Bryant won office and could act on their beliefs, but the case they made that night was that a general recognition of Aboriginal rights to land was overdue, whether the land in question was pastoral or not. They also argued the Gurindji's efforts to support themselves should be encouraged with leases and grants, as with the general population.

What 'Hoppy Mick' Rangiari made of this war of words, delivered about his countrymen at Wattie Creek from a great distance, is unknown. From the sniping opening of the debate, there was ample evidence of the disconnect between politics' partisan bluster and the varied interests of Aboriginal Australia. The next day the budget dominated the news.

As the government's position on Wattie Creek hardened, it was summarised by Peter Nixon, the Minister for Territories, in August 1968. His party refused, he said, to make a:

> [...] series of depressed Aboriginal communities tied to a form of sub-standard living with a barrier between them and the rest of the Australian community.[31]

These were prescient words, and ones that PM Gorton used to sidestep addressing the moral claim by Aboriginal people to land. Nixon attempted to silence Wentworth on the Wattie Creek issue and thereby 'relegate [land rights] to its proper position of relative insignificance'.

---

31   Peter Nixon, 'Statement 9, August 1968', cited in Jeremy Long, 'Frank Hardy and the 1966 Wave Hill Walk-off', *Northern Perspective*, 19, 2 (1996) 1–9, p. 7.

To young people already alienated by the government's support for the war in Vietnam, Nixon's statement was a provocation. Angry protests against the Gorton Government and Vestey's erupted in Sydney and Melbourne. With Hardy's new book on the Gurindji, *The Unlucky Australians*, on the shelves, the author took the fight to the third Lord Vestey (Edmund II) while on a trip to the United Kingdom. There, he led an antipodean demonstration against the Gurindji's 'slave-driving' absentee landlords at London's Smithfield meat market.

As the government's frustrations accumulated, Rangiari's tour of the union halls and student lounge-rooms of Brisbane, Sydney and Melbourne continued. Pictures show his transition from cowboy clobber to the lurid 60s fashions popular among his urbane new friends. He was met by sympathetic, ignorant audiences in venues such as the Bexley Workers' Club:

> [I] talk to everyone and some of them said to me, 'Oh. This is the first time you tell us what's happening by Vestey at Wave Hill. […] Oh dear, they're a hard family. What you trying to do now?'[32]

Aside from demonstrations, the tour bore lasting results. Ultimately the Gurindji leaders' aim was independence, but Moray's vision had always hinged on 'find[ing] a mate' to get there—people who were prepared to provide, and teach the Gurindji the skills they lacked. In Hardy, the elders had found themselves a mouthpiece. A writer and networker was necessary for 'politicking', for winning hearts and minds, but the old men were utterly pragmatic. They also knew they needed supporters who could teach them how to build houses, fix

---

32　Mick Rangiari, 'Talking History: Mick Rangiari', in *Our Land is Our Life: Aboriginal Land Rights in Australia's Northern Territory*, ed. by Galarrwuy Yunupingu (St. Lucia, University of Queensland Press), pp. 33–38 (36).

TAKING A STAND, 1966–1968

their vehicles, and read the mounting piles of correspondence they now received.

Students from Abschol, a university-based lobby group, were the first to hear their call.[33] The old men's priority was a truck for Wattie Creek, and at their request, Abschol agreed to fundraise. With a groundswell of hundreds of donors—including the long-haired folk-singers Peter, Paul and Mary, on tour at the time—a Toyota Dyna was soon bought and laden with supplies. The president of Melbourne University's Abschol branch, David Twitt, delivered the truck to the squatters in person, leaving Darwin on Boxing Day 1968. To Cecil Holmes, an older radical film-maker and journalist riding shotgun beside him while the new tray-top hurtled towards Katherine, he declared himself 'apolitical', and merely visiting the Gurindji to slake his curiosity.[34] Twitt was the first of dozens of young activists from the southern states to travel to Wattie Creek in the next decade.

With Hardy's new book taking the Gurindji's message to the world, they settled in for a fight. Rather than marking the end of the squatters' struggles, the arrival of southern help and a truck signalled their entrenchment. In two years, the occupation at Wattie Creek had merely seen the Gurindji articulate their position, and the delivery of a none-too favourable response from government. The elders had decided to ignore 'Welfare', and make their own future, with whatever help they could get. Neither side showed a sign of compromise or capitulation. An epic battle over Aboriginal land rights was brewing, and Wattie Creek was its epicentre.

---

33 Lingiari later named Rob Oke of Abschol, as the first 'mate' he met on his trips to Melbourne and Sydney after the Walk-off. See NTAS, NTRS 1942, TS 1237.

34 Cecil Holmes, 'The Way to Wattie Creek: "We Will Never Leave Here"', *NTN*, 6 January 1969, p. 3.

Chapter 3

FRIENDS FROM AFAR, 1969–1970

Wattie Creek's Gurindji residents celebrated New Year's Day 1969 with a simple but important ceremony: yanking the starter cord of their new pump. The women's back-breaking work carting water each day from the Daguragu waterhole was over—as long as the pump would last. Between Christmas and the New Year, the men and Abschol's David Twitt had busied themselves laying pipes, digging trenches and installing a union-donated water tank. It was the Gurindji vision in action—'work [...] for ourselves. Little bit of help maybe from white people, but left alone'.[1] To acknowledge their supporters' generosity, Mick Rangiari shooed away kids and dogs, and gave Twitt and journalist Cecil Holmes a pannikin of water from the world's first Gurindji faucet. Afterwards Twitt and Holmes left, the rains came, and the squatters' second wet season in the mud by Wattie Creek began.

After eighteen months' work, their camp was comprised of huts made from bush posts, salvaged tin and fencing wire. Along with wurlies little different from their occupants' earlier 'dog houses' on Wave Hill station, these modest homes were scattered across

---

1   Long Johnny Kijngayari, cited in Cecil Holmes, 'Wattie Creek,' *Aboriginal Quarterly* (Abschol, Australian National University, Canberra, March 1969).

a clearing a couple of hundred metres wide. Car bodies adorned its fringes. The shiny new additions delivered by Twitt—a pump, truck, and water tank—had proved significant goodwill could be harnessed from well-wishers in the south. As the donations were worth the equivalent of tens of thousands of dollars today, though, they had drawn questions, even from supporters. Critics argued that no amount of gift-giving to the Gurindji would resolve their illegal status on their own land, and too much generosity could actually undermine their independence.

Such debates among the Aborigines' supporters highlight the complex issues the Gurindji had raised for mainstream Australia. On a moral level, many people supported the notion of traditional land rights contained in the squatters' petition. Public support for them was mushrooming, though a lot of pastoralists and conservatives were left cold. Their concern was that the issues raised by the Gurindji's request applied not just to the people at Wattie Creek, but to dozens, potentially hundreds, of other dispossessed groups across the country. What would it mean if part of the Australian landmass belonged to Aboriginal people? The debate was complicated by the fact Prime Minister Gorton was now receiving advice from both land rights' most articulate advocates, the new CAA, and its strident, powerful opponents—pastoralists represented by Interior Minister Peter Nixon and his advisers.

Unsurprisingly, the other player in this saga, the Vestey company, was in a double bind. Anxious to protect its lease and cattle from Aboriginal interference on the one hand, it also wished to maintain good relations with the government *and* Australian consumers—while realising it would ultimately have to follow any government decision regarding Wave Hill. As debates played out among the

Gurindji's adversaries, the aim for Twitt and his activist friends was to thoroughly explore what Lingiari and his countrymen wanted, help them achieve their goals, and simultaneously force the government's hand.

In the previous year, the Gurindji's tenacious spokesman Mick Rangiari had repeatedly said his people '[…] want this land here that belongs to us. We want cattle and we want horses'.[2] Although land and cattle were in the leaders' sights, there were fundamental questions for students in Melbourne about how either could be achieved, and how they themselves could support the Gurindji from 3,000 kilometres away.

After David Twitt left Wattie Creek in January 1969, the only way southern supporters could communicate with the Gurindji elders—who could not write—was via the Welfare Branch radio at the settlement. Until this impasse was resolved, the proximity of the Gurindji's NT supporters—a mere 800 kilometres away in Darwin—was invaluable. Moira Gibbs was providing much-needed co-ordination and administration from Darwin, despite the recent death of her husband George, and Cecil Holmes also wrote and lobbied the government. Dexter Daniels and other men from Roper River's leading families were also working to support the Gurindji. Daniels spoke at Gurindji land rights meetings and protests in the south, while his countryman Phillip Roberts extended the Alawa and Nunggubuyu people's support through his work with FCAATSI.

Frustrated by a lack of contact in Melbourne, toward the end of 1969 a group of Abschol representatives travelled to the NT on a fact-finding mission. Mechanic and draft-resister Paul Fox and students

---

2   See Mick Rangiari, cited in Bob Hobman, 'Talking It Over With the Gurindjis', *NTN*, 3 August 1968.

FRIENDS FROM AFAR, 1969-1970

Rob and Kay Oke hitch-hiked most of the way to Darwin, where they slept on the floor of Cecil Holmes. Upon arriving at Wattie Creek in an unregistered NTCAR Land Rover, the Okes found that in line with Prime Minister Gorton's earlier announcement, the development of the Wave Hill settlement was proceeding rapidly. While the squatters scrounged to fix their shanties, washed in a waterhole and cooked on the ground, the settlement already boasted 'a power supply, a cool room, bakeries, [...] portable school facilities, a store, toilets [and] a petrol pump'.[3]

Although the company contracted to build the settlement's houses had wasted months making 150,000 unusable bricks, foundations for twenty-three quality houses had been laid—part of development worth the equivalent of $5 million. The amount was unheard of for a remote Aboriginal settlement. Despite this activity, five miles away at Wattie Creek, government support was almost non-existent. Cabinet's refusal to grant the Gurindji land had left the well-intentioned and politically savvy—though not always practically-skilled—members of Abschol to step into a municipal and humanitarian vacuum. The Okes used their discussions with the Gurindji leaders in December 1969 to shape Abschol's land rights strategy. As contact increased in 1970, the students were also able to integrate events 'on the ground' with their lobbying in Canberra, Melbourne and Sydney. The bush battlers—who had by now been pointedly asking for land over a period of four years—gained more traction through a series of persuasive articles in *The Australian*, written by Hardy. Although regaining their land and running cattle

---

3   Rob and Kay Oke, Paul Fox, David Twitt, *Wattie Creek: Present and Future—Report of the Abschol Field Team* (Melbourne, National Union of Australian Students, December 1969).

were the Gurindji's main goals, Abschol identified housing and a safe water supply as critical, immediate requirements. The activists looked to the University of Melbourne and trade unions for architecture students and tradesmen to help.

On 25–26 May 1970, architecture lecturer Stan Barker flew a few of his students, Frank Hardy, a couple of striking bricklayers and Rod Williams, in his Piper Cherokee to Wave Hill. Williams, described by a Vestey's executive as 'an angry young man with a long black beard', was a rugged actor who Abschol had chosen as their first 'on the ground' recruit for Wattie Creek.[4] He had spent his early years in western Queensland and harboured strong views about the unjust treatment of Aboriginal people. Williams had lived as a nomadic bush shearer and was an actor with Sydney's radical New Theatre. Unlike many of those keen to assist the squatters, he had strong practical skills and firsthand knowledge of rural Aboriginal life.

After the arrival of Barker's plane, a night meeting was called at Wattie Creek. Most of the Gurindji declined to watch the cowboy film shown by the new Welfare officer Len Richardson, electing to 'hear the word' from the south instead. The men sat around a fire, with women and children listening in an outer circle. Hardy regaled them all with tales of recent protests in Sydney: '[…] Policeman on one end pushing one way, other mob pushing the other way, shouting "Give 'em back Gurindji land!"'[5]

When discussion turned to negotiations with the Vestey company, a hush fell. In London, Lord Sam Vestey had signalled his readiness to

---

[4] NTAS, 'Press Conference, Save the Gurindji Committee', 15 July 1970, NTRS 3548, C1-5K.

[5] John Hamilton, 'Dreamtime at Wattie Creek', *The Age*, c. June 1970.

excise some of Wave Hill station for the Gurindji, yet his Australian staff were noncommittal. The Gurindji decided several of them would travel to negotiate with the company in Sydney directly—preferably at Vestey's expense. Hannah Middleton, a freshly-arrived anthropologist living in the camp, suggested a boycott of Vestey-owned tinned meat at the settlement store. It would be another exercise in hardship for the Gurindji, though one they embraced. Pincher Nyurrmiarri was heard reciting the mantra 'Hamper … Imperial … Hamper … Imperial' in preparation for his reproach of the shop manager the next day. After a feast of roast potatoes, the architecture students showed off the model village they had lugged from Barker's plane, by torch and firelight. They had designed houses especially for the Gurindji. Stan Barker put it to the track mob: 'Is this the sort of way […] you would like to live?'[6]

The next morning, 'Young Billy' and elder Hobbles Danayarri enthusiastically began building a one-room mudbrick home under the guidance of Rod Williams, pressing bricks with a union-donated machine. Due to the scarcity of corrugated iron, the house featured a spinifex-thatched veranda. After a few weeks of back-breaking work and a spell laid up with giardia, Williams reflected that the first Gurindji house: '[…] symbolises the strength and determination of these brave people and the permanence of their stand'.[7] Vincent Lingiari, the camp's leader, showed his appreciation:

> We need the people from the south to show us how to build these houses. The station people and Welfare people don't do

---

6   Frank Hardy, 'A Fight for Justice in Black and White', *Sunday Observer*, 27 September 1970.
7   Sydney, State Library of New South Wales (hereafter SLNSW), *Roderick Williams' Papers Regarding Gurindji Land Rights Claim*, c. 1966–1975, MLMSS 6965 / 1–20.

anything for [us], so when they want us to do something for them, like live in their houses, we won't do it.⁸

Staying in the camp's new 'roundhouse'—its open air visitors' digs—the southerners realised there was a social cohesion missing from other places where Aboriginal 'refugees' from the pastoral industry were gathering. In those, people had little say about the location or purpose of their 'community'. According to Williams though, at Wattie Creek:

> You could pick the difference in the people, there was a pride there. They were sitting on their land. [...] They weren't going to move from it; [it was] very different to other places.⁹

Neither did Hannah Middleton see:

> [...] any conflict or disunity about the basic commitment of that group. [...] There was a very high acceptance of what people might have needed to do personally [...]. What conflict [there was] arose at the interpersonal level and it was controlled [...]. It was remarkably harmonious.¹⁰

Many nights, 'fun corroborees' were held—unlike at the government's model settlement, where, 'by eight o'clock everything [was] completely silent'. People in the camp had also busied themselves establishing two large gardens. Pumpkins, cucumbers, tomatoes, onions, lettuce, melons and cabbages were thriving. As the new pump often failed and water had to be carried from the waterhole, watering them was a monumental task. This didn't deter elder Hobbles

---

8   Kim Lockwood, 'At Wattie Creek with the Undemanding Gurindjis', *Northern Territory News* (hereafter *NTN*), [n.d].

9   NTAS, Rod Williams, Interview Recorded by Charlie Ward, November 2009, NTRS 3609, BWF 1.

10 NTAS, Hannah Middleton, Interview Recorded by Charlie Ward November 2009, NTRS 609, BWF 2.

Danayarri and Middleton, who were spurred on by the idea that 'once we had a crop, people would see it was worth the effort'.

* * *

At a series of meetings in August 1970, the Gurindji shared their vision for the future. The men wanted horses and stock for their cattle enterprise, good housing, and to establish their own mustering and fencing teams. They wanted prospectors' rights, and recognised that infrastructure and services were required: a bore for water, more gardens and orchards, toilet and shower blocks, sturdy vehicles and a school, a store, a mechanical workshop and clinic—all at Wattie Creek. Critically, they hoped their own young people would acquire the skills to run and staff them.[11]

The women were in agreement but added certain things: more goats, pigs and chickens, a communal kitchen and laundry, mirrors for the shower block, better clothes and furnishings, a water tap in every house, shade trees and 'flowers to make [the camp] pretty'. Soon afterwards, Pincher Nyurrmiarri elaborated on the elders' vision: 'We been trying to get this land back, you know, and put up block for live, and work the cattle and horses, so we can make money'.[12] What the Gurindji wanted, then, was a cattle station and homestead of their own, a *ngumpit* version of Wave Hill in which the dimensions were reversed. Rather than a station of that size, the cattle operation they envisaged was smaller, more like that of a single herd stock-camp or out-station. In light of their own numbers, their homestead

---

11   Hannah Middleton, *But Now We Want the Land Back—A History of the Australian Aboriginal People* (Sydney, New South Wales, New Age Publishers, 1977), p. 119.
12   See Pincher Nyurrmiarri, *Pincher Numiari [sic]—Gurindji Plans and Attitudes: An Interview by Warwick Neilley* (Abschol and Save the Gurindji Campaign, 1970), p. 4.

would also need to be bigger, or at least contain more housing than that at Jinparrak, the 'new' Wave Hill. Their vision was inspired by the stations they knew, which were unfailingly primitive and could (it appeared) be run by a handful of people.

Ironically, the Gurindji's planned adaptation of a European-type lifestyle was at the time the end goal of the Coalition's assimilation policy, branded in the late 1960s as one of 'integration'.[13] Rather than celebrating the Daguragu elders' visionary adaptation of a pastoral lifestyle and business, though, the Gorton Government spurned them for not embracing its own version of assimilation at the Welfare settlement. They were left high and dry at Wattie Creek.

Aside from handmade boomerangs and other traditional artefacts, the cattle skills accrued by the squatters through working for Vestey's were all they had to trade in the local economy. Fortunately for the old men, running cattle was also something they were passionate about. Supporting the creation of a legal Gurindji cattle enterprise would be a significant undertaking. Abschol realised it would:

> [...] require firstly the granting of land, and then massive, but by no means impossibly large, support in the form of loans and grants from the Commonwealth.[14]

If the Gurindji could get title over a small horse paddock and living area, in other words, they might then be able to get government support for a cattle-focused business venture.

---

13 'Integration' was used to describe a policy which recognised that Aboriginal advancement and participation in mainstream institutions was possible while Aborigines retained their languages and culture. Rani Kerin, 'Charles Duguid and Aboriginal Assimilation in Adelaide, 1950–1960: The Nebulous 'Assimilation' Goal', *History Australia*, 2 (3) (Monash University ePress, 2005) 85.1–85.17 (pp. 85.11–12).

14 Oke et al, *What Now at Wattie Creek: Report of the Abschol Field Team which Visited Wattie Creek in May–June 1970*, (Abschol, Canberra, Australian National University, 1970), p. 6.

FRIENDS FROM AFAR, 1969-1970

National Abschol director Tony Lawson approached the conservative NTLC member for Wave Hill, Dr Goff Letts, for advice. Although Letts, the Territory's former chief veterinary officer, was openly hostile to Frank Hardy and resented the influence of communists among Aboriginal people, he supported the Gurindji's quest for independence and gave them advice on several occasions. The Smorgons, a wealthy Melbourne family, also sought legal advice on the Gurindji's behalf, and a 'pre-incorporation committee' for the Muramulla Gurindji Cattle Company was established in October 1970. 'Muramulla' derived from *ngurramala*, the Gurindji word for 'traditional owner'.

Wishing to increase the Gurindji's opportunities, the committee's mandate also included market gardening, mining, building a store at Wattie Creek, and 'fostering group participation and development of the Gurindji Aboriginal tribe'.[15] Its eight members were the Gurindji's most experienced cattle men: Vincent Lingiari, 'Long Johnny' Kijngayari, Pincher Nyurrmiarri, Mick Rangiari, Lupngiari, Jerry Rinyngayarri, George Manyo and Donald Nangiari. Each signed their name with an 'X' and quickly approved a grant application to search for minerals. Moira Gibbs, agronomist Rob Wesley-Smith and Brian Manning were the company's office-bearers, until they could talk the leaders through the detail at Wattie Creek. So began—on paper, at least—the fifteen year existence of the Muramulla company—a tenuous construction born of the Gurindji's hopes and cattle skills, free legal advice, and the energy of urban students.

The response of Vestey's and other pastoralists was muted while they observed the creation of this 'Aboriginal' cattle company.

---

15   'Muramulla Memorandum', October 1970, Oke Personal Collection.

The industry was developing new strategies to prevent groups like Muramulla from acquiring land the pastoralists considered their own. After the manager of Vestey's Australian arm, Roy Bell, mulled over the Gurindji's demands, he decided Bill de Vos of the NT Cattle Producers' Council (CPC) should act as the company's unacknowledged mouthpiece. Hiding behind the cattlemen's guild was a brilliant tactic which gave Vestey's more leverage than it would have otherwise received. Rather than presenting its views as an obviously self-interested private firm, Vestey's decision frequently created the appearance that its voice was missing from the debate, thus giving the impression the company was merely compliant with the government's wishes. Happily for Vestey's, the government also spoke on their behalf. De Vos wrote privately to the company that following Minister Nixon's statements, 'I came to the conclusion he had left us nothing further to say [...]'.[16] Frank Hardy's accusation that 'Vestey's and the government are hiding behind each other's skirts' was entirely apt.

Despite the common cause of the Department of the Interior and Vestey's, the activists' tactics were beginning to strain their alliance. Vestey's were becoming sick of the negative commentary now directed towards them—especially because the government refused to publicly acknowledge that the company would do whatever Canberra told it to. Vestey manager Roy Bell bemoaned that:

> [...] It seemed to us that the Gurindji issue was running down and could have lapsed into oblivion. [Instead] Vestey's have again been singled out as a target and have been the subject of a vigorous attack [...]. A campaign of direct confrontation is continuing.

---

16   Darwin, NTAS, *Northern Territory Pastoral Lessees Association, Administration and Correspondence Files*, NTRS 3548, C1-5K.

Even Minister Nixon recognised, in an appropriate choice of words, that Vestey's had become 'the meat in the sandwich'.[17]

The company was receiving a barrage of detailed, well-argued criticism from Melbourne's Rob Oke, Tony Lawson (now president of Abschol's parent body), and Jean Leu, a dynamic North Shore housewife who anchored the Sydney campaign. The trio had the attention of Vestey's management—not to mention many of Canberra's politicians. With the reporting of Hardy creating a vanguard, the company was impressed:

> We are dealing with a very well organised opposition who cannot be underestimated: their publicity is good; they are both articulate and vociferous and they are astute enough to pick up any variance in [our] statements or policies [...].

Vestey's 'opposition'—the Gurindji, Abschol and the CAA—had agreed to request an area of 500 square miles from the company. Vestey's realised Minister Nixon might have to succumb:

> It is our opinion that the government will be forced to yield to the extreme pressure, and in the end 500 square miles will be excised [...] and this will be accomplished by pretending that this will be a viable enterprise in the Wattie Creek area. [...] Before very much longer the government will request us to negotiate.[18]

At the same time, the company gave an undertaking it 'would not disturb the Aboriginals camped at Wattie Creek'.[19] The British multinational's image as the Gurindji's foreign oppressor was fading. It was now obvious that the squatters' main antagonist was the government elected to represent them.

---

17 'Vestey's Can't Give Land to Gurindji's', *The Australian*, 28 August 1970.
18 NTAS, Bell, Wattie Creek Meeting, 7 November 1970, NTRS 3548, C1-5K.
19 [J.M.] Hall to Lawson, 3 November 1970, Oke Personal Collection.

In 1969 and early 1970, the person enacting Assimilation policy in Wave Hill's acrimonious environment was Tony Scott. Once an army supply officer, Scott had run afoul of his military superiors in Darwin after a stint accompanying journalist Douglas Lockwood about the Territory. Drawn to work with Aboriginal people, he had joined the Welfare Branch and been trained in Sydney. Before Scott departed for 'Wave', his Katherine superiors read him 'the riot act'. He was warned that 'under no circumstances' was he to go to Wattie Creek, four miles from the Welfare settlement. According to Scott, neither were any:

> [...] Persons of the NT or NSW union movements to be allowed on the settlement. Any uninvited persons were to be reported to the policeman, who was just down the road. [...] When I got there, I read [all the conditions] and I thought 'this is bullshit, [I'm] a prisoner already'.[20]

The heavy-handed rules reflected the government's fears that communists could strengthen the Gurindji's demands for land. But Scott soon learnt that the Wave Hill Welfare settlement was the scene of another battle *within* the government. Warned only about travelling radicals, Scott was unprepared for the pressure unwittingly placed on him by the visits of pro-land rights public servants from the CAA's Office for Aboriginal Affairs.

According to Scott, senior mandarins such as Nugget Coombs, Jeremy Long and Charlie Perkins visited Wattie Creek, and chatted about how he might better support the Gurindji. When Coombs et al returned to Canberra, Scott followed up with them 'over the head' of his bosses in Darwin. His Welfare Branch superiors would

---

20 Darwin, NTAS, Tony Scott, Interview recorded by Charlie Ward, November 2012, NTRS 3609, BWF 50.

arrive later without warning, and question him closely about his activities—which they were mysteriously well-informed of. The stress these visits placed on Scott was considerable:

> Technically the Canberra [CAA] people weren't in a position to make any rules [...]. That's why I turned absolutely white. I had dark hair when I got there—in six months it was snow white!

As predicted by the settlement's police officer (who in all likelihood was the person reporting on Scott to his superiors), the young Welfare officer was soon driven to resign.

Scott had effectively been asked to spy on the Gurindji, prior to his arrival—supposedly in their interests. Unbeknownst to him or Wattie Creek's leaders though, Minister Nixon himself had requested 'discrete but effective' surveillance to monitor the track mob's activities. Vestey's senior Australian staff agreed to the plan. The book-keeper at Wave Hill station, Mrs Williams, was secretly enlisted to forward messages between Nixon's eyes on the ground and the Department of the Interior in Canberra.[21] As a result of Nixon's request, the new policeman at Wave Hill, Constable Bryce Fardell, included the camp on his patrols and provided information to his superiors.

The Gurindji knew they were being watched. Pincher Nyurrmiarri said as much:

---

21   Information released by ASIO shows that aerial and more direct surveillance of the Wattie Creek camp occurred. Visiting members of the press were ASIO informants. See Darwin, NTAS, Bryce Fardell, Interview Recorded by Charlie Ward, March 2010, NTRS 3609, BWF 13; Darwin, NTAS, Swift [Dept. Interior] to Chaney [Administrator], 21 August 1970, NTRS 246, P1, PL 529, Part 2; NTAS, *Police Station, Wave Hill (Kalkaringi), Day Journals, 1916–1999*, NTRS 2127/P2, Item 1; Canberra, NAA, CRS A9626, HG2337, HG 3246.

> They [Welfare Branch staff] never even help him out, Wattie Creek. They always just comin' around, just looking at what you doing here, that's all.[22]

Canberra-based ASIO spies also visited. Not content with the 'intelligence' generated by Tony Scott and his sceptical replacement Ray Hempel, ASIO enlisted Hempel's successor Len Ibbetson directly. Ibbetson, a cigar-smoking Englishman, was so excited by the subterfuge of his '007' role that he stalled his vehicle in the middle of the Victoria River while trying to cross it to impress his ASIO minders.

When Ibbetson was told to refuse the Gurindji and their supporters' permission to use the settlement's radio telephone, it fuelled the perception there was an official campaign to force the squatters off their land. Lyn Riddett, one of the Gurindji's visiting friends, believes:

> The clear impression being given to people at Wattie Creek was 'you are not permanent, you do not have permission to be out there, you have to come into the settlement if you want services, and what's more, we are going to make it quite difficult for you as long as you stay out there'. They were being intimidated, there's no two ways about it.

Mick Rangiari, by now renowned for 'talking up' in the south, promised journalists that if the government refused to help, the Gurindji would build their community themselves.[23]

* * *

---

22 Pincher Nyurrmiarri, *Pincher Numiari* [sic]*: Gurindji Plans and Attitudes: an Interview by Warwick Neilley* (Sydney, Abschol and Save the Gurindji Campaign, 1970).
23 'Students Urge Inquiry on Native Welfare', *The Australian*, 26 September 1970; 'A Gurindji Leader Fronts Minister Over Land Claims', *NTN*, 1 October 1970; 'Tribal Land Dispute', *Sydney Morning Herald*, 30 September 1970.

In early July 1970, Welfare boss Harry Giese and Minister Nixon—the Gurindji's nemesis—travelled to Wattie Creek. Although 'they didn't have much to say' to the elders, Nixon was not taking their activities lightly. Over the coming months, his staff and the Cattle Producers' Council (CPC) privately investigated evicting the squatters and launching an injunction against their supporters. CPC spokesman Bill de Vos counselled Vestey's against the idea: '[...] such proceedings could develop into major, protracted and costly litigation, attracting more publicity to the issue than it deserves'.[24] Similarly, the government's desire to avoid any publicity that might force it to deal with land rights meant the idea was rejected.

Soon after Nixon's visit, he gave a speech in which he laid out the Coalition's position:

> The government believes that it is wholly wrong to encourage Aborigines to think that because their ancestors have had a long association with a particular piece of land, Aborigines of the present day have a right to demand ownership of it.[25]

Nixon questioned an increasingly common belief that freehold land might provide some sort of cure-all for Aboriginal ills, and rejected the activists' portrayal of the Gurindji too:

> It is not really in accordance with the facts to represent the people at Wattie Creek as a vigorous group with capacity and determination needing only land to prosper by their own efforts.

Finally, the Minister asked—with good reason—whether a cattle business on the squatters' proposed 500 square mile excision could support a community of possibly hundreds of people.

---

24 NTAS, de Vos to J Hall and R Bell, 25 Aug 1970, NTRS 3548, C1-5K.
25 House of Representatives, 'Land and the Aborigines of the Northern Territory', Speech by Minister Peter Nixon, (Canberra, 3 September 1970), p. 1.

Nixon's attitude incensed members of the Labor party. After a fact-finding tour of Wattie Creek, MP Manfred Cross accused the government of 'tyranny' and 'conquest', and of refusing to support the Wattie Creek venture because it was on a site of the Gurindji's choosing. 'When it comes to Aboriginals', he railed, 'whoever the Administration might be always knows best'.[26]

* * *

By mid-1970, the work of the Gurindji, FCAATSI, NTCAR, Abschol, unions and church groups was paying off. 'Unquiescent consciences' were stirring in the south.[27] In Sydney, a large public meeting was held in the Teachers' Federation auditorium on 10 July. Activists Faith Bandler and Joe McGinness spoke before Frank Hardy gave an 'impassioned speech' building on his articles in *The Australian*. Fred Hollows, a well-regarded eye surgeon, attended and—swayed by Hardy's oratory—handed in a cheque for $300 ($3,300): an amount so large he was eyed suspiciously by a volunteer.

The passion and numbers were such that a group formed to lobby on the Gurindji issue full-time. Days later, under the name of Sydney's 'Save the Gurindji Committee', they announced their mandate:

> CONFRONT VESTEYS AND THE FEDERAL GOVERNMENT IN THE NORTH AT WATTIE CREEK; and DEMONSTRATE, BOYCOTT AND AGITATE IN MAJOR CITIES IN THE SOUTH.

---

26 Australia, House of Representatives, *Appropriation Bill (No. 1)*, 30 September 1970, pp. 1895–1897.
27 Julie Rigg, 'Support Swells for Gurindji Land Claim', *The Australian*, 20 August 1970.

The group planned an immediate 'mass protest demonstration' and gained 500 members in six weeks. Hardy, with characteristic modesty, later said he 'allowed [himself] to be persuaded to initiate' the Sydney campaign.[28]

In Melbourne, the appearances of Mick Rangiari, Hardy and Dexter Daniels spurred the creation of another 'Save the Gurindji' group, comprised of people far beyond Abschol's student base.[29] In both cities, these committees focused on lobbying, seeking donations and auctioning Gurindji artefacts. They hosted Hannah Middleton, who had been sent by the elders on a speaking tour with a suitcase of their boomerangs and spearthrowers to auction. Donors included the St Albans Cub Pack, the Theosophical Society and the Bundoora Tennis Club.

Rolling demonstrations, sit-ins and pickets in Sydney and Melbourne continued throughout the winter of 1970, targeting Vestey's offices and their Dewhurst butcher shops. Arresting officers confided that they too, were Gurindji supporters. Dexter Daniels—by now known as a 'Roper River Gurindji'—was lobbying for land rights for the Gurindji and his own people, and addressed many of the demonstrations that occurred.

On the afternoon of 31 July 1970, Daniels, Frank Hardy, and Wiradjuri activist Paul Coe met at Redfern's Empress Hotel, a Koori watering hole in Sydney. As the trio roused the passion of the pub's

---

28 NTAS, Press Statement from Save The Gurindji Committee, 15 July, 1970, NTRS 3548, C1-5K; Hardy, *Sunday Observer*, 27 September 1970.

29 The Sydney group was able to draw on the political networks to which Frank Hardy belonged, while in Melbourne administrative support was available through the National Union of Australian University Students (NUAUS), which oversaw Abschol. Abschol members worked in tandem with both the Melbourne and Sydney groups, and their membership overlapped. Rob Oke, Personal Communication, May 2011.

patrons, a crowd gathered outside, preparing to march. Police flooded onto the planned route into the city, their numbers at times exceeding the protesters'. The New South Wales Police Commissioner was even present, creating an air of official opposition to land rights. As protesters spilled out of the Empress into the mob surging up Regent Street, Daniels and Coe provided running commentary, sharing a loudhailer.

When the crowd arrived outside Vestey's Australian headquarters, numbers grew and unrestrained brawling with the police erupted. Schoolgirls were dragged by the hair and thrown heavily on the road. Rod Williams, recently returned from Wattie Creek, went to assist a young man whose face was being battered into the radiator grill of a parked car. Hardy restrained the bush shearer, encouraging him to direct his attention more strategically. One of the protesters' loudspeakers was 'ripped apart by police in an unprovoked attack' and the CPA's national secretary Laurie Aarons received a black eye and cracked nose. Despite the less-than-festive atmosphere, the protest had been billed as a concert, and above the melee, singers strained:

> *Then raise the scarlet standard high.*
> *Within its shade we'll live and die.*
> *Though cowards flinch and traitors sneer,*
> *we'll keep the red flag flying here!*

Williams and Hardy were among forty-five activists arrested. The fines they received were as high as the law allowed, and all were thrown into the city's police cells. A bush-yarning competition was held to maintain morale. To Hardy's embarrassment, his 'Billy

FRIENDS FROM AFAR, 1969–1970

Borker' mantle was taken by Williams' captivating performance of 'The Bastard from the Bush'.

With the campaign at its zenith, it was recognised there was no way of controlling—or predicting—the actions of the masses. While people such as Jean Leu organised art sales, chaperoned the travelling Gurindji leaders and ghost-wrote letters for Hardy, some showed their support differently. A student named Arn Tate of the 'Family of Man' sent a letter to the PM: 'In an attempt to stimulate action from your government I will cease to eat [...], with the aim of drawing attention to the plight of the Gurindjis.' Tate focused on the land issue, and ended his missive with '[...] in the interests of the human race'.[30]

Of more benefit to the Gurindji, a 48 year-old nurse, activist and dedicated lapidarist called Jean Culley introduced herself to the Melbourne support group. With Abschol's backing, Culley decided to drive her Toyota Landcruiser to Wattie Creek and lend a hand. Her brief was to teach the squatters how to polish and mount the area's gems, and offer her services as a bush nurse.[31] Culley threw herself into these and other tasks headlong: those visiting Vincent Lingiari encountered the unusual sight of a white-haired 'secretary' sitting on an upturned flour drum with a typewriter among the old men. In Culley, the Gurindji gained their most persistent and tenacious live-in supporter at Wattie Creek. She would prove an aggravation to a good many of their enemies and at least a few of their friends.

---

30 Arn Tate to Prime Minister Gorton, *c.* July 1970, Oke Personal Collection.
31 It was well known there were semi-precious stones in the Wave Hill area. The precedent set by Don McLeod's 'Strelley mob', in which an Aboriginal group of former pastoral workers in the Pilbara supported themselves through mining, was no doubt relevant to the Gurindji's acquisition of a Mineral Rights Lease, *c.* 1970. See Don McLeod, *How the West Was Lost: the Native Question in the Development of Western Australia* (Port Hedland, Western Australia, self-published, 1984).

A HANDFUL OF SAND

In late August 1970, another supporter arrived. Lyn Riddett was a school teacher who had been perplexed by Australians' denial about the Aboriginal situation for years. When she introduced herself at one of the Sydney group's Sussex Street meetings, Williams vetted her, asking suspiciously 'What do you think *you* could do?' Responding that she could help teach Gurindji children, Riddett went to the Mosman branch of the ALP to garner support. There, she was met with a mix of paternal goodwill and incomprehension. Land rights, she realised, was still a threatening or unknown concept to the party's rank and file.

* * *

When Riddett travelled to Wattie Creek, she flew with Hardy, a pair of journalists and some striking labourers on Barker's plane. When Rod Williams and Paul Fox arrived, driving a donated truck overladen with fruit trees, fencing supplies and a pink porcelain toilet bowl, Abschol's second working bee got underway. The elders' immediate priority was to fence off some land for a horse paddock: a job overseen by skilled fencer Donald Nangiari. Local conditions proved too much for Abschol's newly-arrived labourers, however. After building a one-room house for a few days, they complained about their food, and the poor quality of Abschol's support. As if to aggravate them further, an old woman known as 'Mad' or 'Singin'' Ruby began to harass them. Ruby was a persistent firebug, and to Rod Williams was: '[...] like an amazing old princess. She wore two hats at once, old gowns, lacy dresses [...]. She was like a mirage, an apparition [who] would come into anyone's camp.' A common story was that Ruby's mixed-race children had been removed long ago

by white authorities, and—perhaps as a result—she often screamed 'fuckin' *kartiya*, fuckin' *kartiya*!', or 'Harry Giese bin fuck me!' Ruby was a tragic casualty of what later became known as 'Stolen Generations' policies. She occupied the labourers' sleeping quarters, forcing them to shift camp.

* * *

Williams and other visitors to Wattie Creek in 1970 realised that although land was the Gurindji's main focus, their treatment in the cattle industry also required attention. Many of the camp's stockmen were still working in the industry, and conflict with surrounding stations over pay and work conditions was increasing. Disputes on Inverway and Limbunya stations had occurred in the weeks prior to the arrival of Barker's plane. Workers had been stranded on a neighbouring property for more than a week, allegedly without food. After Welfare officer 'Long Socks Lenny' Richardson refused to assist them, Abschol's Paul Fox brought the men back to Wattie Creek. On another neighbouring station, the manager:

> [...] got a gun and shot around among the houses, and later he pointed the gun at the five or six remaining Aboriginals and asked who was staying. They stayed.[32]

Despite improved conditions on many properties, disputes were increasing. The industry's ground rules (including the payment of the Award) had changed, and the old model of intimidation and dependence was defunct. The Gurindji's bargaining power had increased, and better conditions were being extended to local employees.

---

32 Appley Hoare, 'Working Conditions for Gurindji on Stations around Wattie Creek' (1970), Oke Personal Collection.

As *ngumpit* from the whole region were frequenting the Wattie Creek camp between jobs, contractors and station managers called by to ask Lingiari for workers. This was what the leaders espoused. They expected their countrymen would:

> [...] go out and work for somebody else. When they finish their job they all be comin' here [...]. We got a lot room here, mate. Don't matter where [they're] from—VRD, Limbunya [...] Inverway; all comin' in here. We want to [...] get 'em together and live here.[33]

In one significant advance driven by the activists at Wattie Creek, a group of local pastoralists promised to provide workers with payslips for the first time. The North Australian Workers' Union would do little to support stockmen unless they had membership, so Brian Manning also signed up about a dozen Gurindji men before travelling south to lobby against handling Vestey's products on the nation's wharves.

Looking to reduce the Gurindji's dependence on pastoralists, FCAATSI secretary Phillip Roberts and unionist Joe McGinness bought 700 goats from a Darwin farmer. Some of the people at Wattie Creek had herded (and perhaps tasted) the beasts at Wave Hill station and the Welfare settlement, and wished to supply themselves and Darwin's large Greek community with meat. After eating poisonous Ironwood en route from Queensland, the surviving animals—pronounced 'coats' by the Gurindji—were corralled near Newcastle Waters station. Mick Rangiari and Hobbles Danayarri were dispatched to meet their cloven-hooved charges, but only made it to Top Springs.

---

33 Pincher Nyurrmiarri, *Pincher Numiari* [sic]—*Gurindji Plans and Attitudes: An Interview by Warwick Neilley* (Abschol and Save the Gurindji Campaign, 1970).

It was then that the Gurindji's goat plans over-ran the political commentary surrounding Australia's 'watershed of race relations', as Hardy termed Wattie Creek. By this time, journalists were reporting on 'The Horns of a Dilemma', and quips about Canberra's 'two leg goats' were emanating from Wattie Creek as the squatters formulated their 'coat position'. With the excuse that the Gurindji lacked the land to graze their marooned beasts, authorities also refused to issue the goats with a travel permit. Minister Wentworth attempted to negotiate a solution but was stymied again by his colleagues, who harboured fears that the 'goats might get like rabbits'.[34] People at Wattie Creek believed that Vestey's, who were anxious to prevent feral goats marauding Wave Hill station, had 'thrown a spanner in the works' in Darwin.

Files show the squatters' intelligence was essentially correct—to halt the goats' advance, the cattlemen's spokesman Bill de Vos had lobbied the NT Administration on Vestey's behalf.[35] The government and pastoralists thus used their long alliance to quash the squatters' first attempt at financial independence. The goats' owner returned to his life as a wharfie in Darwin, and gave his animals to the people of Elliott.

* * *

As cyclone-induced rains enveloped Wave Hill at the end of the year, it emerged that the houses built by the activists and Gurindji men would not survive. Hannah Middleton, who was coming to the end of her fieldwork, saw Abschol's mud-bricks begin to collapse:

---

34 Alan Dearn, 'They Prefer Old Camp, So Tribe Will Stay Put on Hill', *NTN* [u.d.].
35 NTAS, de Vos to Hall and Bell, 25 Aug 1970, NTRS 3548, C1-5K; Alan Dearn, 'Government Bans Native Goat Buy', *The Advertiser*, c. August 1970.

> It was a pity, because they started to crumble rather fast. I think we were supposed to paint them every year like you do with adobe houses but we didn't understand that—I certainly didn't. I [also] suspect we should have changed the spinifex in the roof [...].

While the home of camp caretaker Snowy Yalugura and his family decayed around them, the NT Administration announced on 23 December 1970 that its brand new houses at the settlement were ready for occupation. The squatters, contemplating another isolated monsoon under leaky canvas and tin, remained unmoved. The standoff between the Gurindji and their supporters and the Gorton Government continued. Lingiari was adamant the Gurindji would stay by their waterhole until their rights to land were recognised. Minister Nixon was intent on forcing them to the settlement at any cost. Both refused to surrender.

Chapter 4

PROGRESS AND STRAIN, 1971

> They got store. They got garden. They got proper houses. They got trees. Everything coming up big there, just like *kartiya*. They do it all themselves.
>
> Annie Wyatt Nungari.[1]

By January 1971, the Gurindji's camp boasted a store, orchards, gardens, primitive toilets and showers. The government's determination not to draw attention to Wattie Creek due to its paralysis on land rights encouraged the squatters and their young friends. At the end of the wet season the group hoisted a set of bush poles and light bulbs, and when Lingiari switched on a new generator that night, 'quite a ceremony' ensued.[2] For many of the squatters, electric light was entirely novel—its delivery being a feat Vestey's had never achieved for them at Wave Hill.

Aside from the grumbling of a few teenagers, harmony prevailed. The old men's vision for the camp was widely shared and those who wished to stay observed the elders' basic rules: contribute, and don't

---

1   Lyn Riddett to Lex Grey, 29 May 1971, Riddett Personal Collection.
2   Alan Thorpe to John Zakharov, Oke Personal Collection, 22 March 1971.

drink. For those who found these requests too onerous, salubrious housing at the settlement was on offer. The squatters met their own needs where possible, though donations from the 'Save the Gurindji' groups were also used. Wattie Creek residents wanting a ride on the squatters' truck to the settlement—or to use other camp assets—were charged a fee. Support, though tepid, from Welfare Branch staff, was an unexpected bonus. In line with the Gorton Government's assistance for Aboriginal businesses, Len Ibbetson gave the squatters a water pump and occasionally collected their rubbish. The government feared that not supporting the Gurindji's new Muramulla company at all would draw more attention to the land rights cause. Making the most of the conservatives' bind, the Gurindji and their supporters applied for a development loan.

Unlike in previous years, the tempo of activity at Wattie Creek had continued through the 'wet'. Pincher Nyurrmiarri and nurse Jean Culley worked hard to get the squatters' long dreamed of store up and running. While it was funded by a gift from the 'wharfies', Nyurrmiarri and Culley also used their personal savings to stock its shelves. Although the new shop was little more than an unrefrigerated shed with a counter and shelves, it was a huge boon to the Gurindji, eliminating their dependence on the settlement for basic provisions. After several months' operation, Culley reported a modest profit of $350 ($3,750). The squatters were 'happy and proud', and in addition to quickly selling out of stock, this fuelled their bush nurse's perception the enterprise was a 'colossal success'.[3]

It was a hard-earned and stressful victory. Culley, who was horrified by the prices charged by the shop at the Welfare settlement, had

---

3   Jean Culley to Rob Oke, 27 December 1970, Oke Personal Collection, p. 2.

underestimated the running costs of the Wattie Creek business. One factor influencing the store's bottom line—and Culley's blood pressure—were the cultural obligations of local staff to provide goods to their senior relatives on request; a situation that extended into the 1980s. To help recover these losses and bolster the enterprise, customers were charged a weekly levy, with Mick Rangiari and 'Long Johnny' Kijngayari acting as enforcers. Like everything else at Wattie Creek, the business, operating next to the camp's 'roundhouse', was technically illegal. To investigate if this could be resolved, Hannah Middleton contacted Muramulla's pro bono lawyer, Mike Roet.

In March 1971, now-married activists Rob and Kay Oke made their second foray to Wattie Creek, this time en route to East Timor and Europe. Driving a donated second-hand Land Rover and carrying another water pump for the Gurindji, the Okes were impressed with the order and work about the camp. The squatters' days began early. Len Ibbetson drove about the camp, picking up children for school and those working at the settlement for government wages. Groups of women watered the garden and orchard, fed the camp's chooks and milked the goats, all before the heat of the day. The men gathered as well:

> Mick Rangiari collects [them] together by ringing the gong outside the store [...]. Jobs include building a truck shelter, collecting coolibah posts with the Bedford, painting houses and making mud bricks. There is no real [physical work] after lunch because of the extreme heat.[4]

The Gurindji were in good shape: when a visiting doctor tested the health of seventy-five people at Wattie Creek, he found no significant concerns. The track mob's diet was an improvement on that

---

4   Kay Oke, *Daily Activities at Wattie Creek*, Oke Personal Collection [n.d.].

which many had endured on Wave Hill station, but Wattie Creek wasn't a cornucopia, as Lyn Riddett reported:

> We are eking out a very frugal existence. Last night's meal was bread begged from another camp, cheese I had bought on credit from the settlement store, and tea. That was our second meal yesterday, the first being a breakfast along similar lines.[5]

Sporadically eggs, fresh fruit and vegetables, fish and other bush tucker supplemented the beef in the camp, while each week Elsie 'Cookie' Mayawi baked delicious fresh bread.

In early 1971, a few European staff took up the Gurindji's unwanted housing at the settlement, and Warlpiri and Kija and Jaru families occupied the rest. When local police tracker Dandy Danbayarri rented one house at a subsidised rate of $5 ($55) a week, his boss, police officer Bryce Fardell, was dismayed. Danbayarri and his family had gained mains power and better facilities than Fardell himself had. But while living conditions, access to schooling, medical services and shopping were all better at the settlement than Wattie Creek, the bulk of the squatters remained unmoved.

With the NT Administration's 'carrot' of housing having failed, officials sought to lure the squatters from their camp by other means. To Welfare boss Harry Giese and other assimilationists keen to integrate Aboriginal people within the wider community, luring the Gurindji into government-funded housing, services and jobs at the settlement was the first step. The 'separatist' Wattie Creek camp was viewed as an anathema by senior officials, and its residents' steps towards self-sufficiency were thwarted as a result. When the squatters opened their rudimentary store, for instance, Giese's response was

---

5   'Lyn Riddett to Lex Grey', 18 June 1971, Riddett Personal Collection, pp. 17–18.

swift: fresh bread, chicken and vegetables were flown regularly to the settlement shop to lure back Gurindji customers. The Welfare Branch's desire to undermine the squatters' business, foster their loyalty to 'Welfare', and save face was paramount.

Other sections of the NTA tried to increase the Gurindji's dependence as well. When a group of doctors from Victoria applied to provide basic medical services at Wattie Creek, the Department of Health intervened. Similarly, the department had dispensed medicines to unqualified women on cattle stations for decades, but the settlement clinic refused to give basic medical supplies to Jean Culley—a qualified, practising nurse treating up to six people a day at Wattie Creek.

To build on the financial toehold created by the Gurindji's shop, Culley began investigating the gemstones in the area. She consulted mining company geologists with Nyurrmiarri, but the pair was hampered by a lack of basic equipment. Afterwards, Abschol hired Alex Romanoff, a travelling Canadian-Ukrainian geologist, to survey the entire area and teach prospecting skills to Gurindji men. The federally-funded engagement was marred by misunderstandings and payment delays, and in the end achieved little. The Gurindji men had little tolerance for the tedium of surveying, and Romanoff found nothing of financial value.

With prospecting, nursing and the store demanding her time, Culley was over-stretched, and Abschol recruited a bricklayer named Alan Thorpe to complement her work. Thorpe's brief was to assist with the Gurindji's housing and the problems they faced in the cattle industry. Arriving with the Okes in March 1971, the young English immigrant later married a Warlpiri woman and went on to live and work among *ngumpit* people for decades. Upon his arrival, though,

Thorpe's construction plans were swept aside. A dispute erupted on neighbouring Limbunya station, resulting in a six-day walk for the sacked Gurindji stockmen.[6]

With the support of Victorian unions as well as Abschol, Thorpe checked conditions and lobbied the management of surrounding stations with Mick Rangiari. The pair were the first union representatives to apply sustained pressure to the region's pastoralists, and they were often not well-received.

While laws to improve Aboriginal people's working conditions had been introduced progressively since the early 1950s, pastoralists' *attitudes* had progressed little. Rangiari and Lyn Riddett, for instance, were not impressed to find in Vestey's wage payment records that:

> [...] the women weren't paid at the same rate that the men were paid, [they] were called things like 'Minnie Mouse', given these appalling names... the names were derogatory, [yet Vestey's] was trying to impress us.[7]

Many local managers still ran their stations along traditional lines, with Aboriginal people kept at a distance, surviving on inferior food. The conditions and wages of *ngumpit* 'domestics' at Moolooloo station were particularly bad. A segregationist attitude reigned: Aboriginal staff were not allowed in the Europeans' quarters, and the manager shook Thorpe's, but not Rangiari's hand.

With new assertiveness among the Gurindji and their union allies levelling the playing field, the men at Wattie Creek sent a letter to the region's pastoralists stating their terms: at least one day off each

---

6   During the year, conflict between *ngumpit* workers and station management was also reported on Birrimba, Nicholson, Mount Sanford, and Montejinnie stations.

7   Darwin, NTAS, Lyn Riddett, Interview Recorded by Charlie Ward, November 2009, NTRS 3609, BWF 3.

week, electricity, and concrete (not dirt) floors in their lodgings. Jean Culley reported:

> Although [their] pay is not the award and is less than what people should get, that's not really [their] beef. They feel very deeply their inferior position in society—rubbish in the way of houses and food that they are expected to accept—and this is what worries them more than money.[8]

Confirming Culley's belief, the men of Wattie Creek were more than happy to work for Jack Noble, a contract musterer and former head stockman on Wave Hill who had upset the management there by sacking a European cook for giving substandard food to black stockmen. Now an employer himself, Noble's pay was no higher than elsewhere, yet he insisted Gurindji men ate the same food as the whites in his stock camp: a simple but profound sign of respect.

* * *

In Canberra, Coombs and the CAA were flushed with optimism. The government removed Gorton from his role as Prime Minister in March 1971, and his replacement William McMahon was relatively open-minded on Aboriginal land rights. An exciting case was also before the courts.

For several years, Yolngu inhabitants of northeast Arnhemland had been fighting a battle for the recognition of their land rights in parallel with the Gurindji. With rapacious mining interests eying off their country, they had brought a claim before the Supreme Court of the Northern Territory, with Methodist missionaries. The injunction the Yolngu sought against the Commonwealth and

---

8   Jean Culley to John Zakharov, 5 April 1971, Oke Personal Collection.

the Swiss-Australian mining giant Nabalco tested an issue crucial to all Australia's Aboriginal people: would their powerful connections to ancestral land be recognised by the Australian state?

After three years of deliberation, Justice Richard Blackburn announced his decision on 27 April 1971. Blackburn determined that Native Title was not recognised under Australian law, and even if it had once existed, it had since been extinguished by European occupation. As Blackburn acknowledged the profound importance of land to Yolngu while denying them their rights to it, pundits summed up his decision: 'the land might own the Aborigines, but Aborigines don't own the land'. Reaction to the judgment was 'almost universally one of shocked protest', and this paradoxically strengthened the sense, amongst activists and the CAA, that land rights had a strong moral case. Wishing to reduce the political damage caused by the judgment, the McMahon Government moved—in a state 'almost of panic'—to re-examine its land rights policy.

During the winter of 1971, Lingiari travelled south with one of his confidantes, Donald Nangiari, Alan Thorpe, and Jean Culley. Rugged up in sheepskin jackets to stave off Melbourne's winter, the two elders had a productive encounter with one of the country's most powerful men, Australian Council of Trade Unions (ACTU) President Bob Hawke. When Hawke took the Gurindji's complaints to a meeting with Vestey's, the company told him what they'd recently told the activists—if the government chose to lease a portion of Wave Hill to the Gurindji, the company would fall in behind.

Vestey's position was by now an open secret among campaigners, but Hawke didn't care too much for either the British multinational or Billy McMahon, and he took Vestey's defection straight to the media. In the slew of resulting publicity, it was alleged Prime Minister

PROGRESS AND STRAIN, 1971

McMahon had known Vestey's position all along; a likelihood which inspired Hawke to accuse the government of 'bastardry at the highest levels'.

During Lingiari and Nangiari's stay at Lyn Riddett's home in Sydney, the Tiwi-speaking troubadour and public servant Ted Egan asked Lingiari to record Egan's new song, 'Gurindji Blues'. A former Welfare officer then working in the CAA's Office of Aboriginal Affairs, Egan had been outraged by Minister Nixon's rebuttal of land rights, and plaintively summed up the Gurindji's situation:

> *Poor bugger me, Gurindji*
> *Peter Nixon talk long we*
> *Buy you own land, Gurindji*
> *Buy 'im back from the Lord Vestey*
>
> *Oh poor bugger me, Gurindji.*
> *Poor bugger blackfeller Gurindji*
>
> *Suppose we buy 'im back country*
> *What you reckon proper fee?*
> *Might be flour, sugar and tea*
> *From the Gurindji to Lord Vestey?*
> *Oh poor bugger me...*[9]

Egan intended to record 'Gurindji Blues' for release, with proceeds to be directed to Wattie Creek. He and Yolngu songman and leader Galarrwuy Yunupingu recorded the track in the studios of RCA

---

9   Ted Egan, *Sit Down up North: An Autobiography* (Marrickville, New South Wales, Kerr Publishing, 1997), pp. 252–253; 'Gurindji Blues', *Collaborating for Indigenous Rights* (website, National Museum of Australia <http://www.indigenousrights.net.au/file.asp?fID=56> [accessed 8 November 2011]); 'Gurindji's Sing a Lament for Their Land', *Australian*, c. 1971.

Records. Egan invited Lingiari to sing as well, however the taciturn stockman struggled with high notes, and contributed a spoken-word introduction instead.

The song quickly took off after its release, and came to the attention of Egan's superiors in Canberra. The secretary of the Department of the Interior telephoned Nugget Coombs, calling for Egan to be sacked. The ebullient songster overheard Coombs' response:

> Listen [secretary], I don't propose to do anything about this. Firstly, I think it's a bloody good song, and secondly, I think it's a succinct appraisal of the government's pathetic performance![10]

On the same day as recording the single, Lingiari and Nangiari underwent eye surgery performed by ophthalmologist Fred Hollows. Things looked up immediately for Lingiari, who delightedly declared his vision 'good enough I can hunt kangaroo again'.

In early June 1971, the poor condition of the men's eyes propelled Hollows and two colleagues on a journey to Wattie Creek. After a night under a tarpaulin being harassed by 'bloody dogs', Lingiari woke Hollows at dawn. Dozens of Gurindji men were waiting patiently for their first specialist appointment. Running his equipment off a car battery, the eye surgeon quickly discovered:

> It was like something out of the medical history books—eye disease of a kind and degree that hadn't been seen in Western society for generations! The neglect this implied, the suffering and wasted quality of human life were appalling. [...] I went wild, walked over to [the Welfare settlement] and virtually commandeered the radio.

Hollows was about to receive his second shock:

---

10   Cited in Egan (1997), pp. 252–253.

PROGRESS AND STRAIN, 1971

I got on to Darwin and demanded that they send a doctor down to look at the situation. That was when I found out how things worked up there. They sent down an Englishman who was supposed to be a doctor [...] all he could talk about were rules and regulations. He got up on the back of a truck and started lecturing the people about their bad health and telling them that, if they wanted medical services, they'd have to attend the clinic at the settlement. No doubt about it, the medical services were being used as a way of forcing the Gurindji back to work. But it was interesting to see their reaction. When someone starts shouting at a Gurindji he just turns away, and that's what they did then—quietly turned their backs on this fucking idiot and left him there talking to himself.[11]

Hollows' colleague Dr PS Rogers had been asked by Abschol to vaccinate the Gurindji children. Despite requesting permission from the Darwin director of the Health Department, Rogers found on arrival he had been refused a permit to practise medicine in the NT. No reason was given. In the same period, Hollows came under ASIO surveillance, apparently for drawing attention to the extraordinary rates of eye disease among the Gurindji.

* * *

After returning from his trip with Lingiari and Nangiari to the south, Alan Thorpe's opinion of his Melbourne employer Abschol quickly soured. Abschol had doubts about Thorpe too, who was frustrating them with minimal communication and playing hardball during sensitive negotiations with the cattle stations. They sent the

---

11   Fred Hollows and Peter Corris, *Fred Hollows: An Autobiography*, (Melbourne, John Kerr, 1991), pp. 101–106; 'Specialist Appalled at Eye Disease Among the Gurindji', *NTN*, Darwin, 11 June 1971.

Aboriginal rights veteran Stan Davey, now based in the Kimberley, back to Wattie Creek to report on the performance of Thorpe, Culley and others. A few months of remote adversity had embittered Thorpe towards his student and union backers, who he felt had little idea what was going on. When Abschol sacked him, he wrote to them demanding unpaid wages, and said:

> The Gurindji have indicated that they wish me to continue with union activities and you have indicated that you wish me to stop. I would like it cleared up as to who I am up here to help, [Abschol] or the Gurindji.[12]

After finding work as a 'ganger' at the settlement, Thorpe let fly in the press on a trip to Darwin, accusing the Gurindji's Melbourne supporters of 'simply using the situation for political gain [...] without any real regard for the real wishes of the Gurindji'.[13] Thorpe's allegations came weeks after local NTLC Member Dr Goff Letts had accused 'communist stirrers aided by politicians, university groups and other well-meaning but ill-informed people' of making all major decisions for the Gurindji.[14] While Brian Manning took on Letts in the pages of the *NT News*, Thorpe gave his union backers a spray as well. NAWU, Thorpe said, had refused to pay him for the previous six months, because he was 'not sufficiently militant'. He went on to criticise questionable 'Gurindji experts' who 'agitate for what they think the Gurindji's want—or what they believe the Gurindji's should want'. By making such accusations, the 'apolitical' Thorpe had effectively jumped ship, and was now seen to be siding

---

12   Alan Thorpe to John Zakharov, 4 August 1971, Oke Personal Collection.
13   Darwin, NTAS, Alan Thorpe, Interview by Charlie Ward, January 2010, NTRS 3609, BWF 9; 'Claims Gurindjis Political Football', *NTN*, 3 December 1971.
14   'Stirrers Not Behind Our Claim: Lingiari', *NTN*, 18 November 1971.

with Aboriginal rights campaigners' conservative opponents. In case union thugs came knocking, a friend gave him a shotgun for his protection.

At the same time, the work of another Gurindji supporter came to public attention. A public servant working in the NTA (Northern Territory Administration), agronomist Rob Wesley-Smith, and his wife Jan, had begun visiting the squatters after Hardy's book spurred their interest. They provided trees, expert farming advice, and art lessons for the children. 'Wes', as he was known, was a 'rather super young man', according to Hannah Middleton, and in October 1971 he delivered a report mixing pastoral advice with a clarion call to the Gurindji's Melbourne supporters. His sense of injustice inflamed, Wesley-Smith also directed 'friendly fire' about the Gurindji at his government employer.

With Wattie Creek now making the *NT News* for unforeseen reasons, it became clear to activists in Melbourne and Sydney that they lacked the ability—or the right—to control the Gurindji's choices. Thorpe's claims caused them considerable angst. These were not only sour grapes; Thorpe aired a serious disagreement growing between Abschol and the squatters. Following the advice of Wesley-Smith, Brian Manning and politician Goff Letts several months previously, the Gurindji had investigated the possibility of applying to the government for a special purpose lease. To Abschol, this was tantamount to swallowing a government sop and giving up on land rights. Privately, Tony Lawson, the national student union director, was unequivocal:

> If the Gurindji accept any sort of lease they will have lost their bargaining strength with the government. They will become like any of the dispossessed Aboriginal groups. To propose the

idea of a lease is to propose the ending of the Gurindji land rights cause.[15]

When Darwin activists sent correspondence about a lease application to Abschol's parent body on the Gurindji's behalf, it went unanswered. Alan Thorpe fuelled the conflict via the *NT News*:

> Right now the Gurindji's want to seek a lease for the land [...] but Abschol and the other organisations decided a lease application should not be made.[16]

A lease's appeal was obvious to Darwin activists and Lingiari: without some form of title, the authorities were hard-pressed to provide the Gurindji with any proper infrastructure or funding, regardless of land rights. Abschol hit back:

> To charge that Abschol has stopped the Gurindji from applying for leases is ridiculous. [...] On November 9th [1971] Mr Mick Rangiari specifically indicated that he had no wish to talk to the Minister about leasing. If the Gurindji want a lease at Wattie Creek, there has been no lack of opportunity to ask for one.[17]

Ultimately the decision was the Gurindji's to make, and Abschol sent Stan Davey back to make sure the squatters weren't being coerced. A meeting was called in which Lingiari spoke against the lease idea, declaring 'If I had come from Big England then I should carry the lease, but I am on my own land'.[18] This was no doubt sincerity tempered by statesmanship: after Abschol's advisers left, satisfied they had a Gurindji consensus against seeking a lease, Mick Rangiari

---

15   Tony Lawson to Alan. T. Harpe [sic], 30 March, 1971, Oke Personal Collection.
16   'Claims Gurindjis Political Football', *NTN*, 3 December 1971.
17   John Zakharov to Jim Bowditch [*NTN*], 22 December 1971, Oke Personal Collection.
18   Middleton, 21 January 1971; Robert Wesley-Smith, *Report On Future Possibilities at Wattie Creek*, October 1971, Oke Personal Collection.

turned to pro-leaser Rob Wesley-Smith and requested that a lease application be drafted immediately.[19] To the old men, a lease or title of some sort was essential. They badly wanted to run and sell their own cattle, which was impossible without a government-registered cattle brand. In turn, getting a brand required a lease. The NTA had forced the elders down the path of realpolitik.

Infighting between the southern and NT-based activists was increasing. Lyn Riddett was teaching English to—and learning culture and language from—many Gurindji, but Jean Culley and Abschol criticised her. Her academic mentor received a 'deputation' from Abschol to ascertain 'what [she] was to do up there at Wattie Creek', and Melbourne's Abschol president John Zakharov called Riddett interstate to explain herself. Culley faced a similar grilling by the Melbourne activists. Her activities—like assisting young Gurindji to apply for unemployment benefits—had also earned her a description as 'the fly in the ointment' from Wave Hill's Welfare officer Len Ibbetson.[20] This acrimony increased to the point Abschol asked Culley to improve her relationship with the settlement officials, or leave.

Personality and political conflicts distracted the whites from the Gurindji's practical problems. Those caused by the squatters' reliance on creek water, for instance, were many: broken pumps, dying fruit trees, back-breaking water cartage up a six-metre river bank, and possibly an outbreak of disease. Darwin's authorities had reckoned this was likely for four years, yet had done nothing but provide 'a few water purification tablets'. Surveys had shown reliable water was to

---

19 Rob Wesley-Smith, *Diary 1971* [unpublished], 27 December 1971, Wesley-Smith Personal Collection.
20 'Lyn Riddett to Lex Grey', 18 June 1971, Riddett Personal Collection, p. 7.

be found beneath a small rise running between the squatters' camp and the settlement—which also had substandard water.

When the NTA dilly-dallied about sinking a bore, despite pressure from Wesley-Smith and Pincher Nyurrmiarri, Gurindji backer Cecil Holmes provided a larrikin solution in *The Australian* newspaper:

> If there is one bore to be sunk as soon as possible in the interests of the people of Wattie Creek, it would be the Prime Minister of this country, along with his myriad Ministers.[21]

One of these, the new Minister for the Interior, Ralph Hunt, visited the Welfare settlement and Wattie Creek in July 1971 and afterwards announced a win for the Gurindji: a bore supplying both communities would be sunk at the government's expense. Hunt and Giese's priority was to supply water to the Welfare settlement, but the Gurindji's friend in the bureaucracy (Wesley-Smith) leant on a senior official, ensuring the bore to supply both centres was sunk a few hundred yards from Wattie Creek. Activists extracted a commitment from the government that water would be piped to the camp. The Gurindji had lived on the site for four years, and this was the first act of the state acknowledging their desire to stay.

* * *

While Mick Rangiari negotiated with Vestey's in Sydney, he and Waterside Workers' secretary Charlie Fitzgibbon announced that the WWF had collected a huge donation for the Gurindji. A one dollar levy had been raised from every wharfie in the country and as a result more than $10,000 ($100,000) was destined for the elders' project.

---

21 Cecil Holmes, Letter to the Editor, *Australian*, c. August 1971.

They planned to spend it fencing out an area for their proposed cattle operation. The donation was a boon, though a tangle of legal, political and cultural complications emerged. Weeks of discussion took place.

In the same vein as the cattle brand they sought, the squatters saw fencing their land as a potent step towards equality with surrounding stations—as well as being necessary to contain their horses. But where to fence? How could family estates be reconciled with the collective vision of a cattle enterprise? During their four years at Wattie Creek, the senior men had been repeatedly asked to identify, locate and map their sacred sites, the area they wished to reclaim from Vestey's, and their traditional land. The traditional owners of the Wattie Creek area—who included Donald Nangiari, Pincher Nyurrmiarri's wife 'Big Blanchie' Bulngari, her sister 'Little Blanchie' Jingaya (Vincent's wife) and Rangiari's wife Lizzie 'Ngaliwurru' Wapngarri—were among the squatters, yet collectively the group's traditional lands stretched for hundreds of kilometres, beyond Wave Hill station.[22] Where, the wharfies wanted to know, did they propose to place their horse paddock?

Once the Gurindji negotiated these issues, the results had to be translated to the unionists, Culley, and others in turn. The former stockmen's 'maps'—their vast knowledge of their country—functioned, among much else, as the equivalent of property deeds, and were recorded only in song. When presented in ceremonial stanzas of Malngin or Bilinarra, even the most supportive *kartiya* understood nothing. How to bring a local Dreaming story of *wapawurru* (flying fox), say, into the same frame as the European abstraction of paper-based cartography?

---

22   Lyn Riddett, Personal Communication, 20 September 2014.

Notwithstanding all this, when asked by reporters about official reactions to the squatters' proposed fence, Rangiari had bravely replied, 'Don't worry about Vestey's. I don't worry about them', and 'Perhaps the government will be too frightened to pull our fence down'.[23] Despite their spokesman's apparent hubris though, the Gurindji knew they were sailing close to the wind with the Australian state. According to NT wharfie Jack Phillips:

> They wanted to know everything before they put the fence up. Would the government pull it down? Would Lord Vestey pull it down, the manager of Wave Hill station? They wanted to know everything before they started.[24]

It had been an exhausting year for those at the forefront of the land rights debate, yet Christmas brought little peace. On 22 December, the new Minister for Aboriginal Affairs Peter Howson was at loggerheads with Coombs and Dexter of the CAA—a situation that was becoming familiar. 'It was', his journal recorded, 'not the happiest end to discussions for the year [...]. Barrie Dexter put on the look of a pained spaniel who's just been kicked in the guts'. On the same day, Howson issued a warning to his colleagues which, if overblown in its fear of communists, astutely recognised land rights was an issue on which conservative forces were losing ground: 'The Aboriginal issue is going to be the main weapon used by the communists to attack the government in the coming year, and [we] should expect more problems'.[25]

---

23 'Gurindji's Plan to Takeover Part of Wave Hill Station', *NTN*, 13 November 1971; 'Gurindji Claim', *Identity*, January 1972.
24 Darwin, NTAS, Jack Phillips, Interview Recorded by Charlie Ward, December 2009, NTRS 3609, BWF 6.
25 Peter Howson, ed. by Don Aitken, *The Life of Politics: The Howson Diaries* (Ringwood, Victoria, Penguin, 1984), p. 806.

PROGRESS AND STRAIN, 1971

Five years since the Gurindji's Walk-off and four years after the 1967 referendum opened the door for Canberra to govern for Aboriginal people, the fire burning in the NT had taken hold in the nation's capital, and would not go out.

Chapter 5

VINDICATION, 1972

The efforts of Nugget Coombs, Barrie Dexter and Bill Stanner—the Council for Aboriginal Affairs' 'three wise men'—had been thwarted by high-ranking conservatives for years. The only hope they saw of winning a better deal for Aboriginal people lay with the new Prime Minister William McMahon. McMahon was in something of a fix, though. His desire to to make his name as a progressive in Aboriginal Affairs made him receptive to the CAA, even while his loyalty to the Coalition's old guard damaged his reputation with progressives. Nonetheless, when the hapless Prime Minister announced a shift in land rights policy—albeit an incremental and unsatisfactory one—it was Coombs and the CAA's biggest breakthrough yet.

In a speech delivered on the symbolically-charged 26 January 1972 national holiday celebrating the arrival of the First Fleet, 'Silly Billy', as McMahon was unkindly known, combined two very different drafts: one from the CAA outlining their radical approach to Aboriginal advancement, and the other a defence of assimilationist doctrine penned by the Department of the Interior. The public thus heard Coombs' assurances that Aboriginal Australians were free to maintain their own traditions, mixed jarringly with predictions of 'uncertainty' and 'confusion' if land rights were recognised.[1]

---

1   Prime Minister William McMahon, 'Australian Aborigines: Commonwealth Policy and Achievements' (Canberra, Australian Government Publisher), 26 January 1972.

VINDICATION, 1972

McMahon's scattergun performance channelled the divergent schools of thought on Aboriginal issues. It wasn't the speech Coombs had hoped for, but the reaction of the public was immediate and spectacular, foreshadowing a wave of anger that would help to carry Whitlam's opposition to victory at the end of the year.

A group of radical Aboriginal activists responded to McMahon by driving overnight from Redfern to Canberra with a Communist Party photographer. Arriving at 1am, they erected a beach umbrella on the lawns of parliament and proclaimed it an Aboriginal 'embassy'. Within days, more activists arrived to create a direct, larrikin-style provocation to federal politicians. If the Kooris rubbed their dispossession in the government's face, they reasoned, it would force a concession or confrontation on the land rights issue.

As the Tent Embassy grew, a list of demands and a mock ministry was announced. In a pointed swipe at Minister Howson's portfolio of the Environment, Arts and Aboriginal Affairs—referred to by the uncultured as 'trees, boongs and poofters'—the Tent Embassy included a 'Department of the Environment, the Arts, and Caucasian Affairs'.

The Embassy—funded partly by Ted Egan's 'Gurindji Blues'—raised the pitch of political conflict over land rights to a new height. While Minister Hunt sought to change the law so the government could legally demolish the Embassy, the CAA liked the new Aboriginal ambassadors' creativity and believed they had succeeded in rattling the government where the Council itself had failed. Leader of the Opposition Gough Whitlam was photographed at the Embassy listening to the protesters' demands, and emerged to announce that if elected, his government would 'give Aborigines legal, freehold title to land where they could be identified as a

community, tribe, or clan'.² Coombs' face was another seen at the Kooris' sacred fire.

In early February 1972, the head of ASIO, Peter Barbour, advised cabinet it was 'clear that the radical movement in Australia is going to turn its attention from Vietnam and the moratorium to Aboriginal Affairs […]'.³ He was right. To add to the government's woes, McMahon's relations with his Country Party colleagues were souring further and a significant problem was now camped on his doorstep. 'What', he might have wondered, 'had gone wrong?'

* * *

During the Tent Embassy's early days, David Quin, a commerce and anthropology graduate, arrived at Wattie Creek as a replacement for the defector Alan Thorpe. The calm young Sydney-sider had worked in Papua New Guinea's highlands, smoothing the locals' entry to the cash economy. After seeing a job with the Gurindji advertised, Abschol had assessed him as a steadier pair of hands than Thorpe. While Quin quickly learnt Gurindji language and contributed to their mechanical and farming needs, activists in Melbourne scrambled to fund his position. Unlike the maverick Thorpe, Quin dispatched a regular series of reports, often with financial records, from Wattie Creek for the two years of his employment.

Shortly after Quin arrived, in February 1972, the Waterside Workers' donation came through. Jack Phillips, then the vice-president of the

---

2   Tim Rowse, *Obliged to Be Difficult: Nugget Coombs' Legacy in Aboriginal Affairs* (Cambridge University Press, 2000), p. 98.
3   Peter Howson, ed. by Don Aitken, *The Life of Politics: The Howson Diaries* (Ringwood, Victoria, Penguin, 1984), p. 819.

VINDICATION, 1972

WWF's Darwin branch, remembers the squatters' appreciation when he and 'wharfie' Jeff Swain arrived at Wattie Creek:

> The Gurindji treated us like celebrities, they had a big ceremony there, took us out in the bush, sat us down, chanting [...] it went on every night. [Later] they took me down to where they'd started the fence, they'd done about 100 metres with what they had, [and] I was amazed at how strong and straight it was—well they'd worked in the cattle industry all their lives, they knew how to put a fence up![4]

With their fencing work now supported by WWF funds, the squatters maintained pressure on the government. Although the NTA had promised to supply water to Wattie Creek, it had yet to be piped to the camp. In Sydney, Mick Rangiari was characteristically forthright:

> They promised us they would pump [water] to us, but they haven't done it. They say these things to make it look good, but we know they will wait and leave us without water until we stop trying to get our land back.[5]

Land Survey Branch staff surveyed the route of the pipeline into Wattie Creek soon afterwards, however their work was interrupted by heavy rain. Quin, Culley and a number of Gurindji were stranded in Darwin by floods. When the camp eventually dried out, they returned and commenced work on a mudbrick house, planting small gardens and cutting fence posts.

The enthusiasm of some Gurindji Welfare Branch employees was such that they worked in their own time at the settlement, erecting a bough shelter for church services, and planting trees in the rain. Greater productivity was hampered by the government's denial about

---

4   NTAS, Phillips, NTRS 3609, BWF 6.
5   'Gurindji Claim', *Identity*, January 1972, p. 10.

the infertile rock underlying the town. While soil was trucked in for use around its fancy new houses, Welfare officer Len Ibbetson was forced to re-locate a proposed market garden. Ibbetson's hands were tied in other ways at Wattie Creek. Welfare provided services to the squatters, but would do nothing that could be seen as supporting their illegal camp. Ibbetson tried to lure the Gurindji to the settlement instead, operating a well-attended 'baby-minding centre' and adult education classes.

* * *

By March 1972, Wattie Creek's leaders had stared down their anti-lease supporters in the south. Despite the misgivings of the National Union of Australian University Students and Abschol, radical NTLC member Dick Ward drafted the Gurindji's application for a horse paddock lease with Rob Wesley-Smith, and David Quin submitted it to the Lands Branch in Darwin.[6] The request made on the Gurindji's behalf was for a special purpose lease over an area of ten square miles, which they sought in perpetuity and at no cost. Seeking to alleviate the political damage they feared this would do to their land rights campaign, Abschol went to some lengths to point out that the Gurindji refused to pay any rent, and quoted Lingiari saying that without a cattle brand, the lease was not wanted. The southern activists hoped to kill off any perception that the Gurindji had accepted the government's pro-lease, anti-land rights agenda.[7]

---

6   Robert Wesley-Smith, Personal Communication, 11 December 2011; David Quin, 'Report Number Two', 28 February 1972, Oke Personal Collection.

7   The goal of a lease application was also to establish the legality of the Gurindji's occupation, thus enabling the provision of municipal services. See Abschol Press Release, 17 April 1972, Oke Personal Collection.

VINDICATION, 1972

Rob Wesley-Smith was working for the government by day and assisting the squatters by night. Tested by his employer's refusal to take up Vestey's offer, Wesley-Smith took to the press. As a public servant 'stirring the can' on Wattie Creek, he picked up 'Wild Bill' Jeffrey's mantle. Like Jeffrey, who had now disappeared from the limelight, Wesley-Smith held little back. He told the *NT News*:

> The government is despicable and dishonest in its dealing with the Gurindji [...] and is playing politics with leases for Aboriginals instead of acting in their best interests.[8]

The agronomist drew the ire of anti-Communist MLC Dr Goff Letts: 'If Mr Wesley-Smith is keen to leave the umbrella of the public service and get into the bullring of politics, why didn't he trot himself out in the last elections?'[9]

Wesley-Smith's relationship with his departmental minders became strained, and he was charged with improper conduct under the *Public Service Act*, having allegedly supplied '[...] material which was of such a nature as would tend to impair the reputation of the Commonwealth Public Service, orally and in note form.'[10] Wesley-Smith told his superiors that because he had only provided notes to the newspaper—the details of which now escaped him—it was impossible to say whether he had been accurately quoted or not.

*   *   *

As their special 'corroboree' for the wharfies had shown, the Gurindji's traditional cultural and ceremonial life were strong. Had

---

8   'NTA Agronomist Doubts Aboriginal Leases Program', *NTN*, 14 December 1971.
9   'Letts Replies on "Electoral Advice"', *NTN*, c. May 1972.
10 Darwin, NAA, *Muramulla Gurindji Cattle Company*, E80, 1971/2462.

Phillips and Swain come earlier, they would have found many leaders and boys missing: the local boys' 'initiation business' camp began in January and moved to Nicholson and Limbunya stations weeks later. Afterwards, the Gurindji entertained themselves for months with a newly acquired 'devil-devil' dance. A man called Starlight had brought the performance from the Kimberley, and David Quin recalled hilarity at 'the antics of the dancer wearing a devil's mask with its collection of billy goat beards'.[11] Although such *wajarra* (public, 'play-about') corroborees were great fun, they unfortunately failed to halt a slowly-widening gap between the camp's leaders and its young people.

Since the 1940s, observers had noted differences in outlook between the generations of Gurindji.[12] Waiting and struggling in a novel, uncertain environment for five years had only exacerbated the situation, which was unwittingly hastened by 'groovy' *kartiya* activists visiting the camp. One night for instance, a big *wajarra* corroboree ground to a halt when the young Gurindji left—with 'Captain Major' as well—to dance to the latest Joe Cocker album, belonging to geologist Alex Romanoff.

While many of the young Gurindji were keen to work, and were excited by wages their parents could only have dreamed of, some thought cattle work was too difficult or dangerous, and best left alone.[13] Neither did labouring without pay to create their elders' vision

---

11 David Quin, 'Report Number One', 14 February 1972, Oke Personal Collection.
12 Ronald and Catherine Berndt, *End of an Era: Aboriginal Labour in the Northern Territory* (Canberra, Australian Institute of Aboriginal Studies, 1987), p. 204; Darwin, NAA, *District Welfare Officer Reports, Wave Hill Area*, (E242) K66/1/1; Mervyn Meggitt, 'Notes on the Malngjin [sic] and Gurindji Aborigines of Limbunya, N.W. Northern Territory', *Mankind*, Sep 1, 1955, 5, 2 (45–50), pp. 48, 50.
13 Michael George, Personal Communication, Kalkaringi, Northern Territory, 27 October, 2010.

VINDICATION, 1972

appeal to them, and conflict about their contribution to the camp ensued. According to anthropologist Hannah Middleton, one day:

> Long Johnny Kitnaeri and Pincher Ngumiari [sic] seized their boomerangs, held a large meeting and [spent] two hours swearing at the young men with a large audience. [...] They said the young men were too lazy and spent too much time playing marbles and chasing the young girls. They had chosen two nephews [to beat with boomerangs] over whom [...] they had specific control. Vincent stepped in and said, 'No, we're not going to solve it that way with a fright [sic]'. So it all quietened down. From that time onwards [...], the young men were working energetically [...], very ostentatiously.[14]

It was a temporary truce. Many observed the distance between the elders and youth increasing, but few could agree on its cause. The Gurindji's supporters blamed the Welfare Branch:

> Working through the tribal elders seems rarely done by officials from Wave Hill [settlement]. [While] their tribal structure is ignored, it is likely that the [positive] attributes of the Wattie Creek group will be destroyed [...].[15]

Others thought the activists themselves encouraged disobedience:

> The younger members of the tribe, sitting around most of the day, drawing unemployment benefits (or at least many of them), playing cards, drinking, making love, all absorb many of the half-shot ideas of their white visitors. They repeat these, parrot fashion, and from the lips of simple, guileless men come the radical ideas of the political extreme left.[16]

---

14   Hannah Middleton, 'The Gurindji at Wattie Creek', *Abschol and the Anthropological Society of Victoria* (Conference Proceedings, Melbourne, 9 December 1970), Oke Personal Collection.
15   Rob and Kay Oke, Paul Fox, David Twitt, *Wattie Creek: Present and Future- Report of the Abschol Field Team* (Melbourne, National Union of Australian Students, December 1969), pp. 4–5.
16   Brother Paul Webb, (c.1971), Oke Personal Collection, p. 25.

The young people's exposure to the wider world created more tensions. So that Gurindji children could be properly educated—to eventually realise their elders' vision of self-sufficiency—a group of girls enrolled at Kormilda College in Darwin in 1972. Judith Donald, Rosaleen Farquharson, Josepha Kijngayari and Susan Cebu carried their elders' expectations on their shoulders. But while these girls travelled to Darwin and occasionally the southern cities, gaining much broader experience than that available to them at home, their newfound assertiveness challenged some of the older men.

As a result of these tensions, the elders loosened a significant aspect of Gurindji traditional law. Tired of the stresses created by youthful lovers eloping with members of the wrong 'skin', Lingiari initiated a reform allowing young men to pursue the 'promised' wives of male elders. This radical shift reflected his reformist, pragmatic leadership. According to Lyn Riddett and David Quin, Lingiari said he had 'softened' Gurindji law earlier, doing away with capital punishment. Lingiari's father accepted this reform, with the proviso that if it failed, his son should be put to death.[17]

* * *

During the 1972 dry season, the elders' drive to establish their cattle operation continued. Gurindji men fenced off a paddock for quietening horses, and Jerry Rinyngayarri built a saddle shed with material from the old Wave Hill station tip. Such pilfering was allowed by Vestey's, for although Wave Hill station manager Ralph Hayes was sceptical about the Gurindji's plans, he had grown up

---

17   Lyn Riddett, 'The Strike That Became a Land Rights Movement: A Southern Do-Gooder Reflects on Wattie Creek, 1966-74', *Labour History*, 72 (May 1997) 50–65 (p. 58); Quin, Personal Communication, 16 August 2007.

among them and spoke their language. He gave hut frames to the squatters for their village as well.

Notwithstanding the old men's leadership and enthusiasm, at times, little stirred at Wattie Creek. Young men left to work on the stations, and shopping, schooling and work took others to the settlement. When the camp's trucks were broken-down—which was frequently—people had to wait for tools and equipment, and their work was stymied. In mid-April 1972, there was little to do. Quin described:

> Djaldji is making a boomerang in the shade over there with about eight dogs of assorted breeding watching—one or two are scratching the odd flea or tick! Someone just stood up and kicked a few dogs out of the way—yelp! And Tobacco Jack is blowing a few occasional notes on the didgeridoo.[18]

Within days, this reverie was broken by the second Aboriginal action to wrack the Victoria River pastoral industry. On 14 April 1972, three Ngarinyman stockmen—Slim Murrell, Barry Young and a man recorded only as 'Major', all from Victoria River Downs (VRD) station—arrived at Wattie Creek. They made it clear their countrymen were ready to abandon their jobs, and the bush camp they had lived in for generations. Aboriginal morale on the Hooker Pastoral Company-owned station was very low, and conditions were appalling. As with the Gurindji's walk-off, the idea of a mass departure had been brewing for some time. One Ngarinyman elder, 'Old Tim' had been promoting a Wattie Creek-type, independent settlement for the VRD people for at least two years.

The day after the newcomers' arrival, Mick Rangiari, Jerry Rinyngayarri, Jean Culley and David Quin travelled in convoy to VRD to investigate. The activists intended to broker talks between

---

18   David Quin, 'Report Number Five', 10 April 1972, Oke Personal Collection.

the station's management and Big Mick Kankinang and Charcoal Dulung, its Aboriginal leaders. These plans were thwarted when the Gurindji's Bedford truck broke down. Quin, who had vainly worked for weeks to nurse the aging truck to good health, thought it unwise for he and Culley to continue, as accusations about 'white stirrers' inciting trouble would be likely. Culley continued to the station regardless, and was met with hostility.

More than 100 Aboriginal people left VRD and its outstations Moolooloo and Pigeon Hole in the following days. They were driven to the squatters' camp by Pincher Nyurrmiarri's son Charlie, Quin and Len Ibbetson. As Quin predicted, the manager of VRD, Ian Michaels, told officials that the Aboriginal people's exodus was the work of Abschol (especially Culley, who he had previously banned), and the Aborigines had been reluctant to leave.[19] Quin responded that when he had arrived with the Wattie Creek contingent on VRD, the first thing the Aboriginal workers told them was that they were ready to leave. Despite Michaels' claim he had been investing significantly in accommodation for his workers, a Welfare officer concluded it was Michaels himself, and the way he treated his workers, that prompted their final departure: 'I am [...] convinced [leaving the station] was a decision the Aborigines made themselves'.[20]

Now Michaels was free of the administrative burden that accompanied Aboriginal staff and their families, he sent the Ngarinyman people's bank books and their wage and social security cheques to

---

19 Jean Culley to Rob Wesley-Smith, 13 May 1972, Wesley-Smith Personal Collection.
20 Jack Doolan, 'Walk-Off (and Later Return) of Various Groups from Cattle Stations: Victoria River District', *Aborigines and Change: Australia in the 70s*, ed. by Ronald Berndt (Canberra, Australian Institute of Aboriginal Studies, 1977), pp. 106–13 (p. 107).

VINDICATION, 1972

the Welfare settlement neighbouring Wattie Creek. Then—perhaps inspired by events at Wave Hill after the Gurindji Walk-off—he bulldozed the Ngarinyman's camp on VRD station to the ground. Scenes of wild abandon allegedly occurred:

> The people went mad, the Europeans. They carried on like red Indians [sic]. They shot all the dogs and they bulldozed all the huts into a huge pile and they set fire to it and they capered around yelling and screaming and carrying on like idiots. I didn't witness this, but I know well that it happened.[21]

The Ngarinyman mob were now jobless, and NAWU distanced itself from the dispute, claiming the issue was not industrial and those involved were not union members.

Within a fortnight, the remaining Aboriginal people from VRD and its outstations arrived at Wattie Creek, swelling its population to a massive 250 people. The children were enrolled at the settlement school and Len Ibbetson provided the group with food and unemployment benefits. David Quin, noting that even a few extra dogs had arrived, wondered dryly whether Wattie Creek was becoming a 'holiday or perhaps a refugee camp', though according to another visitor, the *ngumpit* stronghold was now 'more hard work than fun'.[22]

Despite the extra pressure their guests put on the Gurindji—and the meagre waterhole from which they were still drawing water—goodwill prevailed. Lingiari was the boss, with authority over the long term Wattie Creek residents, while 'Big Mick' and Charcoal Dulung shouldered responsibility for their own people. The result

---

21　Darwin, NTAS, Jack Doolan Interview Transcript, c.1981, NTRS 226, TS 193.
22　Quin, 'Report Six', p.2; Berenice Nyland, Interview by Charlie Ward, 31 December 2010. In possession of the author.

was a 'very highly organised community which has a straight chain of command'.[23] To repay the Gurindji's kindness, their visitors lent significant manpower to the Gurindji's fencing project.

Small strikes and conflicts erupted on other stations throughout the Dry, further swelling the numbers at Wattie Creek. With more people drawing on Daguragu waterhole, instances of disease— including hepatitis—occurred. To remedy the bureaucracy's inertia regarding the camp's water supplies, a truck began delivering drinking water from the settlement, and 'welfare' employed Gurindji men to build a new pit toilet block in the camp.

The Ngarinyman walk-offs had been a great excitement and preoccupied everyone, but once the visitors had settled in, Jean Culley questioned her place among the Gurindji. The only older *kartiya* present, Culley's opinionated nature alienated her from younger women like Lyn Riddett, and she wondered whether she should stay. Culley had taken leave from a moribund marriage, and since then her spouse had successfully driven their jointly-owned service station in Melbourne into the ground. When Culley was called to attend a court case resulting from unpaid debts owed to the Ampol fuel company, District Welfare officer Jack Doolan commented sardonically: 'one might be forgiven for hoping that it will keep her out of the district for some time'.[24] Undeterred and uninspired in the south, however, Culley simply sold her business, tried to evict her husband from her house, and then returned to her Aboriginal friends at Wattie Creek.

---

23   Jack Doolan, 'Report on Wattie Creek Camp', 3 August 1972, p. 5, Oke Personal Collection.
24   Doolan, 'Report', 3 August 1972, p. 3.

VINDICATION, 1972

The Gurindji's support base was growing. In July 1972, Sekai Holland, a Zimbabwean who later fought successfully for her country's independence, arrived with Abschol's new national director Bryan Havenhand, campaigner Christine Jennett, and Poppies the dog. After learning what they could on the ground, the activists returned to Sydney with Diane Nampijinpa and Shirley Gilgi. The girls' families wanted them to teach mainstream Australians about Gurindji culture and return with useful skills. Gilgi wanted to practise hairdressing, but no formal training eventuated. Once assured she was entitled to travel the city alone, the young woman tackled its eastern suburbs on foot, using trees to guide her. Nampijinpa spent time with Kevin Gilbert, Paul Coe and other Koori activists friendly with Sekai Holland, her host.

Proving that support for the squatters had spread from Victoria and New South Wales, three Adelaide men also dropped in to Wattie Creek. The party's leader Don Atkinson was a lab manager and unionist who had solicited support for the Gurindji at Flinders University. With development experience in Ghana and Kenya, Atkinson had married into a communist family which also supported the Aboriginal cause. Accompanied by his union mates Vic Barnett and glassblower Roy Parrott, the trio drove a tiny Renault loaded with soybeans and fertiliser three thousand kilometres to Wattie Creek. The South Australians planned to deliver money they'd raised in person and take photographs that would assist them to publicise the Gurindji's situation. They also planted their soybeans near the creek and created a filing system for the Gurindji's growing piles of correspondence.

By the time they left for Adelaide, the trio were laden with Gurindji artefacts to auction to raise money for saddles and stock

gear. Driving with a fuel tank improvised from a jerry-can lashed to the roof, Atkinson had 'an assortment of infections, including diarrhoea'.[25] Undeterred, he and his colleagues formed a 'Gurindji Stock Fund' and Vic Barnett organised for Captain Major Lupngiari to visit Adelaide on a speaking tour. The visit of October 1972 was a success, though some wondered if the old Gurindji stockman was showing signs of dementia. Despite or because of his condition, Lupngiari demonstrated the use of a traditional spear during a well-attended appearance at the Teachers' Institute, frightening most of the audience.

* * *

Unfortunately for the Gurindji, Minister Howson's lack of interest in developing land rights policy was acting as a brake on the work of Coombs and Dexter and the CAA. On 20 June, Howson and his adviser Len Hewitt visited Lord Vestey in London to discuss the Gurindji issue. It was obvious to the Minister for Aboriginal Affairs that Coombs had been there before him, 'meddling in matters with which he isn't properly conversant'.[26] When the pro-Aboriginal political scientist Colin Tatz announced on national television that Vestey's were prepared to 'hand over' one thousand square miles of Wave Hill station to the government, it was the final straw for the conservative Minister. Howson believed only Coombs could have been responsible for the leak.

Tatz was right. After a five year campaign, the Gurindji and their supporters had finally broken the alliance of their antagonists. It was

---

25 Philip Nitschke to Jean Culley, 21 February 1974, Oke Personal Collection.
26 Howson, 1984, p. 882.

a huge achievement, but even as the CAA lobbied for an area of 1,200 square miles (about a third of Wave Hill station) for the squatters, the Department of the Interior refused to budge on the issue.

The government's plans to evict the Aboriginal 'ambassadors' camped outside parliament were proceeding. Legislative amendments were passed to criminalise the Tent Embassy, and on the morning of 19 July 1972, 150 police—some of whom had removed their badges—advanced in a phalanx on the ramshackle collection of tents, warning the protesters they would be arrested should they interfere. Many were injured in the melee that followed, and although ALP shadow Minister Gordon Bryant was observed hindering the police, few were arrested.

In this strained environment, the McMahon Government and the ALP opposition began campaigning for the upcoming end-of-year election. The Coalition—which had held power for twenty-three years—had suffered a large swing against it in 1969. Since then, Gough Whitlam had further distinguished Labor's platform from the government's, and was capitalising on the difference.

With land and the other concerns of Wattie Creek's residents intimately connected to *kartiya* politics, they were familiarising themselves with the voting process. The Gurindji had been allowed to vote since 1962, but a high voter turnout at Wave Hill had not been among the Welfare Branch's priorities. This time, Lingiari knew that an ALP Government would be much more supportive of his vision, and he dictated a letter to Whitlam in late October 1972:

> In our law, the first law in this country, that land still belongs to we. Well, if you get into government you got to change your

law to agree with our law. [...] Well, we want to see some word from you in a letter if we are to believe you and vote.[27]

Three weeks later in Blacktown, Western Sydney, Whitlam delivered a comprehensive speech to an elated, beyond-capacity audience bearing badges and balloons. To cheering and foot-stamping, Whitlam told the faithful that universal health insurance, free tertiary education and the abolition of conscription were on their way. On Aboriginal land rights, Whitlam declared:

> We will legislate to give Aborigines land rights—not just because their case is beyond argument, but because all of us as Australians are diminished while the Aborigines are denied their rightful place in this nation. [...] We [...] insist that, whatever the law of George III says, a tribe and a race with an identity of centuries—of millennia—is as much entitled to own land as even a proprietary company.[28]

Whitlam's vision was clear and sincere, in stark contrast to the morass of infighting among the Coalition, unhelpfully augmented by McMahon's outdated beliefs and weak oratory.

Eight weeks before his loss at the polls, McMahon announced that the Gurindji's heavily-contested application for a tiny lease had been successful. It had been hinted for more than a year that the government might provide the Gurindji with a 'sitdown area'—a special purpose lease that it hoped would placate them. But despite intense wrangling in Canberra, McMahon's ten square mile lease was not so much a concession to the CAA or Gurindji as the result of the previous year's Gibb Committee report, which had called on the

---

27 Vincent Lingiari to Gough Whitlam, 27 October 1972, Oke Personal Collection.
28 'It's Time: Whitlam's 1972 Election Policy Speech', <http://whitlamdismissal.com/1972/11/13/whitlam-1972-election-policy-speech.html> [accessed 30 May 2012].

VINDICATION, 1972

government to act for Aboriginal people left jobless by the pastoral industry.

Late in the dry season, David Quin sent word to the Adelaide support group that the Muramulla company had bought twenty-one horses and were owed more by Inverway station. Their lease was also on the way, and Atkinson ordered the Gurindji's precious branding irons to mark their cattle. When the old men received a heavy package from Adelaide there was great excitement. The new brand, 'GDT', stood for 'Gurindji Daguragu Territory'. The squatters' vision of running their own cattle enterprise was coming to fruition. 'It's a permanent settlement', Lupngiari told the Adelaide press. 'We're staying'.[29]

* * *

At the election of 2 December 1972, the Australian people delivered an increase of eight seats to the Australian Labor Party—a small though election-winning margin. On every front, McMahon had been out-performed by the ebullient, charismatic Whitlam. For many Australians raised in the pro-British, regressive pall of the Coalition's decades in power, it was a moment of unrivalled joy and optimism.

Ten days after the count, Coombs telephoned Lord Vestey and informed him that the new Australian government had requested that the CAA investigate the acquisition of a large area of Wave Hill station, 'sufficient to establish a viable cattle enterprise for the Aboriginal people of the region'.[30] It was the breakthrough the

---

29 'Gurindji Seeking Cattle', *Advertiser*, [u.d, c.10 October 1972].
30 Darwin, NTAS, 'HC Coombs to JM Hall', 13 December 1972, Northern Territory Pastoral Lessees Association, Administration and Correspondence Files, NTRS 3548, C1-2D.

Gurindji had been waiting for, and carving up an Australian station proved of little concern to Vestey's, which was preoccupied with continuing its tax evasion following a recent stoush in the English courts. To stay ahead of the taxman, drastically, *ownership*—rather than mere control—of the family's assets had been transferred to a group of loyal trustees on their payroll.

Several days before Coombs' call to England, Ronald Grove, a Vestey trustee and manager of their Argentinian operations, was kidnapped en route to a round of golf in Buenos Aires.[31] Effectively, Grove had become a biological bank account. Held in a cellar for ten days by hooded members of the Argentinian Trotskyist Party, Grove was one of numerous executives to be kidnapped in the region in 1972. The fact some of these businessmen had been executed presumably heightened the Vesteys' concern.

In the Gurindji's experience, Vestey's staff had seemed largely expendable, but it now became obvious there were exceptions to the rule. After a nine-day hiatus following their trustee's disappearance, the Vesteys intervened directly on 10 December 1972 and dissuaded both the Argentinian police and the British Home Office from taking action against the kidnappers. Instead, they sought to broker a settlement themselves. During this time—while final votes were counted on one side of the Pacific, and ransom money on the other—the fate of the Vestey family and that of the Gurindji were in others' hands. A series of 'scare' tapes featuring Grove were deposited across Buenos Aires, and he was freed unharmed. The executive's release cost Vestey's more than $6 million in today's currency.

---

31 'Kidnapped Director Held by Marxists' *New Straits Times*, Kuala Lumpur, December 14 1972, p. 28. <http://news.google.com/newspapers?nid=1309&dat=19721214&id=Bd0qAAAAIBAJ&sjid=I3wFAAAAIBAJ&pg=1538,5561701> [accessed 23 May 2012].

VINDICATION, 1972

In Australia, with left-wing euphoria and conservative disappointment high, this near tragedy for Vestey's was little noticed. Aboriginal land rights was on its way, and Whitlam moved rapidly with one of his deputies to terminate lease applications over Aboriginal reserves. The Department of the Interior, including the NT Administration and Harry Giese's Welfare Branch, was mothballed; public servants were at a loss. According to David Quin at Wattie Creek, McMahon's tiny lease for the Gurindji was stopped in its tracks: 'the Lands Branch in Darwin is not taking any further steps at present with the changed government'.[32]

Whitlam gave the CAA unprecedented government support, and on the strength of 'a piece of paper from the Prime Minister', Coombs sent two of his staff, Nunggubuyu activist Phillip Roberts and old Welfare hand Ted Evans, in an aeroplane to Wattie Creek. The pair accompanied Vincent Lingiari on a flight to assess the area the Gurindji wanted from Wave Hill station. Whitlam was intent on making good on his election promises: that a legal system recognising traditional Aboriginal rights to land—and a fund for Aboriginal groups to buy their land—would be on their way. After a testing six years, the Gurindji and the Labor Party had triumphed.

---

32   David Quin to Vic Barnett, 13 December 1972, Atkinson Personal Collection.

Part Two

Making a Fist of It 1973–78

Chapter 6

A NEW BEGINNING, 1973

> I feel [the Gurindji] have qualities and
> capabilities that have never emerged. They should
> be fostered and encouraged in a special way.
>
> Jean Culley, Gurindji supporter.[1]

After half a century of paternal platitudes from Canberra, Whitlam's election was pivotal for Lingiari and his friends. Spruiking the 'It's time' slogan, the Labor Party pledged to support the Gurindji to achieve their aims. The old men of Wattie Creek deserved some credit for the ALP's new stance, though. The elders had travelled the land for six years talking of their aspirations, and Whitlam, Coombs and others had responded. If the first Australians needed their land and independence, the new Prime Minister thought, they should be helped to have them. It was the seismic shift many believed overdue.

In the tumultuous early months of 1973, Whitlam appointed former activist and teacher Gordon Bryant as the Minister for Aboriginal Affairs. Bryant, having long worked for the Aboriginal cause in FCAATSI, was known for his enthusiasm and—unlike most white Australians—counted many Aboriginal people among his friends.

---

1   Culley to Wesley-Smith, Sunday [Undated, 1976], Wesley-Smith Personal Collection.

With a warm, offhand manner, Bryant took to his job with gusto and an informality that refreshed and disturbed observers equally.

Wanting reform, and fast, the novice Minister announced the new order. A huge new Department of Aboriginal Affairs (DAA) was formed, and Whitlam asked the CAA's Barrie Dexter to lead it. From managing the tiny office that supported the council established by Harold Holt, Dexter's staff increased by 1,000 percent. It was planned that the new DAA would take responsibility from the states, and the Northern Territory—over which the Commonwealth had direct control—would be used as a 'showcase' to develop Canberra's Aboriginal policies. The elephantine Welfare Branch in Darwin was disbanded and its head, Harry Giese, removed. To the progressives, it was time to start afresh. Many 'Welfare' staffers left, though hundreds more took their chances with the new DAA.

For those caught up in this drama, feelings ran high. Giese thought Dexter and Coombs were dangerously ignorant meddlers, while they considered him the tinpot emperor of a failed regime. Giese's removal was quickly mythologised. Despite stories that he was ungraciously sacked by either Bryant, Coombs or Dexter—each of whom allegedly flew to Darwin for the pleasure—Dexter denies sacking Giese, and according to Giese himself, he was demoted by Ray McHenry, his previous underling who had become head of the DAA's NT Division.[2]

Far from being relegated to an office job 'out of the way', as was commonly believed, Giese was given considerable freedom as a travelling adviser. Whether his advice was heeded was another matter. Despite their intense dislike of each other, Giese and Dexter—both

---

2   NTAS, Barrie Dexter, Interview Recorded by Charlie Ward, February 2010, NTRS 3609, BWF 25; Ted Egan, Personal Communication, 13 June 2013; Giese, quoted in Stephen Gray, *The Protectors: A Journey through Whitefella Past* (Crows Nest, Sydney, Allen & Unwin, 2011), p. 195.

A NEW BEGINNING, 1973

consumate bureaucrats—maintained their professionalism, and Giese reported directly to his arch enemy for several years.

Under the new left-wing guard, the progress Giese's Welfare Branch had made for the Gurindji and others was forgotten. Dismissed now as a rusted-on conservative, Giese had once been seen as a southern 'stirrer' himself. As the *NT News* pointed out:

> [...] The original confrontation between Central Australian cattlemen and Mr Giese [occurred] in the early 1950s, when it was made clear that the days of a few shillings a week and a handout of tea, sugar and flour were coming to an end.[3]

To the Territory's cattlemen, Giese's earlier demands for tin huts and pension payments for Aboriginal people now seemed quite reasonable—compared to the agenda emerging from Canberra. Whitlam had different issues to address, high among them the basis of pastoral power in the NT—land.

Having promised much to Aboriginal people prior to the election, the new government set to work. To students at Monash University, Barrie Dexter said that while all and sundry had imposed their wishes on Aborigines in the past, his officers would follow the Aborigines' desires instead:

> Policies and programs must now be designed to enable Aboriginals to decide their own goals and to achieve them. The emphasis is on participation by Aboriginals [...]. Previously, an overall goal, namely 'assimilation' was set, and [measures taken] to achieve it. Now we no longer presume to know the destination or even the direction.[4]

---

3 'End of an Era', *NTN*, 6 March 1973.
4 Barrie Dexter, 'The Commonwealth Department of Aboriginal Affairs—Its Functions and Underlying Principles', in *Seminar on Aboriginal Affairs*, 9 May 1973 (Monash Centre for Research into Aboriginal Affairs, 1973), p. 1.

Notwithstanding the small steps taken by McMahon away from assimilation, it was a massive turnaround for the Gurindji. Whitlam elaborated:

> The basic object of my government's policy is to restore to the Aboriginal people of Australia their lost power of self-determination in economic, social and political affairs.[5]

'Self-determination' then, was the name of the new approach. The new PM went on:

> My government is anxious that 200 years of despoliation, injustice and discrimination have seriously damaged and demoralised the once proud Aboriginal people. The government [...] accepts responsibility for their active and progressive rehabilitation [...]. We will not rest until they have taken up, as a distinctive and honoured component of Australian society, the position to which their rights as the first Australians entitles them.

Whitlam's vision of how this was to occur was complex; even contradictory. While his government planned 'to assume full responsibility [for] Aboriginal Affairs' from the states, it also sought to create small organisations at Wave Hill and elsewhere, which Aborigines could use to manage their own affairs. 'Mainstream' departments, not the special-focus DAA, would also deliver services to the First Australians. Whitlam believed *land*, too, was needed to provide Aboriginal people 'with a base for their economic and social development'. To this end, a Royal Commission into Aboriginal Land Rights, led by Justice Edward Woodward—the Yolngu people's former

---

5   Edward Gough Whitlam, 'Statement by the Prime Minister, the Hon. E.G. Whitlam, Q.C., M.P., to the Ministerial Australian Aboriginal Affairs Council in Adelaide on 6 April 1973', (1973).

A NEW BEGINNING, 1973

QC in their legal challenge against mining—began.[6] To support all these undertakings, a huge funding increase was announced.

Thanks to their years lobbying the ALP, the Gurindji were high among the government's priorities. But at the settlement and Wattie Creek, what would 'self-determination' mean? At Wave Hill there were two groups of Aboriginal people: one seemingly content in a government-built town; the other living illegally in the bush and demanding their land. Until the government got land for the Wattie Creek people, it could do little to help develop their camp, due to its lack of legal tenure. At the settlement, there were no such impediments, and the DAA could use its new mandate to spend money there.

Mulling over such thoughts, Minister Bryant and Barrie Dexter dropped in to see the squatters on a whistle-stop tour six weeks after the election. Such trips would become frequent: it was intended 'true consultation' with Aboriginal people would characterise the government's approach. 'Listen[ing] to the Aboriginal wisdom, rather than [...] imposing my thoughts upon them', was Bryant's aim.[7]

Although the Minister's time at Wattie Creek was as fleeting as previous VIP visits, the encounter was instructive. In line with the new paradigm, Dexter announced he no longer wanted the Wave Hill township to be known as the 'Welfare settlement'. The Gurindji were questioned about their name for the site instead, and Dexter decided that henceforth it would be known as 'Libanungu'. Embarrassingly, this attempt at 'Aboriginalisation' backfired and the new name failed to stick. For the next few years (until another name change),

---

6 The idea of a Royal Commission on the matter was promoted by Nugget Coombs.
7 AIATSIS, 'Draft Statement by the Hon GM Bryant', *DAA 1970—73, Papers of Jeremy Long*, Box 5, Folder 50.

the Gurindji and others continued referring to the town as 'the settlement', while 'Libanungu' was used by government officials—to show their empathy with Aboriginal people. The squatter's camp at Wattie Creek was renamed 'Daguragu': the Gurindji name for the waterhole next to their shacks and humpies. Unlike Dexter's well-meaning but ham-fisted effort, 'Daguragu' had local currency.

During their brief meeting with the Gurindji elders, Dexter and Bryant asked them about the way forward. Did they want to do their own thing at their own pace, or would they like Daguragu to eventually be built up like the neighbouring town? The question was central to the Gurindji's future. The squatters said—or Dexter heard—that they were content for the settlement to continue as a service centre, thus allowing them to live with minimum interference in the bush. With this brief bit of 'true consultation' completed, the Gurindji's main chance to reassess—or even reverse—the conservatives' 1968 decision to build up the settlement and not Wattie Creek was lost.

A few days after Bryant's departure, a headline in *The Australian* trumpeted the political purpose of his visit: 'Gurindji's Win Land' [sic]. Rather than land rights for the Gurindji, this was the ALP cashing in on McMahon's previous announcement. The new government had merely re-endorsed the outgoing government's decision to excise a small (ten square mile) lease from Wave Hill station. Daguragu would get legal tenure, simplifying minimal developments in the camp, but Vestey's occupation of the rest of the Gurindji's land was unaffected.

Bryant, recognising that the Gurindji's battle was far from run, gave them a sweetener: the government would 'see that their land was returned to them'.[8] Although the question of how this could be done

---

8   'Press Statement by the Minister for Aboriginal Affairs, Mr Gordon Bryant', Department of Aboriginal Affairs, 18 January 1973.

A NEW BEGINNING, 1973

(by purchase, or the legal recognition of land rights) was a matter then testing the bureaucracy's best minds, the Minister's assurance meant little to the Gurindji elders. Stung by their scepticism, Bryant told reporters 'I realise that because of the long struggle, it will take Aborigines some time to realise that we mean business'. 'If Lord Vestey is happy', he asked, 'then who can object?'[9]

Lord Samuel Vestey's happiness may have been overstated. Actually, his tolerance of the new Australian government was flagging. Minister Bryant had asked him to fly to Australia for a meeting to discuss the Gurindji's request for a piece of Wave Hill station. This bemused Vestey, as there was nothing his company could do to hasten the process until the Australian authorities themselves issued him with specific instructions. Furthermore, he had discussed the issue at length with Nugget Coombs recently, who was, like Bryant, acting on the government's behalf. Vestey complained about Canberra's shambolic new masters: he was in communication with Coombs, Minister Bryant, and the Attorney-General. Who, he wondered, was in charge?

Compared to other local pastoralists though, Vestey was positively relaxed about the Gurindji's new lease. The president of the NT Cattlemen's Association (NTCA), Bill Tapp, described their new allotment—approximately one thousandth of Wave Hill station—as:

> [...] another handout and another step in the wrong direction. [If land is to be] given away, it should be by proper land ballot, to give everyone a chance, whether they're black, white, or brindle. [...] I'm sure that none of the pastoralists begrudge

---

9   'Gurindji Land Grant Closer', *Canberra News*, 24 January 1973; 'Land Resumptions for Aboriginals to be "Fair"', *NTN*, 24 February 1973.

the Gurindji's getting on and improving themselves, but giving them hand-outs isn't the way to help them.[10]

Tapp thought that if the Gurindji were to be granted a 1,500 square mile pastoral lease (a third of Wave Hill station) as the government proposed, it would be a 'financial disaster'.

The cattlemen's spokesman was not alone. On 8 May 1973, 600 Katherine residents—approximately half the town's *kartiya*—vented their race-related grievances in a public meeting.[11] Chaired by the local Country Party representative and billed as a 'Rights for Territorians' gathering, the group was quickly dubbed 'Rights for Whites'. The meeting sought another Royal Commission—not into land rights but the government's new Aboriginal Affairs policies. The group's 'Committee to End Discrimination' included Bill Tapp and the Gurindji's neighbours, Paul and Betty Vandeleur of Camfield station. Their grievances were many: the neglect of deprived whites at the expense of Aboriginals; Aboriginal people's unsupervised use of their own social security payments, and the government's mismanagement—as the committee saw it—of Aboriginal settlements and cattle projects.

Although the DAA was barely three months old and had not had time to implement any of its new proposals, Barrie Dexter and the DAA's Darwin head Ray McHenry fronted the meeting. Bewildered by the anger in the crowd, they concluded that the concerns of 'Rights for Whites' related mostly to the actions of the previous government.

---

10 'Letts Welcomes Gurindji Lease', *NTN*, *c*. March–April 1973.
11 I estimate that 2,000 of the 2,741 residents of Katherine counted in the ABS census of 1971 were over the age of 18, and that at least 10 percent were Aboriginal. According to primary accounts, Aboriginal people were almost entirely absent from the meeting. See '600 Demand a Royal Commission into Aid', *NTN*, 9 March 1973.

A NEW BEGINNING, 1973

Minister Bryant promised to visit Katherine to discuss the issues raised by the group.

* * *

Eight weeks after the election, the DAA made plans to establish what 'self-determination' meant in practice. Progressive young educators from the Australian National University held a series of seminars for handpicked DAA staff in the tropical township of Batchelor. Despite the distractions of the Rum Jungle Social Club, veterans of the 'top-down' Welfare Branch found that exploring how Aboriginal problems could really be fixed was electrifying:

> [We] were talking in terms of doing things that needed to be done, and being allowed to do them the way that [we] were talking about. It was quite unreal, I think we all ended up on a bit of a high![12]

The DAA also offered a training course in community development, the new *method* of self-determination. Few Aboriginal people were invited, and convenor Liz Sommerlad was the only woman present. Privately, Barrie Dexter wanted to prevent his officers continuing in the tired footsteps of their old boss, Harry Giese. This, Dexter thought, would be a challenge, though the indoctrination process was easier than expected:

> I got to every [former] welfare officer over about three months. I ran two seminars […] to brainwash them [laughs]. It was quite fascinating because I was lecturing them about the fact that we were now in for a change. […] I said 'this might pose problems for

---

12 Darwin, NTAS, John and Ann Rutter, Interview Recorded by Charlie Ward, October 2012, NTRS 3609, BWF 43.

some of you', but they erupted and said 'That's exactly what we've always wanted to do!' It transpired that they'd all been through [training] which preached that gospel. [...] They'd already been brainwashed, even though they were working for Harry![13]

Unbeknownst to Dexter—and perhaps even Harry Giese—critics of the old 'assimilation' policies had been lecturing impressionable Welfare Branch rookies at a government-run college in Sydney for years.

After months of discussion punctuated by confronting 'seventies-style' group work in Batchelor, Sydney and Canberra, the DAA trainees summed up their findings. 'Self-determination', they said, meant allowing Aboriginal people to 'decide the pace and nature of their future development as significant components within a diverse Australian society'.

Once this prescription was approved by the Minister, ex-welfare officer Len Ibbetson would return to Wave Hill and implement it directly with the Gurindji. After Ibbetson completed his unorthodox training—which included infiltrating both the bolshy far-Left Builders' Labourers' Federation and the offices of silvertail property developers *in disguise*—he returned to Wave Hill. For three years, Ibbetson had worked at Wave Hill as the superintendent of a Welfare Branch settlement. Nothing perceptible had changed, but now he was an 'adviser' to 'Libanungu Community'. Did its residents appreciate their town's makeover or Ibbetson's 'brainwashing'? It seems unlikely.

The activists supporting Wattie Creek also had to reckon what effect the new government and 'self-determination' would have on

---

13   This college was the Australian School of Pacific Administration in Mosman, Sydney. NTAS, Barrie Dexter, NTRS 3609, BWF 25.

A NEW BEGINNING, 1973

their campaign. Apparently, Gurindji land rights were a step closer, but the track mob's day-to-day needs in the primitive camp were unchanged. The activists who had spent time at Wattie Creek (now Daguragu) thought that the new government's lip-service about Aboriginal autonomy sold Aboriginal people short, at least in the remote north. After Jean Leu, the coordinator of the Gurindji's Sydney support, visited the squatters for several weeks in the dry season of 1973, she reflected on both the DAA's lofty rhetoric and the number of chickens, horses and cattle the Gurindji had already lost through poor fencing and lax management. She noted:

> The present popular cliché is to let Aborigines 'do their own thing' and 'run their own affairs'—fine, if they comprehend what they are running [...]. To apply this concept indiscriminately, as an overall inflexible policy, is idealistically naive. How can people make a valid choice, or aspire to become a self-supporting community, when their own experiences are so limited, or when they know either nothing, or very little, of available alternatives?[14]

As a case in point, the Gurindji's new lease allowed them to run horses, but buying the animals required better numeracy and business skills than the old stockmen could muster. A few mounts were bought with David Quin's assistance, but their supporters worried that without expert advice, the Muramulla board might be 'taken down' by profiteers. '[...] Evaluating and negotiating the purchase of stock at current market prices is a totally new experience for them', Leu observed. She asked Donald Nangiari—who was soon to be the director of the Muramulla company—how much the Gurindji had paid. 'Some five dollar, some ten dollar', he replied. Later Leu

---

14   Jean Leu to Rob Oke, Oke Personal Collection, 2 June 1973.

ascertained that the six horses bought from the Gurindji's mate Jack Noble had come at the market price of $100 ($950) each. A seventh, un-rideable by Noble or the Gurindji's star horseman Charlie Pincher, had been thrown in for free. Eventually David Quin bought thirty more horses from nearby Inverway station on the elders' behalf.

In other matters, the board members had real expertise. In a letter to Wesley-Smith, Quin said:

> I talked to Vincent about the fencing and paddocking ideas you suggested for conserving grass and increasing fertility in the herd. He realises the need is there and so it is a case of putting it into practice. [...] He told me how they would do this, before I had anything much to say.[15]

At the elders' request though, Quin saw that 'GDT'—their much-wanted official cattle brand—was registered within a fortnight of receiving the new lease.[16] The unprecedented supportiveness and haste this showed from the bureaucracy encouraged Quin and the Gurindji to approach the DAA in Darwin directly, instead of appealing first to the southern 'Save the Gurindji' activists. Dedicated Melbourne supporter Rob Oke saw that the assistance he co-ordinated was quickly becoming redundant: 'Our role would seem to be diminishing rapidly [since the election]. When we stop financing [an adviser] at Wattie Creek, we can probably wind ourselves up.'[17] Unlike in the past, officials at the settlement gave the Gurindji and their supporters 'excellent co-operation on all matters', according to Jean Leu. The DAA's Len Ibbetson even employed Gurindji people to maintain not just the settlement, but Daguragu, on government wages. This suited

---

15   David Quin to Rob Wesley-Smith, 4 April 1973, Wesley-Smith Personal Collection.
16   This occurred on 29 March 1973. Personal Communication, NT Registrar of Brands, 12 May 2012.
17   Rob Oke to Quin and Lingiari, Oke Personal Collection, 4 April 1973.

the 'drivers' of the Muramulla project—old men such as Donald Nangiari, Long Johnny Kijngayari, Jerry Rinyngayarri and Long Jack Jurumbak could not compete financially with the surrounding stations now luring Daguragu's young men elsewhere with award wages.

Small grants were available to Muramulla now, and Daguragu's residents channelled their own social security payments towards the purchase of saddles, horses and cattle. Mick Rangiari remembered:

> Soon as we got that money we used to [...] put it in. 'Okay, we got to buy this with this money—we got to buy a horse. We'll have to save up, we'll have to keep every cheque'. Maybe every fortnight we get it—just put 'em in.[18]

With a small mob of cattle in reach, Muramulla turned to building their own stockyards. These were a high point of Gurindji achievement, through which the knowledge gained over many generations was transferred. Young men provided much of the labour, following advice given by their elders. Watching the process—for he was little able to help—impressed David Quin, requiring as it did:

> Knowledge of the right trees to cut; design [...] and layout; construction techniques and hard work were needed—with the skilled use of adze, axe, crosscut saw and chainsaw. None of the *kartiya* associated with [the Gurindji] since the Walk-off had those skills or knowledge.[19]

In Mick Rangiari's words, 'That big stockyard now, they bin start building. That time was…you know, proud people, eh?'

Running their new cattle was not without its challenges. Although an ASIO spy described him merely as having a 'well-developed sense of

---

18   NTAS, Rangiari NTRS 226, TS 485, (T4), p. 16.
19   David Quin, Personal Communication, 14 July 2012.

humour', Lupngiari's dementia continued. While his cattle industry credentials were unquestionable, the old man's increasing senility—in combination with his cultural authority—was turning him into a hazard, at least from a European economic perspective. According to David Quin:

> Captain Major is still a spanner in the works [...]. He created quite a stir when he shot the [newly bought] big cow for killer—don't tear your hair out. Vincent has tried to sack him but he threatens to shoot people, and means it, too. He is quite mad.[20]

Woes such as dementia brought home a serious issue—the rapid aging of the Muramulla board. At the end of 1973 another elderly man, Donald Nangiari, was appointed as director. Despite his cataract operation two years earlier, Jean Culley privately dismissed him as 'too blind and conservative' for the role. The pragmatic nurse worried that the elders' focus on the livestock enterprise meant obvious issues like the track mob's health and housing were being overlooked. Culley was right, though the old men were happy.

* * *

Muramulla was making progress in line with Long Johnny Kijngayari's aim of working 'for ourselves, [with] little bit of help from white people', but the tiny lease bestowed by Gordon Bryant had done little to fulfil the elders' desire for land.[21] The Woodward Royal Commission on Aboriginal land rights was in its early stages,

---

[20] Canberra, NAA, 'Aboriginal Visitor from NT: Lupgna Giari', *Atkinson, Donald, Volume 2*, A6119/5061; David Quin to Rob Wesley-Smith, 14 August 1973, Wesley-Smith Personal Collection.

[21] Long Johnny Kijngayari, cited in Cecil Holmes, 'Wattie Creek,' *Aboriginal Quarterly* (Abschol, Australian National University, Canberra, March 1969).

A NEW BEGINNING, 1973

and gathering its findings and translating them into law would take years. On the other hand, the government could *buy* the land for the Gurindji from Vestey's, using existing legislation, and authorities were moving to do just that for other Aboriginal groups. Keen to act for the Gurindji, the DAA needed to establish the exact area they wished to reclaim.

Senior DAA staff Ted Egan and Jack Doolan returned to Wattie Creek in a light aircraft. To their relief, the country identified on two flights by Jerry Rinyngayarri, Vincent Lingiari and brothers Pincher Nyurrmiarri, Mick Rangiari and Long Johnny Kijngayari—who had spoken about it for months—was largely identical. Small differences were resolved later in a series of meetings between the elders, Jean Leu, and Jean Culley. Essentially, the Gurindji leaders claimed the western third of Vestey's Wave Hill station, including the Victoria River. The 1,240 square mile parcel of land included Daguragu, patches of good cattle country, and many of their sacred sites.

The DAA's next hurdle was to establish how much the Gurindji's country would cost to buy, and whether it could support a cattle business. Needing expert advice, the DAA contracted their 'go to' consultants, the Australian Agricultural Consultancy Management (AACM). Doolan and Egan planned to rendezvous with the consultants and Gurindji elders at Daguragu in mid-June 1973, but according to Doolan, the 'true consultation' got off to a shaky start:

> About all I had time to say was 'Vincent, we've got some blokes from Canberra here, who want to have a look at Wave Hill for you. You'd better chuck your swag on, old man—we'll probably be away a couple of days'. Vincent and Jerry threw on their swags and away we went in a cloud of dust. [They] should have been advised why the inspection was being done

> [...] so that it could have been discussed at length before the event.²²

The agronomists were not primarily there to consult with the Gurindji but to assess if the prospective block of land to be carved from Vestey's Wave Hill could support a profitable business. Regardless of self-determination's rhetoric, determining whatever vision the elders held for their cattle operation was not their concern.

After Wave Hill station manager Ralph Hayes showed consultant Newton Tiver around, rather than ask the Gurindji about their plans Tiver gave Lingiari a crash course in business, explaining:

> [...] After the initial setting up of the station with assistance from government, it is expected that wages will be paid by the [Muramulla] company to its employees, and that this money will have to come from the profit of cattle.

Confronted with the hard facts of operating a market-focused cattle enterprise, Lingiari vouched for his men, and replied that Muramulla would make sufficient profit to pay its staff. Whether he believed this or just saw his assurance as necessary to get back his land is impossible to know. According to Patrick McConvell, an English linguist just arrived at Wattie Creek, the Gurindji: '[...] argued back, but the decision really lay with the consultant. They'd just been told "this is how to run a cattle station"'.²³

Jack Doolan, who had much experience with Top End Aboriginal people and had worked alongside the Gurindji building their pit toilets, clearly saw:

---

22   Darwin, NAA, 'Visit of AACM Representatives [...] to Wave Hill Station, Libanungu and Daguragu', *Wave Hill Station—Matters Affecting Aborigines*, 13–16 June 1973, NDW 72, 1049.
23   Darwin, NTAS, Interview with Patrick McConvell Recorded by Charlie Ward, November 2009, NTRS 3609, BWF 5.

European priorities are being looked at rather than Aboriginal [ones]. Vincent and his people are more interested in getting back some of their former land, where they can sit down and enjoy their ceremonies, eat their own beef, turn off enough cattle to provide for the necessities of life [...], and work at their own pace.[24]

David Quin agreed. The AACM visit heralded the government's imposition of its formulaic, industry-standard response to the Gurindji's cattle desires. Tensions between the elders' modest goals and the prescriptive demands of the state would plague Muramulla for the rest of its life. After Tiver's two-day inspection of Vestey's Wave Hill though, he left to repeat the exercise with Rembarrnga people east of Katherine.

The AACM had effectively trodden roughshod over a host of problems. The old stockmen's aim of running cattle 'like white European' involved operating some sort of business, but in that regard they had been kept deliberately ignorant during their years in the cattle industry. One issue this raised—of the need for financially savvy, educated staff as part of the Gurindji's new enterprise—highlighted an emerging crack in the government's 'self-determination' approach. Except for having David Quin as a book-keeper, Lingiari wanted Muramulla entirely Gurindji-run. The elders, according to Doolan, 'had their horse breaker picked out, their yard builders picked out, and their manager picked out. They didn't want any [*kartiya* involved]'.[25] According to the rhetoric of self-determination, this choice was the Gurindji's to make, but it was now obvious that an entirely Gurindji-run, taxpayer funded company was a bridge too far for the Whitlam Government.

---

24 NAA, NDW 72, 1049.
25 Darwin, NTAS, 'Jack Doolan Oral History Interview Transcript', NTRS 226, TS 193, p. 44.

A similar shortfall between official aims and Gurindji abilities confronted the DAA at the settlement. There, Len Ibbetson had established two new 'Aboriginal' bodies—Libanungu Council and Wundamarie Housing Association—with which it was hoped residents would manage the development of their communities. Locals had taken to the idea of a Gurindji council, and a group of willing leaders were elected to the board. All seemed well:

> Councillors have acquired a demountable building left by a firm of contractors and have converted it to an office from which they propose to conduct their affairs. Council workers, some of them in their off-duty time, have spread soil [and] planted grass and trees around their office, which they consider to be their own headquarters.[26]

This was heart-warming for Ibbetson, but the workings of a government-funded council—even an 'Aboriginal' one—would require reports, acquittals, quorums and a host of other practices unfamiliar to those reared in the stock camps of Wave Hill station.

In 1973, Western education itself was still a new concept to the elders of Daguragu: primary schooling had only been available at the Welfare settlement since the early 1960s, and the first Gurindji kids had enrolled in high school the previous year. When the resulting shortfall in skills became apparent, the DAA admitted that Libanungu Council—like other 'Aboriginal' organisations springing up at the time—would need to employ a *kartiya* manager for advice. The development of a market garden and poultry farm were expected at the settlement, not to mention general hygiene and road, aerodrome and parks maintenance and administration. It appeared a lot of

---

26   Darwin, NAA, *Wave Hill Community Development*, E460, 1974/242.

whites would be required for 'Aboriginal self-determination' to work in the NT.

While the DAA sought educated European-Australians to 'advise' Libanungu Council, its hapless Gurindji staff were already dealing with enormously increased responsibilities—and amounts of money. When a large funding cheque was sent to the council office, it languished on a desk for several months before a DAA official found it. 'Regrettably', he reported, 'none of the Aboriginals were aware of what this represented'.[27] The government was nonetheless keen to give Aboriginal people as much control as possible, and Billy Bunter—the young council president elected for his literacy and numeracy skills—and Mick Rangiari were asked to decide whether 'their' new housing association could manage the settlement's development. The contract was worth the equivalent of $6 million in today's terms, and they readily agreed.

* * *

During the 1973 dry season, Daguragu's population was still swollen by more than a hundred of the Gurindji's *ngumpit* countrymen who had walked off Victoria River Downs station the previous year.[28] The vision and 'track' of Wattie Creek had inspired the visitors, who were keen to follow a similar path: to set up their own homeland on country excised from VRD. To achieve this, the leaders of the 'six mile mob'—probably Big Mick Kankinang and Charcoal Dulung—

---

27 Darwin, NAA, 'Visit to Wave Hill Centre', 30 January–1 February 1974, *Wave Hill Centre—Policy*, E460, 81/306.
28 After the 'walk-off' from Victoria River Downs Station, the population of Wattie Creek was approximately 250.

lobbied Gordon Bryant and others about obtaining an area they called Yarralin, on the Wickham River.

Success for the Ngarinyman, Ngaliwarru, and Garangburu claimants came quickly. On 8 and 9 October 1973, they met on the site with the LJ Hooker company (VRD's owners) and the DAA. Despite LJ Hooker's reluctance, the department supported the creation of an Aboriginal living area at Yarralin from the outset. Within a week, eighty people left Daguragu and begun building bush shacks and pit toilets in the scrub on the Wickham River. Using the template established by their pioneering Gurindji neighbours, the VRD mob asked Lyn Riddett and David Quin to make a 'signboard' for Yarralin like that which Hardy painted in 1967. Jean Culley—who had lent much support to their walk-off the previous year—was asked to assist, and the DAA funded a position for the purpose. Culley, who had a history of barely-disguised loathing with VRD manager Ian Michaels, thought she was passed over for the job due to his meddling.

While there were now fewer *ngumpit* residents at Daguragu, the number of *kartiya* supporting the Gurindji at Wattie Creek continued to grow. Jean Culley, David Quin and school teacher Lyn Riddett were living in the camp, while Jean Leu (from Sydney) and Don Atkinson, the leader of the campaign in Adelaide, were frequent visitors. This loose network of activists shared the purpose of assisting the Gurindji, though at times they struggled to agree on how to do so. Tensions rose, arguments erupted and factions formed among the whites living outdoors with their Gurindji 'families'. Their observant hosts missed none of it. Culley—who was by now known to local pastoralists as 'the witch of Wattie Creek'—had visited recently with her daughter Paddy and taken a dislike to Quin, the Gurindji's principal

adviser. Culley wrote to his southern backers, telling them that the elders no longer wanted him at Wattie Creek. Riddett and Culley's relationship was also strained, and while these intrigues flourished, another pair of 'friends from the south', Philip Nitschke and his partner Jenny Thiele, joined the group in October 1973. The camp's tensions would soon come to a head.

Nitschke was an opinionated physics graduate from Flinders University who, on Don Atkinson's recommendation, had been quizzed by Lupngiari and Mick Rangiari about taking up a gardening job with the Gurindji. With the elders' backing, Minister Bryant approved DAA funding for the role. Culley's first impression of the physicist-cum-gardener was of a 'quiet and thoughtful man'. He told her that he wanted to avoid the military implications of a physics career. Nitschke's 'quietness' would not last.

A week after the new gardener's arrival, Pincher Nyurrmiarri entered Nitschke's camp. The canny elder advised him to 'lie low' as there was 'trouble going on' at the roundhouse where Quin and Riddett were living. Nitschke watched:

> I was a couple of hundred metres away, but I could hear something going on. Quin started to pack all of his belongings onto his old Land Rover. Pincher [came] over every couple of hours and said 'He's out, he's going, he is taking Lyn with him'.[29]

A woman had been assaulted by one of Quin's Gurindji 'relatives', and when the perpetrator went unpunished, Quin threatened to leave in protest. The elders did little to prevent his departure with Riddett. Soon afterwards, Nitschke was called to a meeting and Lingiari asked him if he would replace Quin as the camp's bookkeeper.

---

29   Philip Nitschke, Interview Recorded by Charlie Ward, 16 June 2007.

Although the Gurindji barely knew him, the elders saw Nitschke as a viable replacement because he had the backing of their trusted friend Don Atkinson. The physicist was also literate, had lots of tools, and enjoyed tackling mechanical problems—once a quality of Quin's too, before his enjoyment had been overwhelmed by the Gurindji's Bedford truck. As Nitschke would learn, the demands of the camp on its advisors were enormous, and beneath Quin's calm demeanour he had been feeling the strain of over-work for some time. Culley reported that the camp's leaders had asked the pair to go, but Quin had been planning to leave for several months.

By this time—quite aside from the dramatic circumstances of Quin and Riddett's departure—the old men surely realised that if their 'friends from the south' were to play a positive role at Wattie Creek, they would also bring with them, or encounter, their own problems. Lingiari told Ted Egan that only one *kartiya* adviser was now welcome to reside in the camp.

* * *

The powerful changes of the new government were becoming apparent at Wave Hill. Award wages were paid to Aboriginal workers at the settlement for the first time. More jobs—although often of limited appeal—were available, and unemployment benefits were also easier to obtain. In the past, the primary male of a Gurindji family was often the only person with an income. Now, women and young adults too had money. With people at the settlement and Daguragu comparatively flush with cash, an age of consumer choice dawned. Goods at the settlement store walked off the shelves and a fashion renaissance began. People took great care of their appearance, and

A NEW BEGINNING, 1973

new 'transistor radios, cassette recorders and wrist watches, even lawn mowers'—were in high demand.[30] By pooling money or doing a season's work on the stations, cars could be bought, and with cars, the simple but profound act of leaving became possible. For the Gurindji, autonomy and individualism had arrived. When a few young fellows left to work elsewhere and kept their wages for themselves, Vincent Lingiari was powerless to stop them.

For cashed-up young men wishing to spread their wings, Top Springs, the closest fuel stop, sold one thing they could not get at home: alcohol. The powerful drug was now available on Daguragu's doorstep, and although the elders wanted their camp to be entirely 'dry', cars were put into service driving the 400 kilometre round trip twice a week to load up with booze.[31] On their return, fighting erupted. Jean Leu described:

> I've lived through those sleepless all-night and half-the-morning booze-ups. [...] Voices threatening to kill, come dawn. One voice repeating hour after hour, 'No-one is going to fuck my wife! I'm the only one who fucks her!' Great verbal histrionics, the [...] throwing of spears and boomerangs (often for effect). The early morning sun filtering through dust raised by warring camps, and Mick's goat nonchalantly standing on his table in the middle of it all, right in the line of flying missiles. [...] Then the nauseating sight of injured people [...].[32]

Fighting and hell-raising after 'grog-runs' occurred more frequently at the settlement than Daguragu. When trouble arose there, it was

---

30 Darwin, NAA, 'Circular Memorandum No. 164 [...]', *Wave Hill—Reports on Community Development*, E460, 1978/242.
31 Darwin, NAA, 'Circular Memorandum No. 164 [...]', E460, 1978/242; Don Atkinson, 'Visit to Daguragu by Sen. Cavanagh [...]', June 1974, Pelczynski Personal Collection; Lyn Riddett, Personal Communication, 28 July 2013.
32 Leu to Atkinson, 4 December 1973, Atkinson Personal Collection.

usually the result of drunken Warlpiri visiting their kin. The new Libanungu Council was quick to respond, but as locals were drinking more too, the focus of the settlement's policeman shifted. Previously, European stockmen and itinerants committed nearly all the crime in the region. Now, the drunken misadventures of Aboriginal people occupied the local constable.[33] The Whitlam Government had not given the Gurindji the right to drink—this occurred in 1964—but it had given them the means to do so.

Like most senior Gurindji, Vincent Lingiari drank rarely if at all, and abhorred the effects of grog. Inspired in part by Rev Graham Paulson, who had taken up residence at the settlement in 1970 and was the nation's first Aboriginal Baptist Minister, he announced he was giving booze away entirely. The old man also pledged his Christianity.

At the settlement, unprecedented harmony between 'Welfare' (the DAA), the Gurindji, and their advisers reigned. Small requests from Daguragu were positively met and usually followed quickly by funding—an extraordinary achievement for an enormous new department with huge responsibilities nationwide. Ironically though, this responsiveness and generosity were symptomatic of problems elsewhere. After Whitlam's announcement about restructuring Aboriginal Affairs, the bureaucracy was in chaos. The DAA's 'showcase' division in the NT had no staff to handle crucial financial and management functions for its first six months. To highlight the resulting confusion—and the fact that the goals of 'self-determination' remained undefined—the Country Liberals in Darwin voiced their concerns:

> The [DAA] have not seen fit to state clearly, precisely and unequivocally what their objective is, [yet] we see that $3,000

---

33 Darwin, NTAS, *Wave Hill Police Journal*, NTRS 2127, Vol. 16–17.

[$25,875] is to be spent on the Aboriginal people [per person] in the NT each year, with no objective in sight.[34]

Despite these criticisms, Gordon Bryant's office continued issuing a sizable stream of cheques. Government money allotted to Aboriginal people was at an all-time high.

Increasing the turmoil were a freshly-empowered group of radical black activists critical of what they saw as the government's tardy efforts to 'Aboriginalise' the DAA. A new group, the NT Council of Rights for Aborigines and Torres Strait Islanders (NTCRATSI) applied heat from Darwin:

> WE WANT ACTION NOW [...]! The department is being set up using the same old tired white faces that kept us down during the previous government. [...] Patrol officers should be Aborigines NOW. There is no time to be lost.[35]

Compounding the strain was the DAA's own tearaway Minister, the ebullient Gordon Bryant. Bryant was as keen as his PM to get things done, and was not overly concerned by protocol or the ramifications of his decisions: problems which he felt were best dealt with by others. The peripatetic Minister made funding decisions on the run with the input of advisers or Aboriginal friends—news that was conveyed far and wide on the black grapevine. Mick Rangiari twigged to Bryant's foibles and buttonholed the Minister twice in person.

On 7 September 1973, DAA secretary Barrie Dexter could take no more. He reported to the Auditor-General that he was unable to control the finances of his own department, and that his relationship

---

34 Northern Territory, Legislative Council, Hon Les MacFarlane, *Hansard: 11th Council–First Session, 20th Sittings. Part One–the Debates*, 26 June 1973 (Darwin, NTLC Printer, 1973), p. 515.
35 NTCRATSI to Gordon Bryant, Barrie Dexter and the Public Service Board, [Date Unknown], 1973, Wesley-Smith Personal Collection.

with Bryant had broken down. The magnitude of these confessions brought the issues plaguing the department to a head. Smelling political blood, Dexter's old foe Ralph Hunt called for him to be sacked, and for a royal commission to be established. Instead, Whitlam removed Minister Bryant nine months into his appointment and replaced him with a 'due process' man, Jim Cavanagh. Aboriginal people who had seen Bryant's availability and derring-do as the only tangible sign of the government's pledge to 'get things done' were outraged. Protests outside parliament house were held. Bryant was unapologetic, reflecting long afterwards: 'If Whitlam had kept out of the road, within two or three years we'd have revolutionised the entire system'.[36]

Bryant had gone, but Dexter's woes were far from over. Whitlam had invited Aboriginal Australia to give its opinions, and the government was now being barraged by complaints. On top of this, an enquiry into the DAA's finances was launched, and the department's most senior Aboriginal staffer, Charlie Perkins, attacked the organisation from within. Perkins wrote in the press that the government's talk about 'Aboriginalisation' was a sham:

> I have been consulted only at the convenience of others [and] treated as a facade designed to impress other Aborigines, rather than being in a position of genuine power.[37]

Perkins' loyalty, it was evident, lay with the nation's Aboriginal people, not Whitlam or his Minister. The issues this raised—of who was really in charge, the bureaucracy or the nation's first people—revealed a

---

36 Cited in Peter Read, *Charles Perkins: A Biography* (Ringwood, Victoria, Penguin, 2001), p. 156.
37 Charles Perkins, 'Promises, Promises, But Blacks Have Gained Nothing', *National Times*, 29 October 1973, pp. 8–9.

hidden fault line through the whole policy of self-determination. Among believers, disappointment was about to kick in.

Perkins, an Adelaide-educated Arrernte man of mixed heritage, was not alone in his frustration. Black and white DAA staff alike questioned whether self-determination could be achieved if the government—not Aboriginal people—directed the bureaucracy's actions. The question dominated the DAA's workshops in Batchelor and Canberra. According to trainer Liz Sommerlad, her trainees all agreed that 'the prime loyalty of the [DAA] adviser is to the [Aboriginal] community, and the department must respect this'.[38] When she invited Minister Cavanagh to clarify the matter though, she and the trainees were shocked. Bryant's staid successor left Len Ibbetson and the other community advisers under no illusion: whatever self-determination meant, it was only to occur as stipulated by the state. After a giddy flush of hope, the limits imposed by the Whitlam Government on Aboriginal people's choices were becoming clear. Many questioned whether self-determination was merely hollow rhetoric. One DAA adviser decided the department: '[...] is not really working for the Aboriginal people, but is a bureaucratic machine which serves its own members, providing they are loyal'.[39] The Gurindji had made the same charge against 'Welfare' at the settlement during the old assimilation era. With Whitlam in power, the hopes of the Gurindji and their friends—not to mention thousands of others—had been raised sky high, but a year on, the stability of the state remained paramount to its decision-makers. Indigenous Australians were set to vent their anger.

---

38 Elizabeth A. Sommerlad, 'Community Development in the Northern Territory', *Aboriginal* News, February 1974, p. 18.
39 Elizabeth A. Sommerlad, *A Training Course in Community Development for Field Workers in a Tribal Aboriginal Context*, Occasional Papers in Continuing Education, No. 6 (Canberra: Centre for Continuing Education, Australian National University, 1975), p. 15.

Chapter 7

INTO THE FRAY, 1974

> May I interrupt you there? You say they [the Council for Aboriginal Affairs] have the expertise. Who, in the name of God, can have more expertise in Aboriginal Affairs than Aborigines?
>
> Senator Neville Bonner to the Minister for Aboriginal Affairs.[1]

He had only been in power for a year, but Whitlam's efforts to empower Australia's first people had disturbed and angered Aboriginal people and whites alike. The mis-steps of the DAA had received extensive media coverage, and included a costly turtle-farming proposal that—as the press reported—had gone belly-up in the Torres Strait. Radical Aborigines saw the department as disingenuous and slow, while conservatives thought its intentions misguided or even dangerous. The people most able and willing to take up (or just criticise) opportunities flowing from the DAA's 'Aboriginalisation' were English-speaking, urban and politicised. The radical agenda of some of these activists (or even their identification as Aborigines) was criticised by paternalistic whites, including ex-Welfare hands still

---

1 Australia, Senate, *Hansard, Parliamentary Debates—Estimates Committee G*, 22 October 1974, p. 405.

INTO THE FRAY, 1974

working in the department. 'Traditional' Aboriginal people like the Gurindji were mostly untouched by these controversies but, in 1974, the elders at Wattie Creek too were drawn into the fray.

Since his arrival among the Gurindji some months previously, Philip Nitschke had embraced his role as their gardener, scribe, lobbyist, mechanic and tutor, with huge energy. His efforts to publicise their situation made those of his predecessors seem half-hearted. But unlike other activists who had attempted to maintain good relations with *kartiya* in the area, Nitschke had no hesitation about fronting Europeans on behalf of the 'track mob' at Daguragu as he saw fit. His confrontational style quickly enraged the settlement's new DAA adviser Trevor LaBrooy—and its other white residents.

When LaBrooy arrived to replace his friend Len Ibbetson in early 1974, the Victoria River was in flood. His 'welcome' included being swept several kilometres downriver before burying an old Gurindji man's body in the dark, soaked by driving rain. A principled public servant, LaBrooy had worked on Queensland's notorious Palm Island Aboriginal settlement. Finding the policies he was expected to enforce there unfair, he had petitioned the then Aboriginal Affairs Minister WC Wentworth over lunch about other work, and was offered a job by Harry Giese in the NT Welfare Branch. As a Justice of the Peace who believed strongly in the rule of law, loyalty to the government and respect for 'common decency', LaBrooy was Philip Nitschke's nemesis. To the young firebrand then flirting with anarchism, LaBrooy's Dutch-British Ceylonese background was a sign of his 'colonialism'. Although both men were on the DAA's payroll, serious altercations occurred within weeks.

Like the Gurindji, Nitschke was dependent on the settlement's services, and needed LaBrooy's goodwill. When a hunting rifle seemingly

went missing in the post—which was being managed by Anna LaBrooy, Trevor's wife—Nitschke angrily accused her of sabotaging Daguragu. The new superintendent was so enraged by this attack that he 'bum-rushed' the younger man from his office with a well-aimed kick. Afterwards, when Nitschke threatened to dispose of him violently, LaBrooy—a former big game hunter—responded in kind.

The young activist was soon disliked by other whites in the area too. Scottish nursing sisters Margaret and Bernadette Glass had just arrived at the settlement (and Australia), and although they were disconnected from local politics, found themselves in Nitschke's sights as well. When Nitschke angrily told them to improve their service at Daguragu, the sisters called for LaBrooy to physically evict him from their clinic and filed a complaint. The nurses' union spokesman doubtlessly had Nitschke in mind when he said:

> There is a new kind of [...] left-wing paternalism. [...] The revolutionaries think they are going to take over. Some of the people implementing the government's policy of self-determination are stirring things up. Some are employees of the ministry, and I think they should be sacked.[2]

By this point, Minister Cavanagh had received a stream of complaints and claims and counter-claims from the combatants at Wave Hill. He defended LaBrooy, pointing out that: 'Mr Nitschke's own inexperience and lack of training may well be an important factor in the situation'.[3] Unbeknownst to the Gurindji's new adviser, the DAA were considering terminating his employment.

---

2   CT McDonald of the Royal Australian Nursing Federation, cited in Cecil Edwards, *Labor Pains* (Melbourne: Hill of Content, 1974), pp. 189–190.
3   Darwin, NTAS, *Northern Territory Pastoral Lessees Association, Administration and Correspondence Files*, Sen. J. Cavanagh, in 'Race Relations Newsletter, No. 9', 26 April 1974, NTRS 3548, C1/2D.

INTO THE FRAY, 1974

The conditions were certainly challenging, and although on better pay than the Gurindji, both Nitschke and the nurses were doing it tough. In 2007 Nitschke remembered:

> The first wet [season] we went through was pretty hard going, the bloody hut was awash with water. It was as hot as hell, there [were] twenty centimetre centipedes hurtling across the floor, sick dogs [were] everywhere, people were diseased. We were bloody trapped for a long period of time when the river was up […]. I don't want to overstate this, but it was tough going.[4]

Similarly, according to local NTLC member Dr Goff Letts, the nurses were living in:

> [An] undersized caravan with a leaky roof and a [tiny] refrigerator […]. They wash their clothes by hand […]. Their air-conditioning has been broken down for some time [and] there is no toilet or shower for them […]. They are in such poor circumstances that the Aboriginal people themselves have built them a bush shelter […].[5]

Daguragu's elders were pleased enough by Nitschke's work, but the fights erupting among the *kartiya* troubled them. Lingiari, ever mindful of the Gurindji's need to maintain good relationships in the region, attempted to prevent Nitschke from visiting Wave Hill station. His concern was warranted; within months, the station manager Ralph Hayes threatened to 'punch Nitschke's head in'.

Hostility towards Nitschke even played out in the Gurindji's camp. One night 'Lynnie' Hayes (brother of Ralph), their old friend Sabu Sing, and the local policeman, arrived for a 'friendly beer' with the Gurindji. As the alcohol flowed, the visitors turned nasty. Pincher

---

4   Philip Nitschke, Interview Recorded by Charlie Ward, 16 June 2007.
5   Northern Territory, Legislative Council, *Hansard: 11th Council–First Session, 20th Sittings. Part One–the Debates*, 23 May 1974 (Darwin, NTLC Printer, 1974), p. 457.

Nyurrmiarri warned Nitschke that unless he left his camp, he would be attacked. Nitschke watched from the darkness as the drunken whites came spoiling:

> [...] the three of them had come over to my camp. My father [who was visiting] came out of the tin shed, and he stood outside where the fire was burning. I could hear the voices through the night, saying 'Where is your shit-stirring son? We're going to teach him a lesson'. My father said 'I don't know, he's gone'. Then they started to give [him] rather a hard time, knocking him around.[6]

Jerry Rinyngayarri, a teetotaller, arrived in the nick of time, and asked the visitors to leave. They got in their Toyota and issued a warning before driving off: 'The weak bastard, we'll get him one day'. Nitschke—who also received death threats—was inclined to take them seriously.

* * *

To encourage greater Aboriginal participation in government decision-making, the DAA had created a new National Aboriginal Advisory Consultative Council (NACC) in a matter of months. The Council was slated to be a key component of Aboriginal self-determination, and hopes surrounding the new body were high. At a meeting in Batchelor, Gurindji and other delegates were told they would:

> [...] get a truly representative Aboriginal body, one big powerful voice to speak to the government. You will be able to decide

---

6   Nitschke, 2007.

your own future and resolve your own troubles [...]. We do not have to go through white people to get what we want.⁷

When the NACC assembled in Canberra in February 1974, its new councillors dictated their agenda. They requested far greater powers, an enormous pay rise, and reserved seats for Aboriginal people in parliament. It was not the 'advice' the ALP had wanted, and Cavanagh responded like an overbearing parent. The council in turn called for his resignation.

This clash at the heart of the government's self-determination project—and the Minister's barely disguised dislike of 'urban', political Aboriginal people—put him on a collision course with Charles Perkins, then the head of the DAA's liaison branch. Perkins, who had been tasked with creating the NACC, was unbowed. He told a national television audience that the Minister had 'as much understanding of Aborigines as of flying to the moon'.⁸ On top of other misdemeanours, this prompted departmental head Barrie Dexter to suspend Perkins.

Dexter's takedown of the most powerful Aboriginal person in the nation increased the ire of new Black Power groups in the south. Despite the former diplomat's work lobbying for land rights with the CAA, threats were made to kill him and he was put under a 24-hour police guard. Minister Cavanagh was also living with a security detail.

In this environment it was not completely surprising that the DAA's Canberra offices were stormed by three Kooris, one carrying a gun. Their leader Bobby McLeod had freshly returned from Wyndham, some 400 kilometres from Wave Hill, and was desperate about his

---

7   AIATSIS, *NACC Consultative Seminar Batchelor*, PMS 645, p. 3.
8   Michelle Grattan, 'Perkins Back at Work: No Charges', *The Age*, 5 March 1974.

people's suffering. Finding that the secretary Barrie Dexter was out, McLeod and his friends held two senior ex-Welfare bureaucrats hostage instead. Perkins was called by the vigilantes to defuse the situation, and after talking down McLeod, went home with the gunman's unfired bullets in his sock.

With Perkins inflaming a mutiny in the Department of Aboriginal Affairs, the press described the operations of the Department as a 'cops and robbers saga played out each day [...] with ever-increasing drama'.[9] Another reporter described 'open hostility between whites and blacks', and a rift that existed 'from the very lowest position to the very highest'. According to the *Nation Review*, things were so strained that when an Aboriginal staffer 'floored a white in the department with a haymaker [punch], nobody was surprised'.[10] At Wattie Creek, Philip Nitschke saw Perkins as a hero fighting the state, and encouraged him on the Gurindji's behalf.

* * *

Now sitting on their 'horse paddock'-size lease with completed stockyards and their own cattle brand, the elders were optimistic about running more cattle. To do so though, they would need more money. The old men reasoned that if they re-opened the Muramulla store, they could direct its profits towards buying cattle, and stock the shop from their own gardens. Then their kids—*karu walija*—would also have better food. When the elders passed a hat around to get the shop going again, $2,000 ($16,000) was thrown in.

---

9   'Race War in Aboriginal Affairs: The White Backlash', *Nation Review*, 9–15 August 1974, p. 1386.
10   *Nation Review*, 9–15 August 1974, p. 1386.

INTO THE FRAY, 1974

Donald Nangiari and the other men assumed that as well as buying cattle, they would increase their herd by the industry's traditional means: the ownership of any unbranded 'cleanskins' Muramulla found within their station boundaries could be transferred from their better-resourced neighbours by searing the letters 'GDT' onto the rump of each beast. Those running small operations on the edge of large holdings in the area had done exactly this for decades, but Ralph Hayes had other ideas. Wave Hill station's manager invited Muramulla to muster a few cleanskins from the rough area around their camp, but he alerted police about the potential of Gurindji cattle thieves elsewhere on 'Wave'. The cattleman was also 'talking tough' about the Gurindji's desire for land. Hobbles Danayarri saw it this way:

> We want to [...] build this place up, our village, our country. [...] Ralph Hayes, he trying to put us back on more small country. He say not our land across Seven Mile. We worrying about the land, we want to know so we can go and get cattle from that land.[11]

A 'catch-us-if-you-can' scenario evolved: when the Gurindji heard Hayes was visiting their camp, they scattered Vestey's cleanskins off into the bush, re-mustering them later.

While Muramulla's relationship with Ralph Hayes was one they could manage themselves, their relationship with DAA 'beancounters' in Darwin and Canberra was proving more difficult. Mixed and unclear messages from the Department had been coming thick and fast. Earlier, and with few strings attached, Minister Bryant had given the elders a generous $30,000 ($284,000) grant to 'carry on

---

11   Hobbles Danayarri to Jean Leu and Union Friends, 13 May 1974, Oke Personal Collection.

funding the Muramulla Co'. As their coffers were seemingly flush, the company had hired fifteen stockmen at the start of the season. The decision to employ so many people drained Muramulla's accounts and caught both the board and the DAA unprepared. Judith Donald, the daughter of Muramulla director Donald Nangiari, was successfully maintaining the company's books with Philip Nitschke—until he was waylaid by floodwaters and she forgot to submit the timesheets of Muramulla staff. The workers—a significant number of the employed people at Wattie Creek—missed their pay.

To help the company get on top of its finances, Jean Culley and former Abschol head Bryan Havenhand suggested that the DAA's grant money should be made accessible to them at the settlement, 'so that the Gurindji will learn to handle money, and they can see by the bank books just what is happening'.[12] Barrie Dexter consented, but the Gurindji's control of their accounts was short-lived.

* * *

In May 1974, Nitschke and LaBrooy's allegations and complaints about Muramulla and each other prompted Minister Cavanagh to investigate the situation for himself. When LaBrooy heard of Cavanagh's visit, he adopted a more conciliatory tone and lent the DAA's rubbish truck to Daguragu. Pincher Nyurrmiarri saw it this way: 'When Minister bloke coming up, that superintendent a bit frightened, so he been clean up a little bit [...]'.[13] LaBrooy maintained the timing was a coincidence. Far from his generosity heralding an

---

12   Jean Culley and Bryan Havenhand, 'Report on a Meeting [...]', 5 June 1974, Pelczynski Personal Collection.

13   Pincher Nyurrmiarri, Open Letter, *Identity*, October 1974, p. 30.

end to the conflict though, disagreement about these matters lingers to this day.

When Minister Cavanagh arrived with Barrie Dexter and Gurindji supporter Don Atkinson on 29 May 1974, they wanted to relay news to the Gurindji about their land request. Whitlam had bestowed a small horse paddock lease on the Aborigines the previous year, and Cavanagh would soon announce the government's intention to excise all the country the elders claimed and buy it from Wave Hill station.

The authorities' justification for buying the Gurindji a pastoral lease at a cost of roughly $160,000 ($1.2 million) was simple: the Royal Commission into Aboriginal Land Rights was dragging on, and the DAA was under pressure to act. Also, Newton Tiver's AACM report had found that the area the Gurindji wanted was 'suitable for the establishment of a cattle station [which] has reasonable prospects of achieving long term commercial viability'.[14] Evidence that the elders wanted to run cattle this way was scarce, but the government would not carve up Wave Hill station without the justification that a profit could be made from the resulting excision.

While Minister Cavanagh's flight was en route to Daguragu, Nitschke and the elders tried to ensure they, not the 'establishment reactionaries' at the settlement, greeted the VIPs. LaBrooy thwarted them, and he and Alan Thorpe (who was now the DAA works manager) met the Minister's plane. During the drive from the airstrip, Cavanagh asked LaBrooy if it was true, as the activists had reported, that he had assaulted Philip Nitschke. When the Minister heard the superintendent's tale of manhandling the scruffy activist

---

14   Darwin, NAA, 'Economic Development Muramulla [...]', *Muramulla Gurindji Co Pastoral Project*, (E460) 1974/1588.

from commonwealth property, Cavanagh tapped him on the arm, whispered 'Well done!' conspiratorially, and broke into laughter.[15]

Upon the VIPs' arrival in the Gurindji's camp, Nitschke requested an audience with the Minister without LaBrooy or other 'Welfare' (DAA staff) present. While Daguragu's elders watched on in bemusement, Cavanagh asked Nitschke to leave as well. Eventually two meetings between the elders and Cavanagh were agreed upon: one with Nitschke, and one with LaBrooy present. Lingiari politely listened as the pair aired their grievances to the Minister, before he moved the conversation to the Gurindji's land.

Barrie Dexter had bad news. First, he admitted it was likely to be another two years before the excision from Wave Hill station could be made, and second, he informed the Gurindji elders that should they muster any un-branded cattle of Vestey's, they would face prosecution. Furthermore, the elders' Muramulla operation would soon be limited to employing two people until they got their excision. In total, thirteen people would soon need to be laid off. All of this shocked Lingiari so much he could barely speak. According to Nitschke, the effect on the group was 'shattering'.[16]

In effect, Dexter had told the elders that if they wanted more government support, their enterprise would be locked into 'caretaker' mode in the interim. It seemed the Gurindji's land rights—if they were ever recognised—would be delivered in the distant future. The old men had tasted government generosity, but remained completely at the mercy of the schedule and requirements of the state. Nitschke sensed injustice:

---

15 Darwin, NTAS, Interview with Trevor and Anna LaBrooy Recorded by Charlie Ward, October 2012, NTRS 3609, BWF 49.
16 Nitschke to Josie Briggs, 10 June 1974, Pelczynski Personal Collection.

> The catch cry of 'self-determination, control and acceptance of responsibility' has become one of the strongest weapons used against the people by the [...] establishment reactionaries. To exercise control, there must be money and power—to crap on about self-determination whilst hanging on to the purse strings is gross hypocrisy.[17]

The stress Cavanagh's visit placed on the Gurindji elders was enormous. After the Minister and Dexter departed, latent divisions among the leadership group flared. Lingiari was rebuked for his passivity and deferral before the visitors. Pincher Nyurrmiarri 'wrote' angrily, leaving out the invective he unleashed on the day, 'Old Vincent didn't tell him [Cavanagh] right story from his heart. Minister didn't find out much from Aborigine at Wattie Creek, what's been happening'.[18] Such criticism of Lingiari by members of his coterie would hasten talk of his succession. While the elder defended himself, saying he had not wanted to upset the Minister and his party, Aboriginal politics itself was changing. Lingiari's civility and respect for authority was increasingly missing from Aboriginal affairs. Aboriginal people elsewhere in the county were becoming— like the more radical Nyurrmiarri and Mick Rangiari—outspokenly critical.

Unaware of or impervious to these tensions, officials continued pressuring the elders about their cattle operation. In July 1974, a group of public servants led by Jack Cooke—a Welfare Branch veteran critical of the DAA—arrived to assess the Gurindji's job prospects. Because Muramulla was only active on its tiny 'horse paddock' lease, Cooke's team assumed that the nine Gurindji stockmen then

---

17   Nitschke to Jean *et al*, Undated [29 May 1974] Oke Personal Collection.
18   Pincher Nyurrmiarri, Open Letter, *Identity*, October 1974, p. 30.

employed were merely 'play-acting'.¹⁹ The visiting inspectors believed the track mob couldn't successfully manage their cattle operation—or Libanungu Council, or Wundamarie Housing Association—alone. To remedy the Gurindji's perceived knowledge shortfall and unproductiveness, a 'competent cattle adviser' was deemed necessary, and Trevor LaBrooy and others leaned on Nangiari, Rinyngayarri and Lingiari to accept this.

Working independently of whites where possible was essential to the elders, and they communicated their preference for a 'half-caste' adviser. Trying to accommodate them, the DAA suggested Sabu Sing, who the Gurindji knew from Wave Hill station. After speaking with LaBrooy, Nangiari believed that unless they accepted Sing, Muramulla would never receive a new truck or more funding from the DAA. Refusing to be cornered, the elders called Sing 'Vestey's spy' and Nangiari issued a statement on their behalf, stating:

> I don't need Sabu Sing here. I know him from little boy. [...] He's a Vestey's man, one of Tom Fisher's son [...]. He never been help we when we been walk off Wave Hill station. [...] I'm sorry for him, but we don't need him.²⁰

When Sing took it on himself to tell Nangiari that 'blokes in Canberra [already] been give [me] the job', the old stockman's anxiety increased. The final arbiter, of course, was Vincent Lingiari. He had been talked around to accepting Sing, but eventually exclaimed 'Fucked if I know, I don't want Sabu out here'.²¹

---

19 AIATSIS, Jeremy Long Papers, *Wattie Creek and Wave Hill*, DAA Project Consultative Team Report, MS 2534, Box 3, Folder 24, 10 July 1974.
20 Donald Nangiari *et al*, 'Letter to the Editor', *Identity*, October 1974, p. 30.
21 Cited in Philip Nitschke to Jean Leu, 8 April 1974, Oke Personal Collection.

INTO THE FRAY, 1974

Weeks afterwards, Gordon Bryant's grant expired and Muramulla switched to the caretaker mode dictated by the DAA. After the company's stockmen were laid off, food for their families became scarce and the hand-to-mouth nature of Daguragu's economy was revealed. Via Philip Nitschke's voluminous correspondence, another breakaway Aboriginal group heard news of the hard times in the Gurindji's camp. The Strelley 'Nomads' had left their pastoral masters in remote Western Australia two decades before the Gurindji and had sustained themselves since with a small mining operation. Patrick McConvell recalls how the Strelley mob were moved to help their fellow battlers:

> The Strelley people got together and flew boxes of tucker to Daguragu. It was bloody amazing. I couldn't believe it. [...] I suppose it really hit me that these two [groups] saw something similar going on in different places.[22]

Activist Stan Pelczynski visited Daguragu on FCAATSI's behalf and was shocked by people's hunger and what he believed to be evidence of malnutrition. The Gurindji were living largely on beef and potatoes. Pelczynski resolved to draw more attention to the issue:

> I rang [my sister] Barbara [then the secretary for the Victorian Council for Aboriginal Rights] and said that the Gurindji have no money, they can't buy things, because the money is not coming, there is starvation here.[23]

Nitschke also went to the press. When Cheryl Buchanan, a young Murri activist representing the student group Race Relations heard

---

22 Nitschke to Atkinson, 10 July 1974, Atkinson Personal Collection; Darwin, NTAS, Interview with Patrick McConvell Recorded by Charlie Ward, November 2009, NTRS 3609, BWF 5.
23 Interview with Stan Pelczynski and Barbara Pelczynska Recorded by Charlie Ward, January 2012.

of the squatters' troubles, she alerted Channel Nine television and set off to Daguragu to investigate herself.[24]

As alarmist press reports abounded, Minister Cavanagh was forced to downplay the seriousness of the Gurindji's situation. Jean Culley also thought the affair had been overdone. Attributing the entire 'starvation' episode to Nitschke's 'emotionalism', she acknowledged there had been a period of 'significant hardship' in the camp, but:

> There is no starvation at Wattie Creek. Never was and never will be. There is plenty of money flowing in from people working at the settlement, and there are a lot of them, including Long Jack, who is helping in carpentry and getting $90 ($720 per week) average.[25]

Nonetheless, a mountain of groceries was donated by well-wishers. The national student union alone offered more than a tonne of food. At Nangiari's suggestion, the supplies were mostly sold in the Muramulla store, with proceeds going to the company.

* * *

In comparison to the settlement, the Gurindji's base for their cattle operation remained a ramshackle camp. Despite their seven-year campaign and the intentions of the DAA, Daguragu's residents still lived in humpies made of bush posts and salvaged iron, while others slept outdoors under scraps of tin and canvas, or in broken-down cars. To the consternation of officials, a Viet Cong flag

---

24 Like many 'Aboriginal' activist groups, the student group Abschol had recently been Aboriginalised and rebranded 'Race Relations'. Bryan Havenhand Personal Communication, 4 November 2011.

25 Jean Culley to Barbara, Rob *et al*, 11 August 1974 and 20 August 1974, Oke Personal Collection.

fluttered overhead. The only facilities were a water tank filled from the government's bore and the Gurindji's self-built shower and toilet block, sitting in mud and stagnant water. No buildings had been erected by Whitlam's government, though construction of a large new shed for the Muramulla store was underway. The real appeal of the camp was intangible anyway, according to South Australian campaigners Don Atkinson and Vic Barnett. Although there were other places that:

> [...] looked less pitiable to the first glance of a middleclass white, [...] the development over the last seven years [at Daguragu] is leading to the strengthening of blackfellow culture, language and skills and consequent self-respect and self-direction, [making] Daguragu a community and not an institution.[26]

While building at the nearby settlement continued, the number of *kartiya* workers there grew—as did their sense of 'ownership' over the town. In addition to the previous government's twenty-three fine new houses, a pre-school, courthouse, service station, nurses' quarters, and market garden were planned. There was even talk of a wet canteen, caravan park and a meatworks. But while *kartiya* were increasingly involved in building and managing the settlement's facilities, according to Culley the Aboriginal residents were being left behind. The same fate, she believed, could befall Daguragu:

> Despite the much vaunted Aboriginal self-determination policy, the expansion at the settlement is so great that the Aborigines are losing track—more and more NACC elections, council, government elections, housing association [*sic*]. They just haven't got a grasp of it all.[27]

---

26   'Gurindji Newsletter', Flinders University, No. 2, 1974, p. 1.
27   Jean Culley to Rob and Barbara *et al*, 20 August 1974, Oke Personal Collection.

The settlement's Warlpiri residents appeared rather subdued to Culley—'not happy like the Gurindji at Wattie Creek'—but she felt slowing the development there was impossible: 'power-hungry whites are driving it, backed by the government'.

Activists, local elders and the DAA all wanted *ngumpit* to be involved in 'their' communities at Wave Hill, but there was little consensus as to precisely how this should happen. A plethora of government jobs were the DAA's solution, but, as noted, with paid positions more plentiful at the settlement, Gurindji elders found it hard to convince people to work voluntarily at Daguragu. The availability of the dole was also contentious. To Gurindji supporters such as Culley and Pelczynski, deterring Aboriginal people from receiving welfare entitlements reeked of discrimination, and they went to considerable efforts at Daguragu to sign people up for the dole. Meanwhile, LaBrooy saw Daguragu residents as 'fringe dwellers' who chose voluntarily—or were even convinced by Philip Nitschke—to be unemployed. Ironically, the peril of social security money was perhaps an issue on which the conservative LaBrooy and radical elder Pincher Nyurrmiarri agreed. Nyurrmiarri, an astute social analyst, didn't want his people 'to be fed like chooks' via the dole.

Wave Hill was not an easy posting for Trevor LaBrooy. The radicalism that had borne the Gurindji's support campaign was peaking, both at Wattie Creek and interstate. While Don Atkinson and Vic Barnett presented a slide show about Daguragu to students occupying the registry of Flinders University—restoring power to the building themselves after it was cut off by authorities—LaBrooy was evacuated from Wave Hill. After an arduous six months, he had contracted trachoma, a common malady among locals. According to

this strongly principled public servant, when he and his wife went to leave from the settlement airstrip on 7 August 1974:

> The wind sock, which is Commonwealth property, had an Aboriginal flag put onto it, which [...] could be very dangerous for air traffic. When we got up close, you could see that barbed wire had been wrapped around the post for quite a distance. Lindsay Jacques tried to get up—he was the airport control officer [and settlement store manager]—but he tore his shirt to shreds and hurt himself [...]. Then Alan Thorpe, the overseer, got up and managed to get it off. This whole procedure was watched by Nitschke, Pincher, Jenny Thiele and others in a vehicle. They were taking photographs [...]. It was done through sheer spite and levelled at me—I am convinced of that—as a parting gesture [...].[28]

Stan Pelczynski, one of the observers, saw the midnight flag-raising as a light-hearted prank, in which the Gurindji put their fencing skills to effective use:

> The Gurindji tied it with wire in such a way that it was very difficult to undo without cutters. When we [came back] in the morning, one of the government people was trying to climb up the post to take it down. We were laughing [...].[29]

After LaBrooy's evacuation—from which he did not return—his position was filled by superintendent Jim Faint. Hostilities ceased. Thankfully, the activists associated with the Gurindji liked Faint: Jean Culley found him 'tolerant, kind, and helpful in the extreme'.[30]

---

28 NTAS, LaBrooy, NTRS 3609, BWF 49.
29 Pelczynski and Pelczynska, 2012.
30 Pelczynski, 1974, Oke Personal Collection; Jean Culley to Rob and Barbara *et al*, 20 August 1974, Oke Personal Collection.

A HANDFUL OF SAND

* * *

Having been given a green light on purchasing land for the Gurindji, the DAA failed to act. The public service was hamstrung. While it awaited the Woodward Commission's findings on land rights, other elements of the bureaucracy had yet to follow through on Whitlam's instructions about buying land for Aboriginal groups. The process of setting up a land fund dragged on, and Minister Cavanagh played for time, warning the Gurindji about further delays. Like others, the normally circumspect secretary of the Melbourne Gurindji group, Rob Oke, had expected haste from the Whitlam Government. He wrote to all members of parliament:

> You, like our committee, must be amazed that twenty months after the Minister instructed his department to arrange for [the Gurindji's land transfer, its date] is still somewhere in the indefinite future. In fact virtually nothing has been done in the last year [...]. For eight years, the Gurindji's [sic] have waited at Wattie Creek. For how much longer will the Australian parliament allow the DAA to postpone the Gurindji's dream of an independent future?[31]

Pressure on the government increased. On 5 October 1974, Cavanagh wrote to Lingiari that land fund or not, the purchase from Vestey's would go ahead.

As with its previous land purchases, the DAA's efforts to buy the Gurindji a cattle station got off to a shaky start. Negotiations were hindered by the department's lack of agricultural and surveying expertise. When a senior DAA negotiator mistook the Victoria River

---

31   Rob Oke, 'Land for the Gurindji's at Wattie Creek', 12 August 1974, Oke Personal Collection.

for the Camfield, Vestey's representatives were alarmed. According to the company's travelling manager, the late Cec Watts, he brought much needed experience to the discussions:

> When they decided to give that country to [the Gurindji] people, it involved seventy miles of frontage on the Victoria River. [The DAA] said 'Oh! How are we going to fence this? We'll zig-zag across the river, there's waterholes here and there and—'. That's where I came into the action. I said 'Like hell we will, you can't maintain a fence like that on a river that comes down like a tide every year and washes all the fences down and cattle everywhere'.
>
> Our attitude was that we were going to make sure that the bloody job was done properly. We had a good contractor—we didn't want some doo-hickey turnout, and I would say that with some of those government departments up there, anything could have happened, with some bright spark wanting to put up a fence![32]

An agreement was reached: the Gurindji would get the river and the land west of it. Vestey's would have seven bores, paid for by the government, to replace their river frontage. With the multinational's acquiescence and hard work by the DAA, the Gurindji's access to their traditional land—to run a commercial cattle operation, if not by virtue of their customary rights—was becoming a reality.

* * *

The elders' quests for land and cattle were consuming all their energy while other key elements of their vision languished. Foremost among these was the special education of Gurindji children, which

---

32 NTAS, Cec and Dawn Watts, Interview Recorded by Charlie Ward, April 2010, NTRS 3609, BWF 14.

had preoccupied the old men from the beginning. Alan Thorpe remembered that in 1971:

> They were always insistent on their kids going to school. The settlement would send the Bedford truck around in the morning, and you'd see parents chasing [the kids] with a stick if they didn't get on. There was one thing that the old people realised, and that was that Aboriginal people needed to get an education, otherwise white people would be running everything for them forever.[33]

The old Gurindji passionately wanted to continue shaping their children's education, and saw their children's attendance at the settlement school as a temporary compromise. Pincher Nyurrmiarri summed up:

> I want a school here in Wattie Creek [...]. If a school starts off here, we'll have two old [men] to teach them same time with the white bloke [...]. They got to teach all sort of law from Aborigine too. I want you people to help me; I'm fighting hard for this school.[34]

Operating their own 'two-way' school was integral to the elders' plan of creating an independent Gurindji society. In late 1974, Nyurrmiarri, Jean Culley and linguist Patrick McConvell were lobbying authorities in Darwin to establish a school at Daguragu, but the Department of Education—little constrained by the DAA's ideas of 'self-determination'—had plans of its own. A 'new school complex at Wave Hill township for use by both [communities]' was announced instead.

In a series of meetings, the Education Department forced the elders to accept that the children of Wattie Creek would continue

---

33 Darwin, NTAS, Alan Thorpe, Interview by Charlie Ward, January 2010, NTRS 3609, BWF 9.

34 Nyurrmiarri to 'Robbie' [Oke], 19 November 1974, Pelczynski Personal Collection.

attending the settlement school. Mainstream education without Gurindji content worried the elders, who felt their kids were learning '*kartiya* way' too much already. Warlpiri children also went to the settlement school, and Lingiari was concerned that the next generation of Gurindji were absorbing the 'other law' of the Tanami desert people, too. Despite the elders' concerns, they were snubbed by the Department of Education. Until their own facility was built at Daguragu—if ever—their desire for their children to be educated tied them inextricably to the town and its affairs.

The costs to the Gurindji of having the government outpost on their doorstep were growing. Since establishing their camp at Wattie Creek, the elders had largely avoided it. Now their arm's length stance was getting difficult to maintain. In addition to their unwanted dependence on the settlement for schooling, groceries, wages and pensions, the problems caused by Warlpiri (and Gurindji people) at the settlement were increasingly being slated home to the track mob. The town was attracting trouble-makers precisely *because* Lingiari and his coterie of strong elders were at Wattie Creek.

Warlpiri had coexisted peacefully with the Gurindji on Wave Hill station for generations. After the Walk-off in 1966, many had gone to Hooker Creek (re-named Lajamanu), a settlement established by the government in 1949 on what was then Gurindji land. Others had elected to stay near the Gurindji at the settlement. Binge-drinking by Warlpiri there—away from their own notoriously strict elders—brought issues of tribal responsibility to a head, and highlighted the need for the two groups to complete a complex series of 'treaties' that they had been negotiating over the previous twenty years.

In December 1974 Daguragu's leaders invited Jerry Jangala and Maurice Luther, two of their Warlpiri counterparts, for talks at

nearby Gordy Creek. According to the DAA, their meeting related to 'potential frictions deriving from traditional matters' at the settlement. The talks followed months of jointly-held ceremonies, in which Gurindji stories and ceremonial responsibilities were transferred to the Lajamanu area's new custodians.[35] Warlpiri elders also authorised Gurindji strongmen to punish any desert trouble-makers in the Gurindji's communities.

To the DAA, and to an extent the leaders themselves, the unclear relationship between the settlement and Daguragu needed clarity, formalisation even. In late 1974, the old Gurindji men bit the bullet. The elders made—or conceded to—another decision that went to the heart of their independence. The outcome was announced by Minister Cavanagh, whose press release of 11 December 1974 declared that Vincent Lingiari:

> [...] had the pleasure of advising [...] that the Gurindji people of Wattie Creek and the townspeople of Wave Hill settlement have united in the name of Libanungu Community Council to work together in all projects associated with the development of Wave Hill town and Daguragu cattle station [...].[36]

After steadfastly refusing the government 'carrot' of twenty-three new houses and myriad other enticements to join 'welfare', it appeared the Gurindji had succumbed. Seemingly Alan Thorpe, now working for Libanungu Council, had driven the push for 'unification'. In practice, the elders had agreed that half of the seats on the new Libanungu Council would be reserved for them, and the council would have authority over both communities. To

---

35   Ford (DAA) to Dexter, 24 December 1974, Oke Personal Collection; Rev Jim Kime, Interview Recorded by Charlie Ward, 3 June 2014.
36   Sen. James Cavanagh, 'Statement by the Minister—Wattie Creek', 11 December 1974.

supporters such as Jean Culley, pressure and bribery had prompted the elders' decision:

> The Gurindji have finally been forced to put their heads in a noose to get some goodies. They needed help badly [...]. Money, money, and more money was what [was] offered [...] and so they gave in. [37]

The elders' loyalty to the new Libanungu Council would prove short-lived, but this flirtation showed their acceptance that for better or worse, a resource-rich, supportive government—not the shiftable activist networks they had known since the Walk-off—were now their most important partners. Perhaps, as the Gurindji had weathered significant humbug due to their argumentative supporters in the months prior, they were easier to persuade. Following Thorpe's lobbying, the old men told Jean Culley and other whites they were only welcome to visit, not live, at Daguragu.

Thus a four year period of *kartiya* assistants living and working at Wattie Creek—mostly funded by public donations—came to an end. Their supporters would return occasionally in the next two years, but the Gurindji's fortunes were now inextricably tied to the state. Initially, the elders had been sceptical of the Welfare Branch's patrol officers at Wave Hill station, and then indifferent when Coalition governments attempted to undermine them at Wattie Creek. By now though, they saw that to realise even a modest version of their vision, they needed the government. Only government had the resources they needed, and only government made *kartiya* law.

An evacuation of supporters began. Philip Nitschke's partner had already gone, due to the camp's stress and hardships, and had been

---

37 Culley to Oke, 13 December 1974, Oke Personal Collection.

working in Katherine. She had decided to move on months earlier—with an American biker, unhelpfully for Nitschke—thus removing a key part of his support and triggering his departure. Jean Culley was the last white to leave before the rains, and towed her caravan to Darwin for some Christmas respite.

When a cyclone approached the northern port town on Christmas Eve, Culley was inside her caravan as the gale lifted it and flipped it on its side. As the cyclone's eye moved overhead, the wind abated and she righted her mobile home with the help of some neighbours—before hell broke loose again, blowing the other way. This time, the caravan was somersaulted in the opposite direction. Amongst the destruction, Culley's arm was broken. Ignoring her injuries on Christmas day, she towed the wrecked caravan to Melbourne, over two thousand miles away.

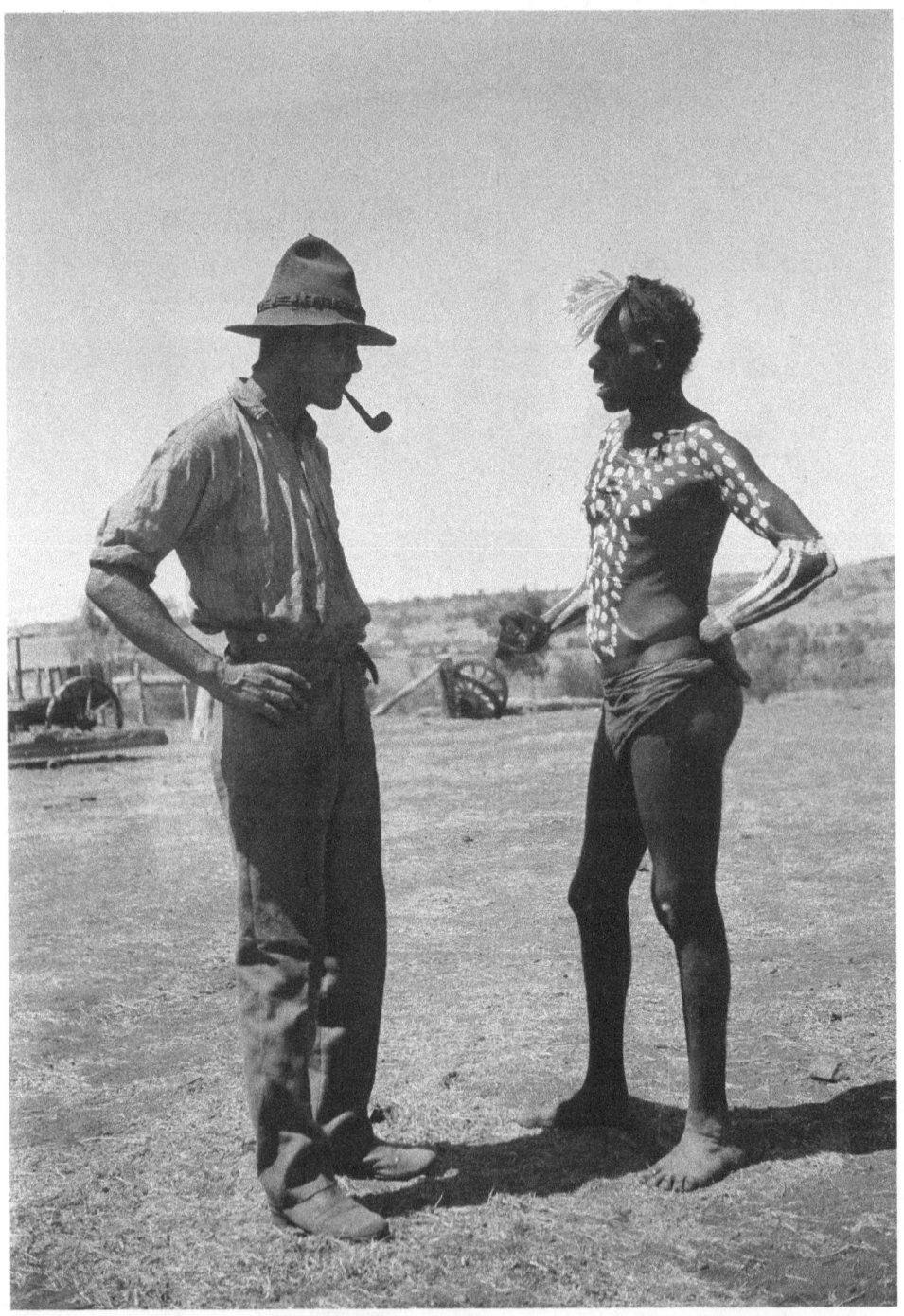

Unknown Gurindji man with traveler Michael Terry, Wave Hill station, c. 1925.
Michael Terry Collection, National Library of Australia, nla.obj-149075782.

Gurindji women, Wave Hill station (Jinparrak), 1927. Jack Henry Collection, Northern Territory Library.

Gurindji men butchering a steer, Wave Hill station (Jinparrak), 1927. Jack Henry Collection, Northern Territory Library.

A game of tug-of-war at Wave Hill station (Jinparrak), 1927.
Jack Henry Collection, Northern Territory Library.

Working cattle, Wave Hill station (Jinparrak), c. 1957. Rob Sampson Collection.

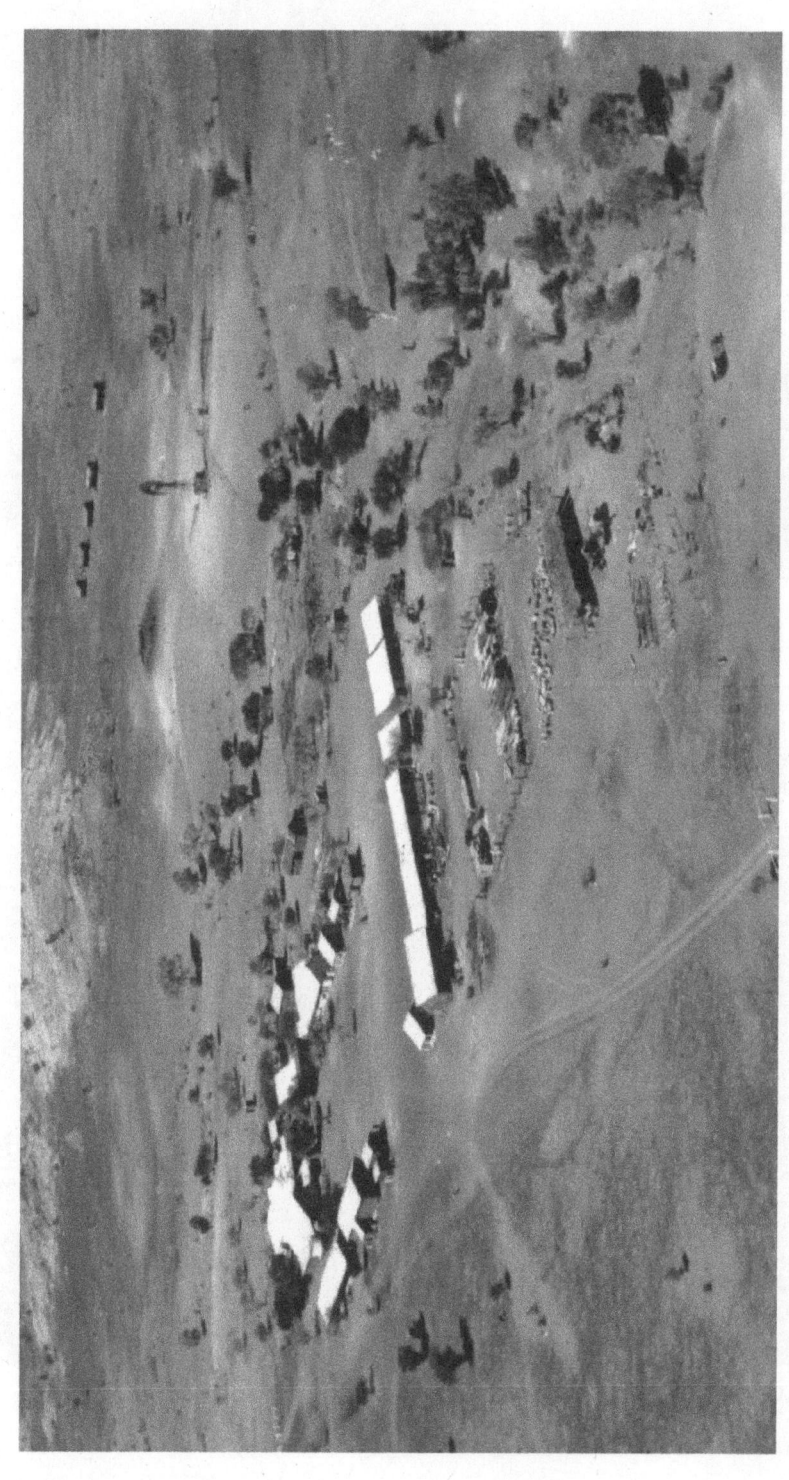

Wave Hill station (Jinparrak), 1950s. Newly built huts for Gurindji, Mudburra and Warlpiri workers are visible at the top of the picture. Their camps are out of frame. Frank Johnston Collection, National Library of Australia, nla.obj-141831363.

The United Aborigines' Mission's 'Two Paths, Two Ways' poster that inspired Vincent Lingiari in the early 1960s. Berndt Museum Collection [Acc. No. 05479], © Rob Douglas

Flanked by Vincent Lingiari, Peter Morris (Vestey's travelling manager) addresses strikers in the Victoria River bed. Tom Fisher looks on, 26 August, 1966. Courtesy of Kim Lockwood.

Peter Morris (Vestey's travelling manager) argues with Vincent Lingiari, 26 August, 1966. Courtesy of Kim Lockwood.

Captain Major Lupngiari and Dexter Daniels arrive in Sydney to raise public support, September 1966. *Tribune*, Communist Party of Australia, with permission of the SEARCH Foundation. State Library of New South Wales.

Gurindji men and the sign painted for them by Frank Hardy at Wattie Creek, 1967. Standing (L–R) Bruce Peter, Sammy Pangkalis, Captain Major Lupngiari, Mick (?), Vincent Lingiari, Mick Rangiari. Sitting (L–R) Starlight (?), Roger Japarta, Joe Randall, Jerry Rinyngayarri, Rodney (?), Old Major, Charlie Pincher, Horace Wulmun, Timmy Vincent. Brian Manning Collection.

An unknown public servant consults Pincher Nyurrmiarri and 'Old Timmy' Yilngayarri on the Gurindji's demand for land, c. 1968. *Tribune*, Communist Party of Australia, with permission of the SEARCH Foundation. State Library of New South Wales.

Long Johnny Kijngayari, Bandy Ripma, Captain Major Lupngiari and Mick Rangiari begin building on Vestey's lease, 1967. Brian Manning Collection.

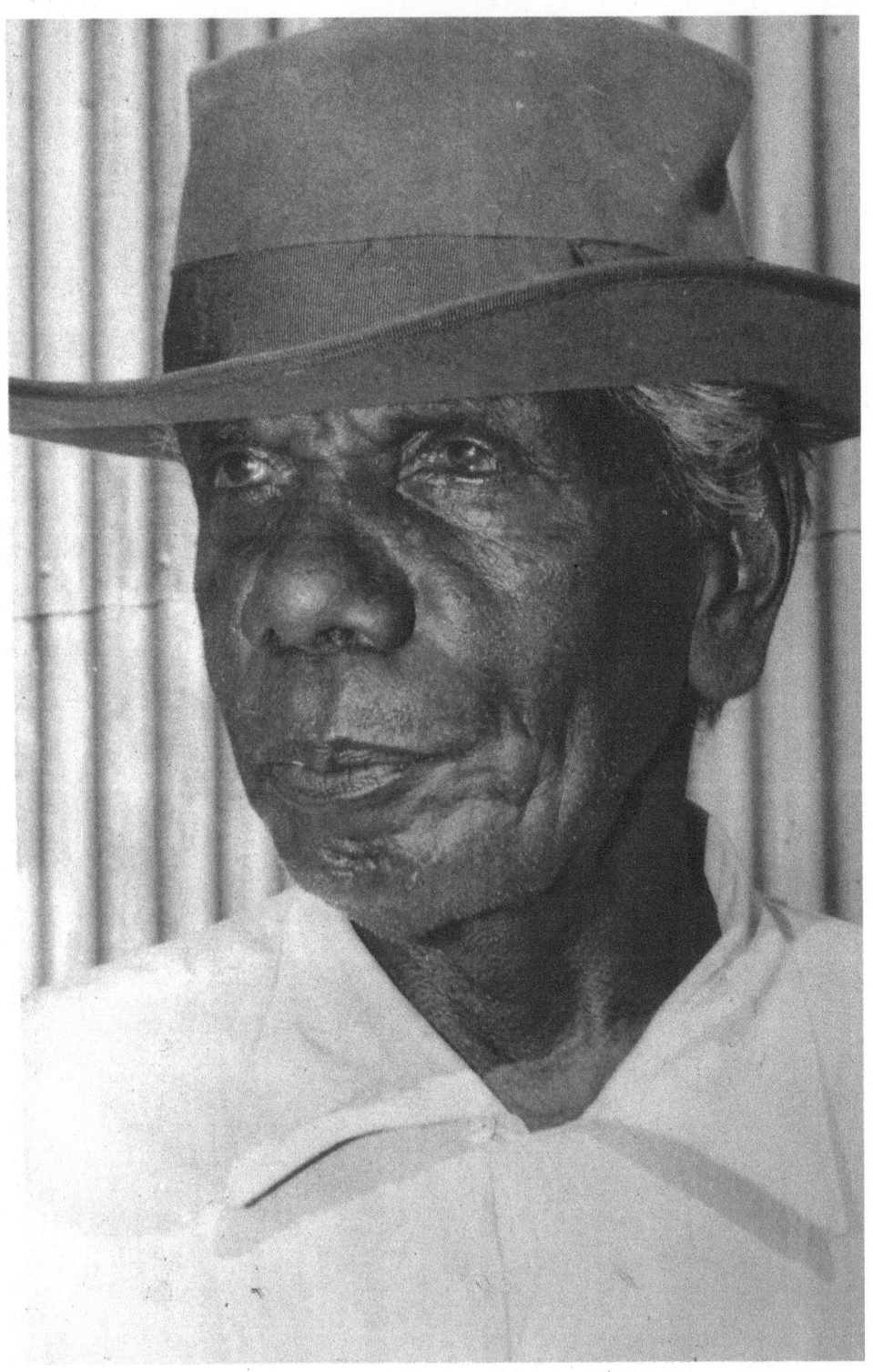

Vincent Jurlama Lingiari, 1972. Courtesy of Rob Wesley-Smith.

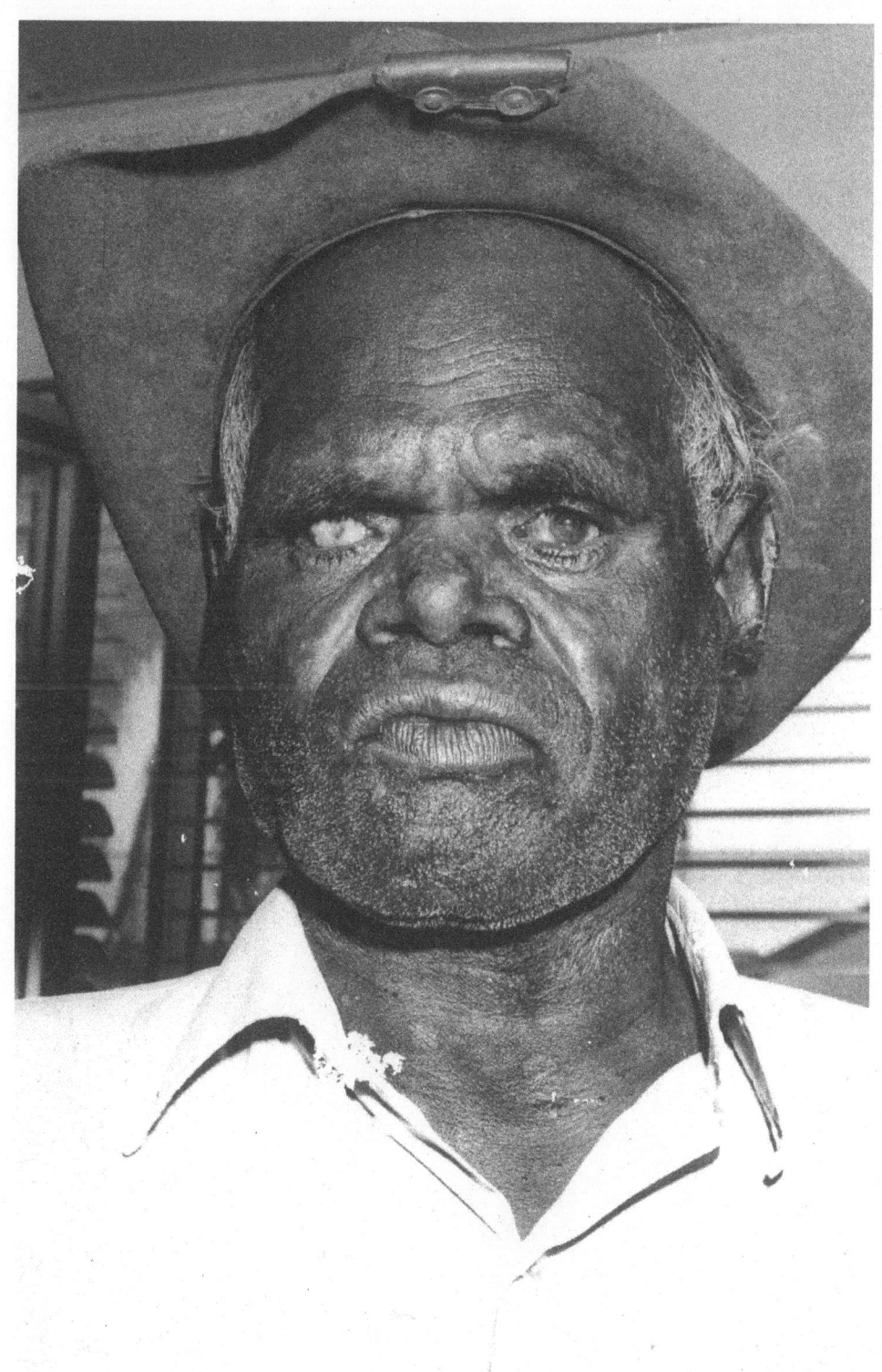

Captain Major Lupngiari, c. 1972. Courtesy of Rob Wesley-Smith.

Pincher Nyurrmiarri, 1969. Courtesy of Rob Oke.

Donald Nangiari, Director of the Muramulla Gurindji Cattle Company, 1971.
Courtesy of Alex Romanoff.

The Gorton Government's $5million 'carrot' to the Gurindji. New government houses at the Wave Hill Welfare Settlement, 7 April 1971. Courtesy of ASIO.

An unoccupied house at the Wave Hill Welfare Settlement, 1971. Courtesy of Rob Oke.

'I wish they hadn't stopped treating us like cattle'. Cartoon by Geoff Hook, *The Sun*, 12 July 1968.

Hobbles Danayarri and Lizzie Wardaliya at their home at Wattie Creek, 1971. Courtesy of Rob Oke.

Gurindji men and Abschol members constructing the Gurindji's first mudbrick houses, 1971. Courtesy of Rob Oke.

Gurindji land rights demonstration, Sydney, 31 July 1970. (L-R) Bobby McLeod, Paul Coe, Sol Bellear, Dick Blair (?), Dexter Daniels, unknown.
Picture Noel Hazard/Communist Party of Australia, courtesy of Brian Aarons.

Rod Williams, unknown and Brian Aarons feeling the heat, Gurindji land rights demonstration, Sydney, 31 July 1970. Noel Hazard, Courtesy of Brian Aarons.

Dexter Daniels speaking about land rights, c. 1970, Sydney. *Tribune*, with permission of the SEARCH Foundation, State Library of New South Wales.

Gurindji land rights demonstration, c. 1971, Sydney. *Tribune*, Communist Party of Australia, with permission of the SEARCH Foundation. State Library of New South Wales.

'Target Personalities and Surrounds, Wattie Creek and Wave Hill, Alan Thorpe's hut circled', 7 April 1971. Courtesy of ASIO.

Sisters Elsie Mayawi, Mona Wirtpaya and Lizzie Yanjaya, 1971. Courtesy of Alex Romanoff.

Hobbles Danayarri building, 1971.
Courtesy of Alex Romanoff.

The Roundhouse: visitors' accommodation
at Wattie Creek, 1971. Hannah Middleton Collection,
State Library of New South Wales.

Harry, a Ngarinyman man, resting with Mick Rangiari's pet pig, c. 1972. Courtesy of Lyn Riddett.

Jean Culley and Long Johnny Kijngayari at Wattie Creek, 1970.
Hannah Middleton Collection, State Library of New South Wales.

Stocking the first store at Wattie Creek, c. 1971.
Hannah Middleton Collection, Courtesy of State Library of New South Wales

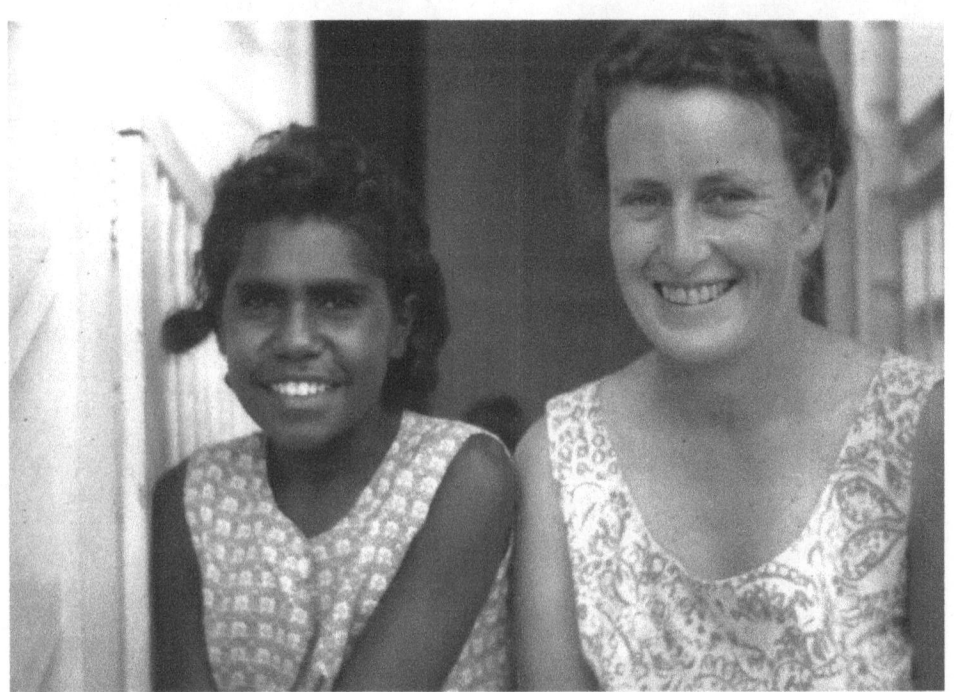

Josefa Kijngayari and Lyn Riddett, Brisbane, December 1971. Courtesy of Lyn Riddett.

Don Atkinson interviewing Lupngiari. Vincent Lingiari looks on, 1972. Atkinson Collection.

David Quin and Jean Leu at Wattie Creek, 1971. Courtesy of Alex Romanoff.

Jerry Rinyngayarri branding horses at Wattie Creek (Daguragu), 1974.
Hannah Middleton Collection, State Library of New South Wales.

Polly Lajayi, mother of Josepha Kijngayari,
c. 1973. Courtesy of Lyn Riddett.

Mick Rangiari and Muramulla Company vehicle bought
with government funds, 1972. Atkinson Collection.

The next generation of cowboys? Teenagers listening to Slim Dusty at Wattie Creek, 1971. Courtesy of Rob Oke.

A wajarra 'public' corroboree for Ngarinyman and Gurindji boys at Wattie Creek, 1972. Atkinson Collection.

Activists observe a Commonwealth employee removing the Aboriginal flag from the Libanungu airsock, August 1974. Courtesy of Stan Pelczynski.

Jimmy Manngayarri and other Gurindji men at the handover of the Daguragu lease, 16 August 1975. Penny Tweedie, National Library of Australia, nla.obj-138156549.

Prime Minister Whitlam and Gurindji men, 16 August 1975.
Courtesy of Rob Wesley-Smith.

Vincent Lingiari, his son Victor Vincent and Prime Minister Whitlam celebrating, 16 August 1975. Courtesy of Rob Wesley-Smith.

Dexter Daniels at Daguragu, 1976. Courtesy of Richard Preece.

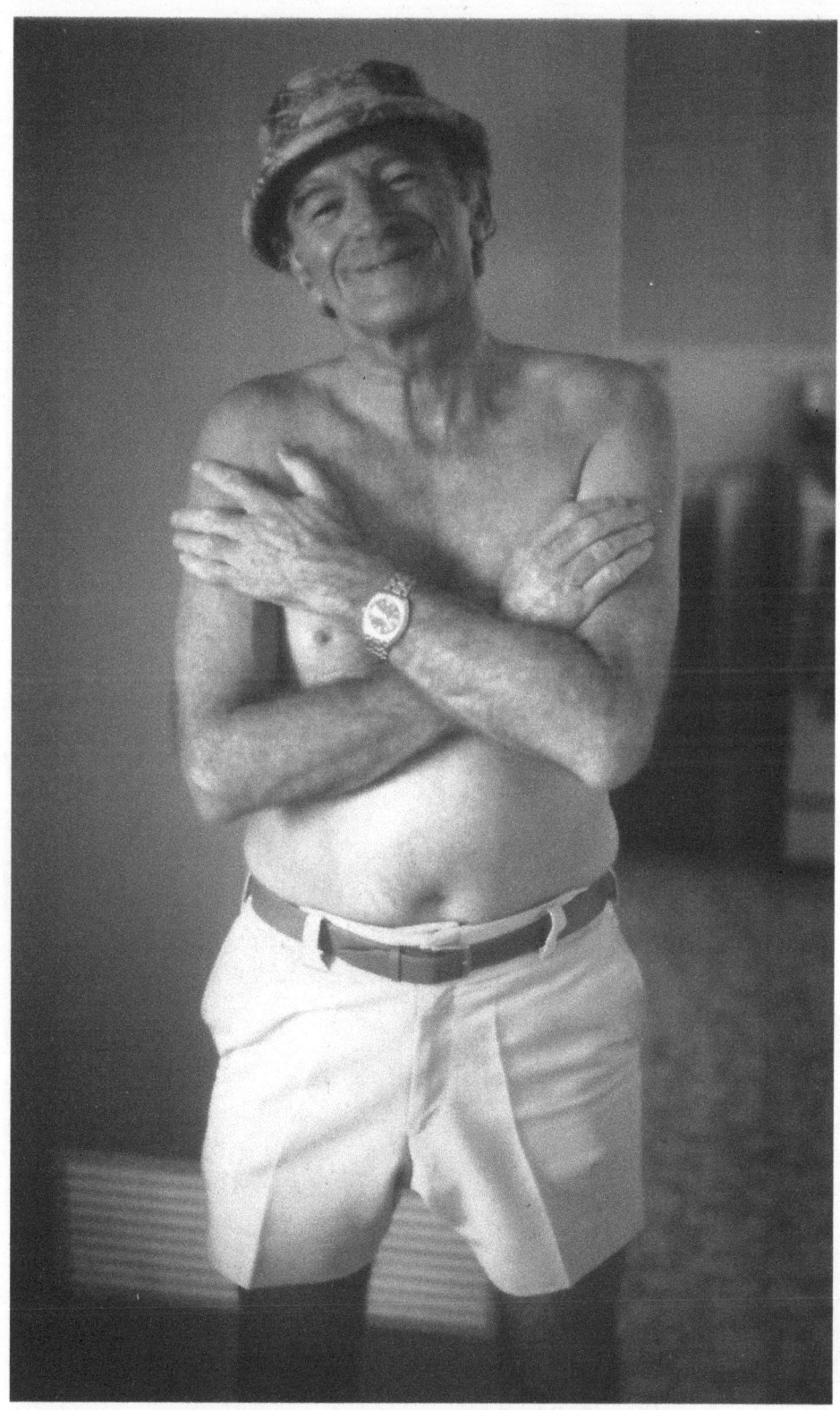
Frank Hardy at Kalkaringi, 1976. Courtesy of Meredith Burgmann.

Pincher Nyurrmiarri, Long Johnny Kijngayari, Dexter Daniels and Richard Preece on Gurindji country, 1976. Courtesy of Meredith Burgmann.

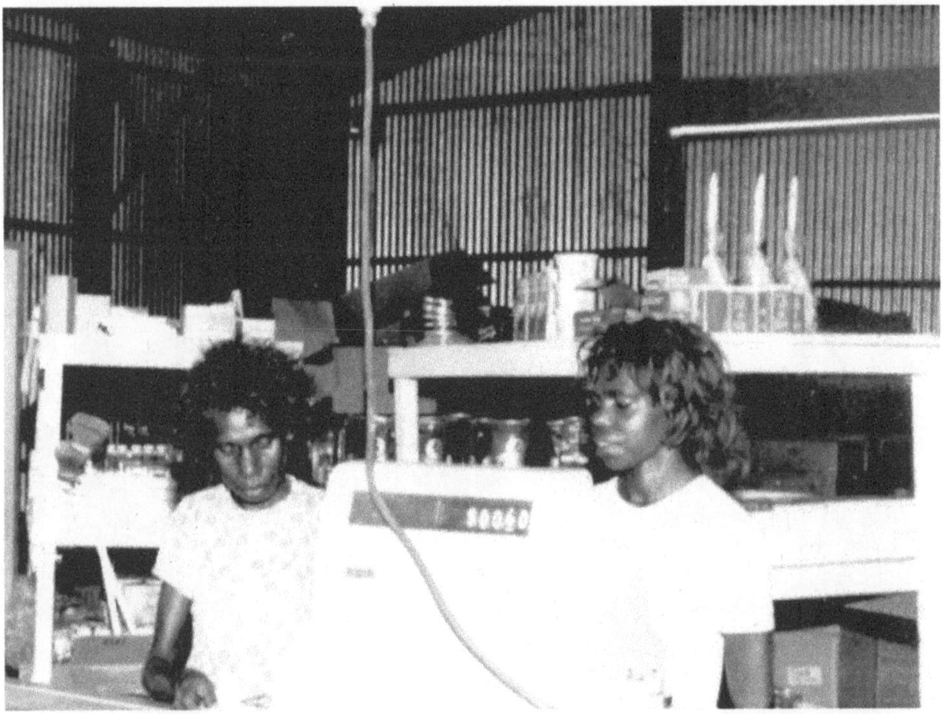

Ellen Splinter and Judith Donald staffing the new Muramulla Company store, Daguragu, 1977. Courtesy of Rob Wesley-Smith.

Daguragu land claim hearing, Justice Brian Toohey with Vincent Lingiari in foreground, July 1981. Courtesy of Rob Wesley-Smith.

The first re-enactment of the Wave Hill Walk-off, Freedom Day, August 1983. Courtesy of Elaine Bullock.

New Generation woman Dawn Rook training at Daguragu Council, 1983. Courtesy of Elaine Bullock.

The New Generation. Trainee plumbers Noel Edwards, Jimmy Butler and George Edwards, 1983. Courtesy of Elaine Bullock

A girls' 'Culture Class' at the Kalkaringi School, 1983. Courtesy of Elaine Bullock.

Vincent Lingiari and Little Blanchie Jingaya, c. 1983.
With permission of Timmy Vincent, courtesy of Rob Wesley-Smith.

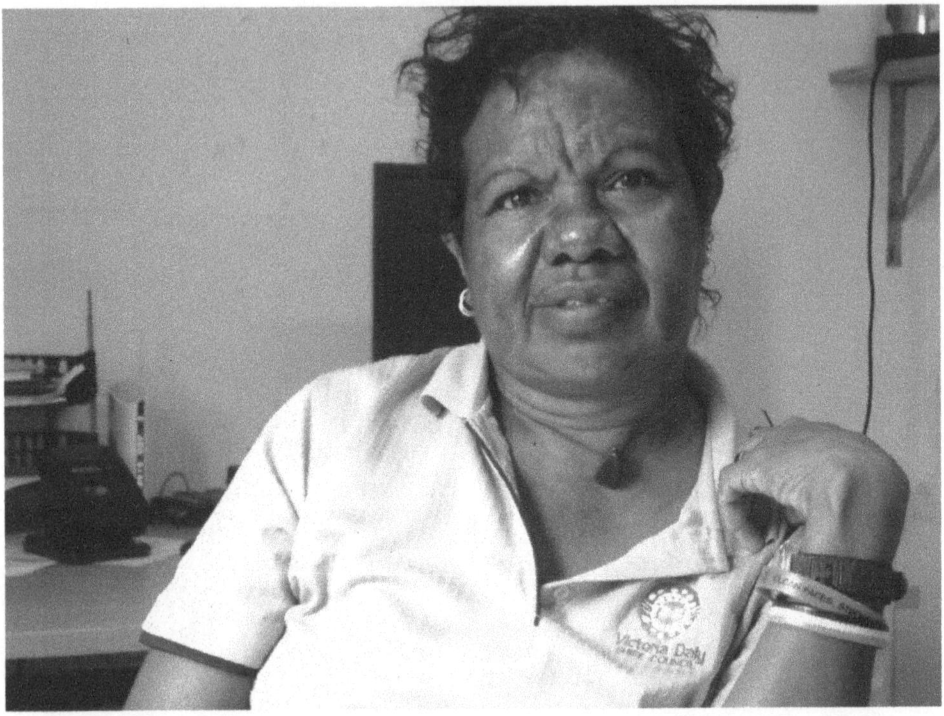

New Generation leader Ros Frith, Kalkaringi, 2012. Courtesy of the author.

New Generation leaders Maurie Japarta Ryan, Michael George, Robert Roy and Michael Paddy, 2006. Courtesy of Trevor Van Weeren.

The next generation, 2016. (L–R) Harry Barkly, Conway Herbert, Ruben Miller, Dylena Miller. Courtesy of Penny Smith/ Karungkarni Art Centre.

Chapter 8

A HANDFUL OF SAND, 1975

After the tumult of 1974, anxiety marred the elders' wet season while they waited for news about their lease. Regrets about their decision to join the DAA's Libanungu Council also plagued them. The group—and Lingiari in particular—were worried the unification they had agreed to was part of a ruse to take over Daguragu. Pincher Nyurrmiarri and others thought Lingiari had made a mistake agreeing to the plan. When Rob Wesley-Smith rode into the camp on his motorbike in January, he was shocked at the old man's physical decline.

As soon as they found a scribe, the elders began distancing themselves again from the government town. Lingiari conveyed his disquiet to Minister Cavanagh: 'The settlement separate now, but when the lease comes, will it cover the lot?' he asked. 'Who owns the settlement?'[1] In 1967, when the Gurindji's petition for land was sent to the Governor-General, they had no interest in the Welfare outpost; they had rejected it in favour of a future at Wattie Creek. Now the government's efforts to include them in decision-making in the growing town had stoked the elders' fears that they might lose control of their own independent community.

---

1   Darwin, NAA, 'Lingiari to Cavanagh' *Muramulla Gurindji Co Pastoral Project*, 20 January 1975 (E460) 1974/1588.

With these concerns weighing on them, the Gurindji were relieved when their first 'mate' Frank Hardy paid them a visit on 30 April 1975. The former communist had been alarmed by Cavanagh's 'unification' announcement several months earlier, and sought to encourage the independence of his old friends. When the DAA's Katherine boss Alex Bishaw arrived at the same time, the pair sought an audience with the elders at Daguragu together. Hardy knew Bishaw as a Labor man from the time of the Walk-off, and both had similar questions for the Gurindji. The purchase of the track mob's land was rapidly approaching, and Bishaw wanted to learn their 'intentions and ambitions, for now is the time for them to decide the direction of their future'. When the visitors sat down with the Gurindji men, the elders' desire to maintain their independence was obvious. The elders felt they had been pressured to join the council at the settlement, and that 'their community [had] been neglected and overlooked in preference to interests at Wave Hill'. Seeing the settlement's prosperity had also caused Lingiari to rethink his humble vision for Daguragu. The Gurindji elders had possibly realised that their initial, modest plan was becoming quickly outdated. Even the cattle stations that had inspired their vision initially were modernising. Septic tanks were replacing pit toilets and electric light had vanquished kerosene lanterns. Not wanting to be left behind, the elders revealed their new desire for a 'program of development reasonably equal to Wave Hill', according to Bishaw.[2]

The first wave of government building at Daguragu was imminent, but the old men's decision signified another turning point for the Gurindji project. For Lingiari, it was a no-win situation. If he refused

---

2   Darwin, NAA, 'Bishaw to Director, *Muramulla Gurindji Association—Wattie Creek Development*, E460, 1975/196.

the government's offer of support for his village, it would remain a primitive, rough encampment on the fringes of what was becoming, by rural NT standards, a modern and well-resourced town. Opening the Gurindji's camp to development 'like the settlement' could take it out of their hands, though. From the government's perspective, Daguragu's development would require specialised, qualified staff, both to build its facilities and then to manage them. The Aborigines' voices might be ignored, or subsumed under planning regulations. Whether the Gurindji would be a part of Daguragu's development remained to be seen.

To strengthen the Gurindji village's identity 'separate from the settlement', another idea was put forward—whether by Hardy, Bishaw or the Gurindji elders themselves is unknown. Rather than Daguragu's leaders joining Libanungu Council, it was suggested the government could fund a second, independent council there. Two communities (plus two councils) equalled Gurindji autonomy and harmony, the idea went. This was acceptable to Bishaw and the Gurindji leaders, who after a night's sleep voted to create their own 'Daguragu Gurindji Council'. The 'unification' Cavanagh had trumpeted five months earlier had collapsed.

With their own council promised, the elders' worries about the government taking over Daguragu were put to rest and the mood of the camp improved. People were buoyed further when Hardy revealed the other purpose of his trip: the NT première of his recently-completed film. Financed in Britain and never shown on Australian television, it was titled, like his book, *The Unlucky Australians*. Every man, woman, child and dog in Daguragu attended the screening. According to the linguist Patrick McConvell—who had been allowed to stay on in the

camp with his family to do language work—the audience's response to seeing themselves onscreen was 'unforgettable'.[3]

Afterwards, inspired by Hardy's portrayal and their new stand-alone council, the Gurindji busied themselves fencing, gardening and mustering 'with no white direction'. The Whitlam Government's support for Daguragu was also finally bearing fruit—the camp was becoming a village. After years of resistance, the Health Department built a small clinic and employed Marie King, the daughter of Daguragu's 'founding father' Sandy Moray as a health worker. Local men laboured with contractors to build Daguragu's first proper houses and install a sewage system. How the track mob felt about these changes is unknown. When proper street lights were erected, many of the Gurindji were delighted as it meant they could continue their card games into the night.

Daguragu's isolation had recently daunted one DAA recruit and forced his departure, but the village's leaders now accepted another young man, Richard Preece, as their community adviser. Taking a career public servant under their wing in this way was a first for the leaders of Wattie Creek, and Preece probably had Hardy to thank. The writer, who was greatly respected by the Aborigines, told them he knew 'in his heart that Preece is a good bloke'.[4] Although Preece had undergone eighteen months' training to prepare him for working in remote Aboriginal communities, he was by his own reckoning extremely 'green'—to the point of frustrating his colleague Billy Bunter, now the DAA's Aboriginal liaison officer. When Preece 'got off on the wrong foot' trying to explain a proposed re-structure that

---

3   John Goldschmidt (Dir.), 'The Unlucky Australians', Associated Television (ATV), 1974; McConvell to Culley, 8 May 1975, Oke Personal Collection.
4   McConvell to Culley, 8 May 1975, Oke Personal Collection.

would see all local DAA workers under a new *kartiya* manager, the Gurindji appeared averse to the message, as well as the messenger. According to Patrick McConvell, most observers were left: '[...] with the impression that [Preece] is confused himself, or trying to hide something. Vincent inclines to the former view, but most of the others fear a con is being worked'.[5] When Preece took the takings from the re-opened Daguragu store away to bank on the Gurindji's behalf, Alan Thorpe exploited their concerns, warning the squatters of encroaching 'government control'. Preece survived this trial by fire and thrived—his career working with bush Aboriginal people continued for forty years.

While Preece supported the Muramulla company's store, Judith Donald, daughter of Muramulla director Donald Nangiari, and Tanya McConvell, Patrick's wife, were working the counter. One of the women's challenges, still, was resisting the demands of Daguragu's senior men—the shop's owners, and therefore (it appeared to them), the owners of its stock. Taking 'freebies' from younger relatives behind the counter put an ongoing drain on the store's takings and caused despair among a succession of *kartiya* staff. 'Donald is no longer dipping into the cashbox, though he seems to be still filching free food', Patrick McConvell reported.[6] While these misdemeanours reeked of corruption to outsiders, unrestrained generosity and providing for certain kin on request were not only valued highly by the Gurindji but formed the basis of their traditional economy.

In early April, the DAA's Len Ibbetson returned to review self-determination's progress. Having now been spurned by the Gurindji, Libanungu Council also appeared lost and lethargic to Ibbetson,

---

5   Sydney, SLNSW, McConvell to Jean, 28 May 1975, in *Gurindji at Wattie Creek (Daguragu), Northern Territory*, Hannah Middleton Papers, c. 1966–1976, MLMSS 5866/15.
6   SLNSW, McConvell, 28 May 1975, MLMSS 5866/15.

who blamed a lack of direction and motivation among its Aboriginal workforce. With greater European guidance, he believed, the council would harness 'the final drive, expertise and impetus which will assist [them] to become a vibrant and active body, and acknowledge their responsibilities with confidence in the future'.[7] It was the same conclusion Ibbetson's DAA colleagues had reached regarding their rapidly expanding cattle plans at Daguragu: closer white supervision was required to manage the Aborigines.

Finding that progress on the settlement's government-funded market garden, tree nursery, and poultry farm was also slow, Ibbetson was disappointed. But were these the goals of local Aboriginal people? Tree nurseries, chicken farms and commercial gardens had never been discussed before the DAA had arrived two years earlier with money to spend. Hobbles Danayarri, Elsie Mayawi and others enjoyed scratching vegetables out of the dirt for instance, but only the government saw the need to manage, regulate and expand such pursuits into businesses supported by forty-hour per-week jobs.

* * *

With all parties now working to a date of 1 July 1975 for the handover of the Gurindji's pastoral lease, negotiations between the track mob, various departments and Vestey's were underway. In anticipation of the Gurindji gaining tenure over their land, Minister Cavanagh invited Lingiari to apply for funding for bores and cattle yards. The elders could do little to respond: Muramulla still lacked an employee

---

7   Darwin, NAA, 'Wave Hill/ Wattie Creek Special Employment Projects Review
    [...]', *Wave Hill—Review of Council Programs and Employment Projects*, 1975–79,
    E460, 1981–89, Part 2.

who could read the Minister's letter, let alone draft an application for funds.

Instead, to deal with the transfer's legal implications, the Gurindji made contact with Geoff Eames, a resilient lawyer working for the new Aboriginal Legal Aid service in Alice Springs. Acting on Muramulla's behalf, Eames travelled with Lingiari and Nangiari to Sydney to talk with Vestey's top brass. After the lawyer picked up the old stockmen from Frank Hardy's home, the trio arrived at Vestey's George Street offices on the morning of 6 June 1975. Things got off to an awkward start: used to the casual manners of Northern Territory stockyards, one of the Gurindji men spat absent-mindedly on Vestey's carpet, grinding it underfoot. The management were horrified, though nothing was said. Phlegm on the rug marked the start of a tumultuous discussion, according to Eames:

> Suddenly it all became very difficult [...]. I started saying 'We are all very happy to be here, it's wonderful to be getting the title—'. One of the company people said, 'I'm not sure what you mean, there's obviously been some misunderstanding. We hadn't said that we agreed to [the sale], we are just here to have further discussions about it'.[8]

It was the visitors' turn to be shocked. Like DAA Secretary Barrie Dexter, Eames and the Gurindji had been confident that Vestey's were in agreement about the terms of the excision proposed by the government two months earlier. The young lawyer called a break:

> Donald and Vincent and I went out [...]. We had a discussion, and I rang Hardy. I told him what had transpired and said 'I

---

8   Darwin, NTAS, Interview with Geoff Eames Recorded by Charlie Ward, April 2010, NTRS 3609, BWF 12.

think we need a bit of support'. [...] We went back in, and I said that I'd spoken to Hardy, and that he'd been very clear that this was a complete backstab. They were very alarmed, and one of them said 'What do you mean by that?', and I said 'I think there are going to be protests about this'. They said 'Do you mean we are going to have to go through the whole London thing again? Are we are going to have people storming through the corridors?' I said 'Well, they will be very angry, and there are plenty of them [...]'.

Then they went away and had a bit of a chat, and when they came back they said 'There's been a great misunderstanding. We are entirely in agreement about excising land for the Gurindji, we thought you were talking about taking the entire station'.

With the old men, Eames and DAA staffers clawing ground from Vestey's, Barrie Dexter anticipated a threat from another quarter: what if the Gurindji's expansionist Warlpiri neighbours attempted to usurp their new lease? Seeking to allay their boss's fears, Dexter's staff sought any evidence of Yapa plans for a corporate takeover. When Dexter was assured that the Muramulla company had no Warlpiri shareholders, the ceremonial handover of title was scheduled for 16 August 1975—the date of Prime Minister Whitlam's earliest availability. Creed Lovegrove, the new director of the DAA's NT branch, visited the Gurindji to inform them of the impending ceremony in person.

Lawyers and surveyors were refining the terms of the excision, but the land also had to be rid of Vestey's cattle. This 'clean muster', it had been agreed, would be done by Vestey's early in the dry season (April-May), and paid for by the government. When the time came, Wave Hill station manager Ralph Hayes employed Gurindji men such as Gus George to do the work. George recalls:

> [...] They told us 'Ah, you mob going to get the country back. You got to put up a boundary fence across the river and [muster] the land on this side [...]. I was working [for Vestey's], to move those cattle back to Wave Hill station area. We couldn't do a clean muster while wild cattle still living in there, we left some cleanskins still there.[9]

The Gurindji would become all too familiar with this problem.

* * *

As the day of the lease transfer loomed, a stream of orders was issued to Richard Preece via the DAA radio telephone at Libanungu. Authorities wanted everything 'just so', as the handover had been plugged as a 'historic and symbolic milestone' before it even occurred.[10] When it emerged that three jets filled with Canberra VIPs were converging on the specially-constructed bough shed and picnic tables set up for them at Wattie Creek, reporter Lenore Nicklin wondered whether the entourage was the biggest 'commonwealth safari' yet seen. Some whites working with the Gurindji at the time were appalled by the bureaucracy's efforts to accommodate the important guests. Rather than witness the contrivance they foresaw—in which the everyday world of the Gurindji would be largely hidden—DAA 'casual' Gavin Perry and others went bush for the day.

This mismatch between local realities and the workings of high political office was revealed when the PM's plane touched down on the morning of 16 August 1975. According to Geoff Eames:

---

9   Darwin, NTAS, Interview with Gus George by Charlie Ward, October 2010, NTRS 3609, BWF 24.
10 Hon. Les Johnson, Minister for Aboriginal Affairs, 'Transfer of Part of Wave Hill Pastoral Lease [...]', Media Release, 31 July 1975, Oke Personal Collection.

> Whitlam flew up in a BAC 1-11. The airstrip [...] wasn't quite long enough for it [laughs]. I remember that when he landed, there were all these dignitaries waiting out there for Gough, but he didn't stop in time and went hurtling through the fence. It was a pretty spectacular start to the day's events.

It was just after midday when Whitlam and his wife Margaret stepped onto Gurindji soil for the first time. According to a very young onlooker, the prime minister 'stood there like a great big giant and [shook] each old people hand'.[11] In her blue slacksuit, Mrs Whitlam also began mixing with the crowd, embracing local infants. The elders' Adelaide mate Don Atkinson, not used to occasions of such public significance, was sporting a creation commissioned from a Singaporean tailor. With the Australian flag fluttering overhead, Jean Culley handed out flyers about the land claim of the Gurindji's neighbours at Yarralin—to Wave Hill station manager Ralph Hayes' annoyance. A succession of former Ministers—all of whom had promised the Gurindji varying amounts of land—milled about: WC Wentworth 'in a crumpled safari suit', the ebullient Gordon Bryant, and the recently-transferred Cavanagh, shadowing his successor Les Johnson. Meanwhile, a 'tethered goat [ate] rubbish with great solemnity' and two chefs hovered nearby 'in spotless white'.

After introductions and greetings, the day's program under the bough shed began. Minister Johnson optimistically reassured the audience that with the government's forthcoming *Land Rights Act*, the Gurindji could convert their lease to proper land rights, making them

---

11   Susan Cebu, 'The Handback [...]', *Mumkurla-nginyi-ma Parrngalinyparla: From the Darkness into the Light—Gurindji Freedom Banners Project*, (Kalkaringi, NT, Daguragu Community Government Council, 2000), (no page numbering).

legal owners 'later in the year'.¹² A grant of $128,000 ($875,000) for the Muramulla company to develop its new lease was also promised. The general manager of Vestey's Angliss group Roger Golding then announced that Lord Vestey would give the Gurindji a gift of 400 cattle—and made a jibe at the protesters who had stormed his company's offices some years earlier. While Golding wished the Muramulla company every success, Lupngiari—a significant player in the Gurindji's struggle—sat back, ignored by photographers, rolling a smoke. Letters and telegrams had been received from dozens of well-wishers. A teenage Gurindji-Tiwi girl, Sandra Cebu, read some aloud, including those from Frank Hardy and Bill Jeffrey, the two *kartiya* who had helped to draft the Gurindji's petition requesting their land, eight years earlier.

On the Prime Ministerial jet that morning, Coombs had urged Whitlam to keep his speech short and invest the day with a sense of ceremony. The shrewd adviser recounted a story told by anthropologist Bill Stanner, how Wurundjeri elders had formalised their people's 1835 land treaty with encroaching settlers at Port Phillip by placing soil into the hand of explorer John Batman. Hearing Coombs' suggestion that the PM might reverse the gesture with Lingiari, Whitlam revised his performance plan for Daguragu on the spot.

When it came to his turn to speak, Whitlam congratulated the Gurindji and their supporters on their victory after a nine year 'fight for justice'. After promising the Aborigines that the Australian government would 'help you in your plans to use this land fruitfully', his speech concluded with the words:

---

12   Hon. Les Johnson, 'Transfer of Pastoral Lease at Daguragu to Gurindji People: Speech by Minister [...]', 16 August 1975, Oke Personal Collection.

> Vincent Lingiari, I solemnly hand to you these deeds as proof, in Australian law, that these lands belong to the Gurindji people, and I put into your hands this piece of the earth itself as a sign that we restore them to you and your children forever.[13]

In finishing, Whitlam handed Lingiari the new deeds to the Gurindji's land, now officially dubbed 'NT Pastoral Lease 805'. Then, to the joy of assembled photographers he stooped down, grabbed a handful of red earth, and poured it into Lingiari's open palm.

According to Vestey pastoral inspector Cec Watts and his wife Dawn, the Gurindji leader—knowing the symbolic import of the soil he had been given—struggled to dispose of it without offending the assembled *kartiya*. The Watts empathised:

Cec: I was standing quite close to Vincent, and Gough gave him this handful of dirt, symbolically, and the old bloke sort of let it drift out of his hand.

Dawn: He didn't know what to do with it.

Cec: Poor old bugger.

Dawn: A bit trickled away …

Cec: He put it behind his back.

Dawn: They could have given him a little box.

Cec: He did well.[14]

Lingiari—who according to one reporter was struck with a case of nerves—responded to Whitlam and the crowd in his own language:

---

13 Edward G Whitlam, *Abiding Interests* (St. Lucia, University of Queensland Press, 1997), p. 188.

14 Darwin, NTAS, Cec and Dawn Watts, Interview Recorded by Charlie Ward, April 2010, NTRS 3609, BWF 14.

A HANDFUL OF SAND, 1975

> The important white men are giving us this land ceremonially [...]. It belonged to the whites, but today it is in the hands of us Aboriginals all around here. Let us live happily as mates, let us not make it hard for each other. [...] They will give us cattle, they will give us horses, and we will be happy. [...] These important white men have come here to our ceremonial ground and they are welcome, because they have not come here for any other reason, just for this (handover) [...].
>
> You (Gurindji) must keep this land safe for yourselves, it does not belong to any different Welfare man. They took our country away from us, now they have bought it back ceremonially.[15]

After Whitlam gave the old man even more dirt for the benefit of the press, DAA photographer Mervyn Bishop's images of the 'handover' became some of the most recognised in Australian Aboriginal history. The power of the photos rested in the symbolism of Whitlam's gesture—made on behalf of millions concerned by Aboriginal dispossession. Interestingly, the ceremony had a European equivalent, known as 'livery in deed', pointing to the more universal nature of its symbolism. In this mediaeval ritual of sale 'the parties went on to the relevant piece of land and the [seller] delivered possession by handing over a twig or a clump of earth to the recipient'.[16]

The handover implicitly acknowledged the moral rightfuness of the Gurindji's stand, and the historical injustices done to them by the Europeans on their country. It was by dint of the Gurindji's hard slog at Wattie Creek that they had successfully brought all this to the

---

15 Vincent Lingiari, 'Vincent Lingiari's Speech', transl. by Patrick McConvell, in *This is What Happened: Historical Narratives by Aborigines*, ed. by Luise Hercus and Peter Sutton (Canberra, Australian Institute of Aboriginal Studies, 1986), pp. 313–315.

16 Thanks to Rob Chapman for alerting me to the archaic conveyancing practice of 'feoffment' in relation to the Gurindji handover. See 'Livery of Seisin', http://en.wikipedia.org/wiki/Livery_of_seisin. Accessed 9 October 2013.

nation's attention—and now, apparently, seen it remedied. The handover day was the old Gurindji men's finest hour, and their victory.

Lingiari made his speech, and a party followed. Chops, sausages and fruit were served before painted-up members of the track mob and others danced. Mindful of the whites' need to mark every occasion by consuming liquor, Daguragu's elders had waived their alcohol ban for the day, but precious little was on hand. Guests quickly learned that the line 'One for Mrs Whitlam, please' would guarantee them a cold beer. The Prime Minister 'poured champagne down his copious gullet' from the bottle, according to Rob Wesley-Smith, before passing it to a startled Lingiari. The old man had sworn off drinking the year before, but he took a swig—and requested Whitlam's help to prevent the ill-effects grog was having on his community.[17]

Amongst such excitement, the Gurindji leader gave the new title deeds to Geoff Eames, his lawyer, for safekeeping. With enthusiastic residents wanting to examine the documents, Eames lost them in the crowd. At that point he was approached by Whitlam, announcing there had been requests for photographs of the black and white statesmen holding the parchment. When the empty-handed lawyer replied meekly that he didn't know where it was, Whitlam's response was quintessential: 'What? It took them 200 years to get their land back, and you've lost it in ten minutes?' Eventually the deed was located, 'all stained with red dirt, it had been passed through so many hands'. After the bonhomie subsided and the VIPs departed for the Wave Hill airstrip, Daguragu's elders were apparently 'disgusted' by the empty beer cans left behind.

---

17   Northern Territory, Legislative Assembly, Hon Roger Steele, *Parliamentary Record–First Assembly. Part One–the Debates*, 13 October 1976 (Darwin, NTLC Printer, 1973), p. 732.

A HANDFUL OF SAND, 1975

In rural Queensland the day after the ceremony, Whitlam claimed on radio that 'for the first time, Aboriginal people have been given rights to their own land'.[18] The PM was gilding the lily, for although he was clear that the government's transferral of a pastoral lease to the Gurindji was just the first step towards returning their land in perpetuity, the 'rights' he'd conferred were merely those enjoyed by Vestey's and other NT pastoralists. Contrary to Whitlam's spin, the reality was that other Aboriginal groups had pipped the Gurindji to the post on that count, too.

Forty years later, the handover itself is commonly seen as the Gurindji's land rights victory, though legally speaking it was anything but. Through their campaigning, which helped inspire the Woodward Commission, the elders had done much towards many Aboriginal groups in the Territory winning land rights—when or if the ALP's *Land Rights Act* was passed. As for *their own* land rights, Whitlam had sold the Gurindji a pup—though a pastoral lease was one many deemed a good stand-in for the real thing. Everybody assumed the Aborigines' lease would be short term, and many, including staunch Gurindji supporters, saw it as a milestone.

Importantly, Lingiari's relief was huge. He looked a younger man afterwards, while Jean Culley believed that in his people's long history, the handover 'could be a turning point to help restore pride and ambition'.[19] Dexter Daniels, the elder's Nunggubuyu ally, was also excited by the Gurindji's success and moved to Daguragu to live. While the ex-unionist worked as a DAA assistant mechanic by day, he was inspired by the impending 'full' return of the Gurindji's

---

18   'Blacks' Land Warning by Whitlam: QLD is Accused', *Courier Mail*, 18 August 1975, p. 2.
19   *Gurindji Newsletter*, No.5, March 1976, Oke Personal Collection.

land and fought for the land rights of the nearby Yarralin mob's as well. Frank Hardy held even loftier hopes. Having missed the ceremony, the veteran agitator returned to Wave Hill with a young Sydney firebrand, Meredith Burgmann. The pair stayed with Richard Preece and Daniels joined them in the evenings. Now the Gurindji almost had their land, Hardy believed they and the Whitlam Government might found a sort of socialist utopia. In the film he promoted that year, Hardy played the journalist-philosopher:

> Not for [the Gurindji] the scornful doubts of their enemies, or the anxious queries of their friends. They believe they can create a viable economy at Wattie Creek within their ancient communal lifestyle, and meet the white man as a brother on equal terms. Let no man say that they can't.

The well-known author thought that if the ALP government could 'break through' the 'enormous pressure from the pastoral groups and others', then:

> [...] We could have an experiment in the self-propelled restoration of a primitive communal organisation of society which the whole world would want to study [...]. There's a lot of hope that something quite unique might happen here at Wattie Creek in the next twenty-five years.[20]

Visions of an Aboriginal idyll at Daguragu were not shared by all. To local pastoralists, the Gurindji were a displaced labour pool, now transformed into fellow landholders. After Ralph Hayes and his men mustered up Lord Vestey's 400 gift animals for the Gurindji, this new relationship soured quickly. According to Cec Watts:

> Ralph had the cattle there, and he said 'What the bloody hell are we going to do with them?' We let them know [...], we said

---

20 Hardy in Goldschmidt (Dir.), 1974.

'We've got the 400 cattle here—you'd better come up and get them'. There was a bit of umm-ing and ahh-ing, they couldn't get horses organised, or get organised at all. It was getting [to be] a bit of a nuisance, tailing these cattle about, and then they [suggested the cattle] could be branded on Wave [Hill station]—which is against the bloody law [...]. That was the last thing we wanted, their bloody cattle running around on Wave Hill, there were enough complications as it was [...]. Finally Ralph said 'Bugger it', and shoved the cattle through the gate. He said 'You got 'em', and that was it. We had no dealings with them from that moment on.[21]

After the handover, DAA staff buttonholed the elders again about accepting an outside cattle adviser and a consultant. While Rob Wesley-Smith advised Lingiari to be 'very careful' about the *kartiya* who would want to work for them, the DAA approached cattleman Stan Andrews about applying for the adviser role. Andrews was then working on the Aboriginal cattle project at nearby Lajamanu, and the Gurindji agreed to trial him if his Warlpiri employers gave him their approval. To fill the second—consultant's—position they planned for Muramulla, the DAA turned to their favoured consultancy, AACM. Lingiari had earlier named Rob Wesley-Smith as the group's preferred choice, but instead John Edey, one of AACM's Adelaide consultants, flew his plane to Daguragu to assess what would be required to develop the Gurindji's lease. Edey informed the elders he would take the DAA job '*if* the Muramulla Gurindji people want such assistance'.[22] Knowing the position of the Department, there was little the elders could do but accept.

---

21   NTAS, Watts, NTRS 3609, BWF 14.
22   Darwin, NAA, Edey to Lovegrove, 18 August 1975, *Muramulla Gurindji Company—Pastoral*, 1975–79, E460, 1975/137.

The possibility of the Gurindji running a low-key operation harvesting cattle on a portion of their land—as they had wanted earlier—was now forgotten. Instead, the old men accepted Edey and Andrews as their employees and the DAA continued its plans to develop the Gurindji's country into a profitable station. $345,000 ($2.36 million) was tagged 'to compensate Muramulla for the provision of further assets in the form of new waters, mustering and fencing'. Despite this substantial outlay, Edey did not foresee a profit 'in the early years', unless 'a rise in beef prices greater than anticipated' came along.[23]

* * *

Despite the promises of self-determination, costing for a truly *Aboriginal* cattle project was beyond the bureaucracy's resources and imagination. Two years earlier, DAA staff had written:

> The manner in which the Gurindji [operate] the project will [...] *depend on the terms of the government making finance available* [...]. The basis of costing and income estimation are determined as for a non-Aboriginal project [...].[24]

Regardless of the official language used, in other words, consultation on how the Gurindji's project would work was ultimately irrelevant. Moreover, nobody involved in the Muramulla project had a good understanding of the two different cultures, or the corporate, pastoral, ecological and commercial knowledge on which its success relied. Now, the non-literate elders found themselves at the helm—but without

---

23   Darwin, NAA, E460, 1975/137.
24   Darwin, NAA, 'Muramulla Gurindji Co Pty Ltd', *Cattle Mustering Venture* [...], 12 September 1973, (F1) 1975/4091.

control—of an organisation with an alien European constitution, subject to laws of which they were largely unaware. In an attempt to make this unwieldy creation function financially, they had been lumped with government-mandated, management-experienced white advisers.

It was October 1975. By granting the Gurindji funding for their cattle operation and access to land, it appeared Whitlam had removed the largest obstacles standing between them and self-determination. Ironically though, by bringing the Gurindji 'into the fold' of the cattle industry, the likelihood of whitefellas taking control of Daguragu and its own enterprise had increased. Student activists in Adelaide pointed out:

> It would be a grave error to believe their struggles are over. Freedom from white control and exploitation is a hard thing to realise. The [DAA] has appointed a cattle manager for the Muramulla company. [Also] Gurindji children go to school at Wave Hill, where three out of the five teachers are Baptists.[25]

These student realists were right. For all the handover's appeal, it had merely won the Gurindji the opportunity to compete as pastoralists on a financial playing field levelled somewhat by grants—a mixed blessing at best. The cattle industry was in a state of near-crisis. The global market was 'acutely depressed' in 1975, and other stations in the region were calling for greater government support.

Neither had the industry's terms been much explained to the elders. Because all and sundry believed the passage of the *Aboriginal Land Rights Act* (*ALRA*) was imminent, little mention had been made to the old men of the 'improvements' the government required on their pastoral lease. Unbeknownst to the Muramulla board, these would

---

25 'Gurindji Struggle Towards Self-determination', *Empire Times*, October 1975, (Adelaide, South Australia, Flinders University).

be far more onerous than those facing their 'developed' neighbours. At rates determined by the government, fencing, bores, and buildings now had to be built on the Gurindji's land each year.[26]

As well as dictating the terms of Muramulla's land use, the government would tightly control the company's funding. After Whitlam's handover, the DAA mailed a long-promised cheque—not to the elders, but to the Department's contracted accountants Wallace, McMullen & Smail. Although the Gurindji were supposedly the recipients of this money—$128,000 ($875,000), four times more than any of their previous grants—they were not mentioned in the accompanying letter. Instead, financial arrangements between the accountants, Muramulla's unwanted AACM consultants, and the department itself were outlined. These transactions resulted in delays, and no wages were paid to Gurindji stockmen for several weeks. According to Patrick McConvell, after the 'high' of the handover ceremony, the station workers' morale collapsed.[27] A Western Desert rock band later summed up Muramulla's new situation as tenants on their own land: 'big name, no blankets'.

As the scale of the government's vision for the Gurindji's land became apparent, their old leaders were ambivalent. According to Jean Culley, even before the handover Vincent Lingiari harboured doubts. These were not made known to the DAA or the public:

> Unfortunately, [the Gurindji elders] have always said they wanted the cattle station. I think if they had known what a tremendous worry it all has been, and the big price they have paid, I don't think they would have gone on the same path. I have spoken

---

26   Muramulla was required to have 2,500 branded cattle by 1977, a 'homestead and outbuildings' to the value of $20,000 ($200,000) by 1978, and to erect 160 km of internal fencing by 1982. See Darwin, NAA, *Muramulla Gurindji Company—Pastoral*, 1975–79, E460, 1975/137.

27   Darwin, NAA, McConvell to Hon Race Mathews, 11 September 1975, *Muramulla Gurindji Company—Pastoral*, 1975–79, E460, 1975/137.

about this with Vincent [Lingiari], and he told me he thinks it is 'too big', i.e. too hard. I told him that now they are on a road, and it's hard to get off. He saw this, and said that he hoped the younger men coming on would help shoulder the burdens [...].[28]

More ominously, the elders' modest vision was increasingly outdated. To make ends meet, stations like Vestey's Wave Hill were turning to mustering by helicopter—an anathema to Lingiari's group—rather than using horse-borne stockmen. In the decade the elders had spent waiting for their land, the industry that had inspired them had moved on.

* * *

Respect and gratitude for Whitlam and his Ministers among the track mob was growing, though public disquiet about the government was also on the rise. The 'big man's' social reforms had the potential to transform Australia, but high unemployment and inflation had damaged the PM's popularity. Malcolm Fraser, the new leader of the opposition, capitalised on this unrest. He attempted to force the ALP to an election by blocking supply bills in the senate that would give the government access to public funds. When Whitlam refused to go to the polls, a crisis ensued—whether constitutional or political is still debated—and his government was controversially dismissed by Governor-General John Kerr on 11 November 1975.

While the nation was transfixed by this drama in Canberra, Labor's journey with the Gurindji and their cattle was cut short. Before the Whitlam government's dismissal, the Gurindji's land rights had seemed within their grasp. The Northern Territory *Aboriginal Land*

---

28 Culley to Wesley-Smith, undated [February 1975], Wesley-Smith Personal Collection.

Rights Act—representing years of work by many Aboriginal people, the Woodward Commission, the Council for Aboriginal Affairs and the DAA—had been before parliament, requiring its last reading. When 'Kerr's coup' occurred, instead of the Act's passage into law, parliament was dissolved and the bill lapsed. The CAA's Barrie Dexter, Nugget Coombs and WEH Stanner were devastated. With the country in limbo, Fraser was endorsed as a 'caretaker' prime minister until an election could be held. When this occurred on 13 December 1975, the Coalition triumphed, claiming a 91 to 36 seat victory. With one of Victoria's landed gentry now leading a new conservative government, Daguragu's elders were thrust into even less certain waters.

Chapter 9

A FIGHTING CHANCE, 1976

> We [...] got a few cattle and horses now. We start to be alright.
>
> But what about them other poor buggers?
>
> Pincher Nyurrmiarri, March 1976.[1]

With their friend Whitlam gone, the Gurindji had cause to wonder—what would Prime Minister Fraser, the new 'boss man' in Canberra, do about their land rights? Before the conservatives' election victory in December 1975, Liberal spokesman Bob Ellicott had sent a telegram to remote communities promising that should his party take power, it would not change *any* Aboriginal policies or funding. Within weeks of Fraser's victory however, the new Central Land Council (CLC) learned its funding would be affected, and Whitlam's land rights legislation would be altered too—possibly heavily. Rather than being reprimanded for lying, Ellicott was awarded the job of Attorney-General.

Fraser was disturbed by what he saw as the Whitlam Government's recklessness and waste in Aboriginal Affairs, and ordered a review.

---

[1] 'Pincher Carries a Torch for the Other Aboriginal Tribes', *The Age*, 31 March 1976.

With rumours about the extent of the new PM's cuts abounding, *The Age* reported that there was 'talk in Canberra [...] of ending all money to the Gurindjis [*sic*]'.² When the size of the proposed budget reduction became known, the new Aboriginal Affairs Minister, Perth solicitor Ian Viner, threatened to resign. Later Viner assured the Gurindji it was 'business as usual' at Daguragu, but nationally 'austerity measures' worth $7 million ($43.7 million) were flagged. DAA staffer Barry Hansen remembers labouring under Fraser's prototypical 'razor gang':

> It was just going to be 'slash and burn' time. It was fairly threatening if you had a particular point of view, or commitment to a project or something. Everything had to be justified.³

Like his Liberal predecessors, Fraser—'the squatter from Nareen'—was beholden to the rural conservatives of the National Country Party, whose opposition to Aboriginal land rights had barely dimmed. More broadly, his cabinet was supportive of Whitlam's policy of 'Aboriginal self-determination', but didn't proclaim itself as such. Instead, the new government branded its approach 'self-management'. This, it said, was designed to: '[...] Develop Aboriginal self-sufficiency and [...] represent initiatives that Aboriginals themselves believe will enhance their dignity, self-respect and self-reliance'.⁴ In other words, the Gurindji could expect more of the same from the DAA under Fraser, but would have to tighten their belts. Fraser's appointment of Viner—an inexperienced non-cabinet member—as

---

2   Dennis Minogue, 'The Dreaming: Wattie Creek's Black Cattlemen Look to the Future', *The Age*, 14 February 1976, p. 13.

3   Darwin, NTAS, Barry Hansen, Interview Recorded by Charlie Ward, September 2012, NTRS 3609, BWF 39.

4   Cited in *Department of Aboriginal Affairs Annual Report 1975–76* (Australian Government Publishing Service, Canberra, 1976), p. 5.

Minister also reflected the fact his government did not see Aboriginal people's advancement as a national priority. Instead, Aboriginal Affairs would return, as a journalist put it, to 'the fringe settlements of the bureaucracy', where it had languished before Whitlam.[5]

Within months, the impact of the Coalition's cuts at Wave Hill became known. All new housing at the settlement and Daguragu was cancelled, and other programs were 'postponed or redesigned'. Only essential services were safe. To show their displeasure, Daguragu residents travelled to Alice Springs—a four-day drive in total—to take part in a large demonstration against the government and its emerging stance on land rights. The Gurindji's recent gains were symbolised by the Libanungu Council vehicle they drove—an impossibility prior to the ALP's establishment of Aboriginal community councils. The Gurindji's fears regarding their lease, land rights and cattle company under Fraser were conveyed clearly by the presence of Vincent Lingiari among the convoy of demonstrators. Travel was by now a rarity for the aging leader.

With Whitlam's legislation now seemingly gazumped, the Gurindji's lease gave them little security at all. In 1976, they—along with all land-connected Aboriginal people in the Northern Territory—were dependent on Malcolm Fraser's government to pass Whitlam's contentious *ALRA* land rights bill. If the law was passed, it would be the greatest restorative gesture offered to Australia's first people since white settlement. Gerry Brennan QC had said as much to Justice Woodward, *ALRA*'s designer, in 1974:

> [This law] will, for all-time mark the high-water mark of possible Aboriginal aspirations. Whatever your Honour does

---

5   Bruce Juddery, 'Disillusionment Likely Among Aborigines', *Canberra Times*, 2 July 1976.

not recommend in favour of Aborigines at this stage will never be granted.[6]

Among other things, Woodward had recommended that powerful land councils be established to hold title and represent traditional owners; that reserves and missions be transferred to Aboriginal people; that mining royalties be payed to them; and that more cattle stations like Daguragu be bought.

These findings had been adopted wholesale by Whitlam, but despite the Liberals' promise that they would continue his plans, Fraser's version of the bill was heavily revised. The watered-down draft drew flak from politicians, pastoralists, fishermen, mining companies, anthropologists, missionaries and Aboriginal people alike. 'Traditional' bush people protesting in Alice Springs was a sign that a new phase in the debate about Aboriginal land rights had begun.

Under Fraser's proposed law, the power of the land councils would be radically reduced, and then transferred to the Minister and the DAA. Similarly, Viner suggested that instead of land councils, Aboriginal legal services could prepare land claims. The right of Aboriginal people to claim land on a 'needs' basis rather than on the basis of traditional ownership had also been removed.

While the Gurindji and their sympathisers were enraged by these apparent concessions to conservative interests, the government was also attacked because they did not go far enough. The Coalition's 'sister' party in the NT, the Country Liberals, had held a decades-long majority in the NT Legislative Assembly, and resented Canberra interfering in their affairs. One Territory conservative warned of an apocalypse if Fraser's bill was passed:

---

6   Cited in Sir Edward Woodward, *One Brief Interval: A Memoir* (Carlton, Vic, Miegunyah Press, 2005), p. 141.

Of all the disasters conceived by Canberra politicians for Territory Aboriginals, none is likely to have as disastrous an impact as [*ALRA*] when the [traditional] owners realise the practical application of what is at present to them only a jumble of words. [...] It is ironical that the Labor Party in Canberra, the 'designer-in-chief' of disasters, has left the [federal] Liberal Country Party to put the match to this one.[7]

As the hyperbole intensified, the issue of the Gurindji's land rights was batted about. The previous Labor Minister Les Johnson had promised the Gurindji that organising their freehold title would be an administrative doddle. Under Fraser though, the true situation became clear: like any other group, Daguragu's elders would have to prove their connection to the country they now leased. In other words, while Minister Viner wished for the 'speedy resolution' of a Gurindji claim, the elders' public assertions of their land rights over the last decade would count for naught. Gough Whitlam, now opposition leader, pressured the government about this new burden when he returned to Daguragu on the anniversary of the handover, in August 1976. Viner responded by reiterating that Daguragu's residents had 'a very good chance of getting freehold title to [their] entire pastoral lease, and their claim [would] be one of the first to be dealt with'.[8]

Before that could happen however, *ALRA* had to be passed without being categorically weakened by the concerted campaign of its strongest critics in the NT Country Liberal Party. As part of their attack, leader Dr Goff Letts offered his own 'resolution' to the Gurindji's situation: rather than granting them land rights over their

---

7   Northern Territory, Legislative Assembly, Hon Rupert Kentish, *Parliamentary Record–First Assembly. Part One–the Debates*, 18 November 1976 (Darwin, NTLA Printer, 1977), pp. 826–827.
8   Min. Viner, cited in *Land Rights News*, No, 4, October 1976 (Alice Springs, Australia, Central Land Council), p. 5.

1,240 square mile lease, Letts thought that the Muramulla cattle company 'could continue with similar tenure to that of neighbouring properties' as pastoral lessees.[9] Instead of receiving the sweep of their traditional lands in perpetuity, in other words, the Gurindji's local member proposed their ownership should only extend to Daguragu and their nearby sacred sites at Mimangu (Seale Gorge): an area of about twenty square miles.

Letts' announcement ended a period in which the elders' land rights victory had seemed guaranteed, and heralded a new threat. Due to moves in Canberra to grant 'self-government' to the Territory, the Country Liberals were on the ascendant with little opposition. Rather than capitulate though, the elders met Letts' 'solution' head on, admonishing the former vet about the importance of their country:

> What do you want to do with this land? We Gurindji have Dreaming and business all around this cattle station block, we want to keep our children here and put our young men in the Aboriginal 'school' for this land.[10]

Surely dismayed to be fighting again for what they thought they had already won, four of the Gurindji's elders appealed to Minister Viner:

> We can see [the CLP] want to cut the land in half because they don't want to give the Aborigines a big land. Mr Whitlam came in to hand over the land forever, but people in Darwin are not satisfied; they want to take the land back. This is Gurindji country all over; that is why the people here are pretty sorry that the white man wants to take it back.[11]

---

9   Letts, cited in *Land Rights News*, No. 4, October 1976.
10   Nyurrmiarri *et al* to Hon. Dr Letts, 17 October 1976, Oke Personal Collection.
11   Nyurrmiarri *et al* to Min. Viner, 17 October 1976, Oke Personal Collection.

A FIGHTING CHANCE, 1976

The Gurindji's lawyer Geoff Eames was now working with the CLC, and flew with traditional owners to Canberra to make their case for 'full' land rights directly to the Prime Minister. During the meeting that followed between Malcolm Fraser, CLC chairman Wenten Rubuntja, Eames and others, the PM reassured the group that Letts and the NTLA would have no input to his government's *ALRA* bill. In making this rash promise Fraser underestimated the rancour of Territory Country Liberal politicians, two thirds of whom also flew to Canberra that night to make their case. Fraser backflipped immediately, promising them that the NT would be able to pass its own 'complementary' legislation.

Believing Fraser was 'pretty hard', the Gurindji sent Pincher Nyurrmiarri to attend a land rights conference and argue for their land with the government. Hosted by Jean Culley and the McConvells, it was Nyurrmiarri's first trip to the big cities of the south. En route to Canberra, the old man was approached by Melbourne Kooris wanting him to teach them 'Aboriginal law'. Because he didn't 'know how the Koori people in the city used to live before', Nyurrmiarri refused.[12] Flying on to the capital, the old stockman was gobsmacked to be offered a hot cup of tea far above the earth. Before he fell ill in Sydney, Nyurrmiarri was impressed by the 'law' depicted in the stone petroglyphs of the Eora people, but took Tanya McConvell to task about the wastefulness of white society, which he thought built and destroyed skyscrapers without rhyme or reason.

Six months after Nyurrmiarri returned to Daguragu, a watered-down version of Whitlam's *ALRA* was passed. In Fraser's version of the Act, Aboriginal freehold no longer included mining rights,

---

12   Patrick McConvell, 'Report on the Visit of Pincher Numiari [*sic*] to Canberra', Undated, Atkinson Personal Collection.

and 'fringe-dwellers' displaced from their traditional lands and living in towns were left high and dry. As the Whitlam Government had proposed, the land of people on reserves would be converted to Aboriginal freehold ownership automatically. The Gurindji weren't so lucky. As predicted, the track mob at Daguragu would have to lodge a claim like other Aboriginal lessees.

Despite these changes, there was jubilation in the offices of the DAA and on the Territory's Aboriginal reserves when the Act was passed. At Ngukurr (Roper River), where long-term land rights activists like Dexter and Davis Daniels and Silas and Phillip Roberts lived, the return of Nunggubuyu country would be automatic. Dexter and Davis Daniels' nephew remembers:

> There was a telegram from Canberra. I was at the ceremony ground leading ceremony. [It said] 'the Aboriginal people have their land rights'. We were so happy! We had a corroboree that night, we celebrated for a week.[13]

* * *

The Gurindji didn't have land rights, but they had the run of their lease. After the handover from Whitlam, the Muramulla board had nominated their Aboriginal staff: Donald Nangiari kept his role as director and his 'full' brother Jerry Rinyngayarri was appointed head stockman. Rinyngayarri had been the Aboriginal 'headboy' of the No. 4 stock camp on Wave Hill station, and was second only to Lingiari in terms of Gurindji law.[14] Consultant John Edey—a former

---

13 Darwin, NTAS, Interview with David Daniels, Recorded by Charlie Ward, October 2010, NTRS 3609, BWF 19.
14 Darwin, NTAS, Interview with Gus George by Charlie Ward, October 2010, NTRS 3609, BWF 24.

government agronomist in the region—flew fortnightly to meet with Nangiari, Rinyngayarri and Stan Andrews. Andrews had left his own job with the Warlpiri and moved his family to the settlement. The number of Gurindji stockmen employed under these four 'bosses'—two Gurindji and two white—varied wildly.

Delighted to have untrammelled access to their land for the first time in sixty years, the Muramulla directors and stockmen got down to work. Vehicles were purchased and Hobbles Danayarri, Lingiari's son Victor Vincent and others erected five kilometres of much-needed fencing before the 1976 wet season. Monthly meetings were held in which Edey and the board discussed stock buying, budgets, development plans, employment and the store. After receiving Lord Vestey's 400 beasts the previous year, the company bought 1,200 head in eighteen months. It was thought—by journalists at least—that the Gurindji herd would grow to reach their lease's capacity within five years. To hasten this process, Edey bought seventeen large 'Droughtmaster' bulls at great cost in Queensland. After the animals were branded by Gurindji stockmen in the old Vestey yards near Kalkaringi, Pincher Nyurrmiarri proclaimed:

> We're starting off now. We want to work the station right away, so we can make a few bob ourselves, when we put the cattle in the meatworks and the money in the bank like white Europeans.[15]

If Gurindji ambition was driving Muramulla's activity, government conditions were directing it. Compulsory 'improvements' to the Gurindji's lease required them to accumulate 6,250 cattle within four years; a homestead and buildings worth $20,000 ($120,000) by 1978; fencing (40 kilometres in the first two years); and nine bores,

---

15 Darwin, NAA, Numiari [sic] to Viner, 8 August 1976, *Wave Hill Centre: Policy and Development*, E460, 1981/306.

to be sunk and equipped by 1985. But while the government required massive spending by the company, it also forced restraint. Due to Fraser's cuts, the DAA informed Muramulla in March 1976 that its budget was to be reduced by 12 percent.

Even before this funding cut, the company had insufficient money to pay all the Gurindji that wanted work. Initially, eighteen people were employed, but Edey warned that the payroll this required would exhaust the company's accounts. Having seen the same thing occur two years earlier, DAA officers agreed; pressure was exerted on Edey to reduce the hours worked by employees. Pincher Nyurrmiarri complained to Minister Viner that the government's miserliness was forcing the inaction of willing workers:

> [...] We got only four blokes working as ringers in the stock camp, because the government cut off the money. How are we going to work the station? We got plenty of cattle. We should have a lot of men working like Ralph Hayes. [...] A lot of the Aborigines don't work now because the money was cut off. [...] We are just sitting around like a big mob of dogs [...]. We worked for the station manager all our life, we were good enough to help them, but the government can't help us now.[16]

Nyurrmiarri's complaint highlighted that at the time Vestey's employed more Gurindji men on Wave Hill station than the elders could hire themselves: presumably a humiliation to Muramulla's board. Minister Viner was unsympathetic though. From his perspective, the unemployed Aboriginal men of the area were simply unwilling to work, either for Muramulla or on surrounding stations.[17]

---

16   Darwin, NAA, Numiari [sic] to Viner, 8 August 1976, E460, 1981/306.
17   Darwin, NAA, Viner to Numiari [sic], Undated, E460, 1981/306.

As self-determination, or as it was now dubbed, 'self-management', required, Stan Andrews' role with Muramulla was to act as an 'adviser'—not a 'boss'—to its Gurindji directors. Andrews was a quiet personality, who refrained from giving orders. The DAA supported Andrews' approach, though other *kartiya* were disparaging. The general view among local whites was that positions such as Andrews' were really to 'manage' Aboriginal people because they were unable to do so themselves. According to Andrews' widow Bev, he and Donald Nangiari navigated these issues each day with the Gurindji stockmen:

> They'd have a meeting every morning. Stan used to advise them what jobs needed doing but he didn't actually say 'Do this, do that'. He used to say 'Well this is what needs to be done', and the old fellow [Donald Nangiari] who was actually given the role of manager, he'd just say to the boys: 'I want this done, I want you to go out and check that bore, that fence', and that's what they did, and they all got on pretty well.[18]

Relations between Nangiari, Stan Andrews and the Gurindji stockmen were functional enough, but according to Culley, the presence of *kartiya* still caused tensions:

> Just by being around, Stan creates a conflict in authority with Donald. There have been several bust-ups in which Donald threatened to leave [...]. There's 'industrial trouble', [...] almost a 'class struggle' between Donald and the stockmen over wages and conditions. Now [...] the younger stockmen go to Stan and complain about Donald or Jerry, and [this] puts Stan in a very difficult position of having to (or having to avoid) defining [sic] himself in a hierarchy as regards them.[19]

---

18 Darwin, NTAS, Interview with Bev Andrews, Recorded by Charlie Ward, November 2012, NTRS 3609, BWF 40.
19 Sydney, Library of New South Wales [hereafter SLNSW], Culley (Melbourne Gurindji Group) to Middleton, 24 February 1976, in *Gurindji at Wattie Creek (Daguragu), Northern Territory*, Hannah Middleton Papers, *c.* 1966–1976, MLMSS 5866/15.

Regardless of Muramulla's internal dynamics, the Gurindji now had a cattle property 'same as other people have got it', at least in a legal sense. Ironically this meant the company was eligible to join the ranks of the elders' antagonist, the NT Cattlemen's Association (formerly the CPC). Lingiari was greatly entertained by the prospect of attending NTCA meetings with his people's former masters, but membership of the pastoral guild remained a poison chalice. Even the Territory's most successful producers were struggling. It was reported that 'white [pastoralists] are considering walking off stations of 5,000 square miles, unable at current beef prices to maintain ten or twenty people'.[20]

Thankfully, the Muramulla company was heavily-subsidised and temporarily immune to the industry's struggles. While the market buckled, nobody, including the DAA, expected Daguragu's elders to return a profit from their new holding immediately. In line with projections, Muramulla spent $77,983 ($420,000) more than it earned in its first year, which was deemed a success.

At the end of the 1976 season, Muramulla's directors, staff and observers (about fifty people in all) gathered for the company's first annual general meeting before a photo mosaic showing their work. Fencing had been erected, bores sunk and upwards of 250 cattle had been branded. Perhaps just as importantly to the old men, they had enjoyed the run of their country again. Getting down to business, Lingiari asked John Edey to tell the directors their financial situation. Edey—who thought the group 'responsible and clear-thinking'—complied, using 'a vertical clear plastic pipe filled with coloured liquid' as an aid. The company had successfully met the government's lease

---

20 Minogue, *The Age*, 14 February 1976, p. 14.

conditions and a Christmas party was planned. In the words of shadow Minister Les Johnson, who visited with Whitlam in August, the Gurindji were 'making a fist of things on their cattle station'.[21]

* * *

With Daguragu itself now zoned as a 'homestead' on the Gurindji's pastoral holding, the way was cleared for the community's further development. A multitude of agencies—empowered by the ALP and funded by Fraser—set to work. Freelance building teams were unleashed with little overall plan, and facilities sprang up like mushrooms. Though the activity buoyed the Gurindji, chaos reigned. The Education Department employed a teacher to work in the tiny 'donga' preschool it had promised, but when the young 'chalkie' arrived for work, her classroom was nowhere to be found. She gave lessons under the bough shed made for the Handover ceremony of the previous year instead, and resigned soon afterwards. The converse also occurred. Although the Health Department had built a small clinic and recruited two Gurindji health workers, the little hospital lacked a nurse to manage and train them.

Amongst these imperfect improvements, and dwarfing them, Wundamarie Housing Association completed a row of houses—'white in colour and white in design'—employing some local men.[22] Unfortunately, within months the substandard dwellings had 'weather strips peeling off or gone altogether, and bits of roof trimming

---

21 Australia, House of Representatives, Hon. Les Johnson, *Parliamentary Debates (Hansard)—First Session of the 30th Parliament (Second Period)*, 5 October 1976 (Canberra, Commonwealth Government Printer), p. 1471.
22 'Brief Report on Wattie Creek', [Undated, but 1976), Pelczynski Personal Collection.

missing'. With Fraser's veto on more housing expenditure, repairs were unlikely. The buildings' Gurindji occupants, 'who seemed to rather like them', used the new dwellings for storage and lived mostly outside.

Still seeing signs of the new communal society he anticipated in this rich tableau, Frank Hardy provided a glowing report of life at Daguragu. The Gurindji were, he said in April 1976, in 'their best shape ever, [...] very confident, and send their best greetings south'.[23] Jean Culley, who was visiting again, agreed:

> The general feeling around the camp is one of wellbeing, and everyone is pretty industrious. Everyone is employed [...] and when you look about there are people working, either building things or cleaning up the grass. There's a far more purposeful feeling about the place.[24]

Twelve Gurindji children—'beautiful young girls in bright print dresses and tall slender boys hugging suitcases'—left the community to begin secondary school at Yirara College in Alice Springs.[25] Lingiari believed that following their education, they would return home to work as carpenters, book-keepers and house-keepers.

* * *

Encouraged by their new lease and money received for their cattle business, Daguragu's elders were still set on creating an independent community, and many in the DAA also believed the Gurindji's

---

23 Frank Hardy, 'Liberals: Pin-Pricking and Cuts for the Gurindjis', *Tribune*, 7 April 1976, p. 2.
24 SLNSW, Culley (Melbourne Gurindji Group) to Middleton, 24 February 1976, MLMSS 5866/15.
25 Minogue, *The Age*, 14 February 1976, p. 14.

dream was closer than ever—if the governance issues of the two communities could be resolved. As noted earlier, in the previous year a second, separate council at Daguragu had been proposed. Musing on the fact that the elders had also briefly accepted the notion of a single council but ultimately rejected it due to its settlement origin, the DAA's Katherine boss John Rutter drove to Wave Hill in the dry season of 1976. He had an idea: if the Gurindji wouldn't come to the council, why not take it to them? Rather than having two councils, Libanungu Council could be disbanded, allowing the seat of decision-making to shift to Daguragu. Even with a few settlement residents on the board, this would give the elders control over both communities—albeit within the government's strict terms. Rutter's vision would, he hoped, reflect and support the area's 'traditional' Aboriginal power hierarchies. When he arrived, his idea set the Gurindji abuzz:

> I only described this proposal briefly and on one occasion to Aboriginal community adviser Billy Bunter and Vincent Lingiari. Both men immediately got very excited and started drawing an organisation in the dirt. Later I borrowed a blackboard from the school in order to describe the concept [...], but half an hour later I found several Aboriginals in control of the blackboard drawing their own version [...]. We were not invited to join the subsequent joint council meeting for an hour, and by then there was little for me to do [...]. After I left Wave Hill, meetings were held at Wattie Creek on three successive days with attendances of up to 300 people. Europeans were not permitted to attend. I understand that the proposal [...] has been accepted by both communities.
>
> Mr Vincent Lingiari told me that this is the way the people had [previously] decided that it was to be, but that efforts to form a single council had been thwarted by Mister Frank Hardy

who came to Wattie Creek and 'kept talking' until they agreed to change.[26]

Hardy's fixation with the Gurindji's independence had blinded him to the true politics of his friends' situation, and they valued his friendship too highly to contradict him.

Now, to concentrate their economic as well as political power at Daguragu, the Gurindji needed to replace their old store with a 'proper', large Muramulla-owned shop. This opened officially in March 1976, in a new, smart iron building. Bev Andrews was employed to manage it while Judith Donald continued to work the till. Despite the overt hostility of racist suppliers in Katherine, the store was stocked with fresh provisions. The community's pride in their enterprise was palpable and shoplifting was unknown. Recognising that the Gurindji's herd was still too small to cope with their appetite for beef, fresh meat was sourced from Bullo River station. Charlie Henderson, Bullo's owner, delivered tonnes of 'killer' to Daguragu in a plane of doubtful quality. When the pilot realised it was overburdened on take-off, unlabelled tins rained from the sky.

Jean Culley and those leaders hoping for complete Gurindji control of Daguragu were disappointed by the appointments of Stan and Bev Andrews. During Culley's visit with her daughter Paddy Zakaria, she reported that although 'everyone seems pretty happy with the tremendous progress', 'the most insidious thing [is that] Stan and

---

[26] In line with Hardy's general vision it is likely he had encouraged the Gurindji to reject proposals from the Settlement to merge the two communities. Hardy—and many others—believed such moves would lead to the usurpation of the Gurindji at Daguragu by either (or both) Warlpiri people and government staff. Darwin, NAA, 'Community Associations Wave Hill and Hooker Creek', *Wave Hill - Review of Council Programs and Employment Projects*, E460, 1981/89 Part 2.

his wife are gaining more and more control over the whole place', and 'whites from the settlement' were stealing from the new store.²⁷ Zakaria understood Muramulla's shop to be 'just another white enterprise, entirely out of the hands of the Gurindji'.²⁸

Despite these concerns, the activists who had supported the Gurindji over the last decade also now believed that the main elements of the elders' vision were within reach. Accordingly, at the request of Yarralin's leaders, Culley, the McConvells and other supporters turned their attention to assisting the land claim of the Gurindji's Ngarinyman neighbours.²⁹ The track mob were left to resolve their problems with the DAA themselves.

* * *

While strong Gurindji engagement at Daguragu continued—albeit largely on the government's terms—DAA officers described 'a state of disarray' at the nearby settlement. To them, the causes of this disorder were clear: a lack of direction, poor 'control of council vehicles' (due to 'so much ceremony going on'), and workers lacking the motivation of their Daguragu counterparts.³⁰ Jean Culley's diagnosis of the previous year was correct: with the abundance of projects, committees and organisations operating at the settlement, residents

---

27 Jean Culley, 'Brief Report on Wattie Creek', [Undated, but 1976], Pelczynski Personal Collection.
28 Zakaria to Oke et al, 14 October 1976, Oke Personal Collection.
29 Big Mick Kankinang to Leu, Culley and Friends, 27 September 1976, Oke Personal Collection; Melbourne Gurindji Group to Viner, 1 February 1976; NTAS, Rob Oke, Interview Recorded by Charlie Ward, November 2009, NTRS 3609, BWF 4; 'Brief Report on Wattie Creek', [Undated, but 1976], Pelczynski Personal Collection.
30 Darwin, NAA, E460, 1981/89 Part 2.

were getting 'left behind'. Rather than scaling back its activity in the hope of reaching its goal of eventual Aboriginal control, the DAA resolved to press on by enlisting 'more suitable European support'.

With a raft of agencies at Wave Hill facing this predicament, *kartiya* had been employed in management roles by the Health and Education departments, the settlement store, its council, housing association and others. The demand for qualified (or just experienced) employees had increased exponentially, and the number of whites at the settlement had ballooned from approximately ten to about fifty, including children—almost a third of the population. Adding to the DAA and Gurindji elders' worries about this was the fact that as the number of *kartiya* increased, their overall professionalism had declined. It seemed an El Dorado for opportunists and no-hopers had opened up on the Gurindji's doorstep.

Rather than reversing these trends, steps were taken that ensured the problem (and the *kartiya*) stayed permanently. On 22 September 1976, 'Libanungu' was gazetted as a township by the Governor-General Sir John Kerr. As Minister Viner explained to Pincher Nyurrmiarri, this meant that the settlement was now officially an open, 'public' town, and both Europeans and Aboriginal people were free to live and do business there. At the same time as the whites' rights within the inequitable local economy were bolstered, the settlement was given a new name: Kalkaringi.[31] Confusingly, the local council retained its old name: Libanungu Council. The government's

---

31 The reason for changing the name of the settlement so soon after its recent 'Aboriginalisation' as 'Libanungu' is unclear. See Patrick McConvell, 'Changing Places: European and Aboriginal Styles', in *The Land is a Map: Placenames of Indigenous Origin in Australia*, ed. by Luise Hercus, Flavia Hodges and Jane Simpson (Canberra, Pandanus Press, 2002), pp. 50–61 (p. 52); Darwin, NAA, 'Extract from the Australian Government Gazette [...]', *Wave Hill Centre: Policy and Development*, E460, 1981/306.

large new school complex at Libanungu (now Kalkaringi), was also officially opened.

The Aborigines struggled with these changes, though none of the *kartiya* at the settlement had any overall plan for the community. Not only that, while 'self-determination' for local Aboriginal people was DAA adviser Richard Preece's aim, there was nothing to guarantee that the staff of other government departments—much less the local shopkeeper—supported the concept. Instead, a growing number of whites at Kalkaringi were disparaging and dismissive towards Aboriginal people. An interdepartmental committee established in Canberra to address these problems—for they had been anticipated three years earlier in Barrie Dexter's Batchelor workshops—had failed to meet. So while the DAA optimistically advocated that Richard Preece 'communicate closely' with Kalkaringi's other whites, instead the young adviser was distracted from his job of empowering Aboriginal residents by a conflict with another powerful *kartiya*, Alan Thorpe.

Since arriving among the Gurindji five years earlier as an activist-supporter, Thorpe had held numerous positions with Libanungu Council and the DAA. Thorpe and Preece had clashed over Thorpe's questionable attempt to 'unify' Daguragu with Kalkaringi and Preece's antipathy had increased when the Englishman improperly— or so Preece believed—took the job of Kalkaringi's shop manager. Since then, according to a number of others, Thorpe had distinguished himself with his maverick approach to running the region's premier commercial outlet. While the store was well-stocked with expensive 'rocking horses, Chanel No. 5 perfume and aftershave lotions', it was often without essential food—not to mention 'mops, buckets, brooms,

and other necessary goods'.[32] It was also soon in significant debt, with an abundance of mostly unsellable Christmas toys on the shelves.

Of far more concern to Preece than what he saw as Thorpe's 'extremely incompetent management' though, was his supposed 'dominance and manipulation' of Libanungu Council—which critics alleged he achieved by marrying an Aboriginal woman.[33] Preece made a failed case for Thorpe's removal, while the performance of both men suffered at the expense of their stoush.

Whatever the substance of the many conflicts between various *kartiya* at Wave Hill, the jobs that self-determination policy afforded them were often superior to those they could get elsewhere. When Thorpe arrived six years earlier, for instance, he was on a bricklayer's wages. As the manager of the store (a role he ostensibly performed on behalf of the Gurindji), he employed six staff and oversaw a $165,000 ($985,000) government loan.

For other European Australians, such opportunities at times provided more incentive to work in an Aboriginal community than any ideals they harboured about empowering its residents. While Thorpe, Preece and other *kartiya* believed they were acting in the Gurindji's best interests, the nature of those interests was debated and at times forgotten. 'Aboriginal self-determination'—loaded as it was with managerial burdens the Gurindji could not, at this stage, hope to shoulder—was beginning to buckle under the Europeanness of its conception.

---

32 Karu Bulangkarni Co. Ltd, the settlement shop's proprietary company, was incorporated in March 1972 so that the Gurindji could legally receive government funds. See Department of Aboriginal Affairs, *Kalkaringi—Book of the Community* (NT Division of the Department of Aboriginal Affairs, 1977, p. 8; Darwin, NAA, 'Community Development Wave Hill [...]', 16 March 1976, and 'Wave Hill Social Club', 21 January 1977, *Community Adviser—Wave Hill*, E460, 1974/1028.
33 NAA, E460, 1974/1028.

A FIGHTING CHANCE, 1976

* * *

At the same time as conflict, incompetence and indifference at Kalkaringi were eroding the DAA's vision for the Gurindji, their errant youth continued to rebel. In the past on Wave Hill station, young men had observed the traditional stockman's lifestyle: binge-drinking once or twice a year after long stints at work in the saddle. Now, according to Jean Culley and others, these binges occurred every week or so at Daguragu and Kalkaringi, and lasted for days.[34] In 1976, this lifestyle was fuelled by a *kartiya* 'grog runner' delivering carloads of booze from the Top Springs hotel after the locals' social security payments were received. Afterwards, 'everyone [would] clear out and leave the place to the drunks'.[35] Patrick McConvell recalls:

> It was very noticeable, the first time that it really happened was in '76. There was a period of three or four months when people came in with grog, and there was a lot of fighting. Quite a number of Mudburra people were living there who had walked off Montejinnie station. I'm not saying Mudburra were responsible for it all, they weren't [...]. Generally people got on, but there was a bit of 'why don't you go back to where you came from?' [...]. People were using axes, really serious stuff, all due to grog.

Vestey's Negri race meeting of August 1976 was marred by violence involving drunk young men from Kalkaringi and Daguragu. After white punters became frightened, 'the Negri'—a highlight on the region's calendar for more than twenty years—was permanently

---

34 'Happy Only When They Are Drunk', *NTN*, 20 August 1975, p. 8; NTAS, Hannah Middleton, Interview Recorded by Charlie Ward November 2009, NTRS 609, BWF 2.
35 Boyd to Atkinson, July 1975, Atkinson Personal Collection.

cancelled. When the young men returned to Kalkaringi, some were involved in another 'bout of drunken brawling and an attempted rape'. According to the incoming DAA adviser, this:

> [...] greatly upset the older men, less for reasons of compassion for the woman involved, but more so for reasons of tribal prohibitions on sexual intercourse [...]. This led to a 'public' flogging at Wattie Creek, where the real source of local authority lies.[36]

Bemoaning that young men 'won't listen to the old fellows now', Pincher Nyurrmiarri saw his interests aligning with the local police: 'I want [...] police and Aboriginal council to work together, steady them down and stop them bringing in the grog'.[37] Grasping for the causes of this growing schism threatening his society, Lingiari felt that the elders' decade-long land rights fight had distracted them from the proper maintenance of their law.[38]

After grappling with such issues for two years, Richard Preece left the Gurindji. He conveyed his thoughts about the inseparable problems of Daguragu and Kalkaringi in a note to Jean Culley: 'Wave Hill is sending me a little closer to insanity every day. I hope the people who originally planned this mess (i.e. Giese and his boys) rot in in hell for it'.[39] If Preece felt he was leaving Wave Hill's new open town and its neighbouring community in a mess, his successor inherited a greater one. While the DAA sought Preece's

---

36 Darwin, NAA, 'Wave Hill [...] Quarterly Report', 31 March 1977, *Community Adviser—Wave Hill*, E460, 1974/1028.
37 Darwin, NAA, Numiari [sic] to Viner, 8 August 1976, E460, 1981/306.
38 Earlier, in the divided calendar year of 'Vestey time', young men had been strictly controlled by white head stockmen during the dry season, and during the 'bush school' and ceremony-rich 'holiday time', they were closely controlled by their elders in accordance with traditional law. Darwin, NAA, 'Wave Hill [...] Quarterly Report', 31 March 1977, E460, 1974/1028.
39 Maiowie to Culley [transcr. Preece], 15 March 1976, Oke Personal Collection.

replacement, a relieving officer—an alcoholic—filled the role, and littered the Department's digs with rubbish and mouldy food. This inebriant's approach to managing a pet was also lax, and on his arrival the newly-appointed adviser John Millhouse found dog shit covering the floors of his home. The resulting stench permeated his new digs and the office below.

Chapter 10

MIXED BLESSINGS, 1977–78

The camp established by the leaders of the Walk-off next to Daguragu waterhole a decade earlier was almost gone. Instead, a community with a 'town' layout, street lighting, and houses connected to both water and power had taken its place. With these novelties—not to mention flush toilets and a host of new consumer gadgets then sweeping the Territory—domesticity became the Gurindji's new frontier. The track mob had never lived in serviced houses before, and unlike whites raised in them from birth, Gurindji parents and children faced them together with little instruction. In the late 70s, the demands of this adaptation peaked—with mixed results, according to Daguragu store manager Bev Andrews:

> [The DAA gave] them these brand-new houses, all lovely paint, dining rooms, lounge suites and everything. Then they'd say 'You have to keep them clean'. Well the Gurindji kept them clean—they used to hose the walls down, and with electricity, you can imagine! They never lived in them. They camped outside, and most of the furniture got used for firewood. Then [the DAA] built them small cottage-type houses, one room places, you know, they liked that.[1]

---

1 Darwin, NTAS, Interview with Bev Andrews, Recorded by Charlie Ward, November 2012, NTRS 3609, BWF 40.

These experiments could be life-threatening. Colin Muir, the Kalkaringi-based electrician from 1975 to 1989, recalled when:

> [...] We shifted a bloke in [to a new house] with his family on a Friday. On the Saturday morning, a fire! Bloody hell, the partition was alight! The place had only just been painted, it was still a bit wet. [...] He had sat beef rib-bones on the griller on the electric stove and switched it on. Of course he didn't know any better—the fat dripped down, and up she went![2]

According to Bev Andrews, the old man was reluctant to leave:

> They were trying to get this old fellow out. You know, 'Get out! You've got to get out! It's going to burn down!'
>
> 'No, no [he said], 'im not cooked yet'. He's standing there, cooking a big rib bone on the flames on top of the [stove]. All the fat was dripping down, but he was [saying] 'No, no, him not cooked yet' [laughs].

Such events were unsurprising—the culinary expertise of Wave Hill's residents had been gained cooking outdoors. For the women, who were also used to washing clothes in cattle troughs, waterholes and coppers, coin-operated washing machines provided similar frustrations.

Lacking any real training, the Gurindji were forced to apply a trial and error approach to basic home activities and the new 'mod-cons' as well. When it came to TV sets, which were just being introduced in the rural NT, the process was costly. Although television signals were broadcast in Katherine and sets were sold there, many Gurindji found their new purchases would not work in Kalkaringi or Daguragu. Colin Muir was often called to fix new televisions suffering for want of a broadcast signal.

---

2   Colin and Maggie Muir, Interview Recorded by Charlie Ward, 24 October 2012. In possession of the author.

A HANDFUL OF SAND

* * *

Leaving such issues behind him, Pincher Nyurrmiarri travelled to Alice Springs for the inauguration of the Central and Northern Land Councils in late January 1977. Fraser's version of Whitlam's *Aboriginal Land Rights (NT) Act* came into effect on Australia Day, but the mood among the land council heavyweights was muted. With *ALRA* becoming law, white Territorians were fearful of an Aboriginal land grab, and acrimony towards the land councils had intensified. Country Liberal Party politicians were warning that the new Act would introduce 'apartheid', and fishermen had threatened a High Court challenge. Attempting to harness this discontent for political purposes, cattleman and NTLA member Sam Calder warned that the Territory would become a 'black state': the goal he attributed to the 'socialists' working for the land councils.[3] In fact, for CLC staff such as Geoff Eames, Wenten Rubuntja, and Rod Hagen, their work was a trial by fire.

In *ngumpit* country, the CLP's efforts to undermine *ALRA* were wasted, and played directly into the hands of Jack Doolan, now a 'pro-Aboriginal' Labor candidate in the upcoming NTLA election. Since assisting the Ngarinyman mob to get established at Yarralin, Doolan, a Korean War veteran, had been drawn into the political brinkmanship over land rights. Incensed by CLP leader Dr Goff Letts' 'complementary' land rights law, which he deemed 'political bastardry of the highest order', Doolan threw his hat in the ring for the Gurindji's seat.[4] While Letts was busy in Darwin and Canberra campaigning against *ALRA* on behalf of his European

---

3   'Calder Warns on Apartheid', *NTN*, 17 March 1977, p. 2.
4   Mark Stanton, 'Wait for Last Vote', *NTN*, 24 August 1977, p. 5.

land-holding constituents, Doolan got 'in a clapped out Toyota, threw [his] swag in the back, and went into Victoria River boots and all'.[5] While rustling up support in the backblocks, he spent two days helping to 'move a stock camp after a mob of cattle broke out of a yard'—time well spent, from Doolan's perspective: 'I probably got a few votes out of it'. Letts was nowhere to be seen.

When the NT Legislative Assembly election of 13 August 1977 was held, the CLP was caught napping and Labor asserted itself as a political power in the north for the first time. The greatest shock was the loss of Letts, the CLP leader, to Doolan—a political cleanskin. The patrol officer's success was due to three things: firstly, he was familiar to the area's Aboriginal people for his work over thirty years; secondly, Whitlam had shown the region's Aborigines that elections—and voting—could affect their lives; and thirdly, *ngumpit* were now convinced that voting ALP would literally pay them better than the conservatives. *Ngumpit* people were not alone in supporting Labor though: other electorates with large Aboriginal populations also punished the CLP. Afterwards, Doolan offered a take-home message: despite the conservatives' strong pastoral base, they had 'badly underestimated the intelligence of the Aboriginal people and their interest in the elections'.[6] Both his ALP colleagues—shocked at their own success—and chastened conservatives agreed.

* * *

Five years after Whitlam's policy turn, self-determination (now 'self-management') was in full swing, though the government was

---

5   Jack Doolan, 'How I Fought Goff Letts', *The Star* [Darwin], 18 August, 1977.
6   David Trounce, 'Doolan Jumps to Poll Lead', *NTN*, 17 August 1977, p. 2.

reluctant to concede control. The role of activist-supporters in mediating the Gurindji's affairs had been taken over by the DAA or consultants such as John Edey. Now, instead of eclectic, self-funded activists railing from Daguragu's 'round house' about Kalkaringi's obstructive officials, DAA advisers oversaw the provision of 'basic hygiene and sanitation services, street cleaning, maintenance of roads, and beautification' there on behalf of Libanungu Council.[7]

The involvement of government agencies had grown, and managing the community created in the Gurindji's name was becoming increasingly complex. Nonetheless, the Muramulla company—the elders' preferred utility—played a role in Daguragu's growth. Surrounded by new lawns and trees, the company's store was the social and economic (not administrative) hub of the community. At night, most of the village turned out for Muramulla's film screenings. Westerns were the most popular with Gurindji audiences, who—despite the 'cowboy' fashion sense of the men—barracked enthusiastically for the 'Indians'. The only distraction on these evenings was the occasional intrusion of a snake.

After a heavy, late monsoon, the Gurindji's cattle fattened and the herd grew to 3,200. This pleased the Muramulla board, but the beasts began trampling through Kalkaringi's streets at night, damaging property and exotic plants. Norm McNair, a recently-arrived language worker, remembers:

> The Droughtmaster bulls lived in town [laughs]. They should have been out among the cattle, but they were living in there! That always struck us as odd. They were very docile, hanging around somebody's tap that might have a bit of green grass around it.[8]

---

7 Department of Aboriginal Affairs, *Daguragu—Book of the Community* (NT Division of the Department of Aboriginal Affairs, 1977, p. 10.
8 Norm and Helen McNair, Interview Recorded by Charlie Ward, March 2010, in possession of the author.

When one of these 750 kilogram beasts fell into a septic sewage tank, a misguided attempt to extract the animal using a rope and a four-wheel drive was launched, destroying the roof of an adjacent house. Another Droughtmaster was 'overfond of vegetation in [his] yard', so a policeman shot it dead.[9] Doolan, the new local member, received complaints about Muramulla's marauding beasts, and he requested that the NTLA 'alleviate the distress caused by the depredations of starving cattle on the luxuriant herbage of the township'.[10] The frustrations of Kalkaringi's gardeners highlighted a more pressing issue: Muramulla was now struggling to meet the government's requirements for 'improvements'—like fencing—on their lease.

In taking a pragmatic approach to its covenants, Muramulla had joined a long tradition of NT pastoralists. In other regards though, real differences were emerging between the Gurindji's operation and those of neighbouring *kartiya*. The overriding priority of European stations was profit for the owners and income for staff; for them, enjoyment of the country was largely a personal matter. In contrast, the Gurindji desired access to their traditional country, the transmission of skills and knowledge to the young, financial independence for Daguragu, and employment and beef for all.[11] The DAA supported these goals in theory, but questions were raised about how they could be achieved. While self-management projects allowed for cultural differences, governments' responsibility to taxpayers did not. Official

---

9   Darwin, NAA, 'Daguragu/Kalkaringi', 20 November 1979, E460, 1981/256; Muir, 2012.
10 Northern Territory, Legislative Assembly, Hon Jack Doolan, *Parliamentary Record–Second Assembly. Part One–the Debates*, 23 November 1977 (Darwin, NTLA Printer, 1978), p. 231.
11 For a full summary of common Aboriginal pastoral aspirations, see Elspeth Young, 'Aboriginal Cattle Stations: Strategies for Self-Management', in *Proceedings of the 17th Inst. Australian Geographic Conference* (Bathurst, NSW, 1981), p. 311.

goodwill was limited, and without the promise of eventual profits from Muramulla, DAA staff acknowledged that the Gurindji men's passion alone was not sufficient grounds to maintain funding.

For Muramulla to keep its government backers happy, the appearance of diligent stewardship was required—encouraging the elders to present themselves as men of financial acumen. Reports like the following were signed by Donald Nangiari and Jerry Rinyngayarri:

> The directors submit the accounts of the company and report as follows: [We have taken] reasonable steps, before the profit and loss statement and balance sheet were made out, to ascertain what action had been taken in relation to the writing off of bad debts and the making of provisions for doubtful debts.[12]

If Muramulla's directors were ever to understand what such statements meant, they would need significant training in business and literacy. Their understanding increased thanks to their meetings with John Edey, who wrote reports for them, but no training was offered.

* * *

While the Gurindji men were engaged with cattle on their traditional land, the DAA continued propping up a range of projects in Kalkaringi and Daguragu. These were unstable and costly affairs, initiated by DAA staff after they solicited 'community support' from a few residents (if a non-committal enthusiasm for the final product—goat meat, say, or child-minding—could rightly be called 'support'). For the DAA, a glimmer of the Gurindji's usual forbearance provided

---

12   Darwin, NAA, 'Muramulla Gurindji Co Pty Ltd—Directors Report', *Cattle Mustering Venture* [...], 1 June 1977, (F1) 1975/4091.

grounds to commission plans and release funding—the Aboriginal 'self-management' policy in action. From this point, waning Aboriginal interest was not seen as sufficient reason to scale back project activity. On the contrary, when support for an enterprise was lacking, DAA advisers would 'get enthusiasm established' among local people. To remedy subsequent disappointments, it was deemed that 'a lack of supervision and direction' were to blame.[13]

Rather than admit that the department had a habit of backing over-ambitious, unpopular failures, officers decided that project 'deterioration'—of Daguragu's market garden, for instance—was caused by *under*funding.[14] Instead of scaling back its support in 1977, the DAA upped the ante. The market garden at Kalkaringi—for the government town now had one too—would concentrate on fruit and vegetables, while its Daguragu competitor would grow and sell decorative plants. Two years later, the department had lost $12,332 ($56,000) on the venture and Kalkaringi's market garden lay abandoned.

Other projects suffered a similar fate. Despite the fact that there was already a 'spasmodically tended' DAA poultry farm at Kalkaringi with four to five hundred birds in 'rather poor condition', more chicken sheds and a new goat enclosure at Daguragu were built. 'The intention'—whose was not named—was 'to keep approximately one or 200 fowls for egg production and to rear goats for milk and possibly meat'.[15] It remained an open question who—if anyone— would take responsibility for these new enterprises at Daguragu: the

---

13   Darwin, NAA, 'Funding of Projects', *Wave Hill—Review of Council Programs and Employment Projects*, E460, 1981/89 Part 2.
14   Darwin, NAA, 'DAA—Application for Funds—Libanungu Council', *Market Garden*, E629, 1977/7/7443.
15   Darwin, NAA, 'Wave Hill [...] Review of Economic Projects', February 1977, *Muramulla Gurindji Cattle Company*, Part 2, E460, 1981/256.

Muramulla Co or the soon-to-be incorporated Daguragu Council. Before the sheds and enclosure were even finished, the DAA learned that selling goat milk was illegal and the idea was aborted.

With DAA projects multiplying and other organisations also leaning on the Gurindji for support and guidance, responsibility fell to a small, strained group of men. Vincent Lingiari's health and eyesight was deteriorating and he had swapped the day-to-day grind of liaison for a strategic, 'statesman'-type role. The old man was now seen as a land rights hero and—after being nominated by Rob Wesley-Smith—had been awarded an Order of Australia 'gong' in Darwin. His fading abilities and his desire to 'retire'—not to mention the attractive 'perks' of council membership—had set the stage for jockeying among his peers. Mick Rangiari, Pincher Nyurrmiarri and Billy Bunter were taking up the load.

For Bunter, the leader with the strongest *kartiya* credentials (though the least ceremonial status, due to his youth and Warlpiri background), the pressure from this work was too much. In early 1977, he resigned from four of his roles, including the presidency of Libanungu Council. The trouble-plagued body was soon to be merged into Daguragu's new council, and older Gurindji power-brokers had painted the Warlpiri man into a corner. Overwork, perceived badmouthing by Alan Thorpe, and the DAA's failure to provide him with a vehicle, despite repeated promises, also forced him to stand down. After the Warlpiri public servant's withdrawal, Mick Inverway, one of his critics, was voted president of Libanungu Council.

This flux among Gurindji leaders was completely eclipsed by the 'hiring and firing' among the whites now at Kalkaringi. Earl Chaffey, Libanungu Council's most recent boss, had 'lost' its outboard

motor, clashed with other *kartiya*, and allegedly pilfered funds. When the possibility of a police investigation was flagged, he began brawling with his wife. John Millhouse, the even-tempered new DAA adviser, was forced to intervene. The son of an adventurous Englishman, Millhouse had a 'way' with people in distress. He'd travelled to the Territory from Adelaide fresh out of school, and seeing the unhappy-looking Aboriginal people on Barkly Tablelands cattle stations, had wanted to contribute. Finding his feet quickly at Wave Hill, Millhouse assisted the Gurindji council board to sack their disgraced municipal officer. Chaffey left the community soon afterwards.

On 4 March 1977, the Gurindji council dismissed their bookkeeper and a mechanic as well. Having now been through four white mechanics, four bookkeepers and four municipal officers in ten months, Libanungu Council had almost self-destructed prior to being decommissioned. 'Naturally enough', DAA officer J. Leggatt conceded, among Aboriginal staff:

> [...] this lack of continuity [...] has caused a poor record for the council in work attitudes. It has meant almost total disregard for council vehicles and machinery and an almost total disrespect for staff members [...].[16]

The DAA now recognised that a 'robber workforce' of whites plagued the region. The pattern they perceived was familiar: after contractors arrived in the community, they manipulated Aboriginal people for more powerful jobs by bribing them with alcohol or other gifts. Although adviser John Millhouse saw Libanungu Council's growing ability to eject such under-achievers as a 'significant step'

---

16 Darwin, NAA, 'Review—Wave Hill/Wattie Creek', 5–10 March 1977, E460, 1981/89, Part 2.

towards Gurindji independence, the DAA paid little attention to the fact that it was usually the department itself that organised, or at least signed off on, the 'robbers'' employment. Instead of admitting its own culpability, at one meeting the DAA's Katherine boss John Rutter gave the Gurindji recruitment advice:

> The community is only as strong as the people you employ to help [...]. Don't employ someone who is a nice bloke and will give you a beer. You have had such a bad mob (of staff), now you are about the only [councils that] don't have their own books.[17]

This would have stung the Gurindji leaders, whose clear goal was to keep their own accounts. In 1977, the 'books' of both Wave Hill's councils were managed by their government-appointed accountants in Darwin.

From the DAA's perspective, such problems would be better solved when Libanungu Council at Kalkaringi merged with Daguragu's new council. John Millhouse was of the opinion that:

> [...] significant decisions affecting the future of the area are made in the main by Aboriginals living at Wattie Creek. [Libanungu] Council will not comment on matters of importance until they have conferred with the Wattie Creek community.[18]

The merger would only be accepted if Daguragu's elders endorsed it, Millhouse thought, and 'the seat of power' remained there.

Local leaders held their first combined council meeting at Daguragu on 1 November 1977. Sixteen councillors and five officials were present. Of the Gurindji elders, Muramulla director Donald Nangiari spoke first:

---

17   Darwin, NAA, 'Minutes—Daguragu/Libanungu [...]', 15 February 1978, *Wave Hill Community Development*, E460, 1978/242.
18   Darwin, NAA, 'Community Associations Wave Hill [...]', 13 August 1977, E460, 1981/89, Part 2.

> We had two councils separate—Daguragu and Libanungu. Much better to have one council [...]. This way we will help each other [and] have one bookkeeper [...]. We want you young people trained, run our place and [get] more money to build up our country. [Soon] everything have to go through council or committee, not the white people.

Billy Bunter had returned to form, and continued:

> All this has been going for a long time now, thinking about when the council get together. It's the time now. This way everything could work, live in peace together. Vincent is getting old [...]. I think everything all sort out now, to have one council.[19]

Contrary to the long-held fear of Hardy and other activists that government efforts to unite the two communities were driven by a desire to bring Daguragu 'under control', by the time Kalkaringi's residents and the track mob were politically unified *at Daguragu*, the DAA merely wished to 'rationalise and recognise the existing [Aboriginal] decision-making process'.[20] In February 1978, John Millhouse happily reported 'the two councils [are] uniting [...]. Daguragu are assuming full control of the township'.[21] For a brief moment, the old strike leaders and their government intermediaries saw eye-to-eye.

Vincent Lingiari was symbolically appointed president of the new united council for a brief period before his son Victor took up the role. Other Daguragu elders were elected. With Daguragu Council bolstering their tribal authority at home and in Kalkaringi, they asserted themselves. 'Strong talk' became common, and white fellas

---

19 Darwin, NAA, 'Wattie Creek Meeting [...]', 1 November 1977, E460, 1978/242.
20 Darwin, NAA, E460, 1981/89 Part 2.
21 Darwin, NAA, 'Project Review Visit [...]', February 1978, *Community Adviser—Wave Hill*, E460, 1974/1028.

were warned to lift their game. Stan Andrews' conduct in his Muramulla job was questioned and the autocratic style of his wife Bev at the Daguragu store was also noted. The Kalkaringi shop committee (which was mostly the same Daguragu-based group as the new council) confronted Alan Thorpe in a two-day meeting over what they saw as his unaccountable management.

A new, hard-line attitude prevailed among the leaders, and several young trouble-makers were banished. At Daguragu Council's early meetings, the board hammered home their expectations and the standards they required of staff. Councillor Banto captured the new attitude: 'We have a council here now, and a policeman'.[22] Drinking at Daguragu would not be tolerated, the elders explained, and workers had to better manage their finances. The misuse of work vehicles—so common at Libanungu Council—was also to cease. The old Gurindji men had a reputation for severity, so these were not idle threats. The NT Children's Court had been told that teenagers at Wave Hill who broke the law were 'shaved bald, bashed unconscious with stones and then "bushed" by elders for some weeks'.[23]

To support the elders' new council, an office was built at Daguragu. As with the previous body at Kalkaringi though, its board—who had barely *seen* local government, much less had training in it—still required *kartiya* guidance. That such whites were required at Wattie Creek but were unwelcome to live there highlighted the elders' continued, unwanted, dependence. This state of play mirrored that on many communities, and privately the DAA acknowledged that full

---

22 Darwin, NAA, 'Minutes—Community Meeting [...]', 1 March 1978, E460, 1974/1028.
23 Elaine Reeves, 'Law Reformers at Work—Turning White Into Black', *National Times*, 4–9 July 1978, p. 18.

Aboriginal self-management remained a pipedream. The DAA's Alice Springs boss Bob Huey wrote:

> Frankly, the Department is kidding itself if it thinks that Aboriginals are effectively or meaningfully involved in the day-to-day management of their affairs'.[24]

The elders recognised that their own plan of a Gurindji-run homeland was languishing, and placed more pressure on their young men to step up. In an early meeting of the new council, Donald Nangiari warned:

> We old people are just about gone. You mob have to start picking it up. You people have elected this council. It's all under Daguragu, you all understand that. You know that foreman, leading hand. He's your boss.[25]

As Nangiari saw it, the need for a transition of power—as well as the creation of a class of young Gurindji administrators—was urgent.

* * *

The DAA's creation of a Gurindji local government council at Daguragu was as far as the state would ever go towards assisting the elders to run their own society. The parameters—and fate—of 'Gurindji self-determination' would be intimately linked to this body's fortunes for the next thirty years. Despite the elders' hopes, the problems that had plagued the old Libanungu body persisted. Casting the net wide to fill the board empowered competitive and

---

24 AIATSIS, Jeremy Long Papers, Huey [Central Regional Director] to Long [Deputy Secretary], 14 August 1976, *De-volution*, MS 2534, Box 6, Folder 59.
25 See Darwin, NAA, 'Minutes—Community Meeting [...]', 1 March 1978, E460, 1974/1028.

inexperienced mid-rankers in the Gurindji hierarchy, alongside reliable elders. While Lingiari's coterie *did* plan to crack down on the behaviour of staff and residents, they were less able to control the use of council assets and work time than they had imagined.

In Daguragu Council's first year, officials recorded a litany of misdemeanours, indiscretions and oversights. Hearing the *kartiyas'* repetitive mantra 'you have your own council now', and being largely unaware of the differences between private and community interests (or 'work' and 'personal' time) guiding politicians elsewhere, 'severe faction fighting' over resources broke out between councillors. Following enquiries, DAA officer Neil Westbury found:

> Two council trucks are unaccounted for—apparently on a trip somewhere near Alice Springs [...]. Notorious characters, namely Mick Inverway, Banto Banto and Wonga Bill [have been] jockeying for positions of influence and using council trucks for their own purposes such as visiting promised wives, exhibiting promised wives, grog runs to Top Springs, and various other jaunts.[26]

Even councillor Wonga Bill—himself the subject of allegations about vehicle misuse—claimed that council vehicles were being used to ferry grog illegally into the communities.

Westbury was unimpressed by the negligible work efforts of the council's staff and board, 'except when it came to being paid'. In a bid to get more 'bang for their buck' from the new council, the DAA reduced its payroll by 25 percent in September 1978. By now, officers believed that Daguragu Council's indulgent style had significantly set back Aboriginal self-management at Wave Hill.[27]

---

26 See Darwin, NAA, Westbury to Casey [DAA], 'Daguragu Council', 14 December 1978, *Wave Hill Community Development*, E460, 1978/242.

27 John Edey agreed, believing that the Muramulla company could only employ hard-working staff due to its limited funding, yet the council was overly tolerant of

How, they wondered, could the other major employers, Muramulla and Wundamarie Housing, force more work from their staff, when the Gurindji's own council was so lax? For their part, the elders felt that if they were required to force greater exertions from their staff, other organisations should do the same.

If Gurindji councillors were to gain the knowledge required to deliver local government, their best chance might have been to learn from some of their European staff. Yet had it been thoroughly attempted, this approach would have had its own serious problems. Few of the Gurindji's white employees were skilled administrators, and the problem of lazy and corrupt *kartiya* had worsened. The brazen thieving of government and council property by Europeans employed to 'help' the Wave Hill communities now dwarfed the indiscretions of Gurindji people. After Fraser's first austerity budget in 1976, poorly-monitored government largesse could be freely exploited. Earlier, under Earl Chaffey's watch over Libanungu Council, an outboard motor had disappeared. Now a large DAA barge used to cross Wattie Creek during the wet season vanished. The pontoon was later seen 700 kilometres away, ferrying supplies across the Roper River. By similar means, DAA-purchased kit homes and new, imperfect four wheel drives were profitably disposed of by *kartiya* contractors and council staff. With such dubious exemplars of professionalism leading Gurindji work crews, Daguragu Council's young president Victor Vincent had good reason to feel overwhelmed. According to Neil Westbury, Lingiari's son took 'a low profile and considers the problems of the council workforce [...] a burden he could well do without'.[28]

---

underperforming workers. Darwin, NAA, 'Muramulla Gurindji Co P/L Report [...]', 14 August 1978, *Muramulla Gurindji Cattle Company Part 2*, E460, 1981/256.

28   See Darwin, NAA, Westbury to Casey (DAA) 'Daguragu Council', 14 December 1978, E460, 1978/242.

A HANDFUL OF SAND

* * *

Despite Vincent Lingiari's plea for assistance with grog issues during the lease handover at Daguragu, excessive drinking continued to plague his children's generation. According to Norm McNair, a language field worker who arrived with his wife Helen in 1977:

> It was pretty deeply entrenched, you could see the pattern. The welfare cheques would come in, gambling rings would set up. [People would] go up to Katherine, get a car and ferry grog in. You'd be aware of the car coming in and within twenty minutes the town would be in uproar. [...] Eventually the cops would come in [...], take a few [people] away, lock them up [and] it would all calm down.[29]

Due to Kalkaringi's 'open town' status, the police were little able to restrict boozing there. Instead, when trouble flared, Daguragu's new councillors stepped in. According to John Millhouse:

> Most of the middle-aged men from Wattie Creek turn out to keep the peace. [...] The leaders of the community, and to a lesser extent men from the township, accept joint responsibility for these matters.[30]

As if to bring home the fact that the Gurindji could not escape the alcohol problem at Daguragu, the body of a resident, 'Young Colin', was found floating in Wattie Creek after a drunken dust-up. By now Gurindji drinkers had given alcohol a name of their own—*ngawa*, meaning water.

In grieving the grog-related deaths of their young, Kalkaringi and Daguragu's residents were not alone. The extreme effects of

---

29   McNair and McNair, 2010.
30   Darwin, NAA, 'Situation Report [...]', 6 March 1978, E460, 1974/1028.

alcohol on Aboriginal communities were the focus of a national enquiry. What made the Gurindji's situation different—in the eyes of others, at least—was their status as leaders of the national land rights battle. Whether or not their elders were aware of it, binge-drinking by young Gurindji was becoming a source of sorrow and disappointment for many of their *kartiya* friends. But because ideals of Aboriginal independence and cultural integrity were central to working in the spread of organisations established by Whitlam, Aboriginal hiccups, obstacles and outright failures were rarely acknowledged. Not only were well-meaning *kartiya* reluctant to speak critically of their Aboriginal friends, in many cases doing so would reflect badly on the whites' own work promoting Aboriginal self-determination. While Vincent Lingiari sought to publicise his people's struggles with grog in a bid to get help, the director of the national Aboriginal research centre AIATSIS omitted the problem at Wave Hill from its publications on the Gurindji.[31] Their 'duty to succeed' was keenly felt.

One enticement for 'Young Colin' and his friends to drink was the fact that it signalled their rejection of the old people's values, but some Gurindji elders also enjoyed a tipple. Libanungu Council's outgoing president Mick Inverway, or 'Yanna', was criticised for his lax approach on the issue.[32] Everyone, old and young alike, was forced to take a stance on the *kartiyas*' poison. The DAA and whiteman's law had proved next to useless in stopping it, but many Gurindji

---

31 Darwin, NTAS, Interview with Patrick McConvell Recorded by Charlie Ward, November 2009, NTRS 3609, BWF 5.

32 Mick Rangiari claimed that due to Inverway's drinking, he was later removed from the Muramulla board of directors. NTAS, Mick Rangiari Interview Transcript, October 1986, NTRS 226, TS 485, (T4), p. 33; NTAS, Wesley-Smith, NTRS 3609, BWF 15; Darwin, NAA, 'Daguragu Community Quarterly Report', 30 March 1977, E460, 1974/1028.

turned to another recently-introduced artefact of *kartiya* culture to help them in the fight against grog: Christianity.

* * *

By the time Lingiari welcomed Baptist Minister Jim Kime to the Aboriginal people's camp on Wave Hill station in 1964, his people had been exposed to travelling missionaries at the Negri races for years. The new religion was very popular among the Gurindji. Indeed, in the early 1970s Lingiari told Rev Graham Paulson that 'he had felt led by God, independent of any white missionary influence, to initiate the [Wave Hill walk-off]'.[33] Later, after Rev Paulson took up residence at Kalkaringi in 1970, he baptised twenty-five Gurindji—including Lingiari and Mick Rangiari—in Wattie Creek. Church services at Kalkaringi were well-attended; local Clancy Banganna became a Baptist 'brother', and Peter Gilgi led the hymn-singing. Lingiari's son Victor Vincent was among the younger generation to join the congregation, and the old man himself lobbied for a church to be built at Daguragu. Before Captain Major Lupngiari succumbed to senility, he ended his letters with an endearing 'God bless you and good bye'.

While Kalkaringi's live-in Baptist missionaries like Paulson and Gordon and Gwen Moore sought to create more Aboriginal Christians, some Gurindji leaders adapted the missionaries' teetotaller doctrine for their own purposes, and received the church's teachings on abstinence and 'moral living' gladly. In 1977–78, the Moores devised a range of measures with Gurindji elders to stop

---

[33] Paulson, cited at: <http://marcuscurnow.wordpress.com/2011/04/01/on-beer-living-water-lent-3-john-41-42/>. Accessed 11 February 2014.

local men (and women, though fewer of them drank) from boozing and gambling their money away. To prevent popular 'grog runs' to the pub at Top Springs, for instance, the elders directed the Kalkaringi store to sell only ten litres of fuel to each person on pay days—not enough to drive to 'Toppy'. Locals overcame these good intentions by siphoning their fuel into one car. With similar hopes, Muramulla company wages were paid only by cheque, and Gwen Moore, then the local Commonwealth Bank agent, issued only five and ten dollar notes to prevent excessive gambling.

Gurindji leaders looked to their own culture to resist the blight of grog as well. Pincher Nyurrmiarri thought that—like in earlier times—expelling young trouble-makers to an isolated bush camp would inspire their compliance:

> I want those Aborigines to get away from the settlement so council men can look after them, because a few of them are causing a lot of trouble [...]. Sometimes they throw stones and break glass when they have a drink. [...] I'm crooked on these Aborigines, my people, who make it bad for we old people.[34]

After complaints from Kalkaringi's nurse and mechanic about losing sleep to noisy drinkers, local councillors 'bushed' the trouble-makers on a truck and sent Warlpiri miscreants to Lajamanu to be punished by their own elders. Despite these efforts, no-one was protected from the strife: Vincent Lingiari's son Peter was arrested while drunk and sent to Fannie Bay gaol in Darwin. After he was released and failed to return home, the worried Gurindji leader asked for help from his *kartiya* friends to find his son.[35]

---

34   Darwin, NAA, Numiari [sic] to Viner, 8 August 1976, *Wave Hill Centre: Policy and Development*, E460, 1981/306.
35   Lingiari to Neilley, Undated [though early 1977], Wesley-Smith Personal Collection.

Desperate for a remedy, Lingiari and the other elders agreed to a proposition put to them by the DAA: the only way to reduce the harm from drinking was by controlling the supply themselves. Wet canteens were foremost among the government's 'solutions' to Aboriginal problem-drinking in communities, and pressure was placed on the old men to accept a licensed club at Kalkaringi.[36] The idea that the club would mostly cater to tourists—and generate income for the council—was used as a sweetener, but it still took the elders months to agree to a public bar on their doorstep. Eventually, Lingiari emphasised the benefit of the canteen's proposed location next to the police station, where any trouble would be controlled by police. Jerry Rinyngayarri summarised: '[...] We want to work it out ourselves, all Aboriginal men, and all the council going to be there to keep an eye on them [drinkers] and what they do. We want to know properly.' The Gurindji elders had acquiesced: the white man's grog was with them to stay. All they could do was try to moderate the damage it caused.

* * *

With the problems of booze assailing the Gurindji, in 1978 lawmakers in Canberra and Darwin created a significant agreement—'over a bottle of Scotch at the Lodge', according to one wag.[37] The anodyne-sounding *Northern Territory (Self-government) Act* reset the terms of the Gurindji's struggle, and that of Aboriginal self-

---

36 This is inferred from a transcription of a detailed discussion between the Gurindji leaders. Darwin, NAA, 'Wattie Creek Meeting [...]', 1 November 1977, *Wave Hill Community Development*, E460, 1978/242.

37 John Reeves, 'Territory-Canberra Relations: The Past, Present and Future', *Northern Perspective*, Vol. 8, No. 1 (1985), 27–33, p. 29.

management in the Territory, entirely. Although the Legislative Assembly in Darwin already made 'laws for the peace, order and good government of the Territory', after a long campaign it became a government in its own right on 1 July 1978. Darwin's state-type powers—including over Aboriginal people—expanded massively.

Under the terms of 'self-government', NT authorities would be required to 'pay due regard to Aboriginal views, needs and circumstances', but what this meant in practice was not defined. Complicating matters was the fact that while the DAA had been busily attempting to 'devolve' power to Aboriginal people under self-management policy, its federal masters were now also 'devolving' critical responsibilities in remote communities to the new Northern Territory Government. Hence on 1 July 1978 Canberra handed over some of its responsibilities at Wave Hill to Daguragu Council— and many more to the Gurindji's old Country Liberal Party adversaries in the NTLA in Darwin. Due to the CLP's hardnosed bargaining, responsibility for Aboriginal councils, schooling, health, infrastructure and housing were later transferred to the NTG as well. The DAA was sidelined and the Gurindji's interface with government splintered.[38] Daguragu Council, like others, had no say in these matters.

Although there was much fanfare and flag-raising to celebrate Territory independence, angry protests occurred at the NTG's first sitting and a vindictive mood infected both sides of the chamber. If the commonly-respected Dr Goff Letts had still been at the helm,

---

38 Bureaucrats recognised that due to the transfer of education to its own department, 'a fragmentation of support' for Aboriginal people had resulted. Darwin, NAA, 'Draft Policy Statements: Health and Education', *Review of Policy Statements— DAA*, E460, 1982/120.

decorum might have prevailed.[39] As it was, after his loss to Jack Doolan, Letts had been replaced by a brash 35-year old lawyer named Paul Everingham—now Chief Minister of the NT.

On coming to office, Everingham—whose Alice Springs law firm had done conveyancing on the Gurindji's lease—proclaimed himself tired of Canberra's 'hit and miss' policies for Aboriginal people. The first Australians weren't, he thought, 'just going to pull themselves up by their boot straps on land rights alone, [but need] other vehicles for self-expression'.[40] The new CLP government hence supported the notion of Aboriginal self-management, but not at the expense of the land-rich pastoralists who sustained the party. Instead of endorsing Aboriginal land rights, then, the new NTG acted on other fronts, trying to improve relationships between Aboriginal people and the police and establishing a liquor commission to reduce the supply of alcohol to communities.

For the 'track mob' at Wave Hill, Everingham's agenda held some potential—they immediately applied to have both Kalkaringi and Daguragu turned into 'dry' communities, for example—but with this second layer of government, the Gurindji now had two taskmasters. Worse, Canberra and Darwin seemed permanently at odds. Dealing with the shiftable agendas of *one* government and its many departments had already stretched them. Realising the elders' dream had just become immeasurably harder.

---

39 Robyn Smith, 'An Inauspicious Beginning: The First Sitting of the Northern Territory Legislative Assembly Following Self-Government in 1978', *Journal of Northern Territory History*, No. 19, (2008) 50–59.
40 NTLA, Hon. Paul Everingham, *Hansard: Second Assembly—Second Session, Part One—the Debates*, 14 September 1978 (Darwin, NTLC Printer, 1979), p. 169.

Part Three

The Harder Road 1979–86

Chapter 11

'A FRAGMENTATION OF SUPPORT', 1979-80

> 'People always regale me with [...] horrific stories about [Aboriginal] pastoral properties, and I'm usually at a loss to know how to deal with it'.[1]
>
> Minister for Aboriginal Affairs Ian Viner

Since the old stockmen started their Muramulla cattle company with southern students in 1970, whites in the industry had been cynical. By the decade's close, there were about twenty Aboriginal-run cattle stations scattered across the Territory, and black pastoralism had found its most outspoken critic: the first Chief Minister of the NT. Live on radio, Paul Everingham described Aboriginal stations as 'running sores and harbours of disease' blotting the landscape.[2] Gurindji elders were alarmed by Everingham's hostility. After seven years of bipartisan support, official opposition to their cattle operation was growing. Worse, courtesy of self-government, Everingham was now the new 'landlord' of the Gurindji's lease.

---

1   Darwin, NAA, Lovegrove to Ford [DAA], 6 November 1978, *Muramulla Gurindji Cattle Company Part 2*, E460, 1981/256.
2   'Everingham and Aboriginal Pastoral Leases', *Central Australian Land Rights News*, No. 11, December 1979 (Alice Springs, Australia, Central Land Council).

Although the Chief Minister publicly declared that 'without land rights, self-management and self-sufficiency for Aboriginals are merely empty phrases', the new NTG revealed its agenda when it massively increased the developable area around Territory towns. While Everingham claimed the rezoning was to provide for a growing population, observers believed it also prevented areas near white settlement being taken by Aboriginal people under the *Land Rights Act*. Some saw it as a declaration—if not of war, than of the NTG's intention to quash the Aborigines' reclamation of their country.

Having noted former County Liberals' leader Goff Letts' plans to refuse them land rights over 99 percent of their lease, Gurindji people were now anxious to have their claim heard quickly under the *Land Rights Act*, like other Aboriginal groups. When Whitlam had handed over their lease four years earlier, the ALP (and later Minister Viner) had promised this was imminent. The Central Land Council's Geoff Eames had discussed a Gurindji claim with John Edey when *ALRA* became law two years earlier, but the CLC had then focused elsewhere, leaving the track mob languishing. Now the Gurindji were agitated by the manoeuvring of the Territory Government, the CLC lodged their claim application on 26 February 1979. They remained vulnerable until it was heard.

Seven months later, the elders' fears were realised. The NT Minister for Lands Marshall Perron sent a warning to the Muramulla company on 1 October 1979. In part, the Minister's letter read:

> [...] the NT of Australia intend after twenty eight days of the giving of this notice to you to forfeit the above lease due to your failure to comply with the conditions of the above lease.[3]

---

3   'Leases "Warning" Claim Denied', *NTN*, 30 October 1979.

According to the Minister, the Gurindji had failed to meet their lease requirements under the *Crown Lands Act*, and would hence be forced to give up their land—unless they could show 'due cause'.

When news of the NTG's intimidation became known—one of thirty-nine identical letters, Perron claimed—it was condemned by federal politicians, the Central Land Council, and the Muramulla company itself.[4] Perron's threat was unprecedented. Because the Gurindji had received no prior warning, and giving 'due notice' in writing was the third—not the first—measure stipulated by the *Crown Lands Act*, the Central Land Council accused Minister Perron of breaching the very Act he was attempting to enforce.[5] Neville Perkins, the NT Labor deputy leader, likewise saw Perron's letter as a forfeiture notice, designed to undermine the security of all Aboriginal pastoral groups.

The Gurindji were perhaps most shocked of all. When asked about Muramulla's most recent hurdle, Mick Rangiari replied 'Them government mob no good, they never want Gurindji people to be happy at Daguragu'.[6] According to MLA Jack Doolan, the elders felt 'betrayed'. They had good reason: Ministers of the Whitlam and Fraser Governments had told them, both in person and writing, that they could never lose their land.

---

4   As far as I can ascertain, no other stations acknowledged receiving one of Perron's letters.
5   Sixty to seventy percent of the NT's cattle stations were in breach of their covenants at the time, though in decades of monitoring by the Commonwealth, none had ever been threatened with eviction. See Edward Ling, 'Blame and Martyrs: The Commonwealth Government's Administration of the Northern Territory's Pastoral Industry, 1911–1978' (Unpublished PhD Thesis, Charles Darwin University, 2010), pp. 231, 382.
6   Tina Jowett, 'Walking to Wattie Creek: the History of the Gurindji People and Their Struggle for Land Rights' (BA Honours Thesis, Sydney, University of New South Wales, 1990), p. 97.

When Muramulla responded to the NTG's attack, the possibility that the company's past funding had been insufficient to meet its covenants was unknown to the Gurindji or their *kartiya* staff. Instead of crying poor, John Edey argued that Muramulla had already met most of the allegedly-breached covenants, and that the rest should be waived on technical grounds. Swayed by public pressure, Minister Perron relented, saying his letter had merely been a 'warning', and the Gurindji's deadline for compliance would be extended. Unimpressed and offended by the whole affair, leaders at Daguragu and Yarralin announced that the NTG's representatives were no longer welcome on *ngumpit* country. The start of the 'marriage' between the Gurindji and their new political masters could not have been worse.

Ironically, throughout this 'forfeiture' stoush, the Muramulla company had been performing better than ever. The annual turnoff of cattle bearing the 'GDT' brand had risen by 400 percent in a few years, and Katherine's meatworks were paying good prices as the market recovered from its slump in the mid-1970s. Muramulla's store was now also riding high: according to Edey, 'the Gurindji viewed the shop at Daguragu with considerable pride and [...] there have been significant social benefits, in addition to the successful direct involvement of Judith Donald'.[7] Turnover of $100,000 ($460,000) a year was expected.

Despite Muramulla's progress, its shop returns and cattle income barely amounted to ten percent of the funding it received. The DAA had been tasked with turning this dependence around, and with pressure growing on John Edey, he in turn leant on the Gurindji elders to employ fewer men and modernise their operation. In 1979,

---

7   Darwin, NAA, 'Edey to Kimmings [DAA]', 7 March 1978, *Muramulla Gurindji Cattle Company Part 2*, E460, 1981/256.

he got his way. Instead of mustering on horseback, helicopters and a light aircraft were used. Unsurprisingly, the Gurindji's semi-wild stock were spooked, and twenty head of cattle died. The disaster confirmed the old men's prejudice. Horseback mustering was central to their love of cattle work, requiring terrific skill, being on country, and imparting knowledge to their nephews and sons. Although Edey and other *kartiya* repeatedly told the board that their time-consuming, collective approach was economically unviable, the elders vowed their company would never muster by plane again.

While the Muramulla board clung to old-school cattle work, change was being forced on them in other ways. In 1978, their head stockman and senior lawman, Long Johnny Kijngayari, died of cancer, and Jerry Rinyngayarri—a newly-licensed driver—was appointed to replace him.[8] Two of Muramulla's key *kartiya*, Stan and Bev Andrews, left Wave Hill as well. With Andrews' position as cattle adviser suddenly vacant, John Edey's workload increased dramatically, and he lobbied the Department to fill the role quickly. The board did not want Andrews to be replaced, but the DAA still questioned the old men's ability to manage Muramulla unaided. DAA staff believed that without a 'motivating' adviser, the Aboriginal people on Muramulla's payroll (besides the young women in the company store) did little work. Trevor LaBrooy reported in Darwin that 'Donald and all others, including Victor Vincent, are adamant that they do not require a resident European adviser/manager', but Andrews' role was filled anyway.[9]

---

8   Kijngayari was not the first of the Wattie Creek and Muramulla leaders to pass away: Lupgngiari ('Captain Major') had died shortly before; and the man who had conceptualised the establishment of a Gurindji homeland at Daguragu, Sandy Moray (Tipujurn), apparently died prior to 1971.

9   Darwin, NAA, 'Social Review Report [...]', *Wave Hill—Review of Council Programs and Employment Projects*, E460, 1981/89 Part 2.

Officials sought to blunt the old men's anger by appointing Bill Purdie, who the elders knew, and his wife Glenda. Purdie had been brought up on Wave Hill station and his family had a long association with the Gurindji. When the couple arrived in March 1980, Glenda took on the book-work of the Muramulla store. Almost immediately though, the company was forced to contend with another death—this time of John Edey, their consultant. Like many bush pilots, Edey had been both highly skilled and cavalier. On one occasion he flew in to Wave Hill after dark—an illegal and dangerous act on the unlit Kalkaringi airstrip. Taking pains not to disturb the local policeman, he mastered a nearly silent, vertical 'corkscrew' descent, landing on the night-blackened runway, terrifying his passenger. The dedicated agronomist believed strongly in the work he was doing with the Gurindji, but his luck ran out in June 1980 when he crashed his plane near Balgo, Western Australia, and was killed.

With Edey—the lynchpin of the Muramulla operation, from the DAA's perspective—gone, the bureaucracy's recruiting headache began again. Departmental officers asked the Gurindji for their views. The old men had by now conceded to the inevitability, or to their need, for a literate consultant, and nominated the department's own Trevor LaBrooy for the role. It transpired though that under the rules of self-government, the NT Department of Primary Production (DPP) had the deciding vote.

* * *

It was in this uncertain environment that the Muramulla men were blindsided by another government challenge. In addition to complying with the NTG's lease covenants—which Everingham

had now shown were to be taken with the utmost seriousness—a nation-wide Brucellosis and Tuberculosis Eradication Campaign (BTEC) arrived at Wave Hill. BTEC would raise the 'bar' the state demanded of Muramulla far higher: to a height, in fact, which the elders would never reach.

First implemented on Tasmania's southern tip, before moving north through the 1970s, BTEC was a land-management revolution dressed as an animal health initiative. Under its terms, every cattle-owner in the nation was required to capture and test every beast on their land, kill any infected animals, and build as much fencing as needed to keep their herd permanently 'behind wire'. This in turn meant smaller paddocks, more watering points for cattle and greater ease of monitoring for landholders. Government assistance was provided, but in the north, where properties were so large some lacked a boundary fence and thousands of cattle wandered free, the logistics of the campaign were barely imaginable. When BTEC arrived at Wave Hill in 1979–80, experts regarded it as 'the most significant impact on the industry since World War II'. The impact was expected to include the destruction of the black pastoral sector.[10]

For the DAA and the cattle operations it funded, BTEC's timing could hardly have been worse. After being robustly criticised for its cattle projects during the 1970s, the DAA was hiving them off to the new, federal, business-oriented Aboriginal Development Commission. The ADC took responsibility for Muramulla from the DAA on 30 April 1980—exactly when BTEC hit Wave Hill. Bovine diseases were barely on the radar of either agency. Lacking expertise,

---

10 David Hanlon and Stuart Phillpot, 'Rural Development Skills: Can we meet the Challenge?', *Vol. 2, Working Papers* (Report Prepared for Department of Employment, Education and Training by RCS Hassall, 1993), p. 28.

both were forced to turn to the NT Government's Department of Primary Production—with which relations were minimal at best. The demands the DPP placed on Daguragu's elders were enormous, and caught them completely by surprise. BTEC would dominate their work for several years.

* * *

At the same time, with the burden of booze having afflicted parts of the Gurindji's society for almost a decade, the fabric of the elders' cultural and ceremonial life was changing radically. Kalkaringi leader Mick Inverway ('Yanna'), was struck by the magnitude of what was happening. When the old law man saw Lyn Riddett at the Mudburra people's Yingawunarri (Old Top Springs) land claim hearing in 1979, he told her that:

> This year when we put the young men in the business, I had to get my son Richard cut [initiated]. I had to find someone a long way away—there were no Gurindji with enough law to cut my son.
>
> 'Why?' Lyn asked.
>
> 'Cos people are dying of the grog'.[11]

The deaths of so many men had made it impossible to continue initiations in the traditional manner. To fill the roles of deceased Gurindji, Yanna and other senior leaders were now forced to 'promote' novitiates to unearned ceremonial positions—or recruit men of the right standing from elsewhere.

---

11   NTAS, Lyn Riddett, Interview Recorded by Charlie Ward, November 2009, NTRS 3609, BWF 3.

'A FRAGMENTATION OF SUPPORT', 1979–80

When people 'died cos of grog', it was mostly in drunken car accidents. Vehicles made the elders' ritual life easier to carry out, but due to taboos about death and not approaching areas where people had died, the impact of alcohol on the Gurindji's ceremonies was further compounded. According to Yanna:

> Too many young people are dying and we can't drive [where that's happened], and if we want to carry business [sacred ceremonial objects], we can't—there's too many dead people on these roads.

The local DAA area officer was now so used to fatalities he no longer recorded all the details. 'Two deaths occurred last weekend in a car accident involving men returning from a binge at Top Springs': enough apparently said.[12]

Despite the direct impact of alcohol-caused deaths on traditional culture, the elders could still use their authority to intimidate troublemakers. According to DAA adviser John Millhouse:

> It is only when ceremonial business is likely to be disrupted that the community seems to be able to take action [against grog]. This has resulted on some occasions in council stopping cars [...] and destroying any alcohol found therein. The connection with 'business' seems to give the councillors immunity from criticism aimed at them by irate relatives.[13]

After drunks assaulted the local policeman and attacked two nurses, Daguragu Council requested for a second policeman to be stationed at Kalkaringi, and also employed a Gurindji 'keeper of the peace' to deal with troublemakers. Banjo Long, the first 'peacekeeper', was

---

12 Darwin, NAA, 'Westbury to Casey', 19 July 1979, *Wave Hill—Review of Projects, Part 2*, E460, 1981/89.
13 See Darwin, NAA, 'Current Situation [...]', 26 February 1979, *Wave Hill Community Development*, E460, 1978/242.

quite intimidating and '[took] his duties very seriously'.¹⁴ These were only stopgap measures though: Daguragu Council was pinning its hopes on the new NTG Liquor Commission to make Kalkaringi and Daguragu 'dry' communities, and halt the sale of take-away spirits and wine at Top Springs. The Commission decided to officially endorse the elders' ban on grog at Daguragu, but it capitulated to *kartiya* drinkers at Kalkaringi. Rather than making the town 'dry' as the elders wished, the Liquor Commission gave Daguragu Council the power to issue (and refuse) drinking permits to Kalkaringi's residents.

The Commission's changes were quickly proved useless. Aboriginal drinkers decided that the penalties of *kartiya* law for breaching the Liquor Act—fines or even gaol—were a risk worth running. Recognising that 'cheap wines are still being regularly imported [to Kalkaringi] with apparent impunity', DAA officials predicted that 'the tribal fighting that has been so much a part of life at Kalkaringi will definitely continue'.¹⁵

The disturbances deriving from alcohol were a symptom of bigger changes among the Gurindji. Daguragu had been transformed by new housing and government construction, though the effect on its residents was hardly that intended. The alienation apparent on other Aboriginal settlements was now settling in. Lyn Riddett had been absent from Wattie Creek for six years, and when she returned in 1979, she was shocked:

---

14   Darwin, NAA, Libanungu/ Daguragu, *Department of Aboriginal Affairs*, CA2605, E242, K9/2/3.
15   Darwin, NAA, 'Community Review [...]', July 1980, *Wave Hill Community Development*, E460, 1978/242; Darwin, NAA, 'Social Review Report [...]', E460, 1981/89 Part 2.

> I drove out there on a Saturday morning, got there late morning. People had been living in conditions in the earlier years that were shocking, but [then] they were clean, and they kept areas around their camps swept and things were washed up and stacked [...], people maintained basic hygiene. When I went back, I was overwhelmed by the filth and the dogs and the bugs and the lice [...], I was absolutely overwhelmed with depression.

Riddett felt that the changes she perceived were linked to the Gurindji's declining sense of pride:

> I don't know what had gone on between 1973 and 1979, but something pretty dramatic had happened [...]. There was just a listlessness [...]. I think people had an enormous pride [earlier] in what they'd done, how they'd stuck it out. You could hear it in the way they talked about themselves. [Earlier] they had been people of stature in respect of government and the union movement—that wasn't there in 1979.

The wholesale development of Daguragu by government had buoyed the Gurindji when it began three years earlier, but with much of their camp now covered by bitumen and building crews, the track mob's sense of control was in decline. Increasingly unable to engage the Gurindji, the DAA was perplexed:

> On the one hand the Gurindji maintain they want a viable cattle project to provide training for their offspring and income for the community. On the other hand they don't seem be able to carry out the work without a resident motivating force [...]. The Gurindji have had [...] a champagne existence in recent years, with ample employment and facilities available to them [...]. They are considerably better off than many other communities [...] and have a large entourage of Europeans to service their every need.[16]

---

16 Darwin, NAA, 'Daguragu/Kalkaringi', 20 November 1979, *Muramulla Gurindji Cattle Company Part 2*, E460, 1981/256.

While *kartiya* staff continued to operate Wave Hill's *essential* services—which had never been included in self-determination's remit anyway—the whitefellas' growing control of inconsequential DAA 'social' projects caused the track mob to withdraw further still. Ideas that had been initiated by the elders had been incrementally overtaken by government agencies. Previously, the choice facing residents was whether to work for the elders, take a government job—perhaps both—or go on welfare. Now, working for the government offered little incentive to reject a social security income.

Earlier, the Gurindji had said they wanted equal services at Daguragu: now, regardless of their growing disengagement, its development continued. A new auto garage was built, though government rules stipulated a fully qualified mechanic was required to oversee it. No Gurindji had the right qualifications, and for a year the workshop sat unused while officials looked for an outsider. For Gurindji elders, the empty building must have served as an unhappy reminder of how far they were from their community's founding goal: Gurindji delivery and control of its services.

* * *

While the track mob's early struggles had spurred the Whitlam and Fraser Governments to act on the issue of land, it was on the Gurindji's training and education that the success of the leaders' vision now hinged. Their views were unchanged: for them, achieving their independence, wellbeing and cultural survival depended not just on reclaiming their country, but on the education of their children. By 1979, bureaucrats too believed that low literacy and poor technical

skills were the main obstacles to Gurindji 'self-sufficiency', yet a school managed by the elders at Daguragu remained as distant as ever.

The federal Education Department had decided in 1974 to refuse the squatters' requests for a school of their own and had built up the Kalkaringi facility for the children of both communities instead. Nonetheless, Lingiari considered 'two-way' schooling at Daguragu so important that he had chosen at times *not* to agitate 'welfare' on the issue too much. The old man feared that if provoked, the government would take schooling away from Gurindji children entirely.[17] Pincher Nyurrmiarri described the elders' position:

> We should have the young fellas working in the shop, in Daguragu. Together they've got to be teached [...]. What about give a chance for Aborigine to take over? [To] give them poor buggers a chance we got [to get] our children in school. They got to be teach by old people [...] so they can work the place. We like to see that, because white European take over all the time [...]. Our children got to take over.[18]

For Kalkaringi's school principals and their bosses in Darwin, however, the wishes of Daguragu's elders were seen—when they were considered at all—as peripheral to the Education Department's raison d'être: running the Kalkaringi school.

When Department of Education bureaucrats were questioned on funding a school at Daguragu, they ducked and dodged. Privately, many thought Wattie Creek was a camp of 'fringe dwellers' bludging from the service-providing settlement. When pressed, a senior NTG officer told the elders that while he personally would 'like a school' at Daguragu, it was an impossibility; he could not 'convince

---

17 Darwin, NAA, 'Project Proposal', *Wattie Creek: Proposed Development Project*, F985, 1973/141.
18 Darwin, NAA, 'Wattie Creek Meeting [...]', 1 November 1977, E460, 1978/242.

the planners in Darwin that the people will stay there'.[19] The Department argued correctly that a school at Daguragu would lead to 50 percent reductions in enrolments, teaching positions and funding at Kalkaringi. The prevailing attitude was that the Gurindji should be grateful for the money the Department had already spent in the town.

Lacking the assistance of their earlier supporters and faced with an immovable bureaucracy, Daguragu's leaders had no choice but to accept the Education Department's terms. Their children got a white education at the Kalkaringi school, but with more cavernous buildings and unknown *kartiya* there than elsewhere, the school was not somewhere the elders could easily contribute. Nonetheless, a talented and dedicated principal and head teacher had been employed in 1978, and many children were engaging properly with schooling for the first time. During Peter Collins and Marg Fenbury's tenure, local elders were able to contribute to their children's schooling as well. Special 'culture classes' were held, though these encounters were often mired in misunderstanding. For one culture class, a *kajirri* (senior woman) directed a bus full of children and staff towards a Dreaming site. The group left after lunch, but by the time the school day ended—knock-off time for the teachers—the class was yet to arrive.[20]

The old people's alienation from the business of their children's schooling was a scenario repeated across the Territory. Norm and Helen McNair, then doing language work at Kalkaringi school, reckoned:

> There [weren't] open buildings with verandas where parents could come in with their children and sit and begin to see what written language was and be part of it. Instead, all of

---

19 Darwin, NAA, 'AGM Meeting [...]', 6 July 1979, E460, 1978/242.
20 Marg Fenbury, Personal Communication, 13 August 2014.

the attention was given to the kids, and all of the owners of the language and the culture were disenfranchised. [...] It all happened the wrong way around.[21]

Notwithstanding a few young Gurindji women working at the school as assistant teachers, the marginalisation of Gurindji knowledge continued. Whitlam's, Fraser's and now Paul Everingham's governments had promoted bilingual education, but applications by the Kalkaringi school for a Gurindji language program were rejected. Even though no Gurindji-speakers had been consulted, the justification given was that the language had 'deteriorated' too badly for teaching it to be beneficial. Rather than the 50/50 'two way' learning envisaged by Lingiari, only one lesson each week—six percent of class time—was taught in Gurindji.

For their kids to progress beyond primary school, the elders had to send them to Kormilda or Yirara boarding colleges in Darwin and Alice Springs. These had their own drawbacks, though. When PM Fraser visited Darwin, he was told the colleges had:

> [...] possible ill-effects on the stability of the social structure of Aboriginal communities. [...] There are doubts as to whether the colleges are providing education which can be meaningfully utilised in the home communities.[22]

When Gurindji students returned from boarding school, they mostly lacked the ability and the confidence to manage local services. Neither did they have much interest in doing so. 'New generation' Gurindji

---

21 School principal Keith Jeans recognised that the involvement of Daguragu's leaders would not increase—while they continued 'not [to] see [the school] as their own'. Personal Communication, 29 May 2014; Norm and Helen McNair [former Summer Institute of Linguistics staff at Kalkaringi], Interview Recorded by Charlie Ward, March 2010, in possession of the author.
22 Canberra, NAA, 'Ministerial Briefing: Kormilda College', *PM's Visit to NT 24–27 April 1978*, A1209, 1978/1050, Part 1.

leader Michael Paddy—then a boarder at Yirara—remembers that if anything, high school sent some of his mates 'off the rails': 'Some kids came back, they used to steal cars, break in to shop. The kids never listened to old people. It was because the lifestyle was changing. A different world'.[23] Adding to the Walk-off leaders' sorrow and disappointment, other kids failed to return home at all.

In a belated attempt to train local residents, the new NTG posted Adult Educators to Kalkaringi. Not only did officials now realise they had badly underestimated the gulf between the effect of schooling on remote Aboriginal people and the skills self-determination required of them, but problems arising from the non-existent relationship between DAA and Education staff in the bush were also noted. If anything, the transfer of schooling from the federal sphere to the NTG had worsened the situation.

After Territory self-government, the NT Departments of Education, Community Development, Health, Transport and Works—*and* the federal DAA—had a stake in the track mob's affairs. From the outset, the NT Government departments—augmented by a smattering of fresh NGOs—marched to their own tunes, not the Gurindji's. The result was so confusing that DAA adviser John Millhouse launched a special committee to co-ordinate them. At one meeting, the chaos of Kalkaringi's *kartiya* housing arrangements was described:

> As things stand at present, we have Health staff occupying Daguragu Council and Department of Education housing, Muramulla staff in council housing, and the shop using Education housing. Furthermore, the area matron has threatened that

---

23 Darwin, NTAS, Interview with Michael Paddy by Charlie Ward, October 2010, NTRS 3609, BWF 30.

the Health Department will withdraw all its staff from Wave Hill if its nurses are evicted from their council accommodation.[24]

With the NTG's 'growing pains' affecting everyone at Wave Hill, Daguragu Council struggled to fill the gap.

* * *

For those wishing since the early 1970s to see the Gurindji managing Kalkaringi and Daguragu through their own council, things had not gone as hoped. Daguragu Council was now at the end of its first year, and after starting strongly, the track mob's stab at 'Gurindji local government' had gone rapidly downhill. An eclectic bunch of Walk-off veterans, young aspirants and stay-at-home fathers—with their Warlpiri counterparts—sat on the board of an organisation whose workings they found alien and impenetrable. Still lacking knowledge of 'public' versus 'private' interests, the councillors had treated the organisation as a personal resource—with little resistance from *kartiya* staff. Many board members saw it as a forum to advance their own standing at the expense of others. As the DAA put it:

> It is patently obvious that with the withdrawal of Vincent Lingiari away from centre stage, no one as yet has proven competent in representing the competing factions. Instead we find any number of people using and being used by various Europeans when the need arises.[25]

White employees, who were often equally incompetent and bamboozled by local culture, had come and gone from the council's

---

24   Darwin, NAA, 'Community Review Report [...]', July 1980, E460, 1978/242.
25   NAA, 'Community Review [...]', July 1980, E460, 1978/242.

managerial roles. The longer term European-Australian residents wished for the emergence of another leader of Lingiari's calibre. Fundamentally divided themselves, they were mostly oblivious to their double standard.

These difficulties had worn down DAA adviser John Millhouse, who was also traumatised by a murder at Daguragu. When the Country Liberals approached him about running in the NT election of June 1980, he seized the chance, and set off on the campaign trail. During his absence, the 'musical chairs' syndrome afflicting the Gurindji continued. Millhouse's DAA job was taken by Gordon Bauman, a fellow survivor from the Welfare Branch, and Daguragu Council sacked their works supervisor Peter Byrnes as well. Byrnes had encountered a group of drunken Warlpiri men harassing Kalkaringi's nurses and resolved the situation with a shotgun.[26]

When Jack Doolan beat Millhouse and retained the Gurindji's seat, the younger man's political dreams were dispensed with and he returned to his wife at Kalkaringi. Finding himself at a loose end, Millhouse successfully applied for the job Byrnes had vacated at the council, although it entailed much lower status and pay. Millhouse took stock of the council's assets to restore some order to the organisation: an eye-opening exercise indeed. He discovered that the councils' mechanic had rented its grader out to a uranium miner, and other equipment was being used by unknown parties then roadbuilding east of Katherine—services for which the council's 'robber workforce' were being handsomely paid. Millhouse's popularity with his new *kartiya* colleagues plummeted.

---

26 DAA staff also harassed the nurses, and the Department of Health threatened to recall their own staff from the community.

Rather than making such looting harder, NT self-government now provided more opportunities for unscrupulous whites. The NTG contracted out many of its services in remote areas, which, according to observers at Wave Hill, was a system 'wide open' to abuse.[27] After Wundamarie Housing Association won lucrative sewerage and other contracts for instance, a *kartiya* employee embezzled a large amount of money and left the community. Numerous 'dodgy' strangers had now lived and worked amongst the Gurindji, who were now highly suspicious of *kartiya*. According to John Bullock, an adult educator working at Kalkaringi, local people:

> Were very cautious, they'd had a lot of people go out there over the years to try and help them. They were very reserved and were concerned about letting themselves 'out' too much to other people. They'd been continually ripped off [...]. It was very easy to do apparently because [their] administration skills were next to zero.[28]

To the chagrin of the DAA, the situation was mirrored all over the Territory. However dishonest the whites were, authorities depended on them. NT Assistant Director Martin Ford described the mass employment of whites in the bush as a 'tragic' result of the Department's 'ad hoc [and] un-coordinated' training for Aboriginal people.[29] Ford and others judged overall progress towards Aboriginal self-management so poor, they considered reversing the department's

---

27 Rolf Gerritsen, 'Blackfellas and Whitefellas: The Politics of Service Delivery to Remote Aboriginal Communities in the Katherine Region', in *Service Delivery to Remote Communities*, ed. by Peter Loveday (Darwin: North Australia Research Unit, Australian National University, 1982) 16–31, p. 20.

28 Darwin, NTAS, John and Elaine Bullock, Interview Recorded by Charlie Ward, October 2012, NTRS 3609, BWF 44.

29 AIATSIS, Jeremy Long Papers, HM Ford [Ass Divisional Director to Secretary], 'Community Self-Management', 5 March 1979, *Community Self-management*, Box 6, Folder 59.

withdrawal from communities—a sacrilegious thought they kept to themselves.[30]

After eight years of supposedly shared endeavour, the DAA and the Gurindji had created two communities which were neither wholly Aboriginal nor European. Instead, they were comprised of an awkward, unstable amalgam of both, constantly in tension between dissolution and dependence. Gurindji people, politicians, and not least the new 'Aboriginal support industry' now relied on the situation to continue. For the mob who had tracked from Wave Hill station, the terms of self-determination's 'deal' were tolerated for what they offered: a degree of physical and material comfort. The Gurindji's own vision of autonomy had been smothered, corrupted and weakened by the terms of Daguragu's funding and development—not to mention the corrosive, gravitational pull of Kalkaringi. The government itself was similarly trapped. Letting Aboriginal people fail by not adequately supporting them (or even by letting them suffer the consequences of their own mistakes) would have dire political consequences—a lesson already learned by the DAA.[31]

Regardless of this relationship's cost for the Gurindji and the taxpayer, the DAA's withdrawal from the bush was in its foundation script, and looming. The responsibility it carried would pass to the 'Aboriginal' councils it had established and the new NTG. Officials knew that Daguragu Council was not up to the job they had created for it, and to avoid causing scandal or irrevocable harm, the DAA created a Katherine-based support agency to prop it up—along with

---

30   Ford also wrote that the pursuit of 'wage justice' and the resultant increase in cash incomes for community members had been highly detrimental to the government's agenda.
31   Darwin, NTAS, Ian Pitman [fmr Director, DAA, NT Division], Interview Recorded by Charlie Ward, July 2014, NTRS 3609, BWF 57.

other councils in the region. Direct government control of Aboriginal communities like in days gone by—in contrast to 'Aboriginal self-management'—was now unthinkable. Instead, as the saying goes, legions of 'missionary, mercenary or misfit' *kartiya* were required. Admitting that self-determination in its original form had failed was not an option.

Chapter 12

TESTING TIMES, 1981–82

Lawyers, anthropologists and stenographers sat with Gurindji elders and their families beneath a make-do canvas awning. It was July 1981 at Daguragu, and the elders' land claim hearing before Justice John Toohey was in full swing. Half the town's whites and the old men themselves gave evidence before the 'bench'—a makeshift trestle. Everything from local massacres to the government's new campaign against brucellosis was discussed, obscuring at times the hearing's purposes: to ascertain the Gurindji, Mudburra, Malngin and Nyininy witnesses' connection to their land, and to make a list of 'traditional owners'.

The entire leasehold given to the Muramulla Co. by Whitlam six years earlier was under claim. With a mining company now eyeing off areas of the Gurindji's lease, the elders were keener than ever to get lasting control over their country. Pincher Nyurrmiarri spoke on behalf of many when he told the judge:

> I want freehold for my children. If I pass away—not only me but a lot of these blokes, a lot of these people here—we want freehold for our children so they can run it themselves if we pass away.[1]

---

1   Pincher Nyurrmiarri, cited in *Daguragu Land Claim 1981*, p. 206.

What the elders—who had repeatedly explained their connection with this country to officials in the past—made of this land claim rigmarole is unknown.

If Justice Toohey had any doubts about the Gurindji, they were soon put to rest by the elders: their knowledge of their land and its Dreaming was encyclopaedic. As much was clear from the first witness, Lingiari's brother Spider Jurluma. In the midst of the old man's serpentine account of his *jurntakal* (snake) Dreaming's progress between hills, caves and waterholes across Nyininy and Malngin country, Justice Toohey asked CLC lawyer Ross Howie:

> 'Mr Howie, where are we now in relation to the claim area?'
>
> 'We are still well to the west, your Honour'.

Ten minutes later, Howie implored the witness:

> Spider, we are really wanting to bring him this way, east, if we can, on to Daguragu, so we do not need all the places over Limbunya way.[2]

According to the Gurindji's long-term supporter Rob Wesley-Smith, who witnessed this exchange:

> It was terribly impressive, [Spider] could have talked for hours. I don't think there was much doubt about their association with the land.[3]

The Gurindji leaders were well-used to making their case for land rights, though the *ALRA* hearing wrung information from them they had never before shared with *kartiya*.

---

2   *Daguragu Land Claim 1981*, ALRA (NT) 1976 Transcripts, Vol. 1, 1981 (pp. 1–244), pp. 37–39.
3   Darwin, NTAS, Robert Wesley-Smith, Interview Recorded by Charlie Ward, September 2010, NTRS 3609, BWF 15.

Since their Walk-off from Wave Hill, the Gurindji had downplayed their diversity with the 'one mob' stance required to overcome government scepticism and indifference. No-one questioned their cohesion, though it became obvious to observers at the hearing with Justice Toohey that the original 'track mob' at Wattie Creek had been joined by families and individuals from other stations. Some of these people had legitimate claims on the Daguragu area—in some cases, stronger claims than the community's elders and Lingiari himself. With the exception of Tipujurn (Sandy Moray), who had now passed on, the Walk-off leaders' cultural authority over the Daguragu area was derived by marriage. Pincher Nyurrmiarri's wife 'Big Blanchie' Bulngari, her sister 'Little Blanchie' Jingaya (Lingiari's wife), and Lizzie 'Ngaliwurru' Wapngarri, Mick Rangiari's spouse, were all full 'owners' of the area, and underwrote their husbands' authority over it. If the Gurindji's land claim was successful, the male relatives of these women would be empowered by the *Land Rights Act* to assert greater control.[4] Such matters were little appreciated in July 1981, however, and Justice Toohey departed, leaving only vague assurances in his wake. In November he sent his report to Peter Baume, the new Minister for Aboriginal Affairs, and the elders' long wait for their land continued.

* * *

The transition to Northern Territory self-government was almost complete and the relationship forged between Gurindji elders and the Department of Aboriginal Affairs after Whitlam's election was largely over. Responsibility for the Gurindji and 'their' organisations had now

---

4 Marie King Pungki Nangkari, the daughter of its 'founding father' Sandy Moray, was too young to exert influence.

been handballed to another government entirely. The Aborigines' new NTG patrons professed to support Gurindji self-management, but Chief Minister Everingham cast doubt on funding them:

> What slice of the budgetary pie should be given to the population minorities [...] who live in inconvenient areas, where distance, terrain and diseconomies of scale make the provision of services such a costly affair? [...] Of course, there are times when government is guilty of being overzealous in its responsibilities to remote communities. We ought not to be chasing after people with services from which they are running away [...].[5]

Elders like Mick Rangiari, Pincher Nyurrmiarri and Lingiari himself had been fighting for their autonomy for a generation. To Wave Hill's leaders, the change to a new regime 'over their heads' must have highlighted their increased dependence on the Australian state. Sheer frustration or despair was justified—at how elusive their goals remained, the conflicts wracking their own society, and the constant misunderstandings, reprimands and apparent betrayals by the *kartiya* with whom they were compelled to work.

Unsurprisingly, when NTG officials appeared in February 1981 to inform Daguragu Council it had overspent its budget, they were given short shrift. Rather than defusing the situation, Minister for Community Development Marshall Perron (Daguragu Council's new NTG 'boss') claimed his officers had 'only pointed out the situation they have got themselves into'.[6] Gone was the Whitlam era's talk of tolerance for Aboriginal mistakes on the road to self-determination.

---

5   Chief Minister Paul Everingham, 'Opening Address', in *Service Delivery to Remote Communities*, ed. Peter Loveday (Darwin: North Australia Research Unit, Australian National University, 1981), p. 1.
6   'Perron Pleads Innocence', *NTN*, 18 February 1981.

While 'Gurindji' organisations floundered, it was a time of plenty for the growing Aboriginal support industry. The new NT Government was flush with federal cash, paying European contractors to build a new police station and housing at Kalkaringi, and seal the road to Daguragu. For the men living rough in 'donga' villages for months to achieve all this, isolation and work weighed heavily. They depended on their mates for entertainment, and social drinking was their favourite past-time.

It was within this milieu that a jovial chef-cum-labourer called Frank Dalton organised a cricket match on the old horse paddock next to the Kalkaringi police station. As the traditional bush sports were horse racing and football (cricket was only played at Christmas), the idea struck a chord, and Dalton was staggered by the response. Station people appeared from all directions, and two kegs of beer were drained before the first ball. It was then that the hospitable cook realised the potential for a recreational enterprise at Kalkaringi.[7]

The Wave Hill Cricket Club was born, with Dalton nutting details out on the fly, and its facilities, aka 'Frank's Bar and Grill', were opened at dawn on ANZAC Day 1981. Dalton was the club's president, the 'host with the most', and everybody's mate. The former drovers' common and Welfare settlement had never seen anything like it, and the town's Christians were dismayed.

For its members, cricket matches and time at Frank's provided precious social contact and light-hearted revelry. Dalton's genius for devising well-lubricated social events saw many of Kalkaringi's *kartiya* jostling for elbow room with pastoralists from near and far. Terry

---

7   Darwin, NTAS, Frank Dalton, Interview Recorded by Charlie Ward, October 2011, NTRS 3609, BWF 27.

Underwood, a club member and friend of Dalton's, remembered one such affair:

> Tributes to three outstanding Territorians [...] along the lines of 'This is Your Life' were organised for Buck Buchester, Gene Tunney and Noel Buntine [a cattleman, policeman and truck driver], and were executed at Frank's Bar and Grill. On the day after each, a cricket match was held between the 'Hero's XI' and the 'World XI'. During Noel's match, the Rest of the World had retired at 0 for 200, and Noel's XI were 9 for 45. Noel sent his eighty-eight year old mother in to bat, whereupon the Rest of the World, inherent gentlemen at heart, immediately conceded defeat.[8]

Fund-raising for good causes accompanied these hijinks, and local patrons were highly generous. When the 'Ash Wednesday' bush-fires occurred in Victoria, the sweat-stained hat of Buck Buchester was auctioned, along with other artefacts, to raise money for the victims.

After encouragement from the local police inspector, Dalton legalised his activities by applying for a liquor licence. Aware many locals were averse to a free-for-all pub opening in their midst, he applied for a limited hours *club* licence. When his bid succeeded, dismayed Gurindji leaders called for a public meeting with the new Liquor Commissioner of the NT.

Many women, the local church mob and others sought to speak to the important *kartiya*, but the gathering was a failure for the tee-totallers of Wave Hill. After hearing the Aborigines' views, the Commissioner concluded they mostly didn't 'understand the purpose of the meeting, or [didn't] care whether the restricted area was

---

8   Terry Underwood, 'Howzat in the Outback', in *Profile Australia's Northern Territory* (Darwin, Sovereign Publications, 1993), p. 21.

restored or not'.⁹ Rather than making Kalkaringi 'dry', he criticised the community's failure to curb its own demand for alcohol, and left. Dalton, his licence intact, negotiated directly with local leaders. Some Gurindji men were amenable to the new bar, and Dalton's status and 'say' increased further after he fell in love with and married a popular Mudburra woman. An accommodation was made: Daguragu Council barred Aboriginal people from joining the cricket club (and hence from drinking at Frank's Bar and Grill), *and* renewed the lease over Dalton's outlet at Kalkaringi each year.

Boozing at Wave Hill was on the rise, not only at Frank's. According to one of Kalkaringi's policemen at the time, gaining the Gurindji's trust was hard, but 'gaining the confidence of Europeans was a lot easier. You simply had to drink with them, and there were ample opportunities for that'.[10] The same officer believed that for most whites, alcohol at Kalkaringi was almost omnipresent:

> Beer was the lifeblood of the community. It provided not only physical and psychological nourishment but a convenient form of currency. If you wanted a lift to Katherine, a blue heeler pup, or some wiring done in your house at Wave Hill, you could always find somebody who would oblige in exchange for a few cartons of cold cans.

Although some Europeans refused to drink, in solidarity with most Gurindji women and elders, Kalkaringi's police were Dalton's enthusiastic patrons. One officer saw drinking after hours with other whites as 'free-flowing conviviality', while 'alcohol abuse' was the cause of

---

9   Darwin, NAA, NT Liquor Commission Chair to DAA, 23 December 1982, *Wave Hill Centre: Policy and Development*, E460, 1981/306; Rev Gordon Moore, 'Wave Hill—Annual Report, 1982', Personal File, Global Interaction.
10 John Jesser, 'The Law in the Wild (North) West', *NTN*, 14 August 1982, p. 15.

poor Aboriginal behaviour. The police station was 200 yards from the club, and its officers fielded a cricket team.

During these heady days, the greatest scandal in Kalkaringi's history occurred. 'Ma' Hawkes of the Top Springs hotel—Dalton's only competitor—perished at work, and Kalkaringi's police were called. Hawkes, otherwise offensively known as 'Old Leather-tits', had kept the 'Toppy' inn for decades, and was known far and wide for her no-nonsense hospitality. Exactly what transpired upon her death—or the role alcohol might have played in what followed—is hard to know, but days afterwards, a dog belonging to one of the local police dug up $28,000 ($106,000) in the Kalkaringi police compound. An officer who had presided with dignitaries over the opening of the new station months earlier was arrested and stripped of his badge. In court it emerged the constable had found the cash under Hawkes' mattress, and helped himself. Despite the fact his police work far surpassed his criminal undertakings, the constable was dismissed from the force.

Kartiya now had monopolised the town's most profitable criminal opportunities, but Aboriginal people were responsible for most petty offences and assaults. Warlpiri and Gurindji teenagers—possibly emulating the 'right' of whites to drink—stole grog from *kartiya* homes, but more troublingly, violence was increasing. In the past, the male perpetrators of any Gurindji misdemeanours were punished effectively by Lingiari's coterie of elders. Now, however, Aboriginal Legal Aid, the police and courts intervened, undermining (and criminalising) the elders' traditional punishments. While the old men were distracted from upholding their law by their work with Daguragu Council and their cattle company, the government was

taking away the 'judiciary' role they held in their own society—a point duly noted by the rebels of the new generation.

Some of the young men had openly challenged Daguragu's leaders for five years, and their sisters and girlfriends increasingly flouted traditional *ngumpit* social conventions as well. Women now had their own incomes, and the traditional forms of 'respect' they showed to men were waning. Boozing distorted the judgement and temper of some men, and as a result Gurindji women were occasionally harmed.[11] Another scourge afflicting mainstream society had arrived, though its causes varied at Wave Hill. Strict beliefs regarding women's sexual choices, increasingly assertive women and the growing disempowerment of traditional male roles and authority were converging. Mixed with alcohol, these factors were causing the Gurindji's social fabric to fray—and then their young women rebelled.

* * *

After the land claim hearing at Daguragu, Polly Lajayi buttonholed Rob Wesley-Smith about Josepha, her daughter. Lajayi, the widow of recently-deceased leader Long Johnny Kijngayari, was worried that the young woman was being harassed by local strongman and 'keeper of the peace' Banjo Long. Since Lingiari's initiative ten years earlier that allowed young men to pursue the 'promised' wives of male elders, the grounds for marriage had become more contested. Some marriages were still planned between younger women and older men

---

11 'Nulla Nulla Man gets Three Years', *NTN*, 17 October 1981; Darwin, NTAS, Wave Hill Police Journal, NTRS 2127, Vol. 16–17; Muir, 2012; Darwin, NAA, *Disturbance at Wattie Creek*, E460, 1978/1035.

through their kinship system, but personal opinion and circumstances increasingly intervened. Josepha was in her early twenties and her mother wanted her to leave Daguragu. According to Wesley-Smith:

> [...]. I was driving through Katherine to Darwin the next day. There were two other girls [who wanted to leave as well], and I said 'that's OK, I'll take them'. The next day Banjo came chasing me in his car, and he went past me and stopped. He got out with a *nulla nulla* and said 'Victor Vincent wants you to go back'—which was a lie. I went back to Wave Hill and there was a whole crowd of people there. They basically pulled the girls out of the car and he came rushing at me with this *nulla nulla* and whacked me. [He aimed for my] head but I ducked and he got my left elbow, which got broken. He was into me, and I punched him with my one good arm pretty hard, which seemed to set him back a bit. I got up and loped off towards where the police lived, then drove myself back to Darwin.

Josepha Kijngayari, the focus of this confrontation, was Kormilda-educated, the daughter of one of its elders, and groomed for a job in her home community. The gulf between this modern (and for the Gurindji, experimental) plan and the traditional path mapped out for her regarding marriage and sexuality was immense, and perhaps until Kijngayari's attempted flight to Katherine, unrecognised by all but Daguragu's young women themselves.

Although the elders sent Billy Bunter to Darwin to apologise to Wesley-Smith and invite him back to Wave Hill, the attack raised serious issues for *kartiya* supporting the Gurindji. How far should they be prepared to go? Whose 'Gurindji' interests should they support? And at what point should they acknowledge that traditional Gurindji approaches to punishment and sexuality were out of step with the modern world?

These issues exercised Wesley-Smith. He had known the Gurindji for more than a decade, and believed that in agreeing to Polly Lajayi's request, he had done the right thing. Also, as a Labor Party hopeful intending to run in the upcoming federal election of 1983, he was wary of his assault's political consequences. When the press reported that the 'ALP activist' had 'broken his arm on a recent outing to Wave Hill', how this happened was deliberately not mentioned. Wesley-Smith was also acting as the NT Council for Civil Liberties (CCL) secretary, and knew well that Aboriginal 'arranged marriage' was a topic of public debate. After Wesley-Smith recuperated in hospital for two weeks, the CCL announced that 'the main issue is not arranged marriages but the alleged forcing of such a relationship upon an unwilling partner'.[12]

Far from receding from public view and being forgotten, the issues raised by Josepha Kijngayari's thwarted escape were thrust back into the spotlight by another Gurindji woman. Nineteen-year-old Lorna Doone had attended Yirara College in Alice Springs and worked in the Muramulla store. She had also enjoyed the sparks of romance with her teenage boyfriend. Within months of the fracas involving Kijngayari, Doone—who her family knew as Nampula (bush fig)—escaped from her own 'promised' marriage to elder George Kalapiti. According to the reports that followed, Doone was bashed by six men determined to force her to marry the sixty-five year-old. After three weeks in hospital, she fled, and was later allegedly forced into a car in Pine Creek by Kalapiti and two Warlpiri men. When the police intervened, Doone was given sanctuary by a sympathetic and vocal MLA in Darwin, Dawn Lawrie. Later it emerged that elements of

---

12 'Promised Brides Issue Complex', *NTN*, 9 February 1982.

Doone's story were fabricated. To the journalists that interviewed her, Doone claimed a twelve-year-old girl was also promised to Kalapiti. A 'Child Brides' headline ran the next day in the *NT News*.

* * *

With child welfare groups and overt racists alike up in arms, Chief Minister Paul Everingham announced his government 'has and will continue to act to protect Aboriginal women who complain to the police of physical attacks [...]'.[13] An Aboriginal social worker and other staff from the new Northern Territory Department of Community Development (NTDCD) were dispatched to Daguragu to investigate. When she arrived at Wave Hill, she found the situation was not as it appeared.

The man at the centre of the allegations, George Kalapiti, had an outstanding reputation among the Gurindji, and had worked as a head stock 'boy' on Wave Hill station. Daguragu's leaders—who were well aware of (and distressed by) recent newspaper reports about their 'child brides'—claimed that Doone had been beaten not by them but her aunties, for straying with *kartiya* stockmen, not her young beau. Senior women backed up the men's story. They took no issue with the marriage, and believed Nampula was in the wrong. Although no evidence was found (and no girl could be identified) to back up Doone's story of a twelve year old bride, the unprecedented attention on *ngumpit* marriage practices shamed the older men, and undermined another aspect of Gurindji culture.

The so-called 'child brides affair' and other acts of female Gurindji rebellion directly rebutted the elders' authority and traditional culture.

---

13   'Govt "Will Act" to Protect Aboriginal Girls', *Darwin Star* 10 February 1982.

They echoed the earlier rejection of traditional values by many young men, and confirmed the elders' fears that '*kartiya* way', absorbed mostly through mainstream schooling, was at cross-purposes with their own beliefs. The clash between between 'old' and 'new' playing out between the generations of Gurindji was inevitable, Kalkaringi's missionaries believed: 'The more [young Gurindji] come into contact with their white counterpart, the more they will want their freedom'.[14]

Josepha Kijngayari and several other young Daguragu women never had the chance to resolve the choices before them. A few years later, Kijngayari was murdered in Kununurra, and as a result, part of her elders' hopes for the next generation and the future of their community also died.

* * *

Muramulla's instability continued. Bill Purdie had departed, having barely warmed his seat as the company's cattle adviser. Facing fresh pressure from bureaucrats, the elders employed Gordon Bauman to replace him in May 1981. Bauman took the job coming fresh from his role as DAA's man-on-the-ground in Kalkaringi. It was an unusual appointment, even by the standards of remote Aboriginal cattle stations. According to one visitor, Bauman, a suburban Melbournite, 'didn't know bullock from bull's foot'.[15] The Gurindji agreed, but hired the former Welfare officer anyway. They had observed his respect for their decision-making, and—sick of being 'under white Europeans'—trusted he would let them get on with

---

14   Rev Moore to Williams, April 1982, Gordon Moore Personal File, Global Interaction.
15   NTAS, Darwin, Transcript of Interview with Stan Davey, October 1986, NTRS 226, TS 462, p. 13.

working their land and cattle without interference. Director Jerry Rinyngayarri asked Bauman to restrain himself to 'office' operations: book-keeping, dealing with government, and liaising with industry regarding cattle sales and transport.

They had limited his contribution to their Daguragu office-caravan, but Bauman remembers the elders allowed him to 'get on a horse and get in the way occasionally, as long as I didn't injure myself. I loved that'.[16] Between his forays in the saddle, he fulfilled his promise, leaving business decisions to the Gurindji elders. With 'European' prudence removed and a stronger market, Muramulla employed a record twenty-four stockman and sold $70,000 worth of stock—increasing its revenue by 30 percent from the previous season. Although the money was absorbed instantly, three decades later Bauman remains proud of the fact that, for a brief period, the Gurindji had total control of their operation.

Regardless of the elders' new freedom *within* their company though, the demands of the government's disease-testing regime (BTEC) on Muramulla were growing. To avoid the destocking of their lease, Rinyngayarri and his men threw themselves into meeting the program's requirements. To manage and test their animals, fifty kilometres of additional fencing—and close co-operation with Department of Primary Production inspectors ('stockies')—was required, straining the patience of both sides. Before one early test for Brucellosis, Rinyngayarri oversaw a muster of 1,300 head of cattle. Without effective yards, however, more than a third of the beasts escaped. The stock inspectors' testing was put on hold until more fencing could be built.

---

16   Gordon Bauman, Personal Communication, 27 July 2014.

Despite the Gurindji's inability to secure their stock, Muramulla's disease test results were a revelation for the inspectors. Their cattle were semi-wild, so DPP staff had expected to confirm Chief Minister Everingham's description of Aboriginal cattle operations as 'harbours of disease'. 'Before we started testing here', related 'stockie' Peter Flanagan:

> [...] everybody regarded Daguragu as a black spot on the map, and then we started and it got to be a very shiny star [...]. [Now it has] a very clean status, it would beat most places in the Territory, and it [is] way above everybody around here.

Among the thousands of Muramulla cattle tested, there was only one 'reactor' that displayed symptoms of tuberculosis. Flanagan showed it:

> [...] to all the boys who were there at the time, Jerry and everybody [...], just to show them what 'TB' was like. It was in the mammary glands, and it had big lesions and yellow pus and stuff like that.[17]

After more cattle from Daguragu were tested at the Katherine meatworks, the DPP placed the property on a provisional 'monitored negative' status—a significant step towards being classified disease-free.

Despite this promising start, BTEC soon mired Muramulla in difficulties. While Rinyngayarri and Victor Vincent were on the front foot about disease testing, the southern end of their lease was inaccessible and impossible to muster. BTEC increased the challenge: all cattle had to be tested not once, but twice per season. After the cattle had been mustered, each test took days. All in all, this amounted to weeks of work, drawn out enormously by

---

17   Flanagan, *Daguragu Land Claim 1981*, p. 512.

Rinyngayarri's refusal to use helicopters—a stance which grated with the DPP. When the Gurindji men abandoned a test, the stockies' tempers flared. Kalkaringi resident Norm McNair remembers a gate being left open, and untested stock getting in with 'clean' animals. 'There seemed to be a series of disasters', he said, 'and that was one of them. I guess the Gurindji got blamed, though I don't know who was responsible'.

Muramulla's adviser Gordon Bauman was witness to the stress BTEC caused the elders, and became disenchanted. As well as observing the prejudice Aboriginal people faced within the cattle industry, Bauman had a front row seat on a damaging personality conflict between Muramulla's DAA and ADC advisers. Deciding that he would have a better chance of lessening the Aborigines' burdens as a lawyer, he enrolled at a southern university and departed. Despite his efforts, Mick Rangiari was critical: 'on a station like this, he couldn't handle it. He wasn't bin cattleman'.[18]

With Bauman gone, Rinyngayarri and Donald Nangiari fought again for a Gurindji man to take up the company's adviser role. Their eyes turned to Lingiari's eldest son, Victor Vincent. Like his father, Victor had a quiet, considered manner, Christian beliefs, an upbringing in the cattle industry, and no schooling. The young stockman had been elected to the Muramulla board in 1978, and taken his father's place as president of Daguragu Council. But while Victor was being groomed as a leader by Baptist missionary Gordon Moore, neither he nor his peers wanted more responsibility.

Again prevented from employing one of their own, the Muramulla board looked out for a more cattle-seasoned whitefella than Gordon

---

18   NTAS, Rangiari, NTRS 226, TS 485, (T4), p. 27–29.

Bauman. After considering Vestey's travelling manager Cec Watts, they hired Wave Hill station's Buck Buchester in April 1982. An old hand who had worked as a Vestey horse-breaker and head stockman for decades, 'Old Buck' had overseen 'cleaning-up' the Daguragu lease in 1975, and knew the country well. Although he was hardly more literate than the board that employed him, Buchester's ability to remember numbers was freakish—a skill he applied to stockwork and supporting the West Indies cricket team. From the ADC's perspective, his illiteracy was something they could overcome: records in the bush were often rough, and the old stockman's figures were beyond dispute.

When Buchester took on the Muramulla job, he came fresh from Wave Hill station, which was well-maintained and being rapidly modernised. To Old Buck's unsentimental eye, the Gurindji's land was a mess. Fences were down and thousands of wild horses (the result of Vestey's horse-breeding program) had the run of the property. Bore casings bought in 1976 lay where they had been delivered, unused. To Buchester, the way to fix these things was obvious, but his new Aboriginal employers did not share his opinions or appreciate the way he conveyed them. Although the old bushman was familiar with the Gurindji—and they with him—thirty years in the industry had imbued him with an authoritarian attitude he found hard to shake. For better or worse though, Buchester was 'family'—both known to the Gurindji and married to a local woman. Instead of showing him the door, the men's working relationship with 'Old Buck' went rapidly downhill.

With changes at the company's helm, Muramulla's Daguragu store was also in flux. The shop had begun swinging between *kartiya* and Gurindji management, like the company itself. When an officer was sent to investigate, he found that:

> In actual fact the shop is a fiasco. The people of Daguragu want a shop but with no European involvement. Thus items are given away to relations for only a fraction of the price charged. Any profits that by chance are made are used by the directors of the cattle company to buy private vehicles etc. When any employee of the shop tries to enforce normal operational procedures, the customers complain that they are being robbed [...].[19]

Fraser's new Aboriginal Affairs Minister Fred Chaney also thought the problems were caused by the Gurindji. To him, 'the shop at Daguragu is not the same as most other community shops. Being completely Aboriginal-run and owned [...] is the main cause of [its] problems'.[20] Whites agreed that when it came to business principles, the Muramulla board were sorely lacking. Norm McNair remembers Daguragu's elders:

> [...] were most adamant that their families could book-up [buy on credit] at the store. Because they were the leaders, they [thought they] didn't have to pay, they could book-up what they wanted [...]. Their rationale was that they were the cattle company, and that it was their store so they could take what they wanted.

Although it had recently been operating with $10,000 ($35,000) worth of stock, in 1982 the store was overwhelmed by its problems, and closed.

These woes fed into Muramulla's broader financial instability and confusion. Yet again, the company had new accountants in Darwin, and getting information from them was painfully slow. The company's

---

19 Darwin, NAA, 'Tonkin to Wright', 18 February 1982, *Wave Hill Social Club*, E460, 1981/100.
20 Darwin, NAA, E460, 1981/100.

flirtation with 'true' Gurindji control had delivered it a healthy injection of cash, but unknowingly it began 1982 in deficit. When the ADC slashed its funding as well, Muramulla was left with an operating debt of approximately $30,000 ($102,000).[21]

* * *

The elders' cattle project was already limping when the NTG foisted another massive project, this time on Daguragu Council. Reforming local government was high on Chief Minister Paul Everingham's agenda. The Country Liberal Party wished to facilitate Territorians having more say over more of their affairs—or to shed many of its responsibilities down the command chain, depending on one's perspective. The NT Department of Community Development (NTDCD) had developed a model to guide this transition, and in 1982 the department informed Gurindji elders. Daguragu's amalgamated council, which the Gurindji and DAA had strived to achieve, would be re-fashioned. The elders' lack of response was deafening. Daguragu Council was struggling to cope with its existing workload, and the idea of its tiny office taking on more responsibilities could not have been less appealing.[22] When NTDCD officials arrived wanting to discuss the transition, local leaders ignored them—the first time public servants had been unable to rouse a response from the formerly ambitious Gurindji.

---

21   The ADC also expected Muramulla to generate a profit increase of 10 percent per annum—an unrealistic figure at the best of times.
22   In this, the Gurindji had much in common with other small populations faced with the development of local government 'from above'. Ruth Atkins, 'Local Government', in *Public Administration* (ed. Richard Spann) (NSW Government Printer, Sydney, 1973), pp. 221–246 (p. 221).

TESTING TIMES, 1981-82

The Gurindji leaders' relationship with the state was increasingly strained, but the snub they directed to the Northern Territory Government also reflected their faltering grip on the organisations of Wave Hill. In 1982, Daguragu Council meetings were rarely held, its *kartiya* managers were ineffective, president Billy Bunter was struggling to cope, and the council's accounts had been transferred to a new support agency in Katherine. By now every 'Gurindji' organisation (except Muramulla, which the elders remained truly invested in)—Daguragu Council, Wundamarie Housing Association, the Kalkaringi store—had been wracked by *kartiya* thieving, fraud or ineptitude. The public servants who they trusted—Alex Bishaw, Len Ibbetson and Trevor LaBrooy, for instance—rarely visited in their senior, Darwin-based roles. Instead, Billy Bunter, Victor Vincent and the surviving strike leaders were liaising with strangers from a bewildering array of government departments and agencies. When things went wrong—which was frequently—Aboriginal people were blamed.

The Gurindji's frustration boiled over. With their activist friends long gone, Muramulla board members Donald Nangiari, Jerry Rinyngayarri, Victor Vincent and Billy Bunter—among others—decided that the best course of action was the one that had shaped their past: a strike. In October 1982, these men and their families gave notice to local employers and 'sat down' at Daguragu. With Lingiari and other elders, they talked of starting over, of creating another new homeland of their own in the south of their lease near McDonald's Yard.[23] The Gurindji expected this 'stop work'—like

---

23 Darwin, NAA, Cartwright to Hearn, 18 October 1982, *Muramulla Gurindji Company*, E1022/3, K1982, 1-7, Pt B.

their spectacular protest of 1966—was a Walk-off they would maintain as long as it took.

According to Gordon Moore, 'all but two houses' left Kalkaringi. From the Baptist missionary's perspective, the people's sit-down was a protest against Frank's Bar and Grill.[24] But there was more than petulance about Frank Dalton's patrons driving the leaders of the Gurindji's second walk-off; their move expressed frustration about the domination of *kartiya* and their opaque institutions at Wave Hill. The arrival of Dalton's club—especially after the Gurindji had tried to make the community 'dry'—was high on their list of grievances, but being ignored by new *kartiya*, the increasing confusion of young Gurindji, and the establishment of other European businesses were equal sources of frustration. A significant number of the track mob were prepared to leave Daguragu, the site of all their struggles and half-realised dreams, to start again. In the words of Billy Bunter, 'we've tried this here and it's not working'.[25]

---

24 Gwen and Gordon Moore also believed the death of the local church leader, Pastor Clancy Barlanga, fed into the 'unrest' they observed in the community. Rev Gordon Moore, 'Wave Hill—Annual Report, 1982', Personal File, Global Interaction.
25 Darwin, NAA, Cartwright to Hearn, 18 October 1982, E1022/3, K1982, 1-7, Pt B.

Chapter 13

RESIGNATION, 1983–86

> The dream was being lost. Their ability to
> maintain themselves and their own station was
> slowly departing.
>
> Kerry Gibbs.[1]

When Jan Richardson, the wife of veteran Aboriginal rights activist Stan Davey, visited Daguragu in early 1983, Pincher Nyurrmiarri implored her to pass a message to her husband: 'tell that old man we need him'.[2] The Gurindji's strike of a few months earlier had dispersed, and little had changed. Now the wily strategist Nyurrmiarri had a special kind of assistance in mind. To penetrate the *kartiya* world, to help the elders take their final shot at control, they needed a white they could rely on. The job advising Daguragu Council was open again.

Seventeen years earlier, Stan Davey had sat down in the riverbed with Nyurrmiarri, Lingiari, Rangiari, Rinyngayarri and others after their Walk-off. The elders had come to like and respect him in the years since, but in addition to being familiar, Davey was brilliantly

---

1 Darwin, NTAS, Interview with Kerry Gibbs, recorded by Charlie Ward, September 2010, NTRS 3609, BWF 18.
2 Jan Richardson, Personal Communication, 12 January 2015.

qualified for the role of Daguragu Council's clerk. As a seminarian in the 1950s, he had discovered his calling relieving Aboriginal disadvantage, and left the church. Davey had helped establish the Victorian Aborigines' Advancement League and FCAATSI, before playing key roles in the successful 'Aboriginal' referendum of 1967 and the Gurindji's own campaign. Eleven years with remote Aboriginal people in the Kimberley, doing community development work with Richardson—as a public servant, or at times a volunteer—had followed. In all regards, Davey was better placed to assist the Gurindji than any of the dozens of *kartiya* who'd preceded him. Richardson had also had a decade of community development experience in the Kimberley. With this couple on their books there was an unprecedented opportunity for the Gurindji elders to achieve their dream.

Davey flew to Kalkaringi in March 1983 and went through the motions of a job interview with his old friends:

> They barely talked to me, apart from welcoming me and sort of talking about other things for a while. They just paid my fare over there and back, and then they told [the NTDCD] 'Yes, that's the person we want'.[3]

The Gurindji employed Richardson as the council book-keeper. Like others returning to Daguragu, she and Davey were shocked. Compared to the 'tight' and committed group they had known earlier, it was obvious the Gurindji had lost their morale and cohesion. Despite his extensive experience, Davey was confronted by the scale of the challenge: 'There is an apathy in the communities here

---

3   NTAS, Darwin, Transcript of Interview with Stan Davey, October 1986, NTRS 226, TS 462, p. 14.

that we did not have to face in the Kimberley. People have lost faith in really being able to deal with their own lives [...]'.[4]

As Davey now saw, for the Gurindji, 'dealing with'—or controlling—their lives was further from their grasp than it had been at any time since they left Vestey's Wave Hill. Although the elders had battled to make their own 'track', and despite self-determination's emancipatory packaging, the terms of their existence had been shaped by far-away law-makers and funding bodies. Policies changed, as the Gurindji now knew, but the stripe of governments had done nothing to lessen the power of the state over the people—especially those in the Gurindji's subsidised communities without 'natural' employment or well-educated populations. After following federal politics closely through one conservative-progressive-conservative cycle, the surviving Walk-off leaders were disillusioned, and disengaging. When PM Malcom Fraser was ousted by a Bob Hawke-led Labor Party within weeks of Davey's appointment, there was little response from the Gurindji—even when Labor's new Aboriginal Affairs Minister Clyde Holding announced the outcome of their long quest for land.

According to Justice Toohey's recommendations, Aboriginal freehold title—'land rights'—would be granted over the Gurindji's lease. The victory came with a bitter twist: under the complex and little-tested conditions of the *Land Rights Act*, the Gurindji were denied some country in their lease's south-west corner. Rather than sacrifice this small bit of scrub and end their battle for land rights, they dug in. With their legendary patience and the backing of the Central Land Council, Daguragu's elders submitted an 'appeal'. The new case got underway while the war between Darwin and Canberra over land rights continued.

---

4   Davey to 'David', 14 September 1984, Richardson Personal Collection.

A HANDFUL OF SAND

* * *

As Stan Davey settled into life at Wave Hill, he dwelt upon the Gurindji's early pride and the battering it had received. Sitting in the raised 'Welfare' house—the former home of Bill Jeffrey, Trevor La Brooy, Richard Preece and a dozen others who'd worked, in their ways, towards Gurindji independence—he wondered about celebrating the famous act that led to Daguragu's founding.[5] Davey imagined the Wave Hill Walk-off itself could be re-enacted, and figures from the Gurindji's historic political battle might attend.

At Daguragu, the elders seized on the idea. They decided to use the event—to be held on 23 August, the Walk-off's anniversary—to convey the selflessness, pride and bravery that had spurred them on, and which they now found lacking among younger Gurindji. Their freedom was what they would celebrate. Contemporary leader Gus George recalls: 'We wanted to have Freedom Day every year to remember [...] old people, and talk about for young people why we have that Freedom Day'.[6] Near their old riverbed camp where the elders announced their stand to the world in 1966, dancing and speeches would be held.

The concept was so popular that on the first Freedom Day in August 1983, Kalkaringi and Daguragu communities were deserted. Everyone was at the river or on the track from old Wave Hill station. Jan Richardson remembers: '[It] was fabulous, the adults re-enacted the walk, with billy cans and dogs and little kids walking too. The big

---

5 Davey was familiar with the large Aboriginal strike in the Pilbara in 1946 and was inspired by the symbolic power of that event. Jan Richardson, Personal Communication, 12 January 2015.

6 Darwin, NTAS, Interview with Gus George by Charlie Ward, October 2010, NTRS 3609, BWF 24.

RESIGNATION, 1983-86

red Muramulla truck came along'.[7] As well as creating a celebration marker for the Gurindji and their friends and supporters, Freedom Day gave the elders a public forum to inspire their youth. The old men's entreaties would be heard by both their recalcitrant teenagers and *kartiya* in the wider world. When Mick Rangiari spotted a visiting reporter on 23 August 1983, he relayed the Gurindji leaders' new 'word' about the reasons behind their strike: 'we did it mainly so our kids would have freedom', he said.[8]

As a morale booster and public relations exercise for the 'track mob', Freedom Day was a coup, though the younger generations voted against it with their feet. The following year's celebration had a much poorer turnout, and Richardson remembers:

> The school lent them a bus, and I have to say, there was something incongruous about all these people getting out of a government school bus to commemorate their independence.

The elders wondered if their youth were at all aware of their parents' striving since the Vestey time. At Freedom Day in 1984, a frail Lingiari mournfully observed that 'the young people don't seem to know what we did for them'.[9]

* * *

When Davey had arrived to take up the job of Daguragu Council clerk in April 1983, its office was in hibernation. The council had

---

[7] A green Bedford truck owned by Brian Manning which he used to deliver supplies to the Gurindji in 1966 was also repaired and driven to Wave Hill by Manning and Kerry Gibbs for early 'Freedom Days'.
[8] 'Fight for Freedom is Remembered', *NTN*, [Date unknown] August 1984.
[9] *NTN*, ibid.

just been reconstituted by the NTG, meetings had not been held for months, and a daunting pile of mail sat unopened. The new constitution also needed ratifying. Although the Territory government touted its new council model as being designed for local adaptation, Gurindji leaders were so disengaged from the NTDCD that they'd adopted the constitution the department sent from Darwin unchanged. Davey and Richardson were dismayed by how 'European' it was, and decided that if the new council was to have a hope of engaging local residents, its rules would need to be revised. Billy Bunter, the then president, agreed, and meetings about 'Gurindji-fying' the council's voting system were held. Possibilities of electing councillors by gender, family groups, community (Daguragu or Kalkaringi), and the eight *ngumpit* 'skin' groups were all discussed.

The leaders eventually decided that each skin group (with their Warlpiri equivalent) would elect their own representative. The result would be a council of eight men and eight women—a neat solution, until it was realised that Kalkaringi's European residents had been overlooked. To remedy this, leaders agreed to bestow a 'skin' group on all *kartiya* so they could vote. When the NTDCD got wind of this innovation, they decreed it unfair that Kalkaringi's forty adult *kartiya* could vote, but were unlikely to ever be elected themselves by a majority Aboriginal population. Although the elders and the DAA had just devoted years of work to creating a council that would specifically channel local Aboriginal power, the NTDCD had a different agenda. Their focus was not on Aboriginal self-management at Daguragu, but Kalkaringi's status as an open town. As a result, the leaders were compelled to create a ninth 'skin group' in Daguragu Council's voting system so a pair of Europeans could also sit on the board.

These deliberations involved local leaders with their council to an extent unmatched since the amalgamation of 1978–79. They had engineered a more democratic system of representation, but having a 'nine-skin' council did little to ensure equal participation when it sat afterwards. Most matters before the council had no equivalents in Gurindji, so meetings were conducted in English—some people, particularly elders, were left behind. And even though the eighteen councillors had been duly elected, not all of them had the cultural authority to make decisions. After council meetings, a waiting game often ensued while a second 'tribal council' of decision-makers was consulted. The older men's power and gender also had to be reckoned with in meetings. Men and women traditionally discussed matters separately. Would the voices of Gurindji women—and younger men too—be heard on the council? There was also the further complication of *kartiya* and other outsiders being elected as members. Davey found the 'ninth skin group' created a great obstacle:

> It only requires two very powerful Europeans to move onto a council, who understand committee routines and systems, and who can do a bit of dominating, and they'll run the council.[10]

One *kartiya* councillor recalls that after Davey stepped down as the council clerk, the ideas of clerks as well as *kartiya* board members were uncritically endorsed.

While local custom vied with democratic principle in council meetings, the 'nine skin' system reflected the old Gurindji leaders' willingness to involve women as political players. At the first meeting of the new NTG-endorsed council on 11 October 1983, Mona

---

10 More world-wise Aborigines from other areas also achieved undue influence in local affairs. Darwin, NTAS, Davey, NTRS 226, TS 462, p. 16.

Cook, the Gurindji's first-ever female office holder, was sworn in as vice president. Jan Richardson was a huge supporter of such developments, and as the council book-keeper (and later its first female clerk) she consulted Gurindji women closely and strongly advanced their interests. One of her first efforts was to get some women a motorcar.

The vigorous use of the council's fleet had confirmed what Richardson and Davey already knew: like other rural and remote people, the Gurindji placed high value on working automobiles. Protracted battles to use private and 'community' vehicles were usually won by powerful men, while women missed out on time behind the wheel.

With a cool logic and the complaints of frustrated female motorists ringing in her ears, Richardson launched an Avon beauty product scheme to raise funds. Operating out of the 'sweetest-smelling council office in the district', the women learnt business skills while flogging off soaps and deodorants, and had a ball.[11] The unprecedented demand for make-up in Kalkaringi and Daguragu that this inspired (plus a government grant) were such that the local mechanic ordered a Toyota for the sales women within a few months.

To keep their new dual cab truck in safe hands, senior women conducted a ceremony putting their 'law' on it, making it off-limits for men. The key to the vehicle was also 'sung' so that no male could touch it. Because few of the aspiring drivers had licences, Roslyn Frith, a young Gurindji-Warlpiri woman who had finished school in Adelaide, was endorsed as the vehicle's sole operator. Negotiations about the key's tight control ensued, and in stark contrast to many

---

11   Jan Richardson, Personal Communication, 12 January 2015.

council vehicles, the women's Toyota enjoyed a hard-working life for several years.

Inspired by such successes, though distressed by the locals' money troubles, Richardson turned her hand to their financial illiteracy. At her behest, the ANZ bank in Katherine agreed to support a Kalkaringi sub-branch, into which locals' wages and social security cheques were paid. Richardson looked to Gurindji culture again and recruited and trained a group of about five cashiers to cater for the Gurindji's different tribal affiliations.[12] On payday every fortnight, the bank tellers clambered aboard the council truck. Richardson tagged along as a trainer with Roslyn Frith, Milton Splinter and others handling the cash. With tellers of the appropriate skin dispensing 'reds', 'blues' and even 'ninjas', this modest banking service was a big step towards fulfilling the elders' vision for Daguragu.

* * *

While the rebellion of young Gurindji women still simmered, mid-ranking female public servants—including Richardson—worked at Wave Hill for the first time. Whereas advisers, consultants and managers in the past (all male) had focused on Gurindji men, the female community workers now wending their way into the bush sought out local women—with different results.

Ros Frith was the first to take advantage of Kalkaringi's new female-friendly politics. Unlike her male peers, Frith stuck at school

---

[12] For Richardson and Davey's approach to community development work, see Jan Richardson, 'Tropical Community Development: Exploring two practitioners' lived experience of community development in the Kimberley region of Western Australia, 1969–1980' (Unpublished PhD Thesis, Darwin, Northern Territory University, 1998).

to the end and was less constrained by the old men's authority. And like Billy Bunter she brought 'Warlpiri confidence' to her leadership, and was elected to the Daguragu Council at nineteen. According to Susan Cebu, a Gurindji-Tiwi friend (and sister of Sandra) who was also elected: 'When Stan and Jan were here they did a lot of wonderful things [...], they taught Ros how to do book-keeping, and she started talking up to white people'.[13]

Learning quickly, Frith's tenure with the council lasted for three years and she soon replaced Bunter as council president. As Frith would find however, while Daguragu's leaders had called for years on young people to 'step-up', in practice the elders weren't always so keen:

> It depends on if they had kids. Some of them would be supportive, but some of them weren't happy with young people taking on the roles, with the young people telling them this and that. Some of them were happy, [saying] 'she's got that recognition, she knows what she's doing, she's educated'. Some of them were really supportive and proud, but some of them weren't, they were thinking 'our kids are now telling us what to do'. [...] They would say 'No, they should be listening to the old people'.[14]

For Frith and the few others who attempted to straddle the two worlds at this level, it was difficult:

> [The elders] were teaching you, and you were teaching them the *kartiya* way. We had our little arguments [...], even though it hurt to argue with an old person. [...] They understood some things, [but] you had to explain to them 'Look, it's part of the

---

13   Darwin, NTAS, Susan Cebu and Roslyn Farquharson, Interview Recorded by Charlie Ward, October 2010, NTRS 3609, BWF 23.
14   Darwin, NTAS, Rosaleen Frith, Interview Recorded by Charlie Ward, October 2011, NTRS 3609, BWF 33.

guidelines, the red tape'. We had to do everything right, so that two-way learning took place.

Frith and other young Gurindji were providing their elders with 'two-way learning' which they themselves had been denied in their schooling. It was still a point that rankled. Keenly aware of the elders' bitterness about the government's failure to provide them with their own school, Davey organised a tour for the leaders to inspect Aboriginal-run schools in the Kimberley. The two-week trip in April 1984 was a success, but the waning energy of the elders—not to mention the priorities of the NT Education Department—meant little came from the exercise.

In the Gurindji's new communities, *kartiya*-type knowledge was essential. Young people adapted more quickly, and criticised the older generation's ways. The gulf between the two was growing and the resulting loss of traditional knowledge was painfully obvious. While Norm and Helen McNair were working to preserve Gurindji language, some of their elderly collaborators concluded there was little point passing on their unique and unrecorded Dreamings to a generation with other interests: 'We saw several old people pass away while we were there, and everything, all their stories, their Dreamings, their songs, all just disappeared'.[15]

* * *

While this cultural tragedy unfolded, Kalkaringi's *kartiya* pursued their own interests with success. Many thought the government's policies to empower Aboriginal people were a waste of time and the

---

15 Norm and Helen McNair, Interview Recorded by Charlie Ward, March 2010, in possession of the author.

Gurindji's problems were their own to solve. As a result, Davey and Richardson's efforts to Aboriginalise Daguragu Council were resisted by an aspirational class of white entrepreneurs—mostly surviving on an Aboriginal customer base. The *kartiya* businesses were more reliable than their government-funded 'Gurindji' competitors, and jeopardised their existence. When a whitefella opened a fuel and takeaway outlet, for instance, the fortunes of Kalkaringi's ailing council-owned shop declined. Similarly, a mechanic went into competition with Daguragu Council's workshop, and former Kalkaringi police officer Dennis Watson began a bus service driving locals to and from Katherine.

Any doubts the whites might have had about setting up shop at Wave Hill were allayed by NTG officials, who told them they should regard the town as '[their] own sacred site'.[16] Nothing had changed after the Gurindji went on 'strike' about these problems in 1982, and Kalkaringi and Daguragu's economic domination by *kartiya* was now complete.

While the whites drank at Frank's Bar and Grill, Daguragu Council issued permits for them to drink in their homes at Kalkaringi as well. Norm and Helen McNair remember the effects:

> Helen: Straight away some of the influential Aboriginal people said 'we want permits too', so it was useless, basically. Kalkaringi was so-called 'dry', but with permits. That was used and abused like anywhere. Once again, what the elders wanted didn't happen, because whites over-ruled.
>
> Norm: [...] and there were a few Aboriginal people who were willing to go along with all that.
>
> Helen: Of course there were.

---

16 Davey to NTDCD, undated, Richardson Personal Collection.

To rehabilitate drinkers, the elders proposed to run their own 'cultural retraining centre' near Lajamanu, with Warlpiri leaders, but some of the old people themselves drank now, too.[17] Norm McNair was distressed:

> These were respected leaders of the community. I just found that quite sad really, because [as they said] 'We've tried so hard for so long'. It just got too much. It was easier to give in and get drunk and forget about it. Some of those leaders were the ones who were shaking their heads about the young people being irresponsible to start with.

Alcohol and the shocking problems it caused had now become *normal* to the people of Wave Hill.

* * *

In 1985, Frank Hardy dropped in to see his mates. With Lingiari and the elders now looking backwards as much as forwards, the reunion gave them all an opportunity to look at the progress made—or not—over twenty years. For any readers attuned to the Gurindji's struggle, Hardy returned bearing little good news. The old radical wrote in *The Bulletin* that while the elders' vision remained strong, it was blurred by 'the blandishments and paternalism of *kartiya*':

> They keep saying to me: 'we kept our word and we stayed at Wattie Creek, but they [the government] didn't keep their word'. They feel the settlement is an economic threat to the future of the Gurindji people. These services established for them are not where they wanted them, and this is a very bitter reality.[18]

---

17 Gurindji Elders to Magistrate, 14 February 1986, Richardson Personal Collection.
18 Richard Pullin, 'Frank Hardy revisits Gurindji to Help with New Problems', source unknown, date unknown [*c.* 1985].

According to Hardy, the building up of 'Welfare' (Kalkaringi) at the expense of Daguragu was the elders' 'main grievance', and for them the school being there was 'the worst thing about it'. Depressingly, two decades after their Walk-off, their desires were little-changed:

> All future building [must] be carried out at Wattie Creek [...]; work must be found for the young men at Daguragu [...]; the cattle must be mustered in future by them; and the cattle station books should be kept [...] in Wattie Creek [...].[19]

The only one of their goals the old men did not lament was land rights. Freehold title had been awarded over 95 percent of their claim, and a finding on the remainder was imminent—though few of Lingiari's generation would have long to enjoy it.

While the Gurindji's land was on its way, Muramulla, its lessee, was struggling. The company's latest accountant was the only signatory on its accounts, and was a source of concern to both the elders and the ADC. Many 'improvements' the government required of Muramulla had also failed to eventuate. The ADC (Muramulla's funding body), BTEC, and the modern pastoral economy all required Muramulla to do this work, but organising it was a struggle. Despite its recent cattle sales, the company was badly short of cash and had little to pay workers. Income from turning off stock had to be spent not on wages, but meeting BTEC requirements. The company couldn't afford to pay the award offered on neighbouring stations, and most of the few 'serious' Gurindji stockmen had taken off to work elsewhere.

One of these itinerant workers was gun rider Charlie Pincher, and when he returned to Daguragu displaying flash clobber and other trappings of wealth, his prestige grew considerably. In addition to

---

19   Frank Hardy, 'In Fear of a Town Called Welfare', *The Bulletin*, 24 September 1985, pp. 64–74, p. 70.

the kudos to be obtained from working on other stations, long-term visitor Kerry Gibbs believes Charlie and others had good reason to leave: 'To sit around the camp, chase cattle and see no actual [financial] reward—it's a pretty good reason to say "Well bugger this, I'm out of here. I'll go where they pay me"'.[20]

The then manager of Wave Hill station, Graeme Fagan, agrees. Although the number of Gurindji people working for their powerful neighbour was in steady decline, some told him in 1986 that unlike the Muramulla Co, 'if you work for Vestey's, you get paid. Three feeds a day and a house to live in—paid!'[21] For the elders, it must have been a painful irony.

The old men's union mate Brian Manning was aware of their frustration, and floated a 'value-adding' plan. On a visit to Daguragu, he and Kerry Gibbs:

> [...] Talked with Vincent about [...] creating employment for women and non-stock workers [by making] a sun-dried meat product, and exporting it to Asia instead of live cattle export. We came prepared with enough seasoning spices and vinegar to make a marinade and conduct a trial. Vincent was interested [...] so he sent off a couple of men to get a killer and we prepared about 100 kilos which we strung up on a makeshift 'clothesline' of barbed wire. After three days [...] I took a sample back to Darwin, which was quite edible six months later. I learned from Victor that the product was considered very good. They ate it all.[22]

---

20   Darwin, NTAS, Interview with Kerry Gibbs, recorded by Charlie Ward, September 2010, NTRS 3609, BWF 18.
21   Darwin, NTAS, Interview with Graeme Fagan, recorded by Charlie Ward, September 2012, NTRS 3609, BWF 42.
22   Brian Manning, 'A Blast From the Past: an Activist's Account of the Wave Hill Walk-off', (The Sixth Annual Vincent Lingiari Lecture, 2002), *Vintage Reds: Australian Stories of Rank and File Organising* <http://roughreds.com/index.html> [accessed 6 December, 2010], p. 13.

Manning's jerky proposal floundered for a lack of government investment.

Despite the fencing erected by Muramulla stockmen and Buck Buchester, the horses the Gurindji depended on were getting away from them. According to Norm McNair:

> They had horses, they had a stallion to breed with the horses, but they had a stage where all the young horses were never castrated, so you had lots of stallions around, and that doesn't do much for [a horse plant]. By the time we left, I didn't think the horses were being managed well.

When the men wanted to muster stock at Lajamanu, Billy Bunter had to ask Jan Richardson if they could borrow her young sons' riding mounts—the Gurindji's entire horse plant was missing.

Such issues were noted by DPP stockies, who had long doubted the Gurindji's ability to muster and test all their cattle and build up their property at the rate required by BTEC. Experience had proved them correct. Not all the cattle on the Gurindji lease were able to be tested, so in 1985 the stock inspectors played their ace. Under the *Stock Diseases Control Act (1923)*, the forcible removal or slaughter of the Gurindji's herd was ordered—the compulsory de-stocking of Daguragu Pastoral Lease 805.

The animals that could not be caught would be killed by helicopter-borne marksmen. According to Buck Buchester, the logic was inexorable: '[The Gurindji] went under [BTEC], they never kept it up, and that's how they de-stocked Wattie Creek'.[23] Compensation would be paid, but it was a stunning blow that *kartiya* cattlemen and

---

23 Darwin, NTAS, Interview with Buck Buchester recorded October 1986, NTRS 3164/295.

government vets agreed was inevitable. Wave Hill station manager Graeme Fagan put it this way:

> Lack of infrastructure is what buggered them. They didn't have anywhere to isolate cattle. They didn't have many paddocks and they were really running a feral harvesting operation, even though they were branding cattle and turning them out once a year.[24]

The elders were far from facing de-stocking alone. Every Aboriginal-run property in the Katherine region suffered the same fate.

* * *

For fifteen years, Lingiari and the old men had worked hard to grow their herd. Now they were forced to back-track. From the elders' point of view, the government's justification probably looked weak: in the testing that *had* been done, only two lonely, pustulent cows with tuberculosis had been found, three years earlier. Even less brucellosis had been found in the Gurindji's herd: one in every two thousand animals. Regardless, destocking meant that a great number were sold or killed, except those which had been confirmed disease-free, and segregated since.

A blame game began. Rangiari and other elders felt their former *kartiya* advisers were responsible for the company's woes.

Interviewer: What was [Stan Andrews] like, a good manager?

Rangiari: Well, he wasn't bin too good, you know. He must have been good in the 'nother hand, but he must have bin little bit robbing people.

---

24   NTAS, Fagan, NTRS 3609, BWF 42.

Interviewer: You reckon?

Rangiari: That's what I bin reckon, you know.

From Rangiari's perspective, Andrews' successor Bill Purdie had also been 'not too good. He been bit of a rogue. [...] He wasn't been stayed too long, because if he could stay a bit longer [...], people complain about it'.[25] Even Gordon Bauman was criticised.

Whites pointed the finger at other *kartiya* involved in the operation as well. Mark 'Fox' Lumsden, a *kartiya* with intimate knowledge of the Gurindji lease, doubts whether Buck Buchester was up to overseeing the development of an entire station:

> He [...] never had the training to put it on its feet properly. Up to a point he did a very good job, but he wasn't [...] what they needed to set them up. [...] He put four or five bores down and equipped them adequately, [and] I think he was alright because he had a dialogue with the Aboriginal people, but he didn't get the [results] that someone with a different set of credentials could have had.[26]

When the Gurindji elders had taken their first illegal steps with cattle on Vestey's Wave Hill station in the late 1960s, conservative governments had ignored them—trying to 'take oxygen', activists thought, from the issues they raised. Then, for a decade under Whitlam and Fraser's policies, the DAA had supported Muramulla with considerable fanfare. Now the Everingham and Hawke Governments seemed intent on dominating the company, and not only through BTEC and the DPP. As the disease eradication campaign's 'hidden' goal of modernisation segued nicely with the ADC's drive to

---

25   NTAS, Rangiari, NTRS 226, TS 485, (T4), p. 26.
26   Darwin, NTAS, Mark Lumsden [former DPP stock inspector] interviewed by Charlie Ward, August 2014, NTRS 3609, BWF 63.

improve profitability, the Gurindji were told that unless they invested their destocking compensation money in more infrastructure, they would lose their funding. Then, after Jerry Rinyngayarri sacked Buck Buchester for his insistence on helicopter mustering, another show of force ensued. The dismissal had barely taken effect when 'three departments of the Darwin administration descended on Wattie Creek, to force [the Gurindji] to give Buck his job back'.[27] The elders complied, and Lingiari complained bitterly that the government was 'using their bag of tricks to stop us running [Muramulla] we own way'.[28]

While all this drained the energy of Muramulla's board, they tried to inspire more passion for cattle in their sons. Plans for an annual rodeo and a 'stock camp school' at Berta Werta or Liku outstations were floated. When the elders asked Stan Davey to organise a training program for young stockmen, most of the 'new generation' participants tried to return home each night, rather than camp on country for weeks as their fathers had done.[29] The young men's poor commitment was dragging the company lower. According to Fagan, who was observing the operation from next door on Wave Hill station, the problem was:

> 'Flexible' staffing arrangements—morning shift, afternoon shift and 'no shift'—they had some really good guys who turned up, and then all the others who came and went, who watched and didn't do much. It was just a hard slog.

Similarly, Norm McNair reckons that by the mid-1980s:

---

27 NTAS, Davey, NTRS 226, TS 462.
28 Hardy, *The Bulletin*, 24 September 1985, pp. 69–70.
29 The 'stock camp school' concept was an attempt to reinstate the structured environment of station stock camps in which Gurindji elders (and *kartiya* overseers) had been able to control young men. See 'Gurindji Adult Education Committee Meeting Minutes', 12 November 1986, Richardson Personal Collection; Michael George, Personal Communication, 27 October 2010.

> There wasn't that much enthusiasm, I guess this breakdown was occurring, enthusiasm was lost. There'd be times when they would get the cattle in and [brand] them and then there'd be great delays. Eventually a few would get together and do a bit, but the momentum really petered out.

In the words of Gus George, 'the young ones not interested in the cattle company side, they were interested in the footy and all that. That's why you can see this thing slowly drop down'.[30]

Now Mick Rangiari's greatest worry for Muramulla was its lack of a strong Gurindji leader:

> What really make me worried—you know, Vincent. Whitlam gave the dirt to Vincent Lingiari [...], and afterward one of his son, Victor [became] a company director. But he's not here, he is away out in the bush. [...] He's supposed to take everything in his hand, he is supposed to be taking over. [...] The place is getting bigger, and someone got to really stand up and run it.

Lingiari's eldest son took on leadership roles as the Gurindji's Central Land Council representative and the DAA's Aboriginal community adviser, but to his father's coterie, these pursuits—and Victor's frequent absences on his outstation—were evidence of his lack of commitment to the company.

The elders' loosening grip on Muramulla and their lease emboldened Wave Hill's young men. Many were keen to impress their families as providers, and saw the surrounding country as a larder with cattle ripe for the taking. BTEC had reduced the Gurindji's herd of 8,600 by half, but if Lumsden is to be believed, the impact of hunting was almost as great:

---

30   NTAS, George, NTRS 3609, BWF 24.

> It [got to] epidemic proportions, it was just everybody driving around with a .303 [rifle]. I'd see them go out with—I used to call it a 'gunship'—a Toyota with three blokes in the back with rifles, and two or three in the front with guns stuck out the doors. They'd just open up on a mob of cattle and they might shoot three and kill one. Some of [the cattle] would just go and die of infection or peritonitis or whatever. First one that fell down, that was it. They'd leave every gate open. It got to a point that if they wanted to go through a fence they'd just cut the fence. If the elders said 'it's our land, our cattle', how do you stop them from doing that?[31]

Today's Gurindji leaders like Michael George and Jimmy Wavehill also believe 'stealing killers' hastened Muramulla's demise. The real impact of the carnage and feasting is hard to know, but 'Fox' calculated that one in nine of the Gurindji's herd were shot and killed each year. Certainly by 1986, the property carried only 2,500 cattle—20 percent of its potential. Jack Doolan wondered whether Muramulla would ever rise again.

* * *

Through education and community development, Davey and Richardson were still giving Gurindji empowerment their best shot. In Daguragu Council's office, curious and ambitious young adults fronted for jobs and training. Ros Frith, Susan Cebu, Michael Paddy, Milton Splinter and others made real progress, but many more found work pressure, the office environment, or training itself not to their liking, and departed. Richardson and Davey remained convinced that the young people's lack of education—including their ignorance

---

31 NTAS, Lumsden, NTRS 3609, BWF 63.

of Western economic, legal and political culture—was their main impediment. When Davey applied for (and took) the job of Wave Hill's adult educator-at-large, he became more disillusioned. The 'churn' of young Gurindji was so great that few emerged with useful skills. Of those who persevered, many cared little for the collective goals of the elders, exploited their positions for their own ends, or were unmercifully harassed by their relatives.[32]

For young council staff like Dawn Rook, refusing the demands of family members was a nightmare. If she or other Gurindji fronting local organisations conceded to their relatives' requests, losing their jobs—their possible toehold in society at large—was the least of their worries. For the track mob, reciprocal exchange was at the heart of their identity, and denying the requests of kin was barely imaginable. For these novice employees to do their jobs, they needed to treat everyone equally, but were ostracised and alienated for doing so. It was another unforseen hurdle for the elders' vision. For while an independent Daguragu would require young people to run its organisations, experience had now shown they would need to be exempt from normal relationships to do so. If it ever came to pass, a Gurindji-run homeland with *kartiya*-style services could only be torn from the fabric of the society the elders wished to preserve.

The Gurindji elders had rejected the archaic pastoral industry in the 1960s, and in the 70s had turned to the state to meet their needs. They'd always known that operating a school, clinic and cattle company—the facilities they wanted—would require *kartiya* knowledge they'd been denied, but twenty years later, that knowledge had also largely eluded their youth. The autonomous 'homestead'

---

32   NTAS, Davey, NTRS 226, TS 462, p. 2.

they'd strived for had also been superseded and outgrown. In its place was a far larger community with its own incorporated council. In addition to Daguragu, the Gurindji's council was responsible for Kalkaringi, a larger town again. The specialised skills and training required to manage these two serviced communities within federal, Territory and local government laws far eclipsed those that Tom Fisher, his book-keeper and hired hands had used in the 1960s to run Wave Hill station.

By 1986, Stan Davey had decided that the elders' aim—and the government's goal—of Aboriginal self-management at Wave Hill was an impossibility. In his reckoning, young Gurindji needed more support to manage *kartiya*-style jobs than Daguragu's elders were prepared to give. As well as the paucity of Gurindji with the motivation or ability to run local operations, Davey believed that both the Territory and federal governments were 'controlling, stifling and suppressing' Kalkaringi and Daguragu, preventing overall Aboriginal control.[33]

Since Whitlam's time, a welter of government-defined 'powers' and responsibilities *had* been handed to the Gurindji, who mostly proved little-interested in their dictated arrangements, took to them in a limited way, or worked them for their own ends. Although whitefellas filled Wave Hill's management roles and governments pursued their diverse agendas, the official mantra of 'Aboriginal self-determination' continued. Self-determination had become a politically necessary, though hollow, contrivance in the north.

As pessimism overcame Davey, Richardson and the elders, the battle for land launched by the old men a generation earlier was

---

33   NTAS, Davey, NTRS 226, TS 462, p. 6; Davey to 'David', 14 September 1984, Richardson Personal Collection.

finally resolved. After Justice Toohey found *ALRA*'s terms inadequate, the government had modified the *Act* and the Gurindji were granted 'land rights' over the remaining 5 percent of their lease. Whitlam's promise at the 1975 handover regarding the 'imminent' transfer of their country to freehold title was fulfilled.

* * *

On 11 May 1986, Minister Clyde Holding flew to Daguragu to hand the Gurindji their 'land rights'. These Aboriginal freehold deeds gave the Gurindji more power over their land, against the government in Darwin, but the 'track mob' had had the run of their country for ten years, and many saw the affair as mere *kartiya* 'paper business'. While a clutch of CLC lawyers, Labor politicians and locals watched on, Minister Holding delivered the Gurindji's land rights without fanfare. Whitlam's handful of sand cast a shadow over the day, but times had changed. The Hawke Government's plans to prevent more Aboriginal pastoral leases being converted to freehold overshadowed the occasion, and the media stayed away. Rather than deliver rousing speeches about mateship, the few elders present chastised the Minister for failing to rein in Kalkaringi's unchecked domination of their affairs instead.[34]

The hope and promise of the early days were over. Nine Ministers had come and gone since WC 'Billy' Wentworth naively pledged a horse paddock to the Gurindji in 1968, and the elders had dealt with them all. Now Muramulla was in freefall and the surviving Walk-

---

34   See Central Land Council, 'Daguragu Station Land Claim', <http://www.clc.org.au/land-won-back/info/daguragu-station-land-claim/>. Accessed 1 October 2014; Jan Richardson, *Diary 1986*, Richardson Personal Collection.

off leaders had turned to past glories. The swings and roundabouts of federal and NT politics, not to mention the vicissitudes of both the open market and government funding, had exhausted them. Gurindji land rights advocate Pincher Nyurrmiarri had been buried months earlier, and Lingiari sat at Daguragu, unable to walk. The battle that began in the bush with the old men's great cry for freedom ended, barely heard. Their fight was over, but their vision remains.

AFTERWORD

In dreadful circumstances a generation earlier, Vincent Lingiari and a group of Gurindji elders had risked their people's security and wellbeing for a vision they held. As we have seen, their subsequent trajectory was extraordinary. Within a generation, the Gurindji track mob left their serf-like position in an archaic industry and became celebrated landholders with apparent control over two modern communities. Driving them were the elders' goals of reclaiming their land from *kartiya*, running their own cattle operation, and creating an autonomous community. They also wanted their children to be educated in a way that would allow them to both operate Daguragu's European-style services, and to take up their roles as the new custodians of Gurindji law and culture. To the elders, it was integral to achieve all of this with a minimum of European support.

In this book, I have described the eventual outcomes of the Gurindji's track and sought to understand the reasons for its successes and failures. Are there any lessons for us from it today, though? Firstly, what of Gurindji land rights, the elders' signature success? The old Gurindji men's concepts of land ownership varied vastly from Europeans' standard beliefs, but in the late 1960s they convinced a large section of the Australian public and the Australian Labor Party to help them remedy the moral wrong of Aboriginal dispossession. As a result, the Whitlam and Fraser Governments' *Aboriginal Land Rights (Northern Territory) Act* 1976 refashioned Northern Territory law so that traditional forms of Aboriginal land ownership could be held within it, ostensibly unchanged. After the Gurindji's land was

AFTERWORD

returned to them under the Act in 1986, they were free to enact their traditional ceremonial responsibilities to their country as they saw fit. The years since have confirmed that land ownership is that rare beast in Indigenous Affairs: an issue apparently responsive to legislation.

Second after land in Lingiari's scheme was his aim of establishing a Gurindji-run cattle operation. A legal 'fix', this time of incorporation, was used to legitimate this goal as well, with different results. Lingiari and his group managed to operate their small business for fifteen years in a remote area without capital of their own, though the elders' ultimate goals for the Muramulla company were never realised. The reasons why the elders and their advisers were unable to make Muramulla financially self-supporting, or to transfer its management to the next generation of Gurindji are many.

From its beginning, the Gurindji's cattle operation was an unstable mix of Indigenous practical know-how, taxpayer funding, and financial and management advice provided by an ever-changing array of European staff, accounting firms and government agencies. Even when Muramulla was functioning at its best in the late 1970s, the goals and assumptions of its Gurindji board members were never aligned with or understood by their governmental backers—and equally those of the government were never absorbed by the Gurindji. The elders had little financial grasp of the pastoral economy they had worked in earlier or the modernised industry they were forced to compete with. Naturally, they failed to anticipate the amount of funding and other resources they would require to make their operation self-supporting.

Muramulla's financial dependence on the state compounded its other difficulties. The conditions attached to the company's funding were heavily prescriptive, but the amounts and timing of that funding

were based not on pastoral but bureaucratic imperatives, and largely unpredictable. The situation was exacerbated by the industry's rapid move towards larger holdings and helicopter mustering, which made the elders' goal of creating a small enterprise with a large number of stockmen untenable.

Cattle nonetheless comprised the Wave Hill region's only viable industry (albeit a subsidised one) and the same business had provided the elders with a rare sense of purpose and value vis-à-vis the wider world. There were few other avenues for young Gurindji men to glean these things, and the elders were therefore determined to hand Muramulla over to the next generation, despite the company's struggles. The only way they could have conceivably achieved this was via significant and ongoing government subsidies, which authorities in the 1980s were increasingly unwilling to provide. Eventually, the cost-cutting emphasis of the NT and federal governments, the growing recalcitrance of their potential workforce, and their own waning abilities put paid to the elders' cattle dream.

In hindsight, the third element of the elders' plan was the most ambitious: creating an independent Gurindji community. Few industries, businesses or communities in remote Australia have ever achieved long-term economic independence from the state, and in a financial sense, Lingiari's dream may have been an impossibility. Merely being 'left alone'—social independence—was foremost in the old men's minds though, and to achieve this they recognised that their children would need to manage the facilities in their community themselves. The elders also saw that to do so, their young people would need to acquire knowledge which they themselves lacked.

Without a bicultural school under the elders' management, Lingiari saw little prospect for either the continuation of traditional knowledge

AFTERWORD

among the next generation, *or* Daguragu's future self-management. Nonetheless, the old peoples' ideal of a school at Daguragu was at odds with the priorities of federal and NTG education bureaucrats, and the elders' requests for such a school were ignored. It will never be known how much the perpetuation of traditional Gurindji knowledge, the educational achievement of Gurindji children, and the elders' aim of realising their independence at Daguragu were set back as a result.

The autonomy of Daguragu community was undermined in other ways by the allocation of government support. Prior to the mid-1970s, the Gurindji people survived in a largely cashless economy, and were clearly committed to using their own skills to build up Daguragu. When unprecedented amounts of funding for infrastructure, wages and welfare payments were suddenly introduced as a result of Whitlam and Fraser's self-determination and self-management policies, the Gurindji's autonomy was compromised in two ways. Firstly, like the invasion of their land in the 1880s, it divorced them from the scale, speed and direction of change in their environment. Secondly, it dramatically hastened the economic transition of their traditionally stratified, hierarchical society into a more homogenous consumer group. This in turn significantly exacerbated existing tensions and conflict that had arisen due to their radically novel circumstances.

State-assisted development eclipsed the elders' vision for their community and increased the complexity and regulation of that community's facilities. To manage those facilities and their problems, non-Indigenous staff were employed in increasing numbers at Kalkaringi and Daguragu. Simultaneously, the mainstream schooling of Gurindji children in Kalkaringi, Alice Springs and Darwin rarely delivered new community leaders, and Gurindji management of local

facilities shifted out of reach as a result. By these means, a society that had masterfully sustained itself by hard work and self-motivation largely lost control of its environment. It is ironic in the extreme that this occurred as a result of government assistance given under policies of Aboriginal self-management.

* * *

While unprecedented government support—and in some instances the lack of it—undermined the elder's vision of an autonomous community, their plans for Daguragu were also challenged by dynamics within their own society. From as early as the 1940s, young Gurindji men had resisted the constraints of traditional life and sought to avoid the physical suffering which resulted from advancing within or from breaking traditional Gurindji law. When their entry to the cash economy and their protection from traditional punishments under *kartiya* law allowed them to in the 1970s, many young people challenged their elders' authority and values—not to mention their plans for an independent community. In the Gurindji's rapidly changing circumstances after their Walk-off, young men and women were freer to leave their community, or not participate in the developmental work encouraged by their elders or the Department of Aboriginal Affairs.

Through travel, schooling, training programs, the local advent of television, and (for some) time in jail, the non-Indigenous world impacted on the next generation of Gurindji far more than it had affected their parents, and offered them a few more choices. In the world the Gurindji increasingly inhabited though, traditional Aboriginal culture was merely a curio. The elders were forced to

AFTERWORD

accept that, increasingly, the rights of an 18 year-old Gurindji youth were the same as those of the most advanced law-man.

The concentrated effects of social, economic and technological change in the remote NT during the 1970s brought Lingiari's group other bitter truths. When the time came for their youth to take over the Gurindji's affairs, the old cattle industry, primitive facilities, and isolation that had informed the elders' vision no longer existed. The *kartiya* world had moved on, and it would fall to the next generation of Gurindji leaders to adapt and regain control.

* * *

Before this could happen, the Muramulla company collapsed. Even though the Gurindji became the recognised owners of their former lease after they received freehold title in 1986, pressure to develop their country continued due to Muramulla's dependence on government funding. To build up its southern half, the elders offered it on agistment to a *kartiya* sharecropper, who built a small homestead at McDonald's Yard to fulfil the 'gentleman's agreement' he made with the old Gurindji. Their country was too rough however, and he departed after three seasons. Rather than seeing their land unworked, the Gurindji sublet the same area to Vestey's—in effect returning half of their newly-won property to Wave Hill station.

When Muramulla dissolved soon afterwards, the company's then director Billy Bunter blamed its book-keepers:

> We were doing really good work, but all of a sudden everything collapsed down. There was trouble with the accountant, John Trezona […]. We never got the monthly reports from the cattle company side. Everything was blind. Nobody let us know what

> happened with the bookwork. [...] Our figures dropped down, and we had to pay back so much money. For what? We'd never done anything wrong.

For his part, accountant John Trezona recalls avoidable losses like a new truck engine worth $5,000 ($12,000) getting 'cooked' on a grog run, and a $12,000 ($28,000) stud bull being butchered and eaten.

Before his death, Bunter described to me Muramulla's end:

> We lost that thing, and they did bugger all. I used to try to get the government and consultant to support us. I never used to have any problem with Aboriginal people not supporting us, so I walked away, I got a job with the Land Council.
>
> I left the cars, tractors, big truck, horses and cattle with the Gurindji people at Daguragu [...]. They had to take the big truck away, the Toyotas away, everything that the station had, they took it away [...]. The old fellas were wondering what was going on. I had to explain everything, what was the truth about what was happening.[1]

Lingiari was now missing from among the 'old fellas'. The great leader died in January 1988 and was afforded Gurindji and Christian burial rites. His grave was marked with a star picket at Kalkaringi.

By the time of Lingiari's death, the Vestey company's flagship Union International was struggling financially, and the call was made to withdraw from Australia. Despite the company's seventy-year tenure at Wave Hill, its departure proved the Gurindji adage correct: *kartiya* leave and we remain. Problems Lingiari had well understood—succession difficulties and family scandals—had compounded Vestey's losses in the global recession of the late 1980s.[2] At home, the

---

1 NTAS, 'Interview with Billy Bunter recorded by Charlie Ward', July 2011, NTRS 3609, BWF 26.
2 With thanks to Tim Rowse, Personal Communication, 17 January 2015.

AFTERWORD

dynasty had been subject to a gargantuan battle with the British tax office and the details of their Byzantine tax avoidance schemes were exposed in the press. Britain's pioneering, ultra-rich food merchants had been brought low.

For the hundreds of workers and scores of communities who had lived in the company's shadow in north Australia, Vestey's departure marked the end of an era. Despite its flaws, the multinational had been a pioneer of Australia's northern development, and its loyal *kartiya* staff were saddened. Wave Hill station was the 'jewel in the crown' of Vestey's vast antipodean holdings, and would also become its last post. As stations across the NT, Queensland and the Kimberley were auctioned in the early 1990s, their records—comprising an archival cornerstone of Australia's frontier history—were sent to the homestead at Wave Hill. The sale of the station was looming, and its manager unsuccessfully lobbied the Stockman's Hall of Fame to take the records for posterity. Running out of time, he burnt them at the homestead tip. Only a book of Wave Hill's improvements was saved.[3] Aside from memoirs and scattered photos, this lonely ledger is the only evidence from Vestey's stations of their long presence in Australia's north. The records from their Sydney HQ were also destroyed.

In July 1992, when Wave Hill station was sold, few Gurindji worked there. At nearby Daguragu and Kalkaringi, the old people's memories of 'Vestey time' were clear, but the company's departure meant little to the new generation. The track mob's cattle dreams had largely turned to dust, and the surviving elders and new leaders leased

---

3   Canberra, Noel Butlin Archives Centre, *Wave Hill Station Improvements Book*, Australian National University, N182; Darrell Lewis, Personal Communication, 13 January 2012.

the entirety of their hard-won land to 'Fox' Lumsden. Over twenty years, Fox and his wife Georgina MacLeod carved a successful business from the Muramulla run. Supporting half a dozen people rather than a community, its small meatworks still supplies beef to the Gurindji.

* * *

Since the Gurindji elders' horses ran wild and their cattle operation folded, new generation leaders have carried forward Lingiari's 'community'-type values, and redefined his vision. Ros Frith, Susan Cebu, Maurie Japarta Ryan, the late Victor Vincent, Michael Paddy and many others have adapted Gurindji political power to a new, post-cattle-industry millennium.

Traditions practised by previous generations of elders have been modified, but whether they have been lost is another story. Visitors to Kalkaringi or Daguragu today realise that Gurindji culture remains strong, vibrant and adaptive. Today, Daguragu resembles other remote communities, but remains a *'ngumpit* place' where whites are unwelcome to live. In 2007 though, the appearance of Gurindji control over their home, the 'birthplace of land rights', was radically challenged. Under the Howard Government's 'Emergency Intervention', federal bureaucrats placed a demountable complex in Daguragu and appointed a Government Business Manager (GBM) to occupy it. This greatly offended the track mob, and Canberra's incumbent 'Ginger Bread Men' maintained such a low profile that the reason for their presence remained a mystery to most locals. Tragically for the people of Wave Hill though, the 'Intervention'—

AFTERWORD

which alongside its racist shock and awe tactics, included increased funding—was a minor prelude to what came next.

When the new Gurindji leaders that I know came of age in the 1980s, they had, like Lingiari's coterie, pinned their political hopes on Daguragu Council. Even then though, 'statism' had triumphed over the type of home-grown independence originally envisaged by Lingiari. The Council was never an adequate vessel for Gurindji *cultural* power, but as the local service provider, employer and political decision-maker, it involved scores of residents in their communities' affairs. *Kartiya* had always held its 'manager' jobs, but the Gurindji believed—and had been officially encouraged to believe—that the council belonged to them. In 2008, Daguragu Council was dismantled by the NT Labor government.

The NTG's enormous Victoria Daly Regional Council (also known as 'the shire') took over, and institutional government support for Aboriginal self-determination at Wave Hill was obliterated. The fortnightly meetings of a dozen Gurindji leaders discussing the intricacies of local affairs that I witnessed in 2004–06 ceased immediately. Bitterness lingers about the takeover, in which Daguragu Council's assets—including a successful business and a bus partly purchased by locals using their own wages—were forcibly possessed. Now, services are centralised and 'Vic Daly' administers diverse Aboriginal communities scattered over an area larger than the country of Greece. Under this economic rationalist edifice, Kalkaringi and Daguragu's 600 Gurindji, Warlpiri and *kartiya* residents have one representative. This unlucky person advocates for the two communities' factions, families and language groups at six meetings a year in faraway Katherine.

This situation is repeated Territory-wide. In the new shire system, dedicated staff do their best in trying conditions, but the problems the shires were meant to fix—inept and unethical clerks, poor financial management, and high staff turnover—remain. For the Gurindji, it has been a disaster. Support previously provided by Daguragu Council for community projects and engagement evaporated, and thirteen Shire Service Managers warmed the seat at Kalkaringi in three years. With 'shire-isation', Territory politicians proved that after three decades of relative stability and a semblance of community control, Gurindji political power was ultimately a plaything of the state.

The Gurindji retain a reputation for feistiness, however. After engineering the removal of the Intervention outpost at Daguragu and refusing a controversial government leasing plan, the track mob's descendants are on the front foot again. Kalkaringi and Daguragu's residents have initiated their own art centre, and formed a corporation designed to re-assert control of their organisations. The community is engaging with the Vic-Daly Regional Council for the first time. Fifty years after the Gurindji's Walk-off, it is a 'new day' again at Wave Hill. Against all odds, Lingiari's legacy lives.

SELECT BIBLIOGRAPHY

Key references and sources quoted directly are displayed as footnotes in the text. Other material informing each chapter is listed here.

Abbreviations
NAA – National Archives of Australia
NTN – Northern Territory News
NTAS – Northern Territory Archives Service
SLNSW – State Library of New South Wales
SMH – Sydney Morning Herald

Introduction

Composing an accurate account of events on Australia's pastoral frontier is notoriously fraught. If *Yijarni: True Stories from Gurindji Country* had been available to me earlier, this process would have been somewhat easier regarding Wave Hill station's establishment. This book is a collection of Gurindji oral histories: *Yijarni: True Stories from Gurindji Country*, edited by Erika Charola and Felicity Meakins (Canberra, Aboriginal Studies Press, 2016). Instead, the brief sketch I paint in the Introduction was informed by the disparate sources listed below.

Interviews
Lauris Farrow, Interview Recorded by Charlie Ward, 28 December 2006. In possession of the author.
NTAS, 'Interview Recorded with Billy Bunter by Charlie Ward', 24 October 2010, NTRS 3609/BWF 2.

Archival
Darwin, NAA, Administrator, Northern Territory [II] - Central Registry, *Wave Hill Station, 1952–54*, F1, 1952/736.
Darwin, NTAS, 'Letterbook', 1914–1931, *Police Station, Wave Hill (Kalkaringi)*, NTRS 2772.
Darwin, NTAS, *Police Station, Wave Hill (Kalkaringi), Copy of Day Journal, 1924–1927*, NTRS 2014, Box PB360.

Published Material

Bobbie Buchanan, *In the Tracks of Old Bluey: The Life Story of Nat Buchanan* (Rockhampton, Central Queensland University Press, 1997, 2006 ed).

Gordon Buchanan, *Packhorse and Waterhole* (Sydney, Angus and Robertson, 1933).

Peter d'Abbs, *The Vestey Story* (Collingwood, Victoria, Australasian Meat Industry Employees' Union, 1970).

Frank Hardy, *The Unlucky Australians*, Sydney, Nelson, 1968 (2006 edn, Melbourne, One Day Hill).

Mary Anne Jebb, *Blood, Sweat and Welfare: A History of White Bosses and Aboriginal Pastoral Workers* (Perth, University of Western Australia Publishing, 2002).

Phillip Knightley, *The Rise and Fall of the House of Vestey* (London, United Kingdom, Warner Books 1993).

Dawn May, *Aboriginal Labour and the Cattle Industry: Queensland from White Settlement to the Present* (Melbourne, Cambridge University Press, 1994).

Patrick McConvell, 'Changing Places: European and Aboriginal Styles', in *The Land is a Map: Placenames of Indigenous Origin in Australia*, ed. by Luise Hercus, Flavia Hodges and Jane Simpson (Canberra, Pandanus Press, 2002).

Ann McGrath, *Born In the Cattle* (North Sydney, Allen & Unwin, 1987).

Peter Read and Engineer Jack Japaljarri, 'The Price of Tobacco: the Journey of the Warlmala to Wave Hill, 1928', *Aboriginal History*, 2, 2 (1978) 140–148.

Jeremy Rifkin, *Beyond Beef: The Rise and Fall of the Cattle Culture* (New York, Penguin Books, 1992).

Newspapers

Stuart Millar and Alex Brummer, 'Heirs and Disgraces', *The Guardian*, August 11 1999, <http://www.guardian.co.uk/theguardian/1999/aug/11/features11.g2> [accessed 21 May 2012].

Theses

Minoru Hokari, *Aboriginal Economy and Cattle Labour: the Economic History of the Gurindji People* (Masters of Economics Thesis, Tokyo, Hitotsubashi University, 1996).

Other

Billy Bunter, 'Carrying Water', *Mumkurla-nginyi-ma Parrngalinyparla: From the Darkness into the Light—Gurindji Freedom Banners Project*, (Kalkaringi, NT, Daguragu Community Government Council, 2000).

Peter Forrest, *An Outline of the History of Daguragu and Locality* (Darwin, Northern Territory Library, 1985).

Cecil Watts, *Western Grazing—A Historical Insight* (unpublished, 1992).

SELECT BIBLIOGRAPHY

Part One—The Quest for Justice 1930–72

Chapter 1: Finding Their Feet, 1930–1966

More than any other work, Pearl Ogden's biography of Sabu Sing, *From Humpy to Homestead* (Winellie, Northern Territory, 1992) conveyed to me the experience of Wave Hill station, the crucible that led to the Gurindji's walk-off. Numerous Gurindji testimonies, including those of Billy Jampijinpa Bunter, added to my understanding. Ronald and Catherine Berndts' *End of an Era: Aboriginal Labour in the Northern Territory* (Canberra, Australian Institute of Aboriginal Studies, 1987) was also essential.

Interviews

NTAS, Darwin, Len Brodie [former Vestey's book-keeper], Interview Recorded by Charlie Ward, January 2010, NTRS 3609, BWF 10.

Darwin, NTAS, John Cooke [former Welfare Branch Officer, Elliott NT, 1966], Interview Recorded by Charlie Ward, May 2011, NTRS 3609, BWF 28.

NTAS, Brian Daniels [nephew of Dexter and Davis Daniels], Interview Recorded by Charlie Ward, October 2011, NTRS 3609, BWF 20.

NTAS, Darwin, Interview with Neil Dudgeon [former jackaroo, Wave Hill station], recorded by Charlie Ward, November 2012, NTRS 3609, BWF 21.

Darwin, NTAS, Ted Evans Interviewed by Mary Stephenson, 1982, NTRS 1942, TS 46.

Darwin, NTAS, Interview with Lyn Riddett [former resident at Wattie Creek, 1971–73], Recorded by Charlie Ward, September 2009, NTRS 3609, BWF 3.

Darwin, NTAS, Walter Rogers [former NTCAR member], Interview Recorded by Charlie Ward, October 2011, NTRS 3609, BWF 34.

Darwin, NTAS, Cec and Dawn Watts [former travelling manager of Vesteys], Interview Recorded by Charlie Ward, April 2010, NTRS 3609, BWF 14.

NTAS, Interview with Rod Williams [Resident at Wattie Creek, 1970], Recorded by Charlie Ward, September 2009, NTRS 3609, BWF 1.

Archival

Darwin, NAA, *Wave Hill Station*, F1, 1952/736.

Newspapers

Peter Buckley, 'A Leader Who Learnt the Hard Way', *Tribune*, 5 October 1966, p. 5.

'Compo for Aborigines: Unknown Words in the Cattle Country', *Tribune*, 21 September 1966.

Christopher Forsyth, 'Mustering for a Showdown', *The Australian*, 19 October 1966, p. 9.

Henry McCarthy, 'Aborigines Join Wages Fight: City Unions Support,' *Tribune*, 11 May 1966, p. 1.

'Missionary Opportunities in the Centre', *The Australian Baptist*, 17 October 1962, p. 11.

Published Material

Bain Attwood, 'The Articulation of 'Land Rights' in Australia: The Case of Wave Hill', *Social Analysis*, 44, 1 (2000) 3–39.

Alison Bingle, *This is Our Country* (Self-published, 1986).

Deborah Bird-Rose, *Hidden Histories: Black Stories from Victoria River Downs, Humbert River and Wave Hill Stations* (Canberra, Aboriginal Studies Press, 1991.

Peter d'Abbs, *The Vestey Story* (Collingwood, Victoria, Australasian Meat Industry Employees' Union, 1970).

Jack Kelly, *Struggle for the North* (Sydney, Australasian Book Society, 1966).

Phillip Knightley, *The Rise and Fall of the House of Vestey* (London, United Kingdom, Warner Books 1993).

Douglas Lockwood, '*I, the Aboriginal*', 1962 (1973 edn, Adelaide, Rigby).

Lyn Riddett, *Kine, Kin and Country: The Victoria River District of the Northern Territory, 1911–1966* (Darwin, Northern Territory, Australian National University, 1990.

Sue Taffe, *Black and White Together-FCAATSI: The Federal Council for the Advancement of Aborigines and Torres Strait Islanders, 1958–1973* (St. Lucia, University of Queensland Press, 2005).

Cecil Watts, *Western Grazing—A Historical Insight* (unpublished, 1992).

Theses

Colin Tatz, 'Aboriginal Administration in the Northern Territory of Australia' (PhD Thesis, Canberra, Australian National University, 1964).

Other

Frederick Bray, *Aboriginals and Halfcastes: Miscellaneous Matters*, Department of Native Affairs, Western Australia, 20 February 1941. In possession of the author.

Brian Manning, Personal Communication, 6 December 2010.

Brian Manning, 'A Blast from the Past: an Activist's Account of the Wave Hill Walk-off', (The Sixth Annual Vincent Lingiari Lecture, 2002), *Vintage Reds: Australian Stories of Rank and File Organising* <http://roughreds.com/index.html> [accessed 6 December, 2010].

Chapter 2: Taking a Stand, 1966–1968

Like all accounts of the Wave Hill walk-off, this chapter makes much use of Frank Hardy's *The Unlucky Australians*. The nature of these transformative times in the northern pastoral industry was also conveyed to me by the National Archives' file *Industrial Unrest*, F1, 1966/2182. Minoru Hokari's article, 'From Wattie Creek to Wattie Creek: An Oral Historical Approach to the Gurindji Walk-Off' (*Aboriginal History*, 24 (2000) 98–116) was also invaluable in communicating the later perspective of senior Gurindji men.

SELECT BIBLIOGRAPHY

Interviews

Darwin, NTAS, Interview with Gus George by Charlie Ward, October 2010, NTRS 3609, BWF 24.

Michael George, Interview by Charlie Ward, Kalkaringi, 27 October 2010. In possession of the author.

NTAS, Rob Oke, Interview Recorded by Charlie Ward, November 2009, NTRS 3609, BWF 4.

Darwin, NTAS, Mick Rangiari Interview Transcript, October 1986, NTRS 226, TS 485, (T1).

NTAS, Interview with Essie Warmuth Recorded by Charlie Ward, December 2010, NTRS 3609, BWF 11.

Archival

Canberra, NAA, 'Petition by Gurindji People to Governor-General re Wave Hill Pastoral Land, Northern Territory', A1734, NT 1968/2509.

Darwin, NTAS, *Northern Territory Pastoral Lessees Association, Administration and Correspondence Files*, NTRS 3548, C1–5J.

Newspapers

'1500 Students to March for Gurindjis', *NTN*, 9 July 1968.

'Aborigine Leaders Visit Sydney', *Tribune* (Sydney, Communist Party of Australia, 12 October 1966), p. 3.

Robert Howarth, 'The Gurindji's Take a Step Into the Twentieth Century', *Australian*, 28 February 1968.

Margaret Jones, 'Taking War to Vestey's Doors', *The Age*, Melbourne, 16 November 1968.

Published Material

Bain Attwood, 'The Articulation of 'Land Rights' in Australia: The Case of Wave Hill', *Social Analysis*, 44, 1 (2000) 3–39.

Deborah Bird-Rose, *Hidden Histories: Black Stories from Victoria River Downs, Humbert River and Wave Hill Stations* (Canberra, Aboriginal Studies Press, 1991).

Jennifer Clark, *Aborigines and Activism—Race, Aborigines and the Coming of the Sixties to Australia* (Crawley, Western Australia, University of Western Australia Press, 2008).

Lachlan Clohesy, 'Fighting the Enemy Within: Anti-Communism and Aboriginal Affairs', *History Australia*, 8, 2 (2011) 128–52.

Margaret Harsant, 'Article Three: Stan Davies [sic] at Melbourne University', *Victorian Abschol Newsletter*, Melbourne, August 1970, Oke Personal Collection.

'Historic Debate', *Aboriginal Quarterly*, 1, 3 (Canberra, Abschol, Australian National University, 1968), p. 5.

Edward G Whitlam, *The Whitlam Government 1972–1975* (Ringwood, Victoria, Viking, 1985).

Correspondents

Fred Friis [former teacher at Wave Hill setttlement], Personal Communication, 20 September 2010.
Jean Rodger [widow of Welfare Officer Ian Rodger], Personal Communication, 6 May 2013.

Other

Peter Forrest, *An Outline of the History of Daguragu and Locality* (Darwin, Northern Territory Library, 1985).
Min. Peter Nixon and Min. William C Wentworth, *Settlement of Aboriginals at Wave Hill, Northern Territory*, 10 July 1968, Press Release, Oke Personal Collection.
Peter Nixon, *Northern Territory Land Rights: a Statement by the Minister for the Interior*, 9 August 1968, Oke Personal Collection.
Rob Oke et al, *What Now at Wattie Creek: Report of the Abschol Field Team which Visited Wattie Creek in May–June 1970*, (Abschol, Canberra, Australian National University, 1970).

Chapter 3: Friends from Afar, 1969–1970

Chapters 3–8 rest largely on the troves of correspondence, reporting and pro-land rights campaign ephemera I encountered in the attic of Rob and Kay Oke and Rob Wesley-Smith's intimidating catalogue. To access the 'other' voice in the debate—that of the pastoral industry and Vestey's—the *Northern Territory Pastoral Lessees Association, Administration and Correspondence Files* in the NT Archives were invaluable.

Interviews

Darwin, NTAS, Brian Aarons, Interview Recorded by Charlie Ward, August 2012, NTRS 3609, BWF 41.
NTAS, Patricia Fardell, Interview Recorded by Charlie Ward, April 2014, NTRS 3609, BWF 53.
Darwin, NTAS, Rob Oke, Interview Recorded by Charlie Ward, November 2009, NTRS 3609, BWF 4.

Archival

Darwin, NAA, *Wave Hill Social Club*, E460, 1981/100. 1968/2509.
Canberra, National Film and Sound Archive (NFSA), *Gurindji Land Rights Protests: Sydney*, Title No: 574167.

Newspapers

'Demonstrators in Supermarket Drive on Vestey's', *Tribune*, 29 July 1970, p. 12.
Frank Hardy, *The Australian*: 'Wattie Creek Revisited', 13 June 1970; 'Tug of War in the Wilderness', 15 June 1970; 'A Dream Denied Becomes a Nightmare', 16 June, 1970.

SELECT BIBLIOGRAPHY

'Horns of a Dilemma', *NTN*, 31 August, 1970.
'Limits on Phone Use', *NTN*, 21 September 1970.
'Natives Must Buy Their Land, Says Nixon', *The Australian*, 4 Sept 70.
'Rights Workers Clash Over Wattie Creek', *NTN*, 2 April, 1969.
Alec Robertson, 'Black & White Join in Demonstration for Gurindji Land', *Tribune*, Sydney, 5 August 1970, p. 12.
'Support Swells [...]', *Australian*, 20 August 1970.
'Wave Hill Houses Ready in January', *NTN*, 24 Dec 1970.

Published Material

Paul Fox, 'Welfare: Another Arm of the Law', *Aboriginal Quarterly* (Abschol, Australian National University, August 1970).
Fred Hollows and Peter Corris, *Fred Hollows: An Autobiography* (Melbourne, John Kerr, 1991).
Cecil Holmes, *One Man's Way* (Ringwood, Victoria, Penguin Books 1986).
Lyn Riddett, 'The Strike That Became a Land Rights Movement: A Southern Do-Gooder Reflects on Wattie Creek, 1966–74', *Labour History*, 72 (May 1997) 50–65.
Frank Stevens, 'Aborigines and the Labour Movement', *Origin*, 3, 2 (30 October 1970) 10–11.

Reports

Australian Government, Australian Law Reform Commission, *Recognition of Aboriginal Customary Laws*, Report 31, Chapter Three: 'Changing Policies Towards Aboriginal People', <http://www.alrc.gov.au/publications/3.%20Aboriginal%20Societies%3A%20The%20Experience%20of%20Contact/changing-policies-towards-aboriginal#_ftnref30> [accessed 27 June 2012].
Hannah Middleton, 'The Gurindji at Wattie Creek', Abschol and the Anthropological Society of Victoria (*Conference Proceedings*, Melbourne, 9 December 1970), Oke Personal Collection.

Correspondents

Felicity Meakins [linguist of Gurindji language], Personal Communication, 8 August 2014.
Rob Wesley-Smith, Personal Communication, 12 December 2011
Rod Williams, Personal Communication, September 2011.
Paddy Zakaria [daughter of Jean Culley], Personal Communication, 2 May 2011.

Other

Tony Lawson to MLC Goff Letts, 30 October 1970, Oke Personal Collection.
'Muramulla Gurindji Company Memorandum of Association', October 1970, Oke Personal Collection.
Rob Oke to Min. Nixon, 11 November 1970, Oke Personal Collection.
Stan Smith, 'A Contentious Issue', 1969, Oke Personal Collection.

Chapter 4: Progress and Strain, 1971

A myriad of sources regarding the popular campaign to support the Gurindji at this time were at my disposal. They are listed below. My reporting of the acrimony within the federal government regarding the 'Aboriginal issue' rests largely on Tim Rowse's political biography of Nugget Coombs: *Obliged to Be Difficult: Nugget Coombs' Legacy in Indigenous Affairs* (Cambridge University Press, 2000) and Peter Howson's diaries: *The Life of Politics: The Howson Diaries*, ed. by Don Aitken (Penguin, 1984).

Interviews

Darwin, NTAS, Jack Noble, Interview Recorded by Charlie Ward, October 2011, NTRS 3609, BWF 29.

Darwin, NTAS, Alex Romanoff, Interview Recorded by Charlie Ward, July 2014, NTRS 3609, BWF 58.

Darwin, NTAS, Alan Thorpe, Interview by Charlie Ward, January 2010, NTRS 3609, BWF 9.

Archival

Darwin, NAA, *Wattie Creek Proposed Development Project*, F985, 1973/141.

Newspapers

'Gurindji's Seek $15,000 Loan: Wattie Creek Plans Take Real Shape', *NTN*, Darwin, 6 January 1971.

'Hunt Defends Government's Stand on Gurindji Claims to Land', *NTN*, 1 June 1971.

David Jones, 'Newest Outback Town', *NTN*, [u.d.].

'Letts Gurindji Letter "Use of the Red Herring"', *NTN*, 25 November 1971.

'Specialist Appalled at Eye Disease Among the Gurindji', *NTN*, 11 June 1971.

'The Gurindji's In Town: NAWU Drive on VRD Stations', *NTN*, 23 March 1971.

'The Gurindji's and Their Land', *Sunday Review*, 16 May 1971.

'Vestey's Ready to Hand Over 500 Acres to the Gurindji', *NTN*, 15 May 1971.

Published Material

HC 'Nugget' Coombs, *Kulinma*, (Canberra, Australian National University Press, 1978).

Reports

Stan Davey, 'Report on visit to Wattie Creek: 19–22 August', 29 August 1971, Oke Personal Collection.

Cecil Gibb *et al*, *The Report of the Committee to Review the Situation of Aborigines on Pastoral Properties in the Northern Territory*, (Canberra, Commonwealth Government Printer's Office, 1973).

SELECT BIBLIOGRAPHY

Northern Territory Administration (NTA), 'Fourth Report of the Sessional Committee of the Northern Territory Legislative Council', 14 November 1967.
Rob Oke, *Report on Trip to Wattie Creek*, March 1971, Oke Personal Collection.
Wattie Creek Newsletter (7), 6 September 1971, Oke Personal Collection.

Correspondence

Jean Culley to Rob Oke, [u.d., *c.* 1971], Oke Personal Collection.
Jean Culley to John Zakharov, 5 April 1971, Oke Personal Collection.
Moira Gibbs to Tony Lawson, 29 December 1971, Oke Personal Collection.
Lex Grey to Lyn Riddett, 27 October 1971, Riddett Personal Collection.
Tony Lawson and Rob Oke to Peter Nixon [*c.* December 1970], Oke Personal Collection
Hannah Middleton to Rob Oke, 30 December 1970, Oke Personal Collection.
Hannah Middleton to Rob Oke, 21 January 1971.
Dr PS Rogers to the Secretary, Melbourne Gurindji Committee, 9 September 1971, Oke Personal Collection.
'Jungmiari' [Zakharov] to Riddett, 26 October 1971, Riddett Personal Collection.

Chapter 5: Vindication, 1972

My account of the Ngarinyman people's walk-off from VRD is based largely on the reportage and personal correspondence of David Quin and Jean Culley, contained in the papers of Rob Oke and others. As was often the case, Stan Davey visited and wrote an important summary: 'Report on Visit to Wattie Creek: 13–14 May, 1971'. Jack Doolan's interview, held at the NT Archives Service, was also of use. Wave Hill Welfare Officer Reports in my own collection have been salutary as well.

My knowledge of the Vestey family's financial affairs was gleaned from the work of Phillip Knightley, the only writer to breach their wall of secrecy. See *The Rise and Fall of the House of Vestey* (London, Warner Books, 1993). The extraordinary business of their executive's kidnapping was told online: 'Por El Rescate De Grove Se Pagaron Sesenta Y Cinco Millones De Pesetas' ('For the Release of Grove Sixty Five Million Pesetas Were Paid'), Be Ward (transl.) *ABC*, Madrid, 22 December 1972, p. 49 <http://hemeroteca.abc.es/nav/Navigate.exe/hemeroteca/madrid/abc/1972/12/22/049.html> [accessed 22 May 2012].

Interviews

Anonymous, Interview recorded by Charlie Ward, 28 August 2012.
Daphne Atkinson [widow of Don Atkinson], Interview Recorded by Charlie Ward, March 2011, in possession of the author.
NTAS, Rosaleen Farquharson and Susan Cebu, Interview Recorded by Charlie Ward, October 2010, NTRS 3609, BWF 23.

Darwin, NTAS, Bryan Havenhand, Interview Recorded by Charlie Ward, April 2014, NTRS 3609, BWF 54.
Berenice Nyland [daughter of Don Atkinson], Interview Recorded by Charlie Ward, December 2010.
Interview with Roy Parrott Recorded by Charlie Ward, March 2011.
Darwin, NTAS, Alex Romanoff, Interview Recorded by Charlie Ward, July 2014, NTRS 3609, BWF 58.

Archival

Darwin, NTAS, W de Vos, 'Memo on Coombs Letter', 15 January 1973, NTRS 3548, C1-2D.

Newspapers

'Aborigines Get Land Gift Offer', *The Australian*, 22 August 1972.
'Aborigines Walk off Station, *SMH*, 19 April 1972.
'Birth of an Icon', *Koori Mail* [Tent Embassy Feature], 25 January 2012, p. 2.
'Dole Payments for Wattie Creek Men', *NTN*, 10 July 1972.
'Government Halts Aboriginal Leases', *SMH*, 8 December 1972.
'Land Grant Doesn't Impress Gurindji's', *NTN*, 14 October 1972.

Published Material

Jennifer Clark, *Aborigines and Activism—Race, Aborigines and the Coming of the Sixties to Australia* (Crawley, Western Australia, University of Western Australia Press, 2008).
Thea Hayes, *An Outback Nurse* (Allen and Unwin, Sydney, 2014).
Clem J. Lloyd, 'McEwen, Sir John (1900–1980)', *Australian Dictionary of Biography* <http://adb.anu.edu.au/biography/mcewen-sir-john-10948> [accessed 27 June 2012].
Laurie Oakes, 'The Campaign', *Whitlam and Frost*, ed. by David Frost. (London, Sundial, 1974), pp. 58–64.
Scott Robinson, 'The Aboriginal Embassy: An Account of the Protests of 1972', *Aboriginal History*, 18, 1 (1994) 49–63.

Correspondence

Don Atkinson to Vic Barnett, Undated [c. March 1974], Atkinson Personal Collection.
Don Atkinson to Vincent Lingiari, 28 September 1972, Oke Personal Collection.
Jean Culley to Rob Oke, c. late 1971, Oke Personal Collection.
Jean Culley to Rob Wesley-Smith, 13 May 1972, Wesley-Smith Personal Collection.
Bryan Havenhand to David Quin, 16 May 1972, Oke Personal Collection.
Bryan Havenhand, 'Gurindji Newsletter', 4 (1972), 18 May 1972, Oke Personal Collection.
David Quin to Vic Barnett, 13 December 1972, Atkinson Personal Collection.
David Quin to Bryan Havenhand, 19 April 1972, Oke Personal Collection.
David Quin to Rob Wesley-Smith, [u.d.], Wesley-Smith Collection.

SELECT BIBLIOGRAPHY

Vincent Lingiari to Roy Bell, 2 March 1972, Wesley-Smith Collection.

Correspondents
Vic Barnett, Personal Communication, 31 October 2013.
Michael George, Personal Communication, 27 October 2010.
David Quin, Personal Communication, 16 August 2007.
David Quin, Personal Communication, 23 July 2012.
Paddy Zakaria, Personal Communication, 30 May 2012.

Reports
'Gurindji Newsletter', Flinders University, No. 2, 1974, p. 1.
'Gurindji Campaign Newsletter' [Sydney Save the Gurindji Committee], July 1972, Oke Personal Collection.
Brian Jenkins and Janera Johnson, *International Terrorism: A Chronology, 1968–74* (Department of State and Defense Advanced Research Projects Agency, 1975).
David Quin, 'Report Number Five', 10 April 1972, Oke Personal Collection.
David Quin, 'Report Number Six', 24 April 1972, Oke Personal Collection.
Wave Hill Welfare Officer Reports, No. 66–72. In possession of the author.

Part Two—Making a Fist of It: 1973–78

Chapter 6: A New Beginning? 1973

Papers in Jeremy Long's 'Wattie Creek and Wave Hill' file stored at AIATSIS (MS 2534) were invaluable in following events at Wave Hill in parallel with the early months of self-determination policy. That transformative policy shift was also brought to life for me by Long's colleague, former DAA Secretary Barrie Dexter (NTAS, NTRS 3609, BWF 25).

Interviews
Jenny Lowe and Barbara Walter [former Wave Hill station staff], Interview Recorded by Charlie Ward, 22 October 2012.
Darwin, NTAS, 'Jack Doolan Oral History Interview Transcript', NTRS 226, TS 193.
Darwin, NTAS, Interview with Trevor and Anna LaBrooy Recorded by Charlie Ward, October 2012, NTRS 3609, BWF 49.
Darwin, NTAS, Tony Scott, Interview Recorded by Charlie Ward, November 2012, NTRS 3609, BWF 50.

Archival
AIATSIS, Russell Hausfeld, *Some Impressions of a Trip to the Northern Territory* (Unpublished, 1961), PMS 4538.
AIATSIS, 'Newsletter No. 3', Department of Aboriginal Affairs, May 1973, p. 1.

Darwin, NAA, *Community Adviser—Wave Hill*, E460, 1974/1028.
Darwin, NAA, *HC Giese correspondence with Secretary*, DAA, NTAC 1982, 34/0.
Darwin, NAA, *Home Management Services: Wundamarie Housing Association 1974*, E460, 1974/1486.
Darwin, NAA, *Termination of Training Allowances* […], E460, 1974/1217.
Darwin, NTAS, *Wave Hill Police Journal*, NTRS 2127, Vol. 16–17.

Newspapers

'A Gurindji Cattle Station "Financial Disaster"—Tapp', *NTN*, 6 March 1973.
'Aboriginal Affairs Inquiry Threatened', *SMH*, 18 October 1973.
'Aborigines Walk Off Station', *SMH*, 19 April 1972.
Anon, '"You'll Get Your Land", Bryant Tells Gurindji', *SMH*, Date unknown.
'Gurindji's Win Land', *The Australian*, 24 January 1973.
'Health Ails Down at Wattie Creek', *NTN*, 17 May 1973.
'Land Talks Confusion—Lord Vestey Says: We'll Co-Operate', *SMH*, 25 January 1973.
'"PM Wasted Our Time": Aboriginal Deputation', *SMH*, 19 October 1973.
'The Katherine Meeting: What Was it All About?', *NTN*, 10 March 1973.

Published Material

Bernard Clarke, *Larrpan Ga Buduyurr: The Spear and the Cloud* (Tranmere, South Australia, 2010).
Jeremy Long, *The Go-betweens: Patrol Officers in Aboriginal Affairs Administration in the Northern Territory, 1936–1974* (Monograph, Canberra, North Australian Research Unit, Australian National University, 1992).
Sir Edward Woodward, *One Brief Interval: A Memoir* (Carlton, Vic, Miegunyah Press, 2005).

Reports

'Statement by the Minister for Aboriginal Affairs, Mr Gordon Bryant, and the Minister for the Northern Territory, Mr Kep Enderby' (Canberra, 18 March 1973).
Jack Cooke, DAA Regional Officer (South), 'The Establishment of the Department of Aboriginal Affairs', Unpublished, Cooke Personal Collection.

Correspondence

Jean Culley to Rob Oke and Barbara et al, 20 August 1974, Oke Personal Collection.
Jean Culley to Rob Wesley-Smith, 3 December 1973, Rob Wesley-Smith Personal Collection.
Jean Leu to Don Atkinson, 24 July 1973, Atkinson Personal Collection.
Jean Leu to Ted Egan [DAA], May 1973, Atkinson Personal Collection.
Jean Leu to Rob Oke, 2 June 1973, Oke Personal Collection.
Jean Culley to Rob Oke, Undated but September 1973, Oke Private Collection.
Jean Culley, cited in Jean Leu to Rob Oke, November 1973, Oke Personal Collection.
Melbourne Gurindji Group, Open Letter, 19 June 1974, Oke Personal Collection.

SELECT BIBLIOGRAPHY

David Quin to Rob Oke, 2 April 1973, Oke Personal Collection.
David Quin to Rob Oke, 8 May 1973, Oke Personal Collection.

Chapter 7: Into the Fray, 1974

Peter Read's excellent account of the friction within the DAA in his book *Charles Perkins: A Biography* was influential in my description of the same (Ringwood, Victoria, Penguin, 2001). The papers of Rob Oke and Stan Pelczynski provided a trove of information, as did Philip Nitschke's prodigious correspondence. Surely every home in Australia received one of his missives. My interview with Trevor LaBrooy provided a useful and different perspective (NTAS, NTRS 3609, BWF 49).

Interviews

Interview with Berenice Nyland [daughter of Don Atkinson], Recorded by Charlie Ward, December 2010.
Interview with Roy Parrott, Recorded by Charlie Ward, March 2011.

Archival

Darwin, NAA, *Muramulla Gurindji Co Pastoral Project*, E460, 1974/1588.
Darwin, NAA, *Wave Hill - Review of Council Programs and Employment Projects*, E460, 1981/89 PART 2.
Darwin, NAA, *Wave Hill—Reports on Community Development*, E460, 1978/242.
Darwin, NTAS, *Northern Territory Pastoral Lessees Association, Administration and Correspondence Files*, NTRS 3548, C1/2D.

Newspapers

'Labor's Black Policy in Tatters', *Nation Review*, 11–17 October 1974, p. 1646.
Mungo MacCallum, 'Cavanagh Has To Go', *Nation Review*, 1–6 March 1974, p. 613.
'Police Guard for Minister', *Daily Telegraph*, 2 March 1974, p. 2.

Published Material

David Hilliard, *Flinders University: The First 25 Years, 1966–1991* (Adelaide: Flinders University, South Australia, 1991).
Philip Nitschke with Peter Corris, *Damned If I Do* (Carlton, Victoria, Melbourne University Press, 2013).
Hansard Northern Territory, Legislative Council, Dr Charles Gurd, Mr Creed Lovegrove, *Hansard: 11th Council—First Session, 20th Sittings. Part Two—Question Paper*, No. 3670, 21 May 1974 (Darwin, NTLC Printer, 1974).

Reports

Sen. James Cavanagh, *Media Release*, 'Aboriginals at Wattie Creek', 7 August 1974, Wesley-Smith Personal Collection.

Barrie Dexter, in 'Seminar of the Fortieth Anniversary of the 1967 Referendum: Transcript, 22 June 2007' (Parkes, Canberra, Office of Evaluation and Audit (Indigenous Programs), Department of Finance and Administration, 2007).
Philip Nitschke, 'Plans for 1974', Wesley-Smith Personal Collection.
Stan Pelczynski, 'Wattie Creek Report', Federal Council for the Advancement of Aborigines and Torres Strait Islanders, 1974, Oke Personal Collection.

Correspondence

Don Atkinson to Vic Barnett, Undated [c. March 1974], Atkinson Personal Collection.
Sen. James Cavanagh to Barbara Chmielewska, 21 May 1974, Pelczynski Personal Collection.
Sen. James Cavanagh to Vincent Lingiari, 5 October 1974, Oke Personal Collection.
Sen. James Cavanagh to Rob Oke, Ministerial No. 2301 and 2181, 2 July 1974, Oke Personal Collection.
Jean Culley to Rob Oke, 13 December 1974, Oke Personal Collection.
Jean Culley to Stan Pelczynski and Barbara Pelczynska 10th [...] 1974, Pelczynski Personal Collection.
Jean Culley to Barbara, Rob, 11 August 1974, Oke Personal Collection.
Jean Culley to Rob and Barbara *et al*, 20 August 1974, Oke Personal Collection.
Donald Nangiari to Jean Leu, 13 May 1974, Oke Personal Collection.
Philip Nitschke to Jean Leu, 8 April 1974, Oke Personal Collection.
Philip Nitschke to Jean Leu, 14 May 1974, Oke Personal Collection.
Philip Nitschke to Jean Leu *et al*, Undated [29 May 1974], Oke Personal Collection.
Stan Pelczynski, untitled notes, 1974, Pelczynski Personal Collection.
Paddy Zakaria [Daughter of Jean Culley], Personal Communication, 27 April 2011.

Chapter 8: 1975, A Handful of Sand

Hannah Middleton's papers at the State Library of New South Wales were a great help in hearing 'the word from Wattie Creek' in the months before and after the handover event. Jeremy Long's *Wattie Creek and Wave Hill* papers at AIATSIS were central to my account (MS 2534, Box 3, Folder 24) of the transfer's official aspects, and interviewing Geoff Eames and Richard Preece in particular enlightened me as to some of the participants' perspectives.

Interviews

Darwin, NTAS, Meredith Burgmann, Interviewed by Charlie Ward, August 2012, NTRS 3609.
Darwin, NTAS, Interview with Gavin Perry Recorded by Charlie Ward, August 2014, NTRS 3609, BWF 61.
Darwin, NTAS, Richard Preece, Interview Recorded by Charlie Ward, September 2010, NTRS 3609, BWF 17.
Gwen Dickman (née Moore, former Baptist Missionary at Libanungu), Interviewed by Charlie Ward, 19 November 2012.

SELECT BIBLIOGRAPHY

National Library of Australia, *Thea Hayes interviewed by Charlie Ward*, 2013.

Archival

Darwin, NAA, *Muramulla Gurindji Association—Wattie Creek Development*, E460, 1975/196.
Darwin, NAA, *Wave Hill-Review of Council Programs and Employment Projects*, E460, 1981/89 Part 2.
Darwin, NAA, *Wave Hill Community Development*, E460, 1974/242.

Newspapers

'ALP Branch Request More Help for Cattlemen', *Katherine Informer*, 4–18 August 1975.
'Happy Only When They Are Drunk', *NTN*, 20 August 1975, p. 8.
Jim Hodge, 'Farmers Get Budget Brush-off', *The Land*, 21 August 1975, p. 1.
Lenore Nicklin, 'Some Earth From Wattie Creek', *Nation Review*, August 22–28 1975, p. 1153.

Published Material

'Australian Political Chronicle, July–December 1975' *Australian Journal of Politics and History* (22, 1, 1976) 74–130, p. 77–78.
HC 'Nugget' Coombs, *Kulinma*, (Canberra, Australian National University Press, 1978).
Nicolas Peterson, 'Demand Sharing: Reciprocity and the Pressure for Generosity among Foragers', *American Anthropologist*, 95, 4 (1993), 860–874, pp. 860–861.

Correspondence

Valerie Bishaw, Personal Communication, 14 December, 2010.
Jenny Boyd to Don Atkinson, 26 June 1975, Atkinson Personal Collection.
Johnson [DAA] to Jean Culley, undated, Wesley-Smith Personal Collection.
Elsie Maiowie [transcr. Preece] to Culley, 15 March 1976, Oke Personal Collection.
Rob Wesley-Smith to Jean Culley, 27 January 1975, Atkinson Personal Collection.
Rob Wesley-Smith to Vincent and Gurindji Friends, 26 August 1975, Wesley-Smith Personal Collection.

Other

Brian Manning, 'Handback and Singing—Track Eight', *From the Darkness into the Light: Gurindji Freedom Banners Project*, Audio CD (Kalkaringi, NT, Daguragu Community Government Council, 2000).

Chapter 9: A Fighting Chance, 1976

From this time, activists were no longer staying—or writing letters and reports—at Daguragu, and my account relies more heavily on government records from this point as a result. There are no shortage of these in the

National Archives in Darwin, as this bibliography attests. The official record of the Muramulla company's government enfranchisement is evidenced in NAA, *Muramulla Gurindji Company—Pastoral*, 1975–79, E460, 1975/137.

Archival

AIATSIS, Barrie Dexter Papers, *OAA/DAA—Public aspects, 1967–86*, MS 4167, Series 19, Item 15.
Darwin, NAA, *Cattle Mustering Venture* [...], 1 June 1977, (F1) 1975/4091.
Darwin, NAA, *Community Adviser—Wave Hill*, E460, 1974/1028.
Darwin, NAA, *Muramulla Gurindji Cattle Company*, E460 1975/196.
Darwin, NAA, *Muramulla Gurindji Cattle Company Part 1*, E460, 1981/256.
Darwin, NAA, *Wave Hill Centre: Policy and Development*, E460, 1981/306.
Darwin, NAA, *Wave Hill - Review of Council Programs and Employment Projects*, E460, 1981/89, Part 2.

Newspapers

David Broadbent, 'The Blacks Take a Battering', *The Age*, 2 December 1976.
'Conference Blasts Land Rights Bill', *NTN*, 9 August 1976, p. 3.
'Cuts Trouble Minister', in 'Back Page', *Sun Herald*, 15 August 1976.
Rob Filmer, 'Stop the Stairs, I Want to Get Off!', *The Herald*, 30 March 1976.
'Fraser Government Let Aborigines Down—Gough', *NTN*, 31 August 1976, p. 1.
Michelle Grattan, 'Delay on Gurindji Freeholds', 2 June 1976, *The Age*, p. 1.
'MLAs Blast March', *NTN*, 12 March 1976.

Published Material

Geoff Eames, 'The Central Land Council: The Politics of Change', in *Aborigines, Land and Land Rights*, ed. by Marcia Langton and Nicolas Peterson (Canberra: Australian Institute of Aboriginal Studies, 1983), pp. 268–277.
Geoff Eames, *Land rights or a Sell Out? An Analysis of the Aboriginal Land rights (Northern Territory) Bill, 1976* (Alice Springs, IAD Press, 1976).
Lorna Lippmann, 'The Aborigines', in *From Whitlam to Fraser: Reform and Reaction in Australian Politics*, ed. by Allan Patience and Brian Head (Melbourne, Oxford University Press, 1979), pp. 173–188.
Ross Howie, 'Northern Territory', in *Aboriginal Land Rights: a Handbook*, ed. by Nicolas Peterson (Canberra: Australian Institute of Aboriginal Studies, 1981), 28–52.
Sir Edward Woodward, *One Brief Interval: A Memoir* (Carlton, Vic, Miegunyah Press, 2005).
Hansard Australia, Senate, Sen. Keefe, *Official Hansard, No. 50, 1976—First Session of the 30th Parliament (Second Period)*, 7 December 1976 (Canberra, Commonwealth Government Printer).
TC Lovegrove, Director of the NT Division of the DAA, cited in Northern Territory, Legislative Assembly, Hon Kentish to Pollock, Question 1481, *Parliamentary Record–First Assembly. Part Two–Questions*, 18 November 1976 (Darwin, NTLA Printer, 1977).

SELECT BIBLIOGRAPHY

Northern Territory, Legislative Assembly, Question 1519, Steele to Andrew, *Parliamentary Record–First Assembly. Part One–Question Time*, 13 October 1976 (Darwin, NTLA Printer, 1977).

Reports
Census, Undated [c. 1976], Wesley-Smith Personal Collection.
DAA Annual Report 1975–76 (AGPS, Canberra, 1976).
DAA Secretary Barrie Dexter, cited in *Third Report from the House of Representative Standing Committee on Aboriginal Affairs, 1975,* Volume II, (Canberra, Australian Government Publishing, 1975), p. 556.

Correspondents
Thea Hayes, Personal Communication, October 2014.
Tanya McConvell, Personal Communication, 23 February 2013.
Paddy Zakaria, Personal Communication, 27 April 2011.

Other
Geoff Newton [former Wave Hill Station saddler], Personal Communication, 3 March 2010
Hon. Les Johnson, Media Release: 'Transfer of Part of Wave Hill Pastoral Lease to Gurindji [...], 31 July 1975, Oke Personal Collection.
Land Rights News, No, 1, April 1976 (Alice Springs, Australia, Central Land Council).
John Millhouse, 'Staff Accommodation Wave Hill [...]', 3 November 1976, Author's Personal Collection.

Chapter 10: Mixed Blessings, 1977–78

The DAA's endeavours to support 'Gurindji self-management' are well-recorded in Darwin's National Archives, as evidenced particularly by the file *Community Adviser—Wave Hill* (E460, 1974/1028). Regarding the controversy surrounding the *Aboriginal Land Rights Act (NT)*, the same can be said of the newsletters of the Central Land Council, other writings of Geoff Eames, and the NTLA Hansard.

Interviews
Gwen Dickman [née Moore, former Baptist Missionary at Libanungu], Interviewed by Charlie Ward, 19 November 2012.

Archival
Canberra, NAA, 'Background Material—NT Self-Government [...]', *PM's Visit to NT 24–27 April 1978*, A1209, 1978/1050, Part 1 & 2.
Darwin, NAA, *Libanungu/ Daguragu, Department of Aboriginal Affairs*, CA2605, E242, K9/2/3.

Darwin, NAA, *Muramulla Gurindji Cattle Company, Part 2*, E460, 1981/256.
Darwin, NAA, *Wave Hill Community Development*, E460, 1978/242.
Darwin, NAA, *Wave Hill Social Club*, E460, 1981/100.
Darwin, NAA, *Wave Hill—Review of Projects, Part 2*, E460, 1981/89.

Newspapers

Central Australian Land Rights News, No. 6, February 1977 (Alice Springs, Australia, Central Land Council), p. 9.
Neil Naessens, 'Election shock for CLP', *NTN*, 16 August 1977.
'Old Mates Meet at Gong Awards', *Darwin Star*, undated.
'Petition on Land rights', *NTN*, 17 February 1977, p. 2.

Published Material

Alistair Heatley, '"And Then There Were Two": The 1977 Northern Territory Legislative Assembly Election', in *Monographs Political and Historical*, ed. by F.H. Bauer (Darwin, North Australian Research Unit, Australian National University, 1978).
Alistair Heatley, *Almost Australians: The Politics of Northern Territory Self-Government* (Darwin, North Australia Research Unit, Australian National University, 1990).
Rev. Ivan Jordan, 'Brief History of Baptist Ministry to the Indigenous People of Central Australia', 8 Dec 1999 <http://www.bwa-baptist-heritage.org/bap-ab.htm> [accessed 14 March 2014].
Stuart Phillpot, 'Understanding Whitefella Secret Cattle Business', in *Working on Country: Contemporary Indigenous Management of Australia's Lands and Coastal Regions* ed. by Jocelyn Davies, Richard Baker, and Elspeth Young (Melbourne, Oxford University Press, 2001), pp. 199–213.
'From the Editor's Diary', *Today*, Vol. 7, No. 3 (Lawson, New South Wales, Mission Publications of Australia), pp. 8–9.

Other

Standing Committee on Aboriginal Affairs, *Alcohol Problems of Aborigines, Northern Territory Aspects: Interim Report of the House of Representatives Standing Committee on Aboriginal Affairs* (Canberra, Australian Government Publishing Services, 1976).
Department of Aboriginal Affairs, *Kalkaringi—Book of the Community* (NT Division of the Department of Aboriginal Affairs, 1977.
Northern Territory, Legislative Assembly, Hon Rupert Kentish, Hon Goff Letts, Hon James Robertson, Hon Ron Withnall, Hon Eric Manuell, *Parliamentary Record–First Assembly. Part One–the Debates*, 17 March 1977 (Darwin, NTLA Printer, 1978), pp. 147–152.
'Internal Audit Appraisal, Wave Hill Community', 27 September 1978, Richardson Personal Collection, p. 1.

SELECT BIBLIOGRAPHY

Part Three—The Harder Road: 1979-86

Chapter 11: 'A Fragmentation of Support', 1979-80

In writing about waste and corruption during this period at Wave Hill, interviewing former Adult Educator at Kalkaringi, John Bullock was informative. Stuart Phillpot's PhD thesis 'Black Pastoralism: Contemporary Aboriginal Land Use—the Experience of Aboriginal-Owned Pastoral Enterprises in the Northern Territory, 1972–1996' (Australian National University, 2000) was invaluable in considering the raft of issues facing the Aboriginal cattle sector. Similarly Mitsuru Shimpo's report on education to the NT Government (*The Social Process of Aboriginal Education in the Northern Territory*, Department of Education (Darwin, Northern Territory, 1978) gave useful context to understand the situation at Kalkaringi's school. The latter was fleshed out for me by my discussions with former staff: Julia Pannell, Marg Fenbury and Peter Collins.

Interviews

Darwin, NTAS, Barry Hansen [former DAA Assistant Regional Director (Central Australia)], Interview Recorded by Charlie Ward, September 2012, NTRS 3609, BWF 39.

Darwin, NTAS, 'Interview with Jack Doolan', *c.* 1981, NTRS 226, TS 193.

Gwen Dickman [née Moore, former Baptist Missionary at Libanungu], Interviewed by Charlie Ward, 19 November 2012.

Darwin, NTAS, Interview with John Millhouse, recorded by Charlie Ward, April 2014, NTRS 3609, BWF 52.

Archival

Darwin, NAA, *Cattle Mustering Venture* [...], (F1) 1975/4091.Darwin, NAA, *Community Adviser—Wave Hill*, E460, 1974/1028.

Darwin, NAA, 'Report and Financials [...], September 1978, Muramulla Gurindji Cattle Company, E629, 1978/7/7581.

Darwin, NAA, *Muramulla Gurindji Cattle Company*, E629, 1979/7/7856.

Darwin, NAA, *Wave Hill—Review of Council Programs and Employment Projects*, E460, 1981/89 Part 2.

Darwin, NAA, *Wave Hill Community Development*, E460, 1978/242.

Newspapers

'Blacks to Govt: Not Welcome', *NTN*, 3 November 1979.

Rob Chalmers, 'Gurindji Lease Intact', *NTN*, 26 November 1979.

Jack Ellis, 'Land Lease Row', *NTN*, 27 October 1979, p. 2.

Terry Ingram, 'Hooker Earns $3.9m Aided by Beef Boom', *Australian Financial Review*, 27 February 1979.

'Lease Notices served on 40', *NTN*, 2 November 1979.
Neil Naessens and Rob Chalmers, 'New Row on NT Land', *NTN*, 7 March 1979, p. 1.

Published Material
Central Australian Land Rights News, No. 11.
Hon Paul Everingham, 'After Land Rights…Self-reliance', *Aboriginal News*, Vol. 3, No. 6, 1979, p. 5.
David Hanlon, 'The Aboriginal Pastoral Industry: A Conflict of Development Objectives', in *Ecology Management of the World's Savannas*, ed. by J.C Tothill & J.J Mott (Canberra: Australian Academy of Science, 1985), pp. 185–189.
'Eradication Success Story: Australia is free of Brucella Abortus', Department of Agriculture, Fisheries and Forestry publication. Accessed 20 May 2014, <http://www.daff.gov.au/__data/assets/pdf_file/0009/2182869/brucella-abortusoct12.pdf>.
Dean Jaensch and Peter Loveday, ed., *Under One Flag: The 1980 Northern Territory Election* (North Sydney: Allen & Unwin, 1981).
Graeme Neate, *Aboriginal Land Rights Law in the Northern Territory: Volume 1* (Chippendale, N.S.W, Alternative Publishing Co-operative, 1989), p. 122.
Jackie Wolfe, *'That Community Government Mob': Local Government in Small Northern Territory Communities* (Darwin, Australian National University, North Australia Research Unit, 1989).

Other
Hon FM Chaney, 'Establishment of the Australian Aboriginal Development Commission […], Press Release, 2 September 1979.
Daguragu Council meeting notes, 17 March 1980, Richardson Personal Collection.
Howie [CLC] to Burchett [Dept. Lands], 29 October 1979, Pelczynski Personal Collection.
Brian Kimmings [former DAA Project Officer], Personal Communication, 19 June 2014.
Maxine Pitts, Personal Communication, 1 May 2015.
Keith Jeans [former Kalkaringi school principal] Personal Communication, 29 May 2014.

Ch. 12—Testing Times, 1981–82

The Daguragu Land Claim transcripts provide a wonderful lateral view of Wave Hill in the early 1980s. My knowledge of the radical Brucellosis and Tuberculosis Eradication Campaign was gleaned with the assistance of the former Chief Veterinary Officer of the NT, Brian Radunz, through an interview and reading his published work. See Brian Radunz, *Territory Stockies and Government Vets: The NT Animal Health System from 1965 to 2012*, Vol. 1 (Northern Territory Government, Darwin, 2013). The pages of the

SELECT BIBLIOGRAPHY

Northern Territory News and *Darwin Star* newspapers provided an account of the misleadingly-named 'child brides affair', which was greatly enhanced by my interview with Rob Wesley-Smith.

Interviews

Darwin, NTAS, Interview with Buck Buchester recorded October 1986, NTRS 3164/295.
Darwin, NTAS, Interview with Jack Doolan, *c.*1981, NTRS 226, TS 193.
Darwin, NTAS, Mark Lumsden [former DPP stock inspector] interviewed by Charlie Ward, August 2014, NTRS 3609, BWF 63.
Colin and Maggie Muir, Interview Recorded by Charlie Ward, 24 October 2012. In possession of the author.

Archival

Darwin, NAA, *Muramulla Gurindji Company*, E1022/3, K1982, 1-7, Pt A, B.
Darwin, NAA, *Muramulla Gurindji Cattle Company*, Part 2, E460, 1981/256.
Darwin, NTAS, 'Child Bride Allegations', *Aboriginal Tribal Marriages*, NTRS 366/P2, AD 82/ 0114.

Newspapers

'Battling with Broken Arm', *NTN*, 15 August 1981.
Sharon Bowditch, '"No Communication" on Exploration', *NTN*, 15 July 1982.
'Policeman Charged', *NTN*, 16 December 1981.
Kerry Sharp, 'Escape from Wattie Creek', *NTN*, 8 February 1982, p. 2.
'Suppression Plea Denied', *NTN*, 17 December 1981.
'Tribesman Speaks Out on Child Brides', *Darwin Star*, date unknown.

Published Material

Tim Rowse, *Remote Possibilities: the Aboriginal Domain and the Administrative Imagination*, (Darwin, North Australian Research Unit, 1992).
Jackie Wolfe, *'That Community Government Mob': Local Government in Small Northern Territory Communities* (Darwin: Australian National University, North Australia Research Unit, 1989).

Other

Gordon Bauman, cited in *Daguragu Land Claim 1981*, Vol. 3, 1981 (pp. 538–735), p. 550.
Gordon Bauman, Personal Communication 22 January 2010.
Financial and Advisory Consulting and Training Services [FACTS], *Daguragu Development Plan*, May 1983.
David Hanlon [former FACTS pastoral consultant to Muramulla Co and ADC], Personal Communication, 3 February 2010.
Robert Lehane, *Beating the Odds in a Big Country—the Eradication of Bovine Brucellosis and Tuberculosis in Australia* (Collingwood, Victoria: CSIRO Publishing, 1996).

Rev Gordon Moore, 'Wave Hill—Annual Report, 1982', Global Interaction.
Plummer [Dept. Primary Production] to Hebblewhite [Dept. Aboriginal Affairs], 6 June 1986, Richardson Personal Collection.
Will Sanders, Personal Communication, 19 November 2013.

Chapter 13: Resignation, 1983–86

Interviews with contemporary Gurindji leaders such as Michael Paddy, Ros Frith and Gus George were of much use creating an account of this period. The records and oral history of Jan Richardson and the late Stan Davey were also essential. An industry perspective of the Muramulla company's diffculties were likewise gleaned from my interviews with Graeme Fagan and Mark Lumsden.

Interviews

Darwin, NTAS, Interview with Billy Bunter recorded by Charlie Ward, July 2011, NTRS 3609, BWF 26.
Darwin, NTAS, Interview with Graeme Fagan recorded by Charlie Ward, September 2012, NTRS 3609, BWF 42.
Darwin, NTAS, Interview with Mark Lumsden recorded by Charlie Ward, August 2014, NTRS 3609, BWF 63.

Archival

Darwin, NAA, 'Muramulla Gurindji Company Meeting', 8 December 1982, Muramulla Gurindji Company, E1022/3, K1982, 1-7, Pt B.

Newspapers

Richard Pullin, 'Frank Hardy revisits Gurindji to Help with New Problems', source unknown, date unknown [c. 1985].

Published Material

L. R. Hiatt, *Arguments About Aborigines: Australia and the Evolution of Social Anthropology* (Cambridge, Cambridge University Press, 1996).
Nicolas Peterson, 'On the Persistence of Sharing: Personhood, Asymmetrical Reciprocity and Demand Sharing in the Indigenous Australian Domestic Moral Economy', *The Australian Journal of Anthropology*, 24 (2013) 166–176.
Graham Phegan, 'Community Government Models for Small Towns in the Northern Territory', *Small Towns in Northern Australia*, ed. by Peter Loveday and Ann Webb (Darwin, North Australia Research Unit, Australian National University, 1989) 86–107.
Elspeth Young, *Outback Stores: Retail Services in North Australian Aboriginal Communities* (Darwin, North Australia Research Unit, Australian National University, 1984), p. 24.

SELECT BIBLIOGRAPHY

Reports

Central Land Council Annual Reports, *1983–84, 1984–85* (Central Land Council, Alice Springs).

'DCGC Study Tour', 16–30 June 1984, Richardson Personal Collection.

Office of the Aboriginal Land Commissioner, *Gurindji Land Claim to Daguragu Station: Further Report by the Aboriginal Land Commissioner Mr. Justice Maurice to the Minister for Aboriginal Affairs*, No. 20 (Canberra, Australian Government Publishing Service, 1985).

Other

Gordon Bauman, Personal Communication, 22 January 2010.

Central Land Council, 'Daguragu Station Land Claim', <http://www.clc.org.au/land-won-back/info/daguragu-station-land-claim/>. Accessed 1 October 2014.

'Daguragu Vote', *7.30 Report, Northern Territory*, Australian Broadcasting Commission (ABC TV), 21 November 1988.

Davey to AIATSIS, 18 June 1984, Richardson Personal Collection.

Jan Richardson, *Diary 1986*, Richardson Personal Collection.

Other

John Trezona, Personal Communication, 15 November 2010.

Afterword

Asides from that listed below, little evaluation of the shire or regional council system has been performed. My opinion is based largely on my conversations with residents and community leaders of Elliott, Ngukurr, Papunya, Kalkaringi and Daguragu communities about their experiences of the Barkly, Roper Gulf, MacDonnell and Victoria Daly regional councils respectively.

Published Material

Bob Gosford, "Doomed to failure": NT local government reform goes "crazy"—Part 2, <http://blogs.crikey.com.au/northern/2010/01/07/doomed-to-failure-nt-local-government-reform-goes-crazy-part-2/>. Accessed 18 May 2015.

Will Sanders, 'Changing Scale, Mixing Interests: Generational Change in Northern Territory Local Government', *Australian Journal of Political Science*, 47 (3), 473–490.

Reports

Desert Knowledge CRC, Ruth Elvin, *Local Government Reform in the Northern Territory: Reforming the Governance of Service Delivery and the View from the Barkly, Working Paper 41*, <http://www.nintione.com.au/resource/DKCRC-Working-paper-41_Local-government-reform-in-the-Northern-Territory.pdf>. Accessed 18 May 2015.

Desert Knowledge CRC, Will Sanders, *Fuelling Large Group Dominance and Repeating Past Mistakes: A Critique of the Northern Territory Local Government Electoral System*, www.desertknowledgecrc.com.au/publications/research.html. Accessed 18 May 2015.

Newspapers

Phillip Knightley, 'How the Vesteys Do It', *The Sunday Times*, London, 12 October 1980.

Robert Milliken, 'Vestey's Sell Most of Australian Ranches', *The Independent*, London, 5 July 1992, <http://www.independent.co.uk/news/business/vesteyssell-most-of-australian-ranches-1531379.html>. Accessed 19 December 2014.

Other

John Trezona, Personal Communication, 15 November 2010.

INDEX

AACM *see* Australian Agricultural Consultancy Management Company
Aarons, Laurie   72
Aboriginal affairs, de-emphasis under Fraser   196–197
Aboriginal Development Commission   viii, 249–250, 298
Aboriginal equal wages case   22–23
Aboriginal Land Rights (Northern Territory) Act   ix, 201–202, 220, 244, 310
Aboriginal policy *see* assimilation; Northern Territory Government, Aboriginal policies; self-determination; self-management
Aboriginal radicalism   148
Aboriginal Scholarships *see* Abschol
Abschol   viii, 53, 54, 56–58, 74–75, 89–93, 100, 111
ACTU *see* Australian Council of Trade Unions
ADC *see* Aboriginal Development Commission
adult education   258, 306
AIA *see* Australian Investment Agency
AIATSIS *see* Australian Institute of Aboriginal and Torres Strait Islander Studies
alcohol, effect on Daguragu   143, 186, 215, 234–235
    effect on Kalkaringi   234–235, 237, 250–251, 270–272, 296–297
    effect on Wave Hill Welfare settlement   143–144, 215–216
ALP *see* Australian Labor Party
ALRA see Aboriginal Land Rights (Northern Territory) Act
Andrews, Bev   210–211, 247
Andrews, Stan   189, 203, 205, 210–211, 230, 247, 301–302
Anthony, Doug   40
Armed forces, Vestey's supply contract   13
ASIO   ix, 68, 100, 133
    surveillance of Fred Hollows   89
assimilation, as government policy   62, 66, 82, 98
Atkinson, Don   111–112, 140, 157, 163, 164, 182
Australian Agricultural Consultancy Management Company   viii, 135–137, 189, 192

Australian Council of Trade Unions   viii, 86
Australian Institute of Aboriginal and Torres Strait Islander Studies   viii, 235
Australian Investment Agency   5
Australian Labor Party   ix, 74, 113, 115
    and NT Legislative Assembly   221
    and Wattie Creek   70, 121, 125
Australian Security and Intelligence Organisation *see* ASIO
Australian Woolgrowers' and Graziers' Council   45
Bagonis, Nick   29
Bandler, Faith   50, 70
Barker, Stan   58, 59
Barnes, Charles (Ceb)   37, 45
Barnett, Vic   111–112, 163, 164
Bauman, Gordon   260, 276–277, 302
Baume, Peter   266
Bell, Roy   64
Berndt, Ronald and Catherine   14
Bingle, A.S.   16
Bishaw, Alex   174–175, 283
Bow Hill police   2
Brucellosis and Tuberculosis Eradication Campaign   ix, 249–250, 277–279, 298, 300–301
Bryant, Gordon   40, 50–51, 113, 121–122, 125–127, 145–146, 182
BTEC *see* Brucellosis and Tuberculosis Eradication Campaign
Buchanan, Cheryl   161–162
Buchanan, Gordie   1–2
Buchanan, Nat   1–2
Buchester, Buck   280, 302, 303
Bulngari, Blanche   31, 95, 266
Bunter, Billy   xxviii, 11, 21, 139, 176, 226, 273, 283, 294, 315–316
Burgmann, Meredith   188
Burnum Burnum   49–50
Byrnes, Peter   260
CAA *see* Council for Aboriginal Affairs
Cairns, Jim   50–51
Calder, Sam   220
Captain Major *see* Lupngiari
Carroll, Paddy   23, 28

– 345 –

Casey, Lord, reply to Gurindji claim 40–41
Catfish waterhole, Victoria River 4
cattle brand, Gurindji need for 93, 95, 102
  see also GDT (cattle brand)
cattle hunting 2, 304–306
cattle industry 191, 206
  advances in 193, 246–247
  treatment of Gurindji 75
  working conditions 75
Cattle Producers' Council x, 64, 69
  see also Northern Territory Cattlemen's Association
cattle stations
  Aboriginal-run 243, 301
  labour disputes 75
  management of 84
  see also Muramulla Gurindji Cattle Company; Newcastle Waters station; Ord River station; Rosewood station; Victorian River Downs station; Wave Hill station
Cavanagh, Jim 146, 147, 153, 156–158, 166, 182
CCL see Northern Territory Council for Civil Liberties
Cebu, Sandra 183
Cebu, Susan 106, 294, 305, 318
Central Land Council x, 195, 244, 245, 287
Chaffey, Earl 226–227, 233
Chaney, Fred 281
Chifley Labor Government 15
Christian missionaries, and alcohol control 236–237
Christianity, and Gurindji elders 20, 144, 236, 279
CLC see Central Land Council
CLP see Country Liberal Party (NT)
Coe, Paul 71–72, 111
Collins, Peter 256
Commonwealth parliament, debate on Aboriginal issues 49–51
Communist Party of Australia x, 22
community development, training 129–130
Cook, Mona 291–292
Cooke, J.A. 25–26, 159–160
Coombs, H.C. (Nugget) 44, 88, 96, 98, 112, 115, 122, 183
Council for Aboriginal Affairs ix–x, 44, 55, 85, 96, 98, 115, 117
Council for Civil Liberties (NT) x, 274
Country Liberal Party (NT) x, 198–201, 220, 239

CPA see Communist Party of Australia
CPC see Cattle Producers' Council
Croker, Sam 1–2
Cross, Manfred, visit to Wattie Creek 70
Crown Lands Act 245
Culley, Jean 73, 80–81, 83, 93, 107–108, 110, 135, 140–141, 171–172, 182, 210–211
Cyclone Tracy (1974) 172
DAA see Department of Aboriginal Affairs
Daguragu 126–127
  autonomy undermined 131, 262, 313–314
  banking service 293
  Cavanagh's visit 156–158
  declared dry 252
  dependence on Kalkaringi 169, 170
  development 207
  and funding cuts 197, 204
  government services to 222
  health clinic 176, 207
  housing 207–208, 218–219
  lack of school 254–256, 295, 312–313
  living conditions 150–151, 161–163, 174–176, 218–219, 252–254
  preschool teacher 207
  relations with government 144, 155–160, 171, 173–175, 189–194, 244–245, 254, 282–284
  stockyards 133, 154
  see also Wattie Creek
Daguragu Community Government Council see Daguragu Council
Daguragu Council xi, 228–233, 251–252, 259–260, 267, 282–283, 289–291, 294, 305–307
  abolition 319
Daguragu Gurindji Council, proposed 175
Daguragu store see Wattie Creek, store
Daguragu waterhole 54
Dalton, Frank 268–269
Danayarri, Hobbles 60–61, 76, 155, 203
Danbayarri, Dandy 82
Daniels, Davis 22, 27, 202
Daniels, Dexter 23–29, 33–34, 37, 56, 71–72, 187–188, 202
Davey, Stan 34, 90, 92, 285–288, 290, 291, 305–306, 307
de Vos, Bill 64, 69, 77
deaths, alcohol-related 250–251
Department of Aboriginal Affairs x–xi, 122, 144–147, 153–154, 189, 224–228, 261–263
  employment of Gurindji 132–133
  NT seminars 129

INDEX

Dewhurst butchers, demonstrations against 71
Dexter, Barrie 44, 96, 98, 122–123, 125, 129–130, 145–146, 153, 180
Donald, Judith 106, 156, 177, 210
donkeys, culling of 14
Doolan, Jack 110, 135, 136–137, 220–221, 260
Doone, Lorna 274–275
DPP *see* Northern Territory Department of Primary Production
Dreamings, Gurindji 39, 265, 295
Droughtmaster (cattle breed) xiv, 203, 222–223
drovers, Gurindji 13
Dulung, Charcoal 108, 109, 139
Eames, Geoff 179–180, 186, 201, 220, 244
Edey, John 189–190, 202–203, 206, 224, 246, 247, 248
education, and self-determination 254, 258
Edwards, Roy 25, 26
Egan, Ted 87–88, 135
Elkin, A.P. 14
Ellicott, Bob 195
equal wages case *see* Aboriginal equal wages case
erosion, of Gurindji country 14
Europeans *see* white men
Evans, Ted 17, 34, 117
Everingham, Paul 240, 243–244, 267
eye disease, among Gurindji 88–89
Faint, Jim 165
Fardell, Bryce 67, 82
Farquharson, Rosaleen 106
FCAATSI *see* Federal Council for the Advancement of Aborigines and Torres Strait Islanders
Federal Council for the Advancement of Aborigines and Torres Strait Islanders xi, 22, 41, 49–50, 55
Federal government *see* Commonwealth parliament; Department of Aboriginal Affairs
Fenbury, Marg 256
Fisher, Tom 16, 18, 20, 28, 29, 30, 42
Fitzgibbon, Charlie 94
floods, at Wave Hill 6
Ford, Martin 261
Fox, Paul 56–57, 74, 75
Fraser, Malcolm 193–196, 201
Freedom Day *see* Walk-off anniversaries
Frith, Roslyn 292–295, 305, 318
GBM *see* Government Business Manager
GDT (cattle brand) xi, 115, 132, 155, 246
gemstone prospecting 83

Gibb Committee report 114–115
Gibbs, George 21–22, 42, 44, 47
Gibbs, Kerry 33–34
Gibbs, Moira 21–22, 56, 63
Giese, Harry 28, 82, 122–123, 129
Gilbert, Kevin 111
Gilgi, Shirley 111
Glass, Margaret and Bernadette 150–151
goats, purchase for Wattie Creek 76–77
Goddard, Tiger 13
Golding, Roger 183
Gordy Creek 30–31, 34–36, 170
Gorton, John 51, 55
government benefits, payment to Gurindji 34–35, 164
Government Business Manager xi, 318
Greenhide Sam *see* Croker, Sam
grog-running 215, 216, 232, 237, 252
Grove, Ronald, kidnapping in Argentina 116
Gurindji xiv, xxx
  access to alcohol 143–144, 215, 234
  attitudes to women 272–275, 291
  and cattle station life 2–3, 6–7
  ceremonial life 103–104, 250, 251, 318
  and Christianity 236
  desire for independence 173–174, 223, 254, 262, 267, 287, 297–298, 312–313
  Dreamings *see* Dreamings, Gurindji
  education 106, 138, 167–169, 208, 254–257, 295, 305–306, 313
  generational difference 104–106, 143, 216, 234–235, 258, 272, 275–276, 289, 294–295, 303–306, 312–314
  health 15
  land claim 244, 264–266, 287, 298, 310–311
  lease proposal 91–93, 102, 114, 127–128
  marriage traditions 106, 272–275
  massacres 5
  notice to forfeit lease 244–245
  observation of decline 253–254
  payment of cash wages 17
  relations with Warlpiri 4, 169–170, 180
  relations with white people xxx, 37, 284
  and Sam Croker 2
  and self-determination policy xxvii–xxviii, xxx, 137–139, 163–164, 190–193, 225, 230–231, 254, 262, 307
  traditional knowledge 257, 312–313, 318
  traditional law 106, 271–272, 275–276, 295, 314

'Gurindji Blues' 87
Gurindji camps, Wattie Creek xx–xxi
Gurindji claim to Wave Hill 39–40, 127, 157, 173, 199–200, 308
Gurindji country, deterioration of 14
　first white man's visit 1
Gurindji Daguragu Territory *see* GDT (cattle brand)
Gurindji girls, education 106
Gurindji land, handover 180–187
Gurindji leaders 12–13, 18, 22, 63, 319
　alcohol control measures 236–238, 251–252, 269, 297
　influence on ALP policy 121
　meeting with Fraser 201
　relations with government xxx, 266–267, 282–284, 302–303, 308–309, 320
　vision for Wattie Creek 61–62, 223
'Gurindji Mining Lease and Cattle Station' 39
Gurindji petition *see* Gurindji claim to Wave Hill
Gurindji supporters, infighting 92–93, 140–141, 151, 213–214
Gurindji women, advancement of xxix, 291–293
Hagen, Rod 220
Hansen, Barry 196
Hardy, Frank 34, 35, 37, 38, 40, 52, 70–73, 174–176, 188, 297–298
　report on Daguragu 208
　The Unlucky Australians xxx, 52, 53, 175
Harvey, Bluey 31, 37, 42
Havenhand, Bryan 111, 156
Hawke, Bob 86–87
Hayes, Ralph 106–107, 136, 151, 155, 180, 182, 188–189
health clinic, at Daguragu 176, 207
Health Department, boycott of Wattie Creek 83, 89
health services, denial of 89
Hempel, Ray 68
Holding, Clyde 287, 308
Holland, Sekai 111
Hollows, Fred 70, 88–89
Holmes, Cecil 53, 54, 56, 57, 94
Holt, Harold 44
Hooker Creek Welfare settlement 20
　see also Lajamanu
Howard government, intervention 318–319
Howson, Peter 96, 112
Hunt, Ralph, visit to Wattie Creek 94

Ibbetson, Len 68, 81, 102, 108, 130, 138, 177–178, 283
Inverway, Mick 226, 235, 250
Ivory, Mick 48–49
Jabada, Duncan 24
Jangala, Jerry 169–170
Jeffrey, Anne 37, 38
Jeffrey, Bill 28, 29, 32, 34–37, 38, 40, 42–43, 183
Jennett, Christine 111
Jingaya, Little Blanchie 95, 266
Jinparrak, as homestead location 6, 7
Johnson, Les 182, 199, 207
Jumiari, Dandy 16
Jurluma, Spider 265
Jurumbak, Long Jack 42, 133
Kalapiti, George 32, 274–275
Kalkarindji *see* Kalkaringi
Kalkaringi xv, 212–213
　church services 236
　housing 258–259
　police scandal 271
　store 213–214, 230, 283, 296
　teenage crime 271
　white residents 211–212, 213–214, 226–227, 261, 268–272, 284, 290, 295–296
　see also Wave Hill Welfare settlement
Kankinang, Big Mick 108, 109, 139
kartiya see white men
Katherine, white dissent to ALP policy 128
Kijngayari, Josepha 106, 272–274, 276
Kijngayari, Long Johnny 12, 21, 40, 63, 81, 133, 247
Kime, Jim 20, 236
King, Marie 176
Kormilda boarding school 257
L.J. Hooker Investments Corporation 107, 140
LaBrooy, Trevor 149–150, 156–157, 164–165, 248, 283
Lajamanu 169, 170, 189, 237, 297, 300
land councils, reduction of 198
land rights, ALP policy 114, 117, 121, 123–124
Land Rights Act, proposed 182–183, 187, 191, 193–194, 195, 197–199
land rights policy, re-examined 86, 96, 98–99
Langsford, W.A. 15
Lawson, Tony 63, 65, 91
Letts, Goff 63, 90, 91, 103, 151, 199–200, 220–221
Leu, Jean 65, 72, 131–132, 135, 140

INDEX

Libanungu *see* Kalkaringi; Wave Hill Welfare settlement
Libanungu Council   138–139, 144, 170–171, 177, 209, 213–214, 227–228
Lingiari, Vincent   11–13, 18–19, 27–28, 29, 30–31, 40, 63, 78, 86–88, 106, 109, 159, 160, 173, 184–185, 187
   anti-alcohol stance   144, 234–235
   Christian faith   20
   illness and death   309, 316
   opposition to lease proposal   92, 102
   Order of Australia   xxvi, 226
Liquor Commission (NT)   252, 269
Long, Banjo   251, 272–273
Lovegrove, Creed   180
Luck, Adrian   37
Lumsden, Fox   318
Lupngiari   13, 17, 22, 26–27, 37, 38, 63, 112, 183
   illness and death   133–134, 247 fn8
Luther, Maurice   169–170
MacLeod, Georgina   318
Malyeri. Elsie   24
Manning, Brian   21–22, 33–34, 63, 76, 90, 91, 299
Manyo, George   63
massacres, of Gurindji   5
McConvell, Patrick   136, 161, 175–176, 211
McConvell, Tanya   177
McGinness, Joe   70, 76
McHenry, Ray   122, 128
McLeod, Bobby   153–154
McMahon, William   85–87, 98, 114
McNair, Norm and Helen   222, 234, 256, 295
Michaels, Ian   108–109, 140
Middleton, Hannah   59, 60, 71, 77–78, 81
Millhouse, John   217, 227, 258, 260
Moore, Gordon   236
Moore, Gwen   236, 237
Moray, Sandy   17–18, 38, 247 fn8, 266
Moray, Tipujurn *see* Moray, Sandy
Morris, Peter   28, 33, 36, 42
Mount Isa, trade unions   13
Mudburra people   23, 215, 250
Muir, Colin   219
Muramulla Gurindji Cattle Company   115, 131–134, 137, 154–156, 158–161, 178–179, 199–200, 202–207, 222–224
   decline and collapse   311–312, 315–316
   and disease testing   276–282, 298–305
   establishment   63–64
   government support   80, 190–191
   and NT government   243–249
Muramulla store *see* Wattie Creek, store
Murphy, Lionel   39–40
NACC *see* National Aboriginal Advisory Consultative Council
Nampijinpa, Diane   111
Nangiari, Donald   12, 74, 86, 88, 95, 131, 133, 134, 160, 202, 205, 224, 283
National Aboriginal Advisory Consultative Council   xii, 152–153
National Party, opposition to land rights   196
National Union of Australian University Students   xiii, 71 fn29
NAWU *see* North Australian Workers' Union
new generation   xvi, xxix, 294–295, 298–299, 303–307, 314
   leaders   318
Newcastle Waters station   23–27
Ngalgardji, Gerry   40
Ngarinyman, and Victoria River Downs   107–109, 139–140, 211
Ngukurr *see* Roper River
ngumpit see Gurindji
Nitschke, Philip   141–142, 149–152, 154, 157–158, 171–172
Nixon, Curly   23
Nixon, Peter   45–46, 51, 52, 55, 65, 67, 78
   visit to Wattie Creek   69
NLC *see* Northern Land Council
Noble, Jack   85, 132
North Australian Workers' Union   xii, 22, 23, 34, 76, 90
Northern Territory, development rezoning   244
Northern Territory Aboriginal people, Commonwealth administration   41 fn16
Northern Territory (Self-government) Act   238–239
Northern Territory Cattle Producers' Council *see* Cattle Producers' Council
Northern Territory Cattlemen's Association   127–128, 206
   see also Cattle Producers' Council
Northern Territory Council for Aboriginal Rights   xii, 22, 28–29, 42
Northern Territory Council for Civil Liberties *see* Council for Civil Liberties (NT)
Northern Territory Country Liberal Party *see* Country Liberal Party (NT)
Northern Territory Department of Community Development   xii, 282, 290

Northern Territory Department of Primary
  Production xi, 249–250
Northern Territory Education Department xii,
  255–256
Northern Territory Government, Aboriginal
  policies 240, 258
  contracting practices 261, 268
  establishment 238–240, 266
  local government policy 282, 319–320
Northern Territory Legislative Assembly
  xii–xiii
Northern Territory Legislative Council xiii
Northern Territory Police 42
Northern Territory Welfare Branch xvi–xvii,
  15–16, 34, 35–36, 46–47, 48, 66–67, 83
  disestablishment 117, 122
NT Council of Rights for Aborigines and Torres
  Strait Islanders xii, 145
NTCA see Northern Territory Cattlemen's
  Association
NTCAR see Northern Territory Council for
  Aboriginal Rights
NTCRATSI see NT Council of Rights for
  Aborigines and Torres Strait Islanders
NTDCD see Northern Territory Department of
  Community Development
NTED see Northern Territory Education
  Department
NTLA see Northern Territory Legislative
  Assembly
NTLC see Northern Territory Legislative
  Council
NUAUS see National Union of Australian
  University Students
Nunggubuyu people 23, 56, 117, 187, 202
Nyurrmiarri, Pincher 12, 40, 43, 61, 63, 80,
  151–152, 159, 164, 226, 285
  death 309
  travel to southern capitals 201
Oke, Kay 57, 81
Oke, Rob 57, 65, 81, 132, 166
Oodgeroo Noonuccal 41
Ord River station 17

Paddy, Michael 305, 318
Paraway see Buchanan, Nat
Parrott, Roy 111
pastoralists 1–2, 4–5, 15, 33, 34, 40, 45, 55,
  63–64, 77, 84–85, 127–128, 188
  see also Buchanan, Nat
Paulson, Graham 144, 236

Pelczynski, Stan 161, 165
Penrith, Harry see Burnum Burnum
Perkins, Charlie 146–147, 153
Perkins, Neville 245
Perron, Marshall 244–246, 267
Petition, for release of Vestey's land see Gurindji
  claim to Wave Hill
Phillips, Jack 96, 100–101
Pincher, Charlie 108, 298
police station, Bow Hill 2
Preece, Richard 176–177, 213–214, 216
public support, Adelaide 111
  Melbourne 71, 73
  Sydney 70, 71–73
Purdie, Bill 248, 276, 302
Purdie, Glenda 248
Quin, David 100, 102, 107–108, 131–132, 137,
  140–142
radicalism 148
Rangiari, Mick xxviii, 12, 29, 43, 49–50, 52,
  63, 68, 71, 76, 81, 84, 94, 107–108, 139, 159,
  226
Referendum (May 1967) 41
Richardson, Jan 285 287, 290, 292, 293,
  305–306
Richardson, Len 58, 75
Riddett, Lyn 68, 74, 82, 84, 93, 110, 140–142,
  252–253
'Rights for Territorians' 128
Rinyngayarri, Jerry 12, 63, 106, 133, 152, 202,
  224, 247, 277, 283
Roberts, Jacob 22
Roberts, Phillip 15, 56, 76, 117
Robinson, Terry 22
Rodger, Ian 43
Roet, Mike 81
Rogers, P.S. 89
Rogers, Walter 28–29
Romanoff, Alex 83
Rook, Dawn 306
Roper River 22, 56, 202
Rosewood station 33
Royal Commission into Aboriginal Land
  Rights xvii, 124–125, 134–135, 166
Rubuntja, Wenten 220
Rutter, John 209, 228
Ryan, Maurie Japarta 318
Save the Gurindji groups 70–71, 80, 132
Scott, Tony 66–67
secondary schooling 257–258
segregationist attitudes, persistence 84, 85

INDEX

self-determination, as government policy   xxvii–xxviii, 124, 129–130, 147, 153, 158–159, 163, 196, 213, 214
  see also self-management
self-management, as government policy   221–222, 225, 238–239, 262–263, 267, 307, 314
  see also self-determination
The Settlement *see* Wave Hill Welfare Settlement
sexual predation, of Gurindji women   3
Shearston, Gary   41
Sing, Sabu   160
Smith, Stan   42
Smorgon family, legal assistance to Gurindji   63
Sommerlad, Liz   129, 147
Splinter, Milton   305
Stanner, W.E.H.   44, 98
station workers, wages   15, 17, 22, 23
Stolen Generation policies, effects of   75
Strelley Nomads, support for Daguragu   161
strike action   23–27
Swain, Jeff   101
Tapp, Bill   127–128
Tatz, Colin   112
Tent Embassy   99, 113
Thiele, Jenny   141
Thorpe, Alan   83–84, 86, 89–92, 157, 170, 213–214, 230
Tipujurn *see* Moray, Sandy
Tiver, Newton   136
Toohey, John   264–266
track mob *see* Gurindji
traditional life, of Gurindji   3–4, 295, 318
  see also Dreamings, Gurindji; Gurindji, ceremonial life; Gurindji, traditional law
Trezona, John   316
Tudawali, Robert   33–34
Twitt, David   53, 54, 56
unemployment benefits *see* government benefits
Union International *see* Vestey's
United Aborigines Mission   20
University of Melbourne   58
The Unlucky Australians (film), Daguragu screening   175–176
venereal disease   2
Vestey, Samuel   4, 5, 58–59
  relations with ALP government   127
Vestey, William   4, 5
Vestey's   4–5
  Argentinian difficulties   116
  continued occupation of Gurindji land   126–127
  demonstrations against   71–72
  gift of cattle to Gurindji   183, 188–189, 203
  government purchase of Wave Hill land   135–136, 157, 166–167, 174, 179
  and Gurindji activism   42
  and Gurindji Wave Hill claim   112, 115–116, 127
  London demonstration against   52
  meeting with Gurindji   179–180
  mistreatment of stockmen   14–15
  and Muramulla Gurindji Cattle Company   63–65
  payment records   84
  picnic races   17, 29, 215–216
  and Wave Hill Walk-out   55, 58–59, 86
  withdrawal from Australia   316–317
  see also Australian Investment Agency
Vestey's managers   84
  see also Bell, Roy; Edwards, Roy; Fisher, Tom; Golding, Roger; Grove, Ronald; Morris, Peter; Watts, Cec
Victoria Daly Regional Council   319
Victoria River Downs station   xiii
  walk-off   107–108, 139
Vincent, Victor   203, 233, 236, 279, 283, 304, 318
Viner, Ian   196–197, 199, 204
VRD *see* Victoria River Downs station
Walk-off.(August 1966)   xxvi, 30–32
  anniversaries   xxvi–xxvii, 288–289
  route   xix
Wapngarri, Lizzie   95, 266
Ward, Dick   102
Warlpiri   xvi
  attracted to Wave Hill   3–4
  at Wave Hill Welfare settlement   169
Waterside Workers' Federation   xiii
  donation to Gurindji   94, 100
Wattie Creek   xx–xxi, 38–39
  Abschol support for   56–60
  as catalyst of land rights battle   xxvi, 53, 185–186
  fencing decisions   95–96, 101
  government position   50–52, 65, 68, 69, 79, 82–83
  living conditions   43–44, 54–55, 57, 60–61, 79–82, 93–94, 101
  ministerial surveillance   67–68

– 351 –

Ngarinyman arrival   108–109, 139
public servants' visits   66, 69, 94, 117, 125
renamed Daguragu   126
resistance to leaving   53, 78, 82, 173
and self-determination policy   125, 130–131, 137, 158–159, 164, 230–231, 267
social cohesion   60
store   80–81, 154, 163, 177, 210, 246, 280–281, 280–281
traditional owners   95, 266
water-supply   43, 54, 60, 93–94, 101, 110
Wentworth's visit   45
as workers' base   76
see also Daguragu
Watts, Cec   167, 184, 280
Wave Hill, location   xviii
   naming of   2
   purchase by Vestey's   4–5
Wave Hill Cricket Club   268–269
Wave Hill station, Gurindji claim   135–136
   Gurindji workers   299
   health of workers   13–14
   homestead   1, 6, 7
   managers   16, 43, 106
      see also Fisher, Tom; Hayes, Ralph; Wilmington, Frank
   pay and conditions   43, 85, 299
   request for pay increase   28
   sale   317
   walk-off *see* Walk-off
   white workers   16
   workers' fertility   14
   workers' living conditions   14, 16, 18–20, 21, 23
Wave Hill Welfare settlement   28, 46–47, 57, 66, 78, 82–83, 94, 101–102, 125, 138, 142–143, 163
   effect of funding cuts   197
   Gurindji involvement   173–174
   schooling   138, 168–169, 255–257
   see also Kalkaringi
Welfare Branch *see* Northern Territory Welfare Branch
Welfare Branch depot, Gordy Creek   31
   see also Gordy Creek
welfare payments *see* government benefits
Wentworth, W.C. (Billy)   44–46, 47, 50, 77, 182, 308
Wesley-Smith, Jan   91
Wesley-Smith, Rob   63, 91, 93, 94, 102–103, 189–193, 272–274

Westbury, Neil   232
wet canteens   238
white men, treatment of Gurindji women   3
white workers, at Wave Hill   16
Whitlam, Gough   xxvi, xxvii, 50–51, 99, 113–114, 117, 121, 124
   visit to Daguragu   181–187
Whitlam, Margaret, visit to Daguragu   182
Whitlam government dismissal   193–194
Williams, Mrs   67
Williams, Rod   58, 59, 60, 72–73, 74, 75
Wilmington, Frank   43
Woodward, Edward   124–125, 197–198
Woodward Commission *see* Royal Commission into Aboriginal Land Rights
Wundamarie Housing Association   138, 207, 261, 283
WWF *see* Waterside Workers' Federation
Yanna *see* Inverway, Mick
Yarralin   140, 182, 211, 220
Yirara boarding school   257, 258
Yolngu   xvii
Yolngu activists   41
Yolngu land rights case   85–86, 125
Yunupingu, Galarrwuy   87
Zakharov, John   93